Developmental Psychology in the Soviet Union

D0929914

Developmental Psychology in the Soviet Union

Jaan Valsiner

INDIANA UNIVERSITY PRESS
BLOOMINGTON AND INDIANAPOLIS

Manufactured in Great Britain

Library of Congress Cataloging-in-Publication Data

Valsiner, Jaan.
  Developmental psychology in the Soviet Union.

  Bibliography: p.
  Includes index.
  1. Developmental psychology—Soviet Union—History.
I. Title.
BF713.V35 1988   155'.0947   87-29864
ISBN 0-253-31626-X

1 2 3 4 5 92 91 90 89 88

Contents

List of Figures

List of Tables

Preface

This book is written with the hope that it might help the reader to understand the complex of reasons that have made developmental ideas prominent in Soviet psychology. The project of writing the present book began at first with the idea of overviewing the most recent developmental work published in USSR and difficult to access internationally. However, it soon became clear to me that such a survey of the present Soviet research would be of limited use, unless the history of Soviet developmental psychology is analyzed in parallel with it. Scientific knowledge does not develop by way of a simple aggregation of new empirical data on top of the old ones. Instead, breakthroughs in any science emerge as a result of new ideas (or, sometimes, technological innovations) that shatter the world view of the scientists and force them to reorganize their theoretical views of the phenomena that they study, and to re-evaluate the existing data. Development of Soviet psychology in the context of Soviet society constitutes a case history of such qualitative reorganization of a scientific discipline. In order to understand the process of this reorganization, its process should be traced in detail. Hence the concentration of the present book on two historical periods in the Soviet psychology—the 1920s and the 1970s–1980s.

The process of work on the present book can be described as that of a detective who is trying to reconstruct the picture of the whole story from scanty bits and pieces of (often limited) evidence. A number of people were helpful in the course of preparing the manuscript. First, I am grateful to George Butterworth whose suggestion to undertake the job of writing this book led me to thinking about the interdependence of science and society in the case of Soviet developmental psychology. Many colleagues and friends helped me to locate and obtain various original publications by Russian and Soviet psychologists, so that a multi-faceted picture of the history of developmental ideas in Soviet psychology could be assembled. They also provided valuable advice in organizing the scanty and often incomplete materials. For all that assistance, I remain indebted to Jüri Allik, Valentina Ivanova, Toomas Niit, Lloyd H. Strickland, Peeter Tulviste, Ina C. Uzgiris, René Van der Veer and Nadia Zilper. Ann Renninger, Julie Robinson and Thomas Kindermann gave their valuable comments and suggestions after reading various drafts of some of the chapters, and René Van der Veer kindly looked through the final version of the whole manuscript and helped to make final corrections. In addition I am grateful to Professor J. L. Black for permission to quote from his book on Russian education. The editorial staff of Harvester Press was very helpful in scheduling the work on the production of the book. I am very grateful to everybody who assisted me in the process of working on this book.

Jaan Valsiner
Chapel Hill, North Carolina
July, 1987

I Introduction: Understanding of Development and its Social-Historical Context

The task of this book—an analysis of how developmental psychology in the USSR has developed and reached its present state—constitutes a case history of the relationships between a science and its cultural-historical framework. The particular science in question is developmental psychology. The cultural framework is that of the Soviet Union. Since no culture can be understood in its static form when a developmental psychologist tries to analyze it, the present book involves an outline of the development of some aspects of Russian society (and later—Soviet society) that were relevant to the emergence and maintenance of Soviet developmental psychology. This explains the historical emphasis that is present all through this book. The contemporary state of affairs in Soviet developmental psychology can be understood best when we take its cultural-historical context into account, and make its structure and development explicit.

This contention of the present author is in effect an application of a core notion in Soviet psychology, introduced by Pavel Blonskii—'behaviour can be studied only as the history of behaviour' (see Chapter V)—to the study of Soviet developmental psychology itself. From that perspective, understanding of some sub-field of psychology in any given country is possible only if one studies the history of that sub-field, embedded within the socio-cultural development of that country. Thus, understanding the contemporary state of developmental psychology in the United States would require an analysis of the history of that discipline in conjunction with the cultural development of the USA, along lines similar to those used for Soviet developmental psychology in this book. Needless to say, the cultural-historical approach to the understanding of the *present* state of developmental psychology in *any* country has largely been absent from the minds of child psychologists. This becomes evident when comparisons between developmental psychologies of different countries are made in

1

psychologists' writings. Such comparisons are usually direct and synchronic—comparing the present state of developmental psychology in one country with that in the other. The results of such comparisons may perhaps reveal some new information about the 'tip of the iceberg'—as the most important aspects of the contemporary state of the psychologies compared remain hidden in the complex webs of the histories of the societies. One of the aims of this book is to resist the temptation to free the contemporary state of Soviet developmental psychology from its social context. Hence the reader should not expect to find a simple overview of contemporary empirical research done by Soviet developmental psychologists in different areas at the present time. Instead, whenever possible, I have attempted to link the ways Soviet developmental psychologists think theoretically and conduct empirical research, with the cultural-historical context of psychology in the Soviet Union. In a number of places in the book that effort made it necessary to provide rather detailed analyses of historical events or situations in the Russian/Soviet society (and philosophy) that constituted the context for developmental psychology. These 'side-trips' are crucial to Western psychologists' understanding of Soviet developmental psychology. Without an explicit analysis of the historical context in which Soviet developmental psychology emerged, and became transformed into its contemporary form, no adequate understanding of its nature is possible.

Historically, the knowledge and understanding of Soviet developmental psychology in the West has generally been limited, with episodic and narrowly thematic occasional upsurges of interest in it. This relates to the other persistent theme in this book—that of inter-cultural communication about developmental psychology. Although some of the major works written by Soviet developmentalists up to the present time are available to the international readership in translation, the majority of ordinary Western child psychologists encounter different problems in understanding psychological writings that originate in the USSR. For example, a state of confusion while reading Soviet psychological papers is frequently experienced by American experimental psychologists who look for 'the data' and their analysis in the conventional statistical form—and have difficulty in finding any. Such difficulty results from the belief that the 'science' of psychology is the same 'science' everywhere, and that it is 'good science' as long as it conforms to the person's own background professional socialization. A similar communication difficulty emerges in the reverse direction. It is reflected in the impressions of Soviet psychologists who, while reading highly empirical papers in American child psychology journals, are disappointed by the obvious lack of theoretical consistency in the majority of papers published in those journals.

These opposite difficulties in the understanding of Soviet psychology by Westerners, and of Western psychology by their Soviet counterparts, constitute a case of scientific communication where the reasons for mutual misunderstandings can be revealed. In this respect, the present treatise is a narrative in the domain of sociology or social anthropology of a social science. Its goal is to analyze the usually hidden ties between the cultural organization of society and the thinking of psychologists, as well as an overview of developmental psychology in USSR.

Soviet psychology: why is it of interest?

The case of developmental psychology in the USSR seems to be of interest to the international public for a number of different reasons. The first of these is a superficial one—the political history of the world in the past six decades has resulted in increased interest in the Soviet Union. Somehow, the widely known 'journalistic events', such as Russian 'bearhugs' on TV screens when foreign dignitaries arrive in Moscow, or the use of a shoe as a tool in international diplomacy at the United Nations, keep up Westerners' interest in the powerful and hard-to-understand country.

The second reason is the natural interest of psychologists and social scientists outside the USSR in the work of their colleagues in that country. However, these two reasons are interdependent— Western psychologists' interest in the work of their Soviet counterparts may be framed by the political discourse about the USSR that is part of the everyday social environment of Western scientists. A simple test of such socio-political framing of psychologists' interests is to look for books (published in English) devoted to psychology in some countries (e.g., India, Italy, France,

Mexico or the Republic of China) rather than others (the USSR, the People's Republic of China). The interest of English-speaking psychologists in psychologies in these different countries seems to be unevenly distributed and, in a curious way, seems to follow the emphases given to those countries as a whole by the socio-political discourse of the mass media in the USA and European countries.

Thirdly, the interest in Soviet psychology may result from the self-presentation efforts of the Soviet social system to propagate its products. Such advertising efforts often take the form of assertions that the Soviet version of the particular promotion object (e.g., Soviet psychology) is better than its Western counterparts, without providing more information about it. Quite predictably, such advertising can have its effect—its recipients become uncomfortable with the little information available, which results in increased curiosity about the mysteries of Soviet psychology. Fourthly, the actual writings of some psychologists from the Soviet Union have triggered the interest of their Western colleagues in the work by these scientists, as well as by others. Thus, if a psychologist becomes interested in the work of a particular Soviet psychologist, such as Vygotsky, it is likely that this interest disseminates to other sides of psychology in USSR.

Finally, the history and the present state of developmental psychology in the USSR can be viewed as a reflection of the social processes within Soviet society. A person taking this perspective uses the available accounts of psychology in USSR as a means to some more general sociological end. In this respect, a cultural-historical study of Soviet developmental psychology may be used to further our understanding of the intricate texture of the functioning of Soviet society as a whole. Such use of a particular social science in the Soviet Union may be a productive direction for research on Soviet society, since details of the actual organization of that society may emerge from such study with greater clarity than is possible within the usual (i.e. politically oriented) analysis efforts that abound in Western countries.

Whatever combination of reasons lies behind the interests of a particular person in developmental psychology in the USSR, the interested person is confronted with a complicated task. An adequate understanding of Soviet developmental psychology requires integration of information from different sources into a holistic Gestalt. It is not only the input information from Soviet psychology that guides the formation of that understanding, but, equally importantly, the Western psychologist's view of the world that is the basis of that understanding. In this respect, the Westerner interested in Soviet psychology forms an understanding of it not as it is, but as it is perceived to be from the perspective of his or her own socialized background. The direction given to those perspectives can easily be labelled 'bias' of some kind. However, in the communication process, such 'biases' are omnipresent and unavoidable, since a recipient of communicative messages about Soviet psychology is an active co-constructor of its understanding, rather than a passive and impartial 'gatherer of data'. In that process of co-construction, the psychologist is inevitably guided by his cultural background. That background leads him to assimilate only selected aspects of the new information and to accommodate his existing background knowledge to it (to use Piaget's terminology). It also makes the process of understanding Soviet psychology by a Westerner a lengthy and complicated process, in the course of which the interest (and motivation to proceed) of only a few may survive. In a way, the compositional structure of this book reflects that difficult process. The diligent and motivated reader may find this book interesting after reading it through, whereas readers who may aim to arrive at some quickly obtainable and simple general conclusion about Soviet developmental psychology are likely to be left unsatisfied. The reason for this lies in the complexity of the subject matter—*no* simple and easy conclusive generalizations about Soviet psychology can be made, given the nature of that psychology. Like most of the intellectual and artistic achievements that have originated in Russia (and, later, the Soviet Union), Soviet developmental psychology is a multiple-sided complex whole. Many particular periods of its history are both innovative and trivial at the same time, different developmental psychologists have been both active 'builders of the Soviet society' and equally active critics of some aspects of that society. Frequent Western efforts to reduce the issue of acceptance of Marxist philosophy by Soviet psychology to the 'either/or' form (i.e., *either* they accepted Marxism on their own, *or* were forced to do so against their will by political authorities) are an example of simplification of a view of the polyphonic nature of Soviet psychology. In reality, much of Russian/Soviet psychology is similar in complexity to the classics of Russian literature or music, which have been greatly appreciated by Westerners over many decades. In this book I will analyze some of the complexity of the theoretical understanding of child development as it has emerged in the web of the Russian culture, especially at the times of rapid change in that culture. However, before that analysis can proceed, the issue of science-society relationships in general needs to be discussed.

Science and society: a general outline of their shared history

The relations between science and society have become a ground for discussion in recent decades, thanks to the diffusion of the philosophical ideas of 'paradigms' (Kuhn, 1962, 1970) and 'research programmes' (Lakatos & Musgrave, 1970) into the thinking and discourse of scientists in many areas, as well as of the interested public. Such wider interest has been further enhanced by Feyerabend's (1975, 1976) criticism of science's orthodox self-reflections.

No one interested in Soviet psychology can avoid having to deal with variable statements, made by authors of different backgrounds, about 'science' and 'the scientific nature' of one or another psychological perspective or empirical research result. Furthermore, s/he is likely to come across statements that negate the 'scientific' status, and assign the label of 'pseudo-science' to some approaches in psychology. For example, many psychological ideas and empirical research practices were labelled using terms of such dubious connotations in the USSR in the 1930s. Likewise, a Western reader may get exhausted after labouring through many pages of semi-philosophical text by a Soviet psychologist, and may end up dismissing it as 'of little value to science'. Some clarification of the terms 'science' and 'scientific' as used in social discourse may help us to keep interested in the real issues of knowledge behind such attributional language use.

Word magic: does calling something 'science' makes it one?
Human beings can create both clarity and confusion through their use of language. Language use makes it possible for us to transcend the immediately available information, and to construct varieties of

knowledge. Usually such construction improves our understanding of the world. Sometimes, however, our language use sets up conditions that make it easy to fuse our thinking and its object world—we may start to consider our reflection on the reality that reality itself.

This philosophical and linguistic-logical feature is analyzed by Michel Foucault (1983) in his treatment of the philosophy of René Magritte's painting *This is not a pipe*. That painting includes a drawing of a pipe, with an inscription in the picture, under the drawing: 'This is not a pipe'. The little game with language use is obvious here—we know all too well that a picture of an object is not a specimen of the objects of the given kind. Furthermore, a linguistic statement *about* an object (or its representation) does not belong to the class of these objects (or their pictorial representations).

Gregory Bateson's analysis of the status of concepts (1971) addresses the same issue. In his example, the general (class) concept 'chair' cannot belong to the class of chairs (that includes a variety of different specimens of particular chairs). One cannot sit on the *concept* 'chair', but one can understand the variety of different chairs, their structure, and properties by operating with that concept in one's mind.

A similar perspective can be taken in respect of the concepts 'science' and 'scientific'. Is a statement 'X is science' one that can belong to the class to which it is referring? Or can a negative statement 'X is not scientific' itself belong to the class of 'scientific' statements? The present author's tentative answer to that question is no. No statement, involving ascriptions of the status of 'science' or 'scientific' to particular theories, methods, data, approaches, etc., can be considered to belong to the class to which it is referring. Such a statement belongs to classes of statements *about* their objects, rather than to the latter. So any statement concerning one or another approach in psychology that claims that the particular approach is, or is not, part of psychology, is not part of psychology itself, but constitutes a part of meta-level discourse about psychology. Such a statement may belong to the class of 'social-political statements about psychology' or, more simply, to the class of 'psychologists' gossip' or their 'boundary maintenance' of the discipline. It may affect what the psychologists do, and how they think, in dramatic ways, but nevertheless that statement does not belong to the class to which it refers.

Psychologists in every country have always been rather interested in meta-psychological discourse. The societies of those countries vary, and so do the ways in which the meta-level discourse about psychology is organized in those societies. The cultural embeddedness of psychology is also directly observable when we analyze psychologists' discourse *about* psychology, and it is much more hidden in their particular statements (about psychological phenomena) that belong to psychology.

In the case of Soviet psychology, it is particularly easy to confuse the two discourse levels—those of psychology and meta-psychology—since these levels are often fused in the writings of Soviet psychologists themselves, in the first place. All the more useful might it then be to keep the distinction of those levels constantly in mind while trying to make sense of Soviet psychological writings. That may reveal some valuable ideas and interesting natural–experimental practices that may often be hidden among lengthy denouncements of the 'unscientific' nature of 'Western bourgeois psychologies' that one encounters in many Soviet texts, published mostly after 1931. It could also reveal the psychological mechanisms by which science and society (the scientist and his social environment) are interdependent in their existence.

Explication of meta-science: organization of science and its change

Perhaps the most widely heard-of treatise of the issues of development of science is Thomas Kuhn's *The structure of scientific revolutions* (Kuhn, 1962, 1970). The central concept that Kuhn uses to characterize the structures of knowledge in sciences is 'paradigm'. It refers to a constellation of beliefs, values, and techniques that are shared by members of a scientific community. On the one hand, that constellation is considered to be sufficiently effective in drawing the adherence of the scientists. On the other— that constellation has to be sufficiently open-ended so that different problems can be solved within it (Kuhn, 1970, p. 10). Paradigms serve as particular knowledge structures in different sciences, and the change in sciences is attributable by Kuhn to paradigm changes—abandonment of a paradigm in favour of another, first by some and subsequently by many scientists. Kuhn's major contribution to the understanding of the history of science has been an emphasis on the nonlinearity of scientific progress and the paradigm-dependence of any scientific research.

Kuhn's interest has largely lain in the history of the 'hard' sciences, in which the connection of the scientists' thinking with their particular social environments need not be obvious or highly relevant. He speaks of the transition from 'pre-paradigmatic' to paradigmatic science. Within the latter, different paradigms organize empirical research by scientists in very different ways— even if the object of research is the same (Kuhn, 1970, p. 152).

The process of scientific revolution in Kuhn's presentation involves the transition from one paradigm through a period of confusion to another paradigm:

All crises begin with the blurring of a paradigm and the consequent loosening of the rules for normal research. In this respect research during crisis very much resembles research during the pre-paradigm period, except that in the former the locus of difference is both smaller and more clearly defined .... The transition from a paradigm in crisis to a new one from which a new tradition of normal science can emerge is far from a cumulative process, one achieved by an articulation or extension of the old paradigm. Rather, it is a reconstruction of the field from new fundamentals, a reconstruction that changes some of the field's most elementary theoretical generalizations as well as many of its paradigm methods and applications. During the transition period there will be a large but never complete overlap between the problems that can be solved by the old and by the new paradigm. But there will also be a decisive difference in the modes of solution. When the transition is complete, the profession will have changed its view of the field, its methods, and its goals. (Kuhn, 1970, pp. 84–5)

Scientific revolutions take place in the domain of professionally educated knowledge that is largely beyond laypersons' knowledge and interests base. Kuhn recognizes the *socially educated* nature of scientific thinking, although he prefers not to deal with the complicated issue of the social goals and rules by which that education takes place. In this respect, scientific revolutions constitute an act of self-re-education, followed by the re-education of one's colleagues:

Looking at a contour map, the student sees lines on paper, the cartographer a picture of a terrain. Looking at the bubble-chamber photograph, the student sees confused and broken lines, the physicist a record of familiar subnuclear events. Only after a number of such transformations of vision does the student become an inhabitant of the scientist's world, seeing what the scientist sees and responding as the scientist does. The world that the student then enters is not, however, fixed once and for all by the nature of the environment, on the one hand, and of science, on the other. Rather, it is determined jointly by the environment and the particular normal-scientific tradition that the student has been trained to pursue. Therefore, at times of revolution, when the normal-scientific tradition changes, the scientist's perception of his environment must be re-educated—in some familiar situations he must learn to see a new gestalt. After he has done so the world of his research will seem, here and there, incommensurable with the one he had inhabited before. (Kuhn, 1970, pp. 111–12)

The individual scientist's re-education of his own world view takes place in a social context. First, it depends on the collective events in the scientists's immediate environment—the scientific community. The scientific community is rarely a club of egalitarian handicraftsmen who have conscientiously adopted the rules of democratic governance. Rather, different forms of organization of the community can be observed in different sciences in different countries at different historical periods. These forms often reflect the social organization of institutions other than scientific ones, which leads to the second aspect of the process of re-education of scientists during the movement to adopt a new paradigm. Namely, the social network of scientists is inevitably interdependent with the wider social-cultural context, even if the actual scientific work conducted by scientists is not well understood, nor its pragmatic societal value immediately obvious. Thus the complex interplay of politicians and their decisions in economic, social, moral, and military matters sets the stage for the social organization of science. Such socio-political 'framing' of science should not be interpreted as if it determines the form of scientific institutions and the content of science in any strict way. Rather, its influence is more subtle and often hidden behind the scientists' self-perception of 'being independent' of society. In that respect, Kuhn notes:

One of the strongest, if still unwritten, rules of scientific life is the prohibition of appeals to heads of state or the populace at large in matters scientific. Recognition of the existence of a uniquely competent professional group and acceptance of its role as the exclusive arbiter of professional achievement has further implications. The group's members, as individuals and by virtue of their shared training and experience, must be seen as the sole possessors of the rules of the game or of some equivalent basis of unequivocal judgements. To doubt that they shared some such basis for evaluations would be to admit the existence of incompatible standards of scientific achievement. (Kuhn, 1970, p. 168)

As will be seen in this book, not all social groups of scientists in cultural conditions other than those of Western Europe and North America have followed that rule in a stringent way. As will be seen in Chapter III, groups of in-fighting Soviet philosophers and psychologists of the 1930s did indicate their interest in using extra-scientific authorities as arbiters in their relationships. In most of the world, the social realities involve quite close interdependence of social politics and social organizations of scientists. That is quite natural, since the latter, even as scientists, remain members of their society at large. Thus, Kuhn's 'rule' of ingroup-management of matters of science may be a product of the world view present in his cultural background, and one that is limited to science organizations sharing that background. It may represent an illusionary way of self-perception for science, while its reality may be questioned on the majority of occasions.

How, then, can the organization of a science in a society be conceptualized so as to understand its subject matter better? Perhaps a general view entailing consecutive mutual constraining by adjacent levels of the hierarchical organization of society is useful for this purpose. Such a view treats science as embedded in the context of a hierarchy of social systems. To extend Bronfenbrenner's (1979) basic idea, these social systems constitute nested structures that regulate the functioning of one another. However, that regulation takes the form of mutual constraining (as opposed to strict determination) of the developmental course of one another.

At the highest, most general, level of the organization of the society, it sets up conditions that determine who among the population becomes involved in one or another area of science. For example, in all societies, becoming a scientist in a particular field involves a lengthy process of education with a selection of the appropriate candidates built into it (in the form of examinations, theses, degrees, honorary insignia, etc.). Furthermore, the content matter and language of exchange of information within a thus 'socially legitimized' science is constrained both by the society and the scientific community itself which may make its 'boundary maintenance' an important task. Undoubtedly, the form of conventions of scientific discourse and boundaries maintained between disciplines are constantly in the process of dynamic change. Thus, Kuhn's 'paradigm changes' can be observed, or new 'interdisciplinary' research areas will become talked about, socially legitimitized, and may flourish. These changes are also wrought by changes in the constraint systems that the society at large sets up for science. Likewise, some information taken from science may play a part in reorganization of the society, by guiding it in one direction rather than another.

A similar (mutual) constraining process may be posited to take place at the level of relationships between scientists and their scientific paradigms (and communities). The particular structure of a paradigm that an individual scientist adheres to constrains his research and guides it in specific directions. It makes some research questions interesting and worthwhile to pursue, and eliminates others as of little relevance. However, the scientist is not a passive recipient of the 'teaching' inherent in the paradigm, but its active co-constructor. He not only follows it, but also checks it, and may at a certain point of his work come to the understanding that the whole paradigm needs to be reorganized. His peers (community) may understand that need and provide assistance by constraining his efforts, or they can equally likely remain embedded in the belief of the adequacy of the old world view. All the participants in the multi-level mutual constraining perspective presented here are active participants in the construction of their science within the society, and thus of the society itself. Again, the case of Soviet psychology, particularly during the 1920s and early 1930s, is an interesting illustration of the active inclusion of scientists in the reorganization of society at large. Soviet psychologists of that time were unable to understand the utopian nature of many of their efforts. Such an understanding is not easy to reach when one is immersed in an environment where there is a wide variety of social utopias.

Interest in developmental issues in Soviet psychology emerged in the context of social thought oriented towards a major reorganization of society. Different social and educational philosophies that were present in the Soviet Union of the 1920s, despite (or perhaps because of) their emphasis on building a 'qualitatively new society', made psychologists' interest in the study of child *development* a most important topic of the psychology of the time. Hence the active efforts by different Soviet psychologists in the second half of the 1920s to find adequate ways to conceptualize development. That was a formidable task—in fact, a task that has been largely unaccomplished in Western child psychologics to the present day (Benigni & Valsiner, 1985; Cairns & Valsiner, 1982). The social environment of Soviet psychologists of the 1920s largely facilitated their efforts towards understanding development, whereas the cultural environments of Western psychologies have rarely provided psychologists with comparable directive guidance towards the same objective in the last six decades.

Constraints on the understanding of development

Besides facilitation by the social environment of psychologists, there also exist universal cognitive issues that constrain psychologists' understanding of development in general. The developmental perspective has been rare in the history of psychology (see Cairns, 1983). The overwhelming majority of empirical and theoretical research efforts in psychology have been within the non-developmental framework of thought. So it is interesting to note that in Soviet psychology developmental thinking has become of central relevance. As a result, a number of efforts to study empirical aspects of child development have emerged in otherwise mostly scholastic Soviet psychological discourse. Predictably, the prevalence of the developmental ethos in the USSR makes an analysis of Soviet developmental psychology potentially interesting for developmental psychologists of other countries.

The conceptualization of development is complicated in psychology for a number of reasons, the most important of which seem to be related with some basic cognitive issues—logic and language use.

Logical constraints on understanding development
The majority of efforts to understand our everyday lives are framed by the thinking on the basis of classical (2-valent) logic. That logic has fortified the ontological side of human thinking. For example, consider a statement 'X is happy' and its negation—'X is not happy'. Simultaneous acceptance of both of these statements is rejected within the Aristotelian logical system, although it is possible within alternative logical frameworks which are generally not used in human everyday thinking (e.g., dialectic logic).

The obstacle that the common-sense use of the classical logic creates for developmental psychology (and for all sciences where development of any phenomena is conceptualized) concentrates on the issue of *sameness* of the specimens within a class. A person, at ages 1, 3, 9 months, 2, 5, 25 and 50 years is considered to be 'the same person' (of different age, of course) in the common-sense. For example, his photographs from each of these ages, put into a family photo album are taken to represent him as he is. At the same time, these photographs provide information on the person's development, which is often not given primacy.

From the developmental viewpoint the classification of age-dispersed materials into a single general category eliminates the issue of development from explicit consideration. This happens because the time dimension is not treated as interdependent with the developing organism, but only as an independent parameter along which specimens or samples of 'the same' class or organism are located. When the developmental side of the phenomena is eliminated from our consideration, the time dimension is of no relevance and is excluded from our thinking. However, if we are interested in development, eliminating the time parameter from our thinking is counterproductive to our goals. At the same time, our traditions of thinking offer very little help in keeping the time dimension in mind, together with the phenomena. Time and development are mutually related—development is irreversible in time, and the irreversibility of time makes development possible. James Mark Baldwin understood this philosophical specificity of development well, when he defined his 'postulates of genetic science':

First. The first or negative postulate: *the logic of genesis is not expressed in convertible propositions.* Genetically, A ... becomes ... B, but it does not follow that B ... becomes ... A.

Second. The second or positive postulate: that series of events is only truly genetic which cannot be constructed before it has happened, and which cannot be exhausted backwards, after it has happened. (Baldwin, 1906, p. 21)

Baldwin's postulates illustrate the difference of a logical system that would be appropriate to the study of development, from the non-developmental Aristotelian logic. The latter complicates the understanding of developmental processes, making it in fact impossible to conceptualize development (as a process) and leading the investigator to think in terms of *outcomes* of some (implied) developmental process that cannot be analyzed directly in the framework of classical logic, with its metaphysical world view. In contrast, a philosophical world view that axiomatically transcends the metaphysics of the classical 2-valent logic may render it possible to study the process of development in its time context. Such a general world view was imported into Soviet psychology in the 1920s from Germany, in the form of Hegel's, Engels', and Marx's dialectical philosophy. The acceptance of that philosophy made it easier for Soviet psychologists to seek ways to study development, relying on principles of dialectics and its complement—dialectical logic. At the same time, the use of the same philosophical world view in the social-political sphere of the Soviet Union played a crucial role in the termination of many of psychologists' efforts in the 1930s (see Chapter III).

However, logical constraints that guide our thinking about development are only one side of the issue. A non-developmental emphasis is often already given to developmental psychologists by the nature of the language concepts available.

Entification as a linguistic constraint

The rarity of explicitly developmentally oriented approaches in child psychology in general may be considered to begin with the linguistic-semantic constraints that our language sets upon our thinking. Here we are not subscribing to any absolute interpretation of the linguistic relatively hypothesis, but rather accept it in the 'soft' version of *constraints on the range of ways of thinking that our language sets up for us* (von Bertalanffy, 1955). The language system does not determine in any strict manner how we think, but it guides our thinking processes towards some (rather than other) ways of thinking about the world.

The major linguistic constraint on developmental thinking is the *entification* that is hidden in the use of language. Entification involves the transition by the language user from describing a process (expressed by a verb or an adjective) to a linguistic form that refers to the static entity (expressed by a noun) which is projected into reality to underlie the process. Thus, users of the English language can easily proceed from talking about how 'Mary met John happily' to the entified state of 'happiness' of the said Mary which is said to *express* itself in actions like that of 'Mary meeting John'—'Mary's happiness was expressed when she met John' (see also Bloom, 1981, p. 37). This tautological cognitive operation—turning process descriptions into labels of static states, which are then attributed to the phenomenon, and subsequently considered to explain the process—is widespread in psychology (see, in general, Ryle, 1949; or a particular case of the concept of 'intelligence', in Valsiner, 1984a). Its roots are firmly embedded in language use as related to human cognition.

Since entification is a general constraint already historically pre-coded in the rules of language use, there are only very limited possibilities for developmental psychologists to avoid it. The most important of these is to transcend the commonsense attributional ways of explaining developmental phenomena. For example, a layperson may explain a child's development of the skill to open supposedly 'child-safe' medicine boxes by a reference to intelligence: 'look how intelligent he [the child] *is!*' At first glance, the nature of the child's task (opening a box that is specially made complicated) may easily afford some agreement by the developmental psychologist with the layperson's attribution of causality to the child's 'intelligence'. After all, 'intelligence tests' in psychology are constructed as giving some problems to solve, and making inference on the basis of the solutions. However, the developmental psychologist has the alternative of discarding the layperson's entified explanation, and studying the process by which the child actually reaches success in opening the box. An abstracted description of the process of problem-solving is an explanation of how the outcome was attained, and requires no entified explanatory concepts. The difficulty for developmental psychologists is to reconstruct such abstract 'process descriptions' in ways adequate to the reality. The entified nature of language concepts increases that difficulty.

Homogenization in thinking as a means of overlooking development

Another constraint that language use sets for our thinking is the *reduction of heterogeneous classes of objects into homogeneous ones* (Nisbett, Krantz, Jepson, & Kunda, 1983; Valsiner, 1984b). Here the heterogeneity of a class of objects is cognitively and linguistically overlooked by replacing the variety of objects by the prototype of the class (e.g., Rosch, 1978). This operation guarantees a certain 'economy' in the thinking process, since when we operate at the level of class concepts implying homogeneity within the class we can conveniently overlook the particularities of the targets of our thinking. However, many aspects of children's actual development may be based on exactly those particular (behavioural or cognitive) aspects of the children that are easily overlooked by virtue of the homogenizing habit of our cognitive operations with classes. For example, the majority of efforts in developmental psychology to describe children's 'trajectories' of development have presupposed that there must be only *one single*, the best, or the most typical 'trajectory', rather than a multitude of individually specific ones. If the latter idea were based on such research efforts, it would at least be a typology of developmental courses (instead of a single course, normative for all children) that psychologists would look for in their empirical studies. Note that even when typologies are sought in psychology, the homogenizing of the class of individual cases *within a particular type* is taking place. As soon as a particular case is ascribed to a particular type, it 'acquires' (in the thinking of the ascriber) the features common to the type, which results in the overlooking of some individually relevant information. In this respect, the replacement of the search for the 'child in general' as a prototype of all children by a small number of 'types' of children simply transposes the homo-genization operation from the general to the intermediate level. Instead of viewing all children as representing a universal 'prototype', they are viewed as representing the 'type' to which they have been ascribed. This may give economy to our everyday thought, but it will not necessarily lead to a better understanding of the actual psychological processes that partake in child development.

Dialectical philosophy and focus on development

As indicated above, one of the reasons why Soviet psychology has had the developmental perspective at its core is the dominance of dialectical philsophical belief systems in Soviet society. Dialectical philosophy is not a Marxist monopoly. In fact, it has been taken from earlier philosophical traditions, and used in Marxist philosophy in different domains of knowledge—natural, social and political. The basic laws of dialectical thinking emerged in their present form in German philosophy of the past three centuries, and entail an axiomatic emphasis on opposite forces confined in the same whole. These opposite forces are in conflict with one another, resulting in the advancement of the internally conflicting whole to a qualitatively new state of organization. The new state of the whole may in some of its parts be similar to an earlier state, but its total organization is nevertheless of new quality.

It is obvious that the basic principles of dialectical thinking make it particularly suitable for conceptualizing development. However, the application of these highly abstract principles of thinking to any concrete area of knowledge is wrought with complications— the same general principles can be applied to the same empirical reality in a multitude of ways. It is easy for a 'dialectical psychologist' to 'over-dialecticize' his research by looking for opposite forces, their conflict, its resolution, etc. in every empirical phenomenon. Criticisms along the line of excessive over-interpretation of human psychological processes that have often been raised against psychoanalytic explanations can be equally valid when directed at overly dialectical perspectives in psychology. At the present time, whether in Western or Soviet psychologies, a reasonable use of dialectical thinking seems largely to be absent. Its absence in Soviet psychology should not be surprising, given the social conditions that Soviet psychology has had for its development, as analyzed in Chapter III.

Summary: the relevance, and difficulty of learning about Soviet developmental psychology

The analysis of developmental psychology in the Soviet Union outlined in this book is of interest from different perspectives. First, it is likely to fill in some gaps in our understanding of what is happening in that psychology today. The contemporary state of Soviet developmental psychology is embedded in the context of its history in conjunction with the history of Russian (and, later, Soviet) society. Therefore, the coverage in this book is explicitly historical and cultural in its emphasis—a rather unusual stance in lieu of most of contemporary Western writings on developmental psychology. It is emphasized in this book that an adequate understanding of developmental psychology in the USSR is possible only when the reader considers psychologists' work in their cultural-historical contexts.

Secondly, the story of the progress of developmental psychology in the Soviet Union is relevant as a case study of the relationships of one particular society, and as an area of knowledge oriented towards revealing aspects of psychological phenomena (those of development) usually discounted in scientific discourse because of logical, philosophical, linguistic and social constraints on investigators' thinking. The explanation of the development of sciences that has been introduced by Thomas Kuhn is put to the test in the context of the case history of Soviet developmental psychology.

Finally, the study of developmental psychology in the Soviet Union may help readers to understand the complexity of academic activities of psychologists who have to (or prefer to) live and work in the USSR, and to appreciate the intellectual richness of some of the psychological work emanating from the Soviet Union. Soviet developmental psychology is a multi-faceted discipline, in which extremely innovative ideas occur side-by-side with very dogmatic recitals of the basics of Marxist philosophy, and where potentially valuable empirical suggestions can easily be dismissed by Western readers because Soviet traditions of empirical data presentation in psychology differ from the consensually rigidified empirical traditions of Western psychologies.

II The Historical Context: Some Aspects of the Past of Russian Society

Russian cultural history is an interesting battlefield of different ideas borrowed from other cultures, integrated with Russia's own traditions, and then considered indigenously Russian and fiercely . defended as such when necessary. As will become clear in Chapters III to V, the same can be said of many ideas in Soviet psychology. Russian (and, later, Soviet) psychology has developed in close interaction with European social, political and scientific thought, although the 'European connection' of these ideas is often overlooked or dismissed as being of only historical interest. In this chapter some aspects of Russian cultural history that can be considered relevant to the advancement of Soviet developmental psychology are briefly outlined.

Soviet developmental psychology and its historical context

The history of developmental ideas in Russian culture constitutes an interesting case of the emergence of a system of thought within a changing society. The seven decades of the history of Soviet psychology were preceded by at least three hundred years of the development of the Russian culture at the intersection of European and Russian indigenous traditions. Likewise, that period saw the gradual expansion of the Russian Empire, which increasingly annexed different territories inhabited by people of non-Russian cultural background. That history of annexation is the basis for the cross-culturally heterogeneous contemporary psychology in the USSR.

Of course, the major event in Russian society that caused a major change in its psychology was the 1917 bolshevik revolution. However, psychology in Russia in the pre-1917 years formed the basis for the development of Soviet psychology along the lines of Marxist thought, imported by the new political group in power and taught to people in USSR through massive re-education efforts in the 1920s. The set of ideas, labelled 'Soviet psychology' in general terms, that emerged in the midst of the social turmoil of the 1920s and became firmly established in the 1930s, was a unification of some of the pre-1917 psychological traditions with the ethos of Marxist philosophy, integrated under the utopian visions widespread in the Soviet society. Four main themes that are characteristic of the new 'Soviet psychology' can be briefly outlined: emphasis on development, interest in collective and inter-individual psychological phenomena, the systemic perspective upon psychological issues, and the fusion of scientific and social issues in the discourse of Russia's psychologists. The developmental nature of the new 'Soviet psychology' as a whole emerged as an integration of pre-1917 dissemination of evolutionary ideas in Russian science (see Chapter III) on the one hand, and of the dialectical Marxist ideas promoted in Soviet society in the 1920s. A number of particular features characteristic of Soviet psychology at the present time have historical roots far back in the history of Russian culture. First, the interest in collective (rather than individual) phenomena in Soviet psychology is embedded in Russian cultural history. Secondly, the emphasis on taking a systemic (rather than reductionistic, atomistic) view of psychological phenomena may be traced to the relationships of Russian natural sciences of the nineteenth century and continental European natural philosophy. Finally, the fusion of scientific and social issues in the discourse of Soviet psychologists had a predecessor in the social activity of many psychologists and philosophers of the pre-1917 era. As McLeish (1975) has argued, that fusion can be attributed to the lack of events in the history of Russian society which could have drawn the line between the religious-moral and scientific domains of thought, similar to the Reformation in Europe.

The history of Soviet psychology illustrates social organization of paradigms in science and their change, particularly because this particular area of science (psychology) is closely tied to the events in society at large. That society, however, has undergone substantial social change in the course of a short period of time. Under these conditions it may become possible to observe the interdependence of science and society—changes in the latter can be seen to restructure the developmental course of the former.

Equally relevant is the fact that some ideas of practices that emerged in the new Soviet psychology were carried quickly (often prematurely) into social practice—only to trigger other social changes that eventually fed back into the course of psychology's development in most direct and dramatic ways.

Russian society and empire before 1917

It is impossible to summarize all the multi-faceted social history of Russia from ancient times, through the period of the formation and flourishing of the Russian Empire, to its downfall in 1917. Fortunately, from the perspective of providing a context for the emergence and development of child psychology in Russia and the Soviet Union, it is not necessary to dive very far into the realm of history. Most of the social issues that have formed the historical context for contemporary Soviet developmental psychology are of quite recent origin. Thus our brief analysis need not go back more than two or three centuries. It originates in the social change wrought by Peter I at the beginning of the eighteenth, and continued by Catherine II towards the end of that century. Events in nineteenth-century Russia were a continuation of the social processes that had emerged in the previous hundred years, and the whole historical development of Russia finally culminated in the social transformation which became possible following the change of political power during the 1917 revolution and its aftermath, the civil war.

The particular aspect of social history that concerns us in the present context is the development of ideas concerning children, their development and education, in Russia. The development of such ideas in any society takes place as the result of the social-communicative process of interaction among adults of different social roles and political positions. Their thinking about children is a small part of their more general world view, which develops both as individual adults develop themselves, and as the culture as a whole develops as a product of the cooperative actions of its members. Thus religious and political ideologies are of paramount importance for cultural beliefs about children. Likewise, for any actual transformation, or even efforts to change these ideologies themselves have their immediate repercussions on the ways in which children are thought about, and raised in practice. This social process obviously relates to the pre-history of developmental psychology in a country, as a scientific discipline. However, the actual emergence and the course of development of child psychology as a science is, in any country, deeply rooted in precisely that pre-history. Many accents to be found in contemporary Soviet developmental psychology would remain unintelligible without an overview of the social pre-history of psychology in Russia.

The development of Russian society since 1700 has clearly been dependent on wars and revolutions, only some of which actually involved Russia itself. Thus, Peter I's successes in the war with Sweden for access to the Baltic Sea at the beginning of the eighteenth century resulted in increased connections of the Russian Empire with Western Europe. The events of the American and French revolutions, as well as Pugachov's uprising, altered the course of the promotion of social ideology of European Enlightenment that was initially favoured by Catherine II. Instead of liberal ideas, German-type bureaucracy began to govern Russian society. The Napoleonic wars provided another opportunity for changes in the Russian society, which led to the Dekabrist uprising, its severe suppression, and the rethinking of social and child-education ideology as its aftermath. The Crimean war was another trigger for recognition of the need for social change, and the Russian-Japanese war resulted in a violent and severely suppressed efforts towards this. Finally, the First World War sowed the seeds of the 1917 revolution, the course of which guided Russian society into the form that gave rise to a new approach in developmental psychology in the 1920s. That, again, took place amidst a ferment of discussions, controversies, infights, and the eventual establishment of the power role of the communist party throughout the country in forms that borrowed heavily from pre-1917 practices enriched only by the imported Marxist thinking.

In the course of this stormy history of Russian society, two general lines of issues were of paramount importance to the developing thinking about children. First, all child-related issues were necessarily rooted in the system of beliefs of the Russian Orthodox Church. Secondly, these issues had their semi-secular side in the need of the Russian state to educating at least some of its children for particular political and technological goals, while keeping their loyalty to the state and its religion. Furthermore,

Russian society has over centuries been a segregated class society, with different roles prescribed for different classes. Different socio-economic strata have in turn responded differently to one or another innovation brought into Russian culture from outside. As a result, Russian society has developed as a heterogeneous mixture of indigenous Russian culture and different kinds of imported features from other cultures. Some of these imported aspects have been assimilated very well (in fact, so well that they may easily be considered 'genuinely Russian'), others have resulted in continuous and at times violent friction between different factions in society. Still other imported cultural issues have been rejected from the outset, so have not become parts of Russian culture.

Religious ideologies: Russia and Europe

Russia became Christianized in the year 988, taking the Byzantine version of Christianity as its state religion. Although this happened before the official breakdown of the Christian church as the result of the 'Great Schism' of 1054, that acceptance of Christianity set Russian cultural development on a different route from that of Western-European cultures. It is interesting to note that Byzantine Christianity was *imported* into a heterogeneous cultural area that remained politically divided into separate states until Ivan the Terrible established the centrally governed Russian state in the sixteenth century. The imported nature of Byzantine Christianity played an important part in the development of Russian culture, becoming assimilated to the existing religious belief system which it also changed (but did not replace in full).

McLeish (1975) has emphasized the difference between Russian and European development of cultures in terms of the religious frameworks in which they were embedded. In contrast to Europe, Russia never underwent anything comparable to the cultural events of the Renaissance, or the religious Reformation. As a result, the differentiation of the spheres of secular and religious life (a major result of the Reformation and the advent of capitalist production in society) that emerged in Western Europe remained largely unknown in Russia. The specifics of the Eastern Orthodox Christianity may have played a part in guiding any cultural event in Russia comparable to the Reformation in Europe. McLeish has compared the two trends in Christianity:

The essential difference between the two branches of the universal Church consisted in the *orthodox* character of the Eastern Church. This is testified to in the fact that discussion over dogma virtually terminated in the seventh century— the legacy of the Bible and of the Fathers of the Church was regarded as providing a completed body of knowledge necessary for salvation. This knowledge, rather than being developed and interpreted, was required to be preserved intact without admixture and without loss. Religious energies, which in the Western Church were channelled into controversy (and sometimes bloody wars), were concentrated on ritual. This had the function of bringing the individual and the community into direct contact with the Deity. The *ikon* was regarded not merely as a symbol but as a vital link transmitting grace and power to the believer. (McLeish, 1975, p. 17)

An emphasis on the 'no doubt' status given to religious dogma is certainly a powerful tool in the hands of anybody trying to establish social control over others. Russia's history, of course, is full of different religious dissent movements and their often violent conflicts with political power. One aspect, though, seems to support McLeish's position—Russian dissenters usually established a new undoubtable dogma, following which they clashed inexorably with the state power (supported by the Russian Orthodox Church). Rational argumentation about different dogmas, efforts to prove the truthfulness of one over the others by argument rather than by dominance-by-force, has not been widespread in Russian history. (As will be shown in Chapter III, disputes of Soviet philosophers and psychologists in the 1920s and later followed this pattern quite well.) Furthermore, discussions about ideas, even in the eighteenth and nineteenth centuries of more intense cultural contact with Europe, were limited to the few who were educated in the European tradition, rather than widely shared by many people (even among the well-to-do). It can be argued that the role of the Russian Orthodox Church over Russia's cultural history has set the stage for paradoxical relations between the 'indigenously Russian' and 'imported foreign' aspects of culture in literally every area of intellectual life—literature, ideology, politics and science. The tendency—widespread among Russian intelligentsia historically—to 'seek the truth' has simultaneously resulted in very sophisticated philosophical, literary, musical and scientific work on the one side, and extremes of dogmatism in philosophy, social policy, and science, on the other. The impact of that tendency on the beginnings of contemporary Soviet psychology in the 1920s is noteworthy—many highly erudite psychologists or physiologists (e.g., Chelpanov, Kornilov, Pavlov, Bekhterev) were involved in disputes, displaying their strong conviction in the truthfulnes of *their* particular theoretical standpoint.

Citizenship and education in eighteenth-century Russia

The paradoxical nature of the education of people beyond religious socialization by the Church in Russia became very evident at the time when Czar Peter I made an effort to modernize some aspects of Russian culture along West European lines at the beginning of the eighteenth century. In addition to promoting European technology (in connection with his military interests), Peter I attacked a number of traditions in the cultural sphere that were related to the orthodox heritage of Russia. Many popular accounts of Russian history of the times of Peter I make much of that czar's fascination with cutting the long beards of the aristocracy at his court, to make them more like the courtiers of European monarchs. However, Peter I's reform efforts certainly extended beyond such merely symbolic issues, and included among others the introduction of new educational establishments. At the level of schools, it involved the education of sons of the Russian aristocracy in foreign languages and sciences (Kniaz'kov & Serbov, 1910, pp. 35–56). This expansion education was a significant part of the technological modernization of the Russian military establishment. It opened up new areas of knowledge for young people in Russian culture. At the same time, the introduction of education in Russia was of a pragmatic nature—its goals were to improve useful know-how in the service of the state.

This practical orientation of secondary education reveals the deep roots of the Russian 'state school' *gosudarstvennaia shkola*) idea embedded in the needs of the central government, rather than in any Enlightenment type of social policy of improving the educational state of people for their own sake. The ambivalence of the relationship between state goals and Enlightenment philosophies became particularly prominent in the reign of Catherine II. She—being an imported ruler herself (a German princess married into the family of a Russian czar)—proved to be an European-oriented enlightener for some, and a despotic ruler of the people at the same time.

Catherine II introduced the Russian society the idea of *general* education—education that transcends the immediate practical needs of the state, yet keeps all the education that people receive in the service of the state. During her reign, and after considerable infighting between proponents of different educational systems (all of Western European origin—cf. Ermilov, 1906), the system built along the Austrian model (of 1774) for general education was finally adopted in 1786. By that time, Catherine II's earlier fascination with ideas of the French Enlightenment (for example, by virtue of her active correspondence with, and support of, Voltaire) had greatly receded. The Russian general education system introduced in 1786 differed from its Austrian model in significant respects, the most important of which was that it granted educational facilities to urban dwellers, but not to rural peasants. It also did not introduce the rule of *obligatory* education, but emphasized that the new schools should accept students on *voluntary* basis (Kniaz'kov & Serbov, 1910, p. 128). Thus, the educational system clearly was used unevenly by different classes in society. For example, in 1801 the system was estimated to include 72% of the students from the aristocracy, bourgeoisie, clergy, and the merchant class (Kniaz'kov & Serbov, 1910, p. 154). Education indeed had become possible for those who could afford it and may have wanted it, and in turn the state was guaranteed the use of people educated by this system, in different functions of its apparatus.

The establishment of the core ideology of individual-society relations

Interestingly, it is the educational undertaking by Catherine II in the context of her Enlightenment-related efforts to educate Russian people that explicitly defined loyalty to the monarchy as the major psychological demand for all citizens of the Russian Empire. In her treatise *Book on the duties of man and citizen* that was meant as the definitive guideline for the newly established educational system (translated in full in Black, 1979, pp. 209–66), the need for socialization of children to become loyal to the state occupied a prominent place. Labelled in a laudatory way, the *love for the fatherland* was defined as it

... consists in showing esteem and gratitude to the government, in obeying the laws, institutions and just rights of society in which we live, in respecting the advantages of society and using them for the general good, and in striving as much as possible to perfect these things so that we might partake of the glory of the society to which we belong and might do our utmost [to promote] its well-being. (Black, 1979, pp. 246–7)

The parallel between the parent-child and ruler-citizen relationships can be found very much on the surface in Catherine II's treatise:

Everyone knows that a parent tries to protect his children from all dangers. So the Sovereign provides security from foreign enemies to the whole country, like a father who loves his children. A parent keeps order and harmony between his children. Similarly the Sovereign maintains justice and defends every subject who is offended unjustly by his fellow-countrymen. A parent provides his children with various necessities and benefits. The Sovereign too extends order, prosperity and benefits befitting every rank all over [his realm]. (Black, 1979, p. 247)

Remembering that the function of this writing by Catherine II was to aid the socialization of people towards loyalty to the ruler and the state, the above quote reveals the effort to build up such loyalty by reference to its similarity to basic tenets of family life. The use of this parallel can be seen as a very appropriate psychological means of socialization at a time when the educational system became established in Russia. However, an extension of this parallel may lead to the development of parallel loyalties—to the head of the particular family, and to the head of the Empire. Therefore, the monopoly of the state (over the parents) became an issue. Catherine II spelt out four ways in which the citizens should demonstrate their love for the fatherland:

1. ... *the first duty* of a son of the fatherland is *not to say or do anything reprehensible in the eyes of the government*, such as the following disgraceful acts; complaining, malicious conversations, defamatory or impertinent remarks [aimed] at a state institution and the government. [These] are crimes against the fatherland and warrant harsh punishment.
2. ... *the second duty* of the sons of the fatherland is *compliance* [with the laws]. Everyone is obligated to obey [laws] even when the obedience seems difficult and when one thinks that the laws ought to be different.
3. Often the general well-being cannot be achieved except by having some people feel some kind of an encumbrance. Yet the common good must be preferred to the personal [good]. Private individuals cannot see everything in the state and learn enough about the condition in it to determine correctly how one or another law contributes to the general and personal good. Those who govern can and must know all this better and more reliably. For this reason *trust in the foresight and*

jurisprudence of those who govern is the *third duty* of sons of the fatherland.
4. The obedience of sons of the fatherland must be active. That is, every son of the
fatherland must really use all his abilities and property for the good of the state,
especially when they are needed by those who govern. *Doing this* is the *fourth
duty* of a son of the fatherland. The needs of the state are varied; they cannot be
known to every citizen; they can be greater or less according to circumstances . . . .
Therefore a son of the fatherland must show his willingness to serve his country
with his abilities and possessions not according to his own reasoning and volition,
but rather according to what his government demands from him, and he is
obligated to fulfill that demand willingly in all situations. (Black, 1979, pp. 248–9)

These demands of undivided loyalty to the government have
served as the basis of all subsequent Russian (and later Soviet)
ways of thinking about the individual's relationship to society.
Whereas in Catherine's time those demands need not have differed
much from similar citizenship requirements in other European
countries, what is remarkable in the context of Russian society is
that these rules survived with little change in the course of the two
centuries subsequent to their introduction. They formed the basis
on which the meaning of 'partiinost' in Soviet science was built in
the first decades of the Soviet rule (see Chapter III). They have also
remained the major basis of child socialization in the Soviet Union
(as will be exemplified in Chapter VII).

Slavophiles and Westernizers: views on the improvement of society in nineteenth-century Russia

The development of Russian society in the nineteenth century
included the further advancement of two tendencies in Russian
culture. One of these—the 'Slavophilic' social movement—
involved the ideology of return to Russian indigenous ways of life
of the times when Russia's connections with Western Europe were
still rare (prior to reforms of Peter I). The other movement among
Russian aristocracy and intellectuals of other backgrounds
emphasized the need for closer cultural ties with Europe. This
movement of 'Westernizers' advanced to the excesses of taking
over aspects of culture from European countries at times, thus
serving as a suitable stimulus for the Slavophiles to move towards
excessive emphasis on 'truly Russian' ways of life. Many of the
Russian progressive thinkers (as they are labelled by contemporary
Soviet sources)—Belinski, Herzen, Turgenev, etc.—followed
Westernizing ideals in their wishes and activities to change
Russian society. However, both Slavophiles and Westernizers

approached the task of reaching their respective goals of social change in a basically similar way. They made their goals into *the* normative ideal obligatory for society, and fought fiercely with their opponents in words and deeds to attain these ideal goals (Egorov, 1973). It is in the context of the fight between Slavophiles and Westernizers in Russian society that developmental ideas emerged and were maintained in the nineteenth century.

The influence of European natural sciences on Russian thought

Developmental ideas that were advanced and gained ground in European thinking in the nineteenth century can be roughly divided into three streams, each of which had its own historical path in its dissemination in Russian society. First, developmental ideas constituted the core of the advancement of evolutionary thinking in biology (Lamarck, Darwin, Wallace, Spencer, Huxley, Haeckel). This domain of ideas was largely confined to the discourse of biologists and natural philosophers in the beginning, and later became more widespread in European societies in connection with its conflict with the dominant religious world views. The second stream of thought where developmental ideas were advanced and from where they began to affect societies was the tradition of the dialectical philosophy of Hegel, which was borrowed and modified by Marx and Engels in conjunction with their theoretical and applied sociological undertakings. This domain of developmental thought became part of the socio-political process of European societies. Finally, the third line of developmental thinking emerged in the context of the embryology of Karl Ernst von Baer, Wilhelm Preyer, and others. Each of these three domains was only partially related to the others. Quite often, representatives of one domain were at least ambivalent about the role of the others. Thus Marx and Engels were hesitant to accept Darwin's evolutionary theory unconditionally, because of its connection with Malthus' population theory. Von Baer, likewise, remained relatively reserved towards Darwin's theory (Raikov, 1961).

The dissemination of developmental ideas in Russia proceeded along separate lines in each of these three domains. Perhaps the source of developmental ideas for Russian scientists in the last century that was (at least geographically) closest was the embryological and natural-scientific thinking of Karl Ernst von Baer (1792–1876) of Baltic German origin, who served as a member of the Russian Academy of Science in St Petersburg. Von Baer's contribution to the advancement of developmental ideas in nineteenth-century Russia served as the basis for Severtsov's further advancement of these in his phylo-embryogenetic theory in the first decades of the twentieth century (see Chapter III). Through Severtsov, von Baer's developmental ideas reached the attention of Russian psychologists in the 1920s (Basov, Vygotsky, and others; see Chapters IV and V).

The dissemination of Darwin's theory in Russia was remarkably quick—it was spread by the activities of Western-oriented Russian natural scientists working under the ethos of a substantial intellectual upsurge in Russian society during the 1860s, wrought by Russia's defeat in the Crimean War. The speed with which Darwin's basic works were translated into Russian illustrates the active quest by Russian cosmopolitan intellectuals for the new, developmental, system of thought. Thus, *The origin of species* (1859) appeared in its first Russian translation in 1864, followed by a second edition one year later. *The descent of man*, translated by Sechenov, appeared in 1871, and at least three other of Darwin's books (*Variation of animals and plants under domestication, The expression of emotions in man and animals*, and *Voyage of the Beagle*) followed in the 1870s. Russian translations of Wallace's works did not lag behind—his *Natural selection* of 1870 appeared in Russian in 1878.

Russian biological thinkers as well as the rest of the 'liberal intelligentsia' of the time considered Darwin's ideas an obligatory part of their education, and sometimes turned to deeply committed worship of it as the 'absolute truth' (Kline, 1955, pp. 307–8). On the other hand, it is necessary to remind ourselves that the 'Russian intelligentsia' of those times (and also at our time) was a highly segmented and self-segregated social group in which different kinds of integrated sub-groups had no contact with one another. Thus, the groupings that glorified Darwinian ideas were separate from others (religion-centred intellectuals) who would not consider these ideas in any way valuable, and vice versa. As

Kline points out, the first decades of the dissemination of Darwinian ideas in Russia were quite different from the public controversy about those ideas that was present in Western Europe. That preliminary period of dissemination of Darwinian thinking in Russia

... is remarkable chiefly for its *lack* of anti-Darwinian statements on behalf of representatives of the Church, since this period (extending to 1884) was marked in the West by many violent clashes, in print and on the public platform (between T. H. Huxley and Bishop Wilberforce, for example). To be sure, during this period only one Russian theological journal, *Pravoslavnoe obozrenie*, was printing theoretical articles. In any case, its editors apparently did not regard Darwinism as a threat to faith or morals, or else had not yet decided how to meet this threat, for only two articles were published during this entire twenty-four-year period which touched upon the question of Darwinism. (Kline, 1955, p. 313)

It was only later, starting in 1885 (the publication of N. Danilevskii's *Darvinizm: kriticheskoie issledovanie*) that conflict between Darwinist biologists (with Timiriazev in the lead) and Church-related Slavophile thinkers came out into the open. It culminated in 1887–89, when both sides accused each other of a variety of more or less serious breaches in accepting or misunderstanding Darwinian thinking (Kline, 1955).

On one particular issue in Darwin's theory there happened to be conspicuous agreement between Russian Darwinists and anti-Darwinists: Both proponents and opponents of Darwin in Russia expressed their disagreements with *inter-individual competition* as the key factor in the evolutionary process. Instead, Russian thinkers of the latter half of the nineteenth century preferred to emphasize *cooperation* of organisms in their adaptation process. The idea of cooperation as the way by which organisms adapt to environments was first expressed by a young Russian biologist, N. Nozhin, in 1866 (Kline, 1955, p. 309), and was repeated by Chernyshevskii and others. A more explicit and widely-known perspective on the role of cooperation in evolution was represented in the thinking of Prince Peter Kropotkin, whose role in the history of anarchistic ideology is the main domain in which he is an original contributor.

Kropotkin, however, did not claim original authorship of the idea of the role of mutual aid as a factor in evolution. Instead, he pointed to the influence of the zoologist Kessler of St Petersburg

University, whose lecture 'On the law of mutual aid' at a Russian Congress of Naturalists in January 1880 was said by Kropotkin to have '... struck me as throwing a new light on the whole subject' (Kropotkin, 1908, p.x.). Kropotkin's own venture into the field of evolutionary thinking was his reaction to the propagandist efforts by Thomas Huxley, whose presentation of the Darwinian idea of 'struggle for existence' he considered excessive, and inaccurate as far as Darwin's original emphases were perceived by him. The first of his essays on the topic—'Mutual aid among animals'—appeared in 1890 as a direct rebuttal of Huxley's *Struggle for existence and its bearing upon man* two years before. It was only later that Kropotkin continued to elaborate the theme, extending his conception of 'mutual aid' to savages, barbarians, lifestyle in mediaeval cities, and his contemporary society. All these essays later become chapters in his well-known book *Mutual aid: A factor of evolution* (1902).

As the title of his book implies, Kropotkin emphasised the role of mutual aid in evolution as *a* (and not *the*) factor in the evolutionary process. He advocated the idea that inter-organismic struggle for life exists in parallel with mutual aid, and that the role of the former must not be interpreted as the overwhelming mechanism of evolution. Kropotkin claimed:

As soon as we study animals—not in laboratories and museums only, but in the forest and the prairie, in the steppe and the mountains—we at once perceive that there is an immense amount of warfare and extermination going on amidst various species, and especially amidst various classes of animals, there is, at the same time, as much, or perhaps even more, of mutual support, mutual aid, and mutual defence amidst animals belonging to the same species or, at least, to the same society. *Sociability is as much a law of nature as mutual struggle.* Of course it would be extremely difficult to estimate, however roughly, the relative numerical importance of both these series of facts. But if we resort to an indirect test, and ask Nature: 'Who are the fittest: those who are continually at war with each other, or those who support one another?' we at once see that those animals who acquire habits of mutual aid are undoubtedly the fittest. They have more chances to survive, and they attain, in their respective classes, the highest development of intelligence and bodily organization. (Kropotkin, 1908, pp. 5–6)

Kropotkin provided numerous examples from the behaviour of animals of different species, as well as that of humans in different times, in favour of not discarding inter-individual cooperation as an important aspect in the organization of development of animal species and human societies. He did not specify in what ways 'struggle for existence' and his 'mutual aid' interact in reality. Nevertheless, he came close to an analysis of that interaction in his criticism of Herbert Spencer's synthetic philosophy:

Mutual aid indeed is not only the most strong means for every animal species in its struggle for existence against hostile forces of nature and other hostile species, but it is also *the main tool of progressive development*. It gives longevity even to the weakest animals (and, consequently, provides for accumulation of experience), guarantees their reproduction and mental development. (Kropotkin, 1920, pp. 35–6)

Kropotkin's emphasis on the cooperative (systemic) and future-oriented nature of development later (as will be seen in the next chapters) became one of the main features of Soviet developmental psychology.

Developmental ideas in Russian social thought

Differently from the assimilation of the idea of development in biological sciences and embryology, the philosophical line in the assimilation of developmental ideas in Russia was closely connected with the social-political friction between different political parties. In fact, the emergence of a left-wing political force which imported Marxist social ideology from Western Europe set the stage for assimilation of the idea of development among other aspects of dialectical philosophy. The history of assimilation of Marxist philosophy in Russia, both pre- and post-1917, is closely related to the utopian ideals and messianic ideology of the political group that turned that philosophy into its militant ideology.

The Marxist emphasis on viewing social phenomena as developing entities was a corollary to the dissemination of social-democratic political ideology in Russia. An interesting facet of such dissemination of developmental ideas is revealed in the early work of A. Bogdanov (alias A. A. Malinovskii), whose later utopian writing became well-known (e.g. 'Red Star'), and whose philosophical system of 'tektology' (Bogdanov, 1922) is a forerunner of the General Systems Theory.

That Russian social democrats of the end of the nineteenth century who were interested in philosophy should arrive at explicitly developmental world views is no surprise. It follows from their attachment to the dialectical materialistic thought of Karl Marx and Friedrich Engels, who built their philosophical system (and social politics) on the foundation of Hegel's dialectical thinking. Furthermore, like other intellectuals in Russia at the end of the nineteenth century, social democrats could benefit from the proliferation of the Darwinian evolutionary theory in Russian society. Thus, when viewed from both sides—those of natural science and dialectical philosophy—Russian social-democratic thinkers were well prepared to look at the world from a developmental standpoint.

Bogdanov fits that general pattern quite well. In a book entitled *The main elements of the historical view on nature: nature, life, psyche, and society* (1899) he proposed a developmental world view that integrated evolutionary theory with dialectical philosophy, dealing explicitly with the issue of understanding development.

Bogdanov's explicit interest was in understanding processes of change that take place in nature and society. According to him, such understanding could be reached only if the *historical approach* to natural and social processes is used. Every process was viewed by Bogdanov as taking place in some context (which was also a dynamic process, rather than a static state). The *form* of the dynamic systems can be studied in two ways—by looking at the *internal* and *external* history of those systems. Changes of the internal relationships of the system were defined by Bogdanov as the internal history of its form. In a similar way, the study of the system's process of relationships with its environment was defined as the external history (Bogdanov, 1899, p. 49).

Bogdanov followed a basically environmentalistic perspective in his view on the relative role of the external and internal histories of a system in determining its dynamic state. The environment was assigned the leading causal role, with the qualification that environmental effects on the internal state of the system often operate with a time-lag. However, by attributing the leading causal role to environment, Bogdanov did not deny the relevance of the internal history of the system:

Changes in the internal relationships of a form are triggered by changes in the external relationships and follow the latter over time. The character of the internal changes is fully determined, first, by the character of external changes, and, secondly, by the already existing internal relationships of the form. (Bogdanov, 1899, p. 51)

It is interesting to note the presence of two features in Bogdanov's thinking. First, the emphasis on external (environmental) determination of the internal changes of a system follows the lines of both evolutionist and Marxist thought. Secondly, Bogdanov's emphasis on the primacy of external history in the causation of internal changes is not absolute, and does not constitute a simple causal (environmental relations directly cause internal relations of a system/form) attribution. Instead, he explicitly recognized the relevance of the pre-existent internal 'basis' of the form, that participates together with environmental input in the construction of the 'internal history' of the system. The influence of the external relations on the internal relations of a system can be delayed in time, and is partial (rather than absolute) in its character.

Bogdanov's interactionistic conceptualization of development in nature and society is remarkably modern in the sense of contemporary psychology. Bogdanov's conceptualization of the interaction of the internal and external histories of a system involved a sub-division of the system into its 'central' and 'peripheral' parts. This separation made it possible for him to integrate the role of internal relations with environmental input in the development of the given system. Bogdanov claimed (1899, p. 52) that the 'internal history of the central elements [of the form] is determined by the history of the whole' (by the internal history of the whole form, including its central and peripheral elements in a structured arrangement). In contrast the structure of the 'peripheral elements in the process of their change, is determined both by the external environment, and by the internal relationships of the whole' (Bogdanov, 1899, p. 53). Bogdanov's systemic emphasis is evident in his efforts to explain the development of the forms in nature and society. His thinking moved along a very natural trail: since all forms are interdependent with their environments, but structurally (although dynamically) organized, then some parts of the structure ('peripheral elements') are more closely related to the environment than others ('central elements'). The peripheral elements are on the one hand linked with the environmental input, while remaining parts of the whole organism (therefore—linked with central elements) on the other. The change in the system as a whole is therefore co-determined by the environmental input and the internal history (of the core of the system), and can be delayed (relative to the timing of the external influences) due to the functioning of the peripheral elements. It is obvious that Bogdanov's 'environmentalism' was actually similar to what is called an 'interactionist' standpoint in our contemporary psychology.

The development of a system takes place through 'crises' (a feature of central importance in Marxist philosophy) that involve the 'emergence' of a new form while an 'old' one 'perishes'. Bogdanov's scheme of system-environment relationships in which the central and peripheral parts of the system are distinguished from one another lead him to explain development in a way that antedates many of the inclinations of Russian/Soviet psychologists of this century:

In the process of development, *primary change* takes place in the case of those internal relationships of the form that are closer and more immediately related with the fight for existence. After that, other internal relationships *change accordingly*—in that, their change takes place as much later, as they are located further away from the immediate fight for existence with the external world, and relate remotely to that world. (Bogdanov, 1899, p. 117)

The developmental adaptations that take place in the immediate encounter of the organism with the world were labelled *primary adaptations*, on the basis of which more 'remote' phenomena—*secondary developmental adaptations*—are constructed, with a possible time-lag. Later Russian/ Soviet traditions of talking about the 'primary' and 'secondary' 'signal system' (Pavlov), or Bekhterev's habit of explaining psychological phenomena by reference to increasingly complex 'associative reflexes' (see Chapter III) are conceptually not very different from Bogdanov's account. Furthermore, Basov's analysis of the 'internal' and 'external' stimulation and their integration (see Chapter V) bears resemblance to Bogdanov's theoretical scheme of development through organism-environment interaction.

Both in the area of natural science and in the field of social-political philosophy in Russia in the second half of the last century, the basis for explicit acceptance of developmental ideas was gradually formed. Similarly to the further advancement of developmental ideas in post-1917 society, the issues of development in Russian society were inevitably embedded in the context of social-political events. Ideas of development were offspring of the developing society and its complex turmoils.

Conclusions: Russian cultural history and development ideas

This introduction has outlined the two major conceptual issues, the mutual relations of which in a historical vein will be analyzed in this book. On the one hand, reasons for the rarity of developmental thinking in psychology were briefly outlined. On the other, the history of a number of selected aspects of Russian cultural history that relate to assimilation of developmental ideas were presented. However, none of those dealt with psychology in the narrower delineation of this discipline. In the next chapter, the major lines of developmental thought as it emerged in the history of Russian/Soviet psychology are presented.

III Developmental Ideas and the History of Psychology in Russian/Soviet Society

Developmental ideas were disseminated in Russian behavioural science in the latter half of the nineteenth century, and continued to spread during the first two decades of this century that preceded the 1917 revolution. Two traditions of behavioural science became established in Russia, both of which played important roles in the advancement of developmental ideas. The first tradition emerged from the context of biological evolutionary theory, where the names of two scientists are particularly important. Developmental ideas constituted an important part of the zoopsychological theorizing of Vladimir Vagner. Also, the evolutionary thinking of Aleksei Severtsov was extended from the realm of biological morphology to that of behavioural psychology.

The second tradition that provided relevant input for the development of Russian developmental psychology was the neurophysiological tradition that started with the work of Ivan Sechenov. It was followed by two reflex-based neurophysiological thought systems that were influential in the first half of this century—those of Ivan Pavlov and Vladimir Bekhterev. This neurophysiological approach to development continues to be relevant in contemporary Soviet physiological sciences, with some connection to contemporary Soviet developmental psychology. The work of Sechenov, Pavlov and Bekhterev included selective emphasis on various aspects of development, although it would be an overgeneralization to consider it developmental in its core.

Taken together, the traditions of Russian evolutionary biology and neurophysiology formed a solid natural-science basis for advancement of developmental ideas in psychology. The role of Vagner's zoopsychology and Severtsov's evolutionary theory are particularly important in creating that basis.

Evolutionary theory and Russian developmental psychology

Developmental ideas became integrated into Russian psychology of the turn of the twentieth century due to the work of two scientists—Vladimir Vagner (or Wagner, as his name is often transliterated, particularly in German publications), and Aleksei Severtsov. Both started their scientific activities in pre-1917 Russia, and continued in the first decades of the post-1917 period, during their old age (Vagner lived from 1849 until 1934; Severtsov from 1866 to 1936). Both of them were evolutionists, although the areas of application of their evolutionary thinking differed. Vagner was the founder of Russian comparative psychology (zoopsychology). Severtsov approached developmental issues in the context of morphology, and although his interest in psychological factors involved in the evolutionary process has been mentioned in some Soviet historical accounts of psychology (e.g., Smirnov, 1975, pp. 141 and 211), his more specific contributions to the advancement of developmental thinking have rarely received sufficient attention.

Developmental ideas in Vagner's zoopsychology

The scientific contributions of Vladimir Aleksandrovich Vagner to evolutionary thinking and zoopsychology in Russia range from empirical observations of the behaviour of different species (spiders, birds—Vagner, 1890, 1907) to treatises of methodological and theoretical importance (Vagner, 1910, 1913, 1924–9, 1929).

Already in his first general analysis of the methodological relevance of comparative psychology, Vagner emphasized the relevance of including the developmental (ontogenetic) aspect in the comparative framework of zoopsychology. In his doctoral dissertation *The biological method in zoopsychology* Vagner stated:

... it is not enough to compare psychological phenomena of some animals with those of others, it is also necessary to compare these phenomena of life of one animal at different stages of the development, starting from the first moments of the appearance of these psychological phenomena until the very last times of their presence. (Vagner, 1901, p. 19)

The study of psychological phenomena in the course of their carrier-organism's lifetime was emphasized by Vagner as his ontogenetic method, in parallel with the phylogenetic study of psychological phenomena. Vagner's emphasis on the ontogenetic study of psychological phenomena in different species in comparative-psychological research efforts made it possible for him to observe the relative independence of morphological and behavioural aspects of organisms' development. He advanced the thesis of *parallel lines of development* of behavioural and morphological sides of organisms in ontogeny (Vagner, 1913, p. 235). New behavioural (psychological) forms can develop in an organism's ontogeny which do not relate to any new development in the morphology of organs on which the behaviour is based. Likewise, changes in morphology need not give rise to any behaviourally novel forms. In this sense, the morphological and behavioral 'lines' of development proceed in parallel. However, these lines of organisms' development can sometimes also coincide—at some stages in development one line may have a direct role in the formation of the other. Vagner's recognition of 'loose coupling' between morphology and behaviour was a significant theoretical contribution to evolutionists' thinking about the role of behaviour in the evolutionary process.

The necessity for solving the puzzle of the role of behavior in evolution was apparent to Vagner, who understood the limited explanatory power of the idea of natural selection very well. Natural selection, according to Vagner, '...does not *create* anything by itself, it only *censors* the finished product: leaving some, eliminating others' (Vagner, 1929, p. 51). Therefore, he thought it important to look for mechanisms of development that produce the outcomes which are subsequently censored by the natural selection process. Ontogenetic investigations were expected to provide an insight into the processes of development.

Vagner's idea of parallel lines of development was later advanced further by himself and applied to the issue of biological and cultural development of the species in his last major work *Psychological types and collective psychology* (Vagner, 1929). Vagner contrasted the automatic-selective nature of natural selection with the constructive nature of inter-organism interaction ('collective psychology') as the mechanism of development:

Among animals involved in the fight for survival, the *natural selection* of those most fit to the conditions of the given environment served as the factor that directs progressive evolution. That selection itself created nothing; it only automatically eliminated all that did not coincide with the demands of the life conditions of the given time and place.

In the fight of psychological types with one another, collective psychology is the factor which directs progressive evolution.

Between those two factors of evolution—natural selection and collective psychology—both similar and different features exist. Their similarity exists in that as a result fights are eliminated through the insistence on the right of existence by either one or the other.

Their difference is, first, that while the organism eliminated by natural selection perishes, that left aside by collective psychology continues to live and fight for its life. Secondly, *natural selection is automatic and its laws immutable, whereas collective psychology is constantly changing, it develops and progresses in conjunction with the development of its constituent elements.* (Vagner, 1929, p. 132)

The contrast of the flexibility of 'collective psychology' with the rigidity of the laws of natural selection here seems to mimic the contrast between behaviour and morphology that Vagner used two decades earlier in his introduction of the idea of parallel lines in development. The issues of 'collective psychology' were a popular topic of discourse in the Russia of the 1920s, as is evident from publications by a number of leading psychologists of the time under that title. At different levels of phylogenetic development, the relative importance of natural selection and 'collective psychology' vary. In the human case, Vagner claimed that 'collective psychology in the social life of humans plays the role analogous to that played in the animal kingdom by natural selection' (Vagner, 1929, p. 205). That analogy also entailed the selective censor's role to be taken over by 'collective psychology', from natural selection in biology.

Vagner's ideas were influential in the emerging developmental psychology of the 1920s in the USSR. His influence on Vygotsky's thinking is beyond question. More importantly, his ideas served as the basis for most of contemporary Soviet zoopsychology (see Fabri, 1975), and most of the developmental psychology that emerged in the framework of the 'Leningrad school' of Soviet psychology (Malakhovskaia, 1975; Tihh, 1966, 1970).

Ontogeny, phylogeny, and psychology in Severtsov's developmental thinking

The inclusion of a brief analysis of Severtsov's ideas here—in the context of a work of developmental *psychology* in the USSR— may seem far-fetched at first glance. Aleksei Nikolaevich Severtsov was an embryologist and an evolutionary theoretician whose connections with the Russian psychological establishment both before and after 1917 were less than extensive. His biological empirical work was conducted over many decades, and was exclusively devoted to issues of morphogenesis in different animal species (see Adams, 1980 for a thorough overview of Severtsov's work). The only theoretical work that Severtsov published that intersected with issues of psychology was his *Evolution and the psyche* (*Evoliutsia i psikhika*, 1922) in which he discussed the role of behaviour in the process of evolution. Severtsov's major theoretical works on the theory of evolution were exclusively concentrated on issues of how morphological phylogeny relates to ontogenetic (embryologic) development of organisms (Severtsov, 1921, 1929, 1934).

There are, nevertheless, good reasons for not overlooking Severtsov's theoretical contributions to the scientific approaches to the study of development that were important for Russian biologists and psychologists of his time, and that emerged as the single definitive line of the psychology that developed in the USSR from the 1920s onwards. Severtsov's role in the advancement of Russian/Soviet evolutionary biology was immense. His pedagogical activities at the universities of Tartu (1898–1902), Kiev (1902–10) and Moscow (1910–30) resulted in a situation where almost all the notable evolutionary morphologists in the USSR by the 1930s were in one or another way educated by Severtsov (Adams, 1980, p. 196). This practical influence is even more noteworthy if we remember that between the two World Wars, Soviet evolutionary biology became the leading intellectual tradition of world evolutionary theory. It is in the context of the serious evolutionary thinking of Soviet biologists, including Severtsov, that Soviet developmental psychology emerged and advanced in the 1920s.

Severtsov's particular ideas about development deserve a closer analysis. Like Vagner, he was interested in understanding how the *process* of development proceeds, and the developmental phenomena he was particularly interested in were those of phylogeny and ontogeny. His interest in evolution started (like that of Vagner) from the background of German evolutionary and embryological thinking of the nineteenth century, in which Haeckel's recapitulation idea ('biogenetic law') was held in prominence. At the time of the emergence of his interest in more general theoretical issues around 1908 (cf. Severtsov, 1934, p. 3), discussions of the relevance of evolutionary theory to individual organisms' development were as active as the disputes around sociobiology in the present day. The use of evolutionary ideas in speculative ways as explanations of outcomes of developmental processes did not satisfy Severtsov. In a speech delivered in 1910 at a meeting of Russian naturalists and medical doctors, he criticized his contemporaries' wide (ab)use of evolutionary explanations:

In order to explain the fact of evolution, a certain internal teleological principle, some kind of *vis evolutiva* that is endowed with feelings and will, is inserted into the organism. Does it not remind you of the electrical and magnetic liquids used in old physics? The proposition that evolution takes place because of the existence of a certain evolutive force is nothing more than the reiteration of the very fact of evolution. It inadvertently brings to mind the classic explanation of the sedative effect of opium, given by a doctor in a play by Moliere: *'Opium facit dormire'*—*'Quia est in eo virtus dormitiva, cuius est natura sensus assupire'*. *Virtus dormitiva–vis evolutiva*, isn't it the same line of thought ...? (Severtsov, 1921, p. 307)

Severtsov quickly proceeded beyond idle speculations about the biogenetic law of Mueller-Haeckel, and attempted to discover the laws of the process of evolution. In his efforts to understand how phylogeny relates to ontogeny, he developed a theoretical system that has become known as that of phylo-embryogenesis (Russian: *filembriogenez*). Severtsov's first step to relate phylogenetic and ontogenetic sides of evolution was to bring the *time* dimension of individual development into the discussion of the role of evolution in the survival of individual organisms. He emphasized that the conditions of the fight for survival of animals of the same species, who live in the same environment, differ at different periods of their lives. The young offspring differ from their parents in terms of the conditions under which they have to survive. A species that serves as a food resource for the adult animals of another species may be a major predator of the offspring of that species. Within the same species, the ways of relating to the environment by the developing organism differ at different stages of their ontogeny. Such ontogenetic stage-specificity of relations with the environment is supported in development by adequate timing of the maturation of different organs. Severtsov relies on the principle of heterochrony in the ontogeny of different organ systems of the given animal. Those organs ontogenetically essential to the individual's fight for survival at a certain stage of development are described by him as maturing exactly by that time (Severtsov, 1921, p. 189). That ontogenetic heterochrony is the product of the phylogenetic evolution process that operates not at the level of the 'fit' of organs in general (that is, without specification of the conditions of time and environment), but at the level of their 'fit' according to the particular age stage and environmental conditions of the organism. The changes in the phylogenetic process can occur either through alterations at *early* stages of embryonal development, or through reconstruction of the *final* state of affairs of the individual organism's development.

Severtsov's theoretical account of the development of species and individual organisms was systemic and holistic in its nature. Thus he considered that both *progressive* and *regressive* changes acted in a coordinated fashion, leading to further development. Furthermore, the evolution of particular organs within the developing organism as a whole takes place at the intersection of both external (environmental) and internal (the place of the organ in the system of other organs) conditions. Severtsov stated:

In respect of the evolution of animals, taken as a whole, we must say that it consists of the evolution of different organs. As we saw, every organ in its evolution adapts on the one hand to the conditions of the surrounding environment, and on the other to the rest of the organs of the given animal. That is, evolution is a harmonious process, in which all parts of the process are appropriately coordinated between themselves. Evolution takes place through the parallel action of *progressive* and *regressive* changes in the organization and functions of animals. Depending on which of these processes prevails in the phylogenetic process, we characterize the *general* nature of the evolutionary process as progress, or regress. But here we must remember that those *regressive* changes ... are adaptations that are useful for the general economy of the organism, and as such are also factors of biological progress that is, in the end, characterized by the success by the species in the fight for survival. That regress does not lead the organism to death: the extinction of species does not originate in regressive changes, but in the disadaptation and in insufficient ability to adapt to new, changing conditions. (Severtsov, 1921, pp. 116–17)

Such emphasis on the coordinated and systemic view of biological evolution is repeated in the work of Russian psychologists later in the 1920s. For example, Basov's emphasis on the coordination of internal and external stimulation domains in the process of child development (see Chapter V) is rooted in Severtsov's theoretical thinking (Basov, 1931a, pp. 78–80 and pp. 118–19). Severtsov's theoretical contribution to developmental psychology was likewise made explicit by Vygotsky, who suggested that his systemic-holistic view of development could serve as the foundation for a 'new psychology' (Vygotsky, 1982a, p. 184).

Severtsov's only, but purposeful, excursion into the analysis of psychological issues in relation to evolution (Severtsov, 1922) illustrated another aspect of his evolutionary perspective that consolidated over the 1920s and culminated in his analysis of the *directions* of the evolutionary process (Severtsov, 1934, Sewertzoff, 1929). Namely, he discussed the role of behaviour in the evolutionary process, in the case of environmental conditions which themselves are constantly undergoing change. That environmental change may take place at different speeds for different aspects of the environment. According to Severtsov, animal behaviour serves as a *means* of adaptation to *quickly changing* environmental conditions. If the animal's environment undergoes a quick change, the animal responds with a change in behaviour, leaving its morphology intact in its old form. That response to the environment 'increases the plasticity of animals in relation to quick changes of the environment quite significantly' (Severtsov, 1922, p. 40). Furthermore, Severtsov emphasized the increasing complexity of behavioural adaptations to changes in the environment among species at the higher evolutionary levels. In his *Evoliutsia i psikhika*, he pointed to the transition to a qualitatively new (progressive) level of existence in the case of human beings, because of the ability to change their environment with the help of tools:

The human being, starting from its very early stage of evolution, begins to substitute new organs by novel means. When animals, in order to adapt to new conditions of existence, develop new morphological features that require long time periods for their evolution, the human being invents (remaining at the same morphological organization) new objects that practically substitue for the organs: clothing, that provides warmth; fire for cooking; the stone axe, that increases the power of his blows; the spear, that enables hitting the enemy at distance; bow and arrow that allow further increase in that distance, etc. (Severtsov, 1922, p. 52)

This account of human adaptation at a qualitatively new level represents Severtsov's emphasis on four different kinds of forms of adaptation—*aromorphosis* (Russian: *aromorfoz*), *idioadaptation, degeneration,* and *coenogenesis* (embryonal adaptation: see Adams, 1980; Sewertzoff, 1929). The first two of those forms— aromorphosis and idioadaptation—are particularly relevant in the present context. According to Severtsov,

'aromorphosis' [is] ... change of general and universal nature, due to which the organization of the animals [i.e., a species] rises to a higher level, and that provides the possibility for further progressive change ... 'idioadaptation' [includes] all changes of adapting kind, all adaptations to strictly determined conditions of environment that do not increase the general energy of life activity of the animals. (Severtsov, 1934, p. 86)

Leaving aside the reference to 'general energy of life activity' (a term comparable in indeterminateness to the 'vis evolutiva' that Severtsov himself was highly critical of two decades earlier), we can see that the author of the theory of phylo-embryogenesis tried to come to grips with the issue of relations between quantitative and qualitative transitions in the process of evolution. Under some conditions of organism-environment relationships, the idioadaptations are the mechanisms that improve the fit of the organism to its existing environmental structure. The idioadaptational role of behaviour was considered particularly relevant by Severtsov (1922). However, under other conditions, aromorphosis may take place, and the species moves to a qualitatively new ('higher') level of existence. The idea of aromorphosis in animal evolution made it possible for Severtsov to describe the psychological development of the human species by allowing it to transcend the traditional adaptational (in his terms, idioadaptational) framework of gradualistic interpretations of Darwinian evolution. In animal evolution, aromorphosis is the major aspect of development that introduces qualitative 'jumps' into phylogenesis. Once aromorphosis takes place, it leads to novel and flexible ways of coping with changes in environment; in the case of mammals, wrought by the modification of their brain organization (Severtsov, 1934, pp. 123–4). Finally, moving from animal evolution to human history, the new capacity for making and using external implements in relation to the environment emerges. It can be viewed as a meta-level aromorphosis, following Severtsov's line of thought. The acceptance of the qualitatively special nature of the human species does not deny that species a place in the evolutionary ladder. Instead, it reserves for it the highest role in that scheme.

Severtsov's contribution to the theoretical side of developmental ideas in science is substantial and well worth more elaborate analysis. His impact upon psychologists in the USSR of the 1920s is evident. It is also interesting that Severtsov's solution to the problem of quality-quantity relationships in evolutionary theory closely paralleled the ways in which that issue had been treated in the nineteenth century German dialectical *Naturphilosophie* of Friedrich Engels. Engels' contributions to Marxist philosophy happened to gain increasingly wide popularity in Soviet Union in the latter half of the 1920s (especially following the translation of his notes on different matters of natural science, as *Dialectics of nature* in 1925). In Severtsov's work, psychological and evolutionary aspects of development became integrated in ways that assigned the former an active, albeit limited, role in the process of evolution.

Russian neurophysiology and issues of development

The second tradition of natural science in Russia that deeply influenced the advancement of Soviet developmental psychology was the neurophysiological tradition of researchers that started with the work of Ivan M. Sechenov (1829–1905). Sechenov's neurophysiological contributions are widely known and analyzed (Iaroshevskii, 1968). However, his treatment of specifically developmental issues has received little attention.

Sechenov's developmental ideas in *The reflexes of the Brain*
It is usual to consider Sechenov's *Reflexes of the Brain* to be the forerunner of the Russian/Soviet tradition of an emphasis on the nervous system as the basis of psychological phenomena. Sechenov is repeatedly credited by Soviet historians of psychology (Iaroshevskii, 1966, 1968, 1985; Petrovskii, 1967) with the introduction of the objective reflex-based foundation into Russian psychology. Less known are the developmental ideas that were introduced by Sechenov in this classic work, in conjunction with the analysis of the psyche in terms of reflexes.

Sechenov's personal scientific education was closely tied to his contemporary European scientific medical-biological knowledge. He received his education in Germany and Austria, and later worked for a short period in Claude Bernard's laboratory in Paris (cf. Sechenov, 1907). His major work—*Refleksy golovnago mozga* (*Reflexes of the Brain*) was written during the summer of 1863 after his return from Paris, and was originally designed to be published under the title *An attempt to introduce physiological bases into psychological phenomena.* This title was changed under the demand of the censor (cf. Sechenov, 1907, p. 125), and the work was first published in that year in a medical journal. Its publication fed into the ongoing social-political controversy in Russian society, making Sechenov a target for suspicions by the czarist government and an authority among its opponents (Iaroshevskii, 1968). Three years later, it appeared in a second (updated) edition in book format (Sechenov, 1866).

The idea of development is evident in Sechenov's *Refleksy* ... in conjunction with his explanation of the emergence of 'voluntary movements' in ontogeny:

Everybody judges a person's character on the basis of his external activity. That character, as everybody accepts, develops in the person gradually from the crib. In its development, the most important part is played *by the person's encounter of life, i.e., upbringing* [*vospitanie*] *in the wide sense of the word.* (Sechenov, 1866, p. 75)

This emphasis on the development of the psychological processes, in conjunction with the interaction of the individual with the environment, is the forerunner of later elaborations of the idea in Russian psychology. Furthermore, the distinction of 'involuntary' and 'voluntary' behaviour that has become the core of later developmental psychology in the USSR (e.g., Vygotsky's separation of 'lower' versus 'higher' psychological processes on the basis of their involuntary versus voluntary nature), was used explicitly by Sechenov in his *Refleksy* ... . Let us look in greater detail at Sechenov's version of the separation of 'lower' from 'higher' psychological processes:

In the child's and almost every adults' vocabulary there is not a word that is not learned—orally or by way of writing ... The very process of articulation of words by a parrot and a child is indeed similar. But what immense difference in speaking ability exists between the two! The parrot learns only some phrases in the course of decades, the child learns thousands in the same time. The former's speech is mechanical, but in the child from an early age the phrases already have a meaningful character. That character depends mostly on associations between auditory and visual-kinesthetic impressions.... (Sechenov, 1886, pp. 84–5)

For Sechenov, it was the establishment of reflex-type associations together with the development of inhibitory control over the behavioural expressions of some of the associations that explained the functioning of the human mind. At the same time, Sechenov emphasized that the developing child is active in his relationships with the environment (Sechenov, 1866, pp. 89–90). Of course, that active relating to the environment serves as the basis for establishing new reflexive associations. Sechenov's account of thinking illustrates his combining the ideas of association with emergence of inhibition of behaviour in the course of development:

... auditory sensations have the important advantage over others that they associate even at an early age in the strongest manner with muscle sensations—in the breast, throat, tongue, and lips, i.e., with the sensations involved in one's own speech. On that basis the auditory memory is strengthened by the kinesthetic one. When the child thinks, he immediately and at the same time speaks. In 5-year old children thinking by words is expressed by whispering, or at least by movements of the tongue and the lips. (Sechenov, 1866, pp. 123–4)

Sechenov's idea of the inhibition of the motor-end movements (1866, pp. 146–7) of the speech organs while the association structure in the brain is developing is very similar to later Russian and Western associationistic explanations of mechanisms of development (Pavlov, Bekhterev, Watson). Sechenov's grasp of the development of thinking antedates twentieth-century conceptualizations of the issue. The process of 'internalization of external experience' that became the core of social-cognitive developmental psychology in this century has its forerunner in Sechenov (Iaroshevskii, 1968, pp. 280–2). Likewise, Sechenov anticipates Luria's theoretical emphasis on the role of speech in controlling the action of a developing child (Luria, 1979). Sechenov's heritage is the basis for the whole reflex-based view of the development of psychological processes in Russian neurophysiology (Bekhterev's reflexology, Pavlov's thinking and experimentation on conditional reflexes). Sechenov's associationistic view of psychology made it necessary to integrate developmental issues into his thinking, since the acceptance of the idea that new associations can be formed implies an emphasis on development, even if on a small scale. His *Reflexes of the brain* included this developmental aspect, which alerted generations of Russian physiologists and psychologists after Sechenov to the issues of development. Furthermore, Sechenov's work was the first example of the Russian/Soviet tradition of the study of psychological processes in which behavioural phenomena are treated in research together with the neurophysiological processes that organize them. In contrast to the traditions of most behavioural research in the West, the focus of Russian investigators has been on the brain mechanisms that underlie behaviour (even if, at times, these mechanisms have been only implied and not directly studied).

The origins of reflexology of later Soviet psychology: Russian neurophysiological traditions

When an ordinary Western psychologist of the present day asks himself what he knows of Soviet psychology, the name most likely to come to mind is that of Pavlov. This reflects an interesting twist in how understanding of psychology in another culture is subject to selective dissemination of knowledge. First, it has been claimed that the behaviouristic traditions in Western (particularly American) psychology have benefitted from Pavlov's ideas in the first decades of this century. Secondly, different accounts of Soviet psychology, starting from the 1950s, would reflect the Soviet claim that psychology in the USSR is 'Pavlovian' in nature.

In reality, the 'Pavlovian' label attached to Soviet psychology as a whole is a gross simplification of reality. At best it would fit the fad of 'Pavlovization' of Soviet psychology in the early 1950s. As will be seen later in this chapter, that fad amounted to little beyond a change in the style of Soviet psychologists' discourse. Furthermore, its roots are in the social-political events of the post-Second World War era in the USSR.

It is interesting that the notion of Pavlov's great influence on the development of Western (particularly American) behavioural psychology is also largely an overstatement. In fact, it could be argued that at least within the boundaries of the discipline of psychology from the beginning of the twentieth century up until the late 1920s, the influence of Vladimir Bekhterev's ideas was of greater relevance than that of Pavlov. Furthermore, it was Bekhterev's, more than Pavlov's, influence that facilitated the advancement of behaviourist ideology in the United States in the first decades of this century (Watson, 1916, 1919). Pavlov's ideas were actually very slow to become of interest in the United States, despite the increasing dominance of the behaviouristic ethos of American psychology starting in 1913 (Behrens, 1985). Although Pavlov himself entertained great hopes for the acceptance of his ideas in American behavioristic psychology of his time and was in intensive personal contact with a number of American psychologists (see Windholz, 1983), the actual acceptance of Pavlov's ideas in America was fraught with ambivalence (see Guthrie, 1930; Lashley, 1930; Pavlov, 1932). It is perhaps accurate to say that Pavlov's name has more widely been used in American psychology to legitimize various behaviouristic empirical endeavours, than has his actual empirical methodology and neurophysiological theorizing been adopted (see Razran, 1965, for a detailed review). In contrast, Bekhterev's actual influence has been diminished in retrospective accounts of the history of psychology.

Ideas relevant to understanding development were part of the thinking of both Bekhterev and Pavlov. An analysis of the developmental aspect of their contribution is therefore appropriate here.

Vladimir Bekhterev and the energetistic perspective on development

Bekhterev's contribution to Russian psychology is wide in scope. His administrative work included the establishment of the first psychological laboratory in Russia (in 1885 in Kazan), and the opening of his Psychoneurological Institute in St Petersburg in 1907. His reflexological ideas were largely formulated before 1917 (e.g., Bekhterev, 1904, 1907), and his Psychoneurological Institute played an important role in the development of psychology in Russia prior to 1917 (see Kozulin, 1984, Ch. 2).

Bekhterev's prolific writing on a wide range of topics in psychology, psychiatry and neurology, as well as his organizational efforts in promoting research in psychology (despite his later personal distaste for that term) made him a seminal figure in the scene of social and behavioural sciences in Russia during the first three decades of this century.

Bekhterev's contributions to the study of development extend across both the theoretical and empirical domains. In the latter, he was the author of a number of treatises on child development (1909, 1910, 1912, 1916). These studies covered numerous issues, from the development of infants in the first six months of life, to the objective study of children's drawings, and to the issue of the aesthetic education of children. In the theoretical sphere, Bekhterev's acceptance of the concept of energy as the centre of his theoretical system (1904, 1907, etc.) led inevitably to the need for conceptualizing changes in observable psycho-neurological phenomena, and to addressing the problem of development.

Bekhterev was the first Russian behavioural scientist who explicitly formulated the beginnings of an activity-theoretic perspective that later became the core of Soviet developmental psychology in different versions (Vygotsky, Leontiev, Zaporozhets, Basov, Ananiev and others). In his *Psikhika i zizn'* (*The psyche and life*), Bekhterev introduced the canon of the *active relationship of the organism with the environment*:

… one could think that all changes in organisms are determined by the conditions of the environment. However, one should not forget one important characteristic—the active relationship of the organism to the environment which makes it possible for the organism to be independent of the surrounding conditions to a certain extent, and even adapt those to the organism's own needs …. (Bekhterev, 1904, p. 103)

The life of an organism is determined by the integration of its internal 'forces' and external stimulation in the course of activity (Bekhterev used the Russian word *deiatel'nost* in that context). It is on the basis of 'active participation by the organisms in their adaptation' that their 'hidden energy' is revealed (1904, p. 107). In the context of organisms' active relations with their environment, two kinds of psychological influences on adaptation take place: the 'immediate' or 'involuntary' on the one hand, and the 'wilful', 'voluntary' on the other (p. 105). As can be seen, the separation of 'lower' and 'higher' (voluntary) psychological functions that later became important in Soviet psychology (see Chapter IV) is reflected in Bekhterev's early writings.

Bekhterev's own thinking did not stay the same over time. Over the decades at the beginning of this century, it moved towards greater mechanistic explanation of psychological phenomena by the extensive use of the 'associative reflex' concept. Thus, his later writings are quite hostile to the idea of psychological phenomena that are not reducible to reflexes.

Although the majority of Bekhterev's publications have become bibliographic rarities and have thus been out of sight (and mind) of the majority of psychologists, his major general work *Obshchie osnovy refleksologii cheloveka* (*General foundations of human reflexology*), first published in Russian in 1917, went through four Russian editions in 1923, 1925 and 1928, the third of which appeared in German translation in 1926 (cf. Bechterew, 1926) and has been available in English translation (Bechterev, 1932). That latter translation was based on the last (4th, 1928) Russian edition of the work. It thus constitutes a summary of Bekhterev's 'later' theoretical heritage, written at the time when he was a direct participant in the infights of Soviet behavioural scientists in the 1920s.

Bekhterev's analysis of human behaviour in terms of associative reflexes coincided historically with Pavlov's physiological research on animal behaviour, unified by the concept of conditional (conditioned) reflex. This parallel development of ideas and empirical work of the two schools of research not just in the same country but in the same town (St Petersburg) led to increased mutual rivalry and occasional verbal hostility between Bekhterev and Pavlov (see Kozulin, 1984, Ch. 2; Iaroshevskii, 1985). Bekhterev's 'associative reflex' is very similar in conceptual nature to Pavlov's 'conditional reflex'. The context for the development of associative reflexes is of interest first, if we want to understand Bekhterev's concept of development.

According to Bekhterev, the basis for the formation of associative reflexes in human ontogeny is the structure of inborn *organic* reflexes ('instincts' in the terminology of his contemporaries). Based on these, the child-environment interaction leads to the establishment of other reflexes:

All organic reflexes presuppose an innate or inherited biological need manifested in the form of a tendency, which subserves the existence of the individual and, consequently, the existence of the species. Such are the organic reflexes in the form of the need for food and self-preservation in general, for warmth, light, oxygen, movement, and, when the organism is tired, for rest; and, lastly, urges sexual in character, which ensure the life of posterity.

In connection with the organic reflex of nutrition, a responsive reaction, which may be called *the parent reflex*, is developed on the part of the parents, and especially of the mother giving suck. *This reflex is really acquired, but it has a partly organic basis in the mother's nursing the child at her own breast*, and in the procuring by the parents of other forms of nutrition for the child, and, in general, the care exercised by the parents for his welfare. Thus, here we have really to do with a reflex partly organic, partly acquired.

Another organic and, at the same time, acquired reflex results from the child's need for companionship, because of his helplessness and the insecurity of his existence when he is deprived of the society of others, and, above all, of the mother. These reflexes, which, on the one hand, develop under conditions of family life, and which, on the other, are sustained by the conditions of adult social life, may be called, first, *the family or family-social reflex*, and second, *the social reflex*. (Bechterev, 1932, p. 140, emphases added)

This quote from Bekhterev's writing illustrates the ease with which he pointed out new kinds of reflexes. Instances in reality are quickly explained by references to 'parent', 'family', or 'social' reflexes, without much elaboration of the conceptual nature of these inventions.

Bekhterev's idea of the *development* of reflexes in ontogeny involved the development of further associative links between previously present reflexes:

... higher or association reflexes [*sochetatel'nyi refleks*] originate on the basis of organic innate or organic acquired reflexes. Thus, on the basis of the simple organic reflex of sucking there gradually develops a visual association-sucking reflex, so that the nipple of the breast need not be put into the infant's mouth, but he himself, under the influence of visual impulses, seizes the nipple or some similar object, for instance, the finger, etc., with his lips. Later, with the development and increasing variety of natural conditions, a complex of association reflexes aggressive in character develops, and these are associated with nutrition, the acquisition of nutritive products, and other objects. In a similar way, a complex of association of higher reflexes is developed on the basis of organic reflexes in the form of the need for warmth, light, and fresh air, and they lead to the appropriate acquisition by the individual of warmth, light, and fresh air. Since, in this acquisition, the presence of monetary signs is, among others, an anterior and concomitant stimulus, these signs, in turn, become stimuli which lead to the excitation of appropriate aggressive reflexes associative in character, reflexes which lead to the acquisition of money. (Bechterev, 1932, p. 141)

Here, too, Bekhterev describes in one sweeping paragraph all the development of a child, from striving for the breast to striving

for money. The ease with which Bekhterev explained away
phenomena by references to reflexes and the development of their
combinations was paralleled by his equally active fight against the
use of cognitive or in any way 'soul'-related terminology.
Bekhterev's 'reflexology' shared with other branches of behaviouristic thought of his time the claim to 'objective' study of
behaviour. By his definition,

... that science which I have duly called reflexology consists in the study of the
organism's correlative activity [*sootnositel'naia deiatel'nost'*] in the wide sense of
the word, and by correlative activity we mean all the organism's inherited and
individually acquired reactions, beginning from innate and complex-organic
reflexes up to, and including, the most complex acquired reflexes, which in man
go by the name of actions and conduct and comprise his characteristic behaviour.
(Bechterev, 1932, p. 171)

Bekhterev's elimination of mentalistic concepts from his
psychological theory coincided with his elimination of differences
between the mental and the behavioural of physiological through
the use of the concept of 'energy' in ways that by far transcended
the use of that term in physical sciences. First, 'nervous energy'
was claimed to be akin to 'physical energy'. Secondly, Bekhterev
claimed that separate 'physical' and 'nervous' energies do not exist,
but instead are united in one, 'neuro-psychical' energy (1932, p.
292), to which the principle of conservation applies. The use of
'energy' as an abstract explanatory device appeared in Bekhterev's
thinking from the 1890s (1896, 1904), and recurred in his writings
consistently throughout the rest of his life (see Bechterev, 1932,
Ch. 28). Bekhterev's use of the energy concept, taken from late
nineteenth-century physics and biology, was subsequently used by
him widely; he extended it to psychological and social phenomena
with vigour and determination, often resulting in overextension of
the use of the concept. Along parallel lines, Friedrich Engels'
dialectical view of nature was largely based on the same scientific
energistic basis. Thus it is of no surprise that Engels' dialectics
(increasingly widespread in the Soviet Union from 1925) made it
easy for Bekhterev to relate his energistic reflexology to Marxism
in the 1920s (Bekhterev & Dubrovskii, 1926).

The idea of explaining psychological phenomena through the
use of the energy concept obviously provided the halo of
'objectivity' to Bekhterev's viewpoint thanks to their alignment

with problems of physics. Similarly to the state of affairs in other reductionistic ideologies in the history of psychology (e.g., the attribution of objectivity to behaviour in behaviouristic traditions), the *actual* objectivity of energetic explanations remains, of course, undetermined. However, the energetic viewpoint opened the door to addressing issues of change and development, since Bekhterev's emphasis on energy exchange between the organism and its environment led him to an open-systemic view of life processes.

Bekhterev was in the habit of constructing a number of basic 'principles' of energy-related events, some of which are relevant for understanding his thinking about development. The following of his 'principles' are of interest in this respect:

The principle of continuous change: Bekhterev accepted that nature is in constant flux and change. Everything moves, flows, changes. He related his pet idea of 'correlative activity' with that process of continuous change:

No sufficiently strong external stimulus goes without exerting an influence on the mechanism of correlative activity. This mechanism reacts with an appropriate reflex, *but this reflex changes the state of the organs which participate in its execution* and, at the same time, *changes, in some degree, the very mechanism of correlative activity, and this change, in turn, changes the form of the reaction to the same stimulus in the future*, for the modified mechanism cannot manifest the same reaction previously evoked by the given stimulus. (Bechterev, 1932, p. 299, emphases added)

It is obvious from this quote that Bekhterev's thinking about change involved the understanding of development as a basic event emerging from organism-environment interdependence. The cyclical nature of that interdependence—the environment triggering a response in the organism, and the response produced by the organism facilitating change in the organism for encountering future stimuli—leads the organism to develop further. Different paths can be taken in that development, dependent on the matching of stimulation and reflex responses:

... the human individual too is not constant, but changes with every new influence, every manifestation, every new reflex, for if this reflex is a reproduction of a former reflex, the individual is enriched by the facility he has acquired, irrespective of the fact that his reflex is not quite identical to its predecessor.

But if the reflex, because of combinative activity, is new in character, the individual is enriched also in regard to the quality of external manifestation. Thus, in both cases, the correlative activity, which lies at the basis of development of the person, changes and, as the manifestation of reflexes is unintermittent, it is obvious that the person himself is being unintermittently changed, and, indeed, *at every moment, the person changes as a result of the realisation of reflexes.*

It is clear from this that a person, since he is original as a result of hereditary conditions and the peculiarities of his social education, *is, at any given moment, something changing and irreproducible, and each moment invests him with something he has not previously experienced* and which, therefore, creates habit. (Bechterev, 1932, p. 300, emphases added)

The idea of qualitative transformation of the person under conditions of new activity that results in irreversible courses of persons' lives is evident here. Furthermore, Bekhterev emphasizes the closeness of the principle of continuous change to the principle of evolution.

The principle of evolution: Bekhterev's view of evolution was inseparable from his emphasis on change, but was not limited to the latter:

The constant change itself is not yet evolution, since change is a result of constant movement, whereas *evolution is the development of some forms from other ones*, and, consequently, continuous or quick replacement of some forms by others ... to evolution we ascribe not only change itself, with which all movement is related, but also *the transformation or emergence of novelties in respect of external and internal form* ... the evolution, involving development of new forms, is in essence a creative act, and the principle of evolution is in essence the principle of creativity. (Bekhterev, 1921, p. 319, emphases added)

In ontogeny, according to Bekhterev, the reflex systems of the person develop in conjunction with his activity within his environment. He emphasized the developmental nature of the complexes of associated reflexes in ontogeny:

If we take the ontogenetic development of animals and man, it is again possible to trace, by attentive observation, how, on the basis of simple reflexes in the infant, as well as in any new-born animal, association reflexes develop; how concentration, which is a real dominant, develops; how association reflexes differentiate, and are combined with other reflexes; how they thus become more and more intricate, by becoming complexes of reflexes, conduct, and action ... (Bechterev, 1932, p. 302)

The emphasis on the emergence of new forms in evolution was not interpreted by Bekhterev in terms of progressive development only. He was (along lines parallel to Severtsov's ideas of aromorphosis as contrasted with regression) also duly aware of regressive transformations of forms in the process of evolution. His treatment of the issue of regression in evolution was particularly evident in his treatment of societies and social groups, their emergence, self-maintenance, and decline (Bekhterev, 1921). Furthermore, Bekhterev's ideas of social evolution coincided with those of Kropotkin (see p. 48) in the reluctance to exclude cooperation from the picture of evolution in the traditional Anglo-saxon way (see Bekhterev, 1921, p. 327). Bekhterev's ideas of evolution seem to have been one of the bases for Basov's developmental theory of forms (see Chapter V).

The principle of historical sequence: This principle involves understanding that 'no phenomenon in nature originates and is manifested until all the necessary preconditions have been realised' (Bechterev, 1932, p. 318). In other words, development of phenomena involves some inherent temporal schedule along which it takes place:

Every process in the development of correlative activity obeys one universal principle, according to which no new and more complex form of existence can be realised before the appearance of the necessary simpler forms which determine it. The phylogenetic development of correlative activity also obeys this principle, as does the phylogenetic development of living beings in general.

The ontogenetic development of the person also obeys this principle, and even education and teaching must necessarily accord with it, for no enrichment of the mind is possible for the developing person until all the knowledge necessary for it has been previously acquired. (Bechterev, 1932, p. 318)

The principle of historic sequence illustrates Bekhterev's awareness of the limits that organisms' and people's life histories set upon their immediate further development. New associative reflexes can develop at any time only within certain limits set by the general schedule of development, which is based on the history of life up to the given moment.

A number of other principles used by Bekhterev (those of adaptation, reciprocal action, differentiation, and selective generalization: see 1932, pp. 325–46) are also of importance for the developmental aspect of his theory of the organism-environment relationship. All these principles, taken together, constitute the framework within which much of the developmental research in Russia, and from which the reflexological tradition in Soviet psychology, emerged (Denisova & Figurin, 1969; Figurin & Denisova, 1969; Shchelovanov, 1969).

Bekhterev's developmental thinking is usually not given special attention when his role in psychology in Russia and the USSR is discussed. Rather, his contributions to the proliferation of 'materialistic' and 'reductionistic' (or behaviouristic) views in psychology are usually the central issue when his role in the history of psychology is considered (e.g., Petrovskii, 1967). However, his actual contribution to the advancement of ideas of development in Russia was significant. Bekhterev's influence can be traced in the empirical work of Soviet developmental psychologists of different times and 'schools' (see Chapters V, VII, VIII). Both in the Soviet Union, and in the psychologies in Western countries, Bekhterev's influence on the thinking of psychologists has been similar (albeit usually unacknowledged) to that of Pavlov.

Ivan P. Pavlov and Soviet developmental psychology

It is interesting to trace the comparative history of Bekhterev's and Pavlov's popularity in Russian/Soviet psychology over time. Kozulin has described the difference in roles very adequately:

Bekhterev left hundreds of disciples who, on the eve of the Revolution, filled most of the departments of psychiatry and neurology in Russia (except for those in Moscow). Within a decade of his death, however, there were only a handful left who dared to call themselves Bekhterev's students and to develop his theories. Pavlov, in contrast, was always reluctant to call anybody a disciple, yet today his self-proclaimed protegés occupy most of the top positions in Soviet psychology. In contemporary texts Pavlov is lavishly praised as the founder of modern neurophysiology and the most profound theorist of the behavioural sciences; Bekhterev is simply mentioned in historical surveys as a prominent neurologist. (Kozulin, 1984, p. 40)

In many ways, Pavlov's physiological views have a similarity to those of Bekhterev, although their personal ways of doing science were very different (see Babkin, 1949, Ch. 7). Pavlov was primarily a natural scientist whose personal relationship with the issues addressed in the psychology of his time were ambivalent. On the one hand, he fought fiercely against mentalistic concepts in physiology, and authoritativly demanded experimental purity in research in the natural sciences. On the other, however, he used concepts similar to the mentalistic in the invention of explanations of a number of behavioural phenomena, especially towards the end of his life. Pavlov's fierce defence of associationist ideology (see Windholz & Lamal, 1986) in science against its opponents (especially his aggressive dismissal of Gestalt psychology—see Windholz, 1984a) largely took the direction of ascribing the all-explanatory conceptual role to conditional reflexes.

In order to understand Pavlov's relationship to the history of developmental ideas in Russian/Soviet natural science, it is useful to trace his views from the 1890s to the 1920s. Pavlov developed as a natural scientist of international stature in the tradition of German physiology of the nineteenth century. Like other Russian natural scientists of his time (Severtsov, Bekhterev, Vagner), one of Pavlov's concerns was to get rid of vitalistic conceptualizations of the functioning of biological organisms. Different intellectual strategies leading to the avoidance of vitalistic concepts can be envisaged. These can be roughly divided into associationistic and structuralistic ones. Whereas the former eliminate traces of vitalistic thinking about biological organisms by reconstructing the 'machinery' of an organism by reference to the combination of parts of that organism, the latter accomplish the same objective by revealing the organism's holistic structural organization properties. In the latter case, the explanation of the origin and nature of the structural properties usually remains beyond the task of the investigation, in which case vitalistic explanations of those properties can easily be attributed to them. That attributional 'danger' is less evident if an investigator reconstructs the complex functioning of an organism by reference to the combination of its parts that work together.

In his efforts to be 'objective' in his research, Pavlov essentially got trapped in the paradox inherent in positivistic science. On the one hand, the purge of subjectivity from the discourse about the organization of experimental work undoubtedly made it possible for him and his colleagues to treat physiological phenomena with great empirical rigour and exactness. On the other hand, positivistic scientists usually avoid analyses of the source of their more general hypotheses, and hope that 'the data speak for themselves' en route towards inductive generalizations. That belief was evident in Pavlov's efforts to construct his theory of 'higher nervous activity' inductively, starting from empirical demonstrations of the conditional reflexes, and ending in explaining any psychological phenomenon by reference to association of these reflexes of different kinds and complexity.

The question of the development of organisms was of no special interest to Pavlov—at least as long as it could not be studied experimentally on an animal model under well-controlled laboratory conditions. When the question of developmental ideas in Pavlov's work is addressed, it is limited to the issue of *formation* of *conditional reflexes* in conditions controllable experimentally. The principles of reflex formation thus established in an inductive way may then be carried over to the world outside the laboratory, and to species other than *Canis familiaris*. It must be stressed that Pavlov himself was relatively cautious of such generalizations across conditions, although at the same time he considered the conditional reflex principle applicable as the objective explanatory concept across species (Pavlov, 1927, lecture 23). However, his disciples were less cautious about such generalizations which culminated in the 1950s in excessive emphasis on Pavlovian thinking in physiology and psychology.

In analyzing issues of development in Pavlov's physiological thought it is necessary to start from a terminological problem—the translation of Pavlov's central concept of *uslovnyi refleks*. The standard rendering of this concept into English, starting from Pavlov's early journal publications in English (e.g. 1906), and followed by two book-format translations of Pavlov's work in the 1920s (1927, 1928) has been *conditioned reflex*. The translators of both of these books were Pavlov's co-workers for a time (G.V. Anrep—translator of Pavlov, 1927; W. Horsley Gantt—Pavlov, 1928, 1941), and must have been aware of the translation problem involved in that term. The translation of the Russian word *uslovnyi* as *conditioned* adds a nuance in the English translation— it involves an explicit emphasis on the *externally formed* nature of the *uslovnyi refleks*. It is true than in Pavlov's laboratory the research on *uslovnyie refleksy* (plural in Russian) involved experimental manipulations towards the end of forming such reflexes. In this sense—that the *uslovnyi refleks* was indeed *formed* by external manipulation of laboratory conditions—the translation 'conditioned' may be fairly adequate. However, the more accurate translation of the concept that better represents Pavlov's original idea (see also Kozulin, 1984, p. 42), would, in English, be *conditional reflex*. The relevance of this linguistic nuance becomes evident in reading the following quote (from

Pavlov's speech at the 1903 Madrid congress on medicine) where the distinction between unconditional and conditional reflexes was first introduced in the comparison of physiological and psychological phenomena (experiments):

In its physiological form our experiment—provided, of course, all extraordinary conditions are excluded—always gives the same results; this is an *unconditioned reflex* [compare with 'unconditional reflex'—J.V.]. The results of a psychical experiment, however, recur with more or less constancy, otherwise we could not speak of it as a scientific experiment. The difficulty of the psychical experiment lies in the greater number of factors which must be considered. Thus the reflex obtained is *conditioned* [compare with 'conditional'—J.V.]. (Pavlov, 1928, pp. 52-3)

The conditional reflexes of a given animal, however, have their own history of development that Pavlov clearly recognized, and discussed in the context of its value in evolution:

In our psychical experiments there appear before us as stimulators of the salivary glands not only such properties (appearance, sound, odour) of various objects which are unessential for the work of these glands, but absolutely all the surroundings in which these objects are presented to the dog, or the circumstances with which they are connected in real life. For example, the dish in which it is presented, the furniture upon which it is placed, the room, the person accustomed to bring it, and the noises produced by him—his voice, and even the sound of his feet— though at the moment he cannot be seen. Thus in the psychical experiment the connections of the objects exciting the salivary glands become more and more distant and delicate. Undoubtedly we have here before us an extreme degree of adaptation. We may admit that in this special case such a remote and fine reaction as that of the salivary glands to the characteristic step of the person who usually feeds the animal has no other physiological importance than its subtleness .... The importance of the remote signs (signals) of objects can be easily recognized in the movement reaction of the animal. By means of distant and even accidental characteristics of objects the animal seeks his food, avoids enemies, etc. (Pavlov, 1928, p. 52)

The establishment of remote signals as a means for adaptation of the animal is obviously developmental in nature. The learning process it involves was transformed by Pavlov into the 'purified' form of experimental formation of conditional reflexes in laboratory conditions. In these conditions, the conditional reflexes are formed by the experimenter (and can thus be called 'conditioned'). The experimenter sets up controlled conditions for the development of such reflexes. However, the reflexes themselves are *conditional* to the circumstances of the animal-environment relationships that are set up by the experimenter.

Pavlov was interested in the establishment of conditional reflexes in animals as a road to understanding the organization of the work of the nervous system, rather than for the sake of knowledge about behaviour *per se*. In this respect, his approach to behaviour differed from his contemporary American investigators of behaviour (see Windholz, 1983), among whom Pavlov credited Thorndike with preceding his own experiments on conditional reflexes by a couple of years (Pavlov, 1928 p. 40). He also had a good insight into how the roots of interest in the objective study of behaviour in America differed from his own:

The Americans, judged by the book of Thorndike set out on this new path of investigation in quite a different manner from us. From a passage in Thorndike one may conjecture that the practical American mind applied to everyday life found that it is more important to be acquainted with the exact outward behaviour of man than with guesses about his internal states with all their combinations and changes. With these considerations concerning man, the American psychologists proceeded to their laboratory experiments on animals. From the character of the investigations, up to the present, one feels that both the methods and the problems are derived from human interests.

I and my co-workers hold another position. As all our work developed out of physiology, so it has continued directly in that path. The methods and the conditions of our experimentation, as well as the scheme of the separate problems, the working up of the results, and finally their systematisation—all this has remained in the realm of the facts, conceptions and terminology of the central nervous system. (Pavlov, 1928, p. 40)

A comparable distinction between Pavlov's and contemporary American research on brain and behaviour became evident in the course of the famous discussion between Pavlov and his American colleagues at the beginning of 1930s (Guthrie, 1930; Lashley, 1930; Pavlov, 1932). The interest in the basic principles according to which the nervous system of an organism functions was primary for Pavlov. His interest in behaviour as such was of secondary relevance, important only as it allows inferences about the work of the brain. That may have been the reason for Pavlov's almost total use of the dog model for experimenting on conditional reflexes. Later in his life, in conjunction with his disagreement with Köhler's views on anthropoid learning, Pavlov did include research on chimpanzees in his scientific activities (Frolov, 1937, Ch. 6; Windholz, 1984b). The only excursion outside the realm of animal models that is relevant for child psychology was the work of Nikolai Krasnogorskii who, as a young assistant in Pavlov's laboratory, demonstrated the possibility of the formation of conditional reflexes in human children (Krasnogorskii, 1907, 1908). Characteristically, Pavlov saw the relevance of Krasnogorskii's work as the extension of the reflex principle to the human species (Gureeva & Chebysheva, 1969, p. 127), rather than viewing it from a developmental perspective. After these first demonstrations, Krasnogorskii continued his work on conditional reflexes of dogs. He returned to the study of children only later (in the 1920s), in conjunction with his work as a paediatrician, and emerged in the 1950s as one of the proponents of the application of the teaching of higher nervous activity as an explanatory system for child psychology.

If in the course of the first decade of the twentieth century Pavlov's teaching of the conditional reflex was formulated and experimentally demonstrated, then the following decades resulted in further elaboration of his ideas in close connection with empirical research. In time Pavlov came close to explaining almost every psychological phenomenon in terms of conditional reflexes. This wide application of the term is reminiscent of Bekhterev's willingness to use his 'associative reflex'. The aspect of development entered into Pavlov's thinking perhaps most directly in the area of transition from the 'primary' to the 'secondary' signal system in evolution. The latter was seen as a result of evolution:

Until the time when *homo sapiens* appeared animals were connected with the environment so that direct impressions fell upon the different receptors and were conducted to the corresponding cells of the central nervous system. These impressions were the several signals of the external object. However, there arises in the developing human an extraordinary perfection, the signals of the second order, the signals of the primary signals in the form of *words* — the spoken, the heard, the seen word. Finally it came about that through these new signals everything was designated that the human being perceived both from the environment and from his inner world, and these signals commenced to serve him not only in communicating with other men, but also when he was alone. The chief significance attached to the word was the predominance of those new signals—yet it remained a word, only a second signal of reality. And we know that there are numbers of people who operate only with words from which they deduce everything, would experience everything without coming into contact with reality. And on this they wish to base their own life as well as to direct the lives of others. (Pavlov, 1941, pp. 162–3)

This description of the development of the second signal system by Pavlov in 1935 occurred in the context of describing inter-individual variability in the 'types' of the nervous system. Pavlov's long experience (over thirty years) with the conditional reflex had led him to construct a classification of personalities under the label of 'types' of nervous system. Although Pavlov accepted the idea that organisms develop, and despite studying the microgenetic aspect of development (conditional reflexes) over three decades, he did not address the issues of development as such in a more systemic theoretical framework. It was the organism's stable state, its adaptation to environment through restoring an equilibrium with the environment, that Pavlov was interested in (see Pavlov, 1906, p. 614). As that adaptation necessarily involves dynamic changes, Pavlov studied those changes in the form of conditional reflexes. However, he did not address the issue of the ontogeny of these reflexes in any systematic way. In this Pavlov's contribution to the advancement of developmental ideas in Russian/Soviet behavioural sciences is less than that of Bekhterev, who was active in numerous ways in research on children and the development of their reflexes.

During the decades following the 1917 revolution in Russia, both Pavlov's and Bekhterev's ideas had a long-term influence on Soviet behavioural science. That influence, however, underwent interesting social transformations, in unison with the changes in the Soviet society from 1920s onwards. It is exactly the integration of Soviet developmental psychology in society that makes an historical analysis of that psychology interesting. However, in order to be able to make sense of the intricate ties between the thinking of developmental psychologists on the one hand, and the social discourse that surrounded them on the other, a relatively detailed overview of social changes in Soviet society and science is needed.

The nature of the social change in Soviet society in the 1920s

The 1917 revolutions (both February and October) and their subsequent transition into the civil war led the people of the former Russian Empire into an altered state of existence. Aside from serious material hardships caused by war and famine, the newly victorious force that had established political control in the country moved gradually but consistently towards the goal of changing not only the lives of the people, but also their ways of thinking about their lives.

It was evident that in the first years following the civil war the leadership of the bolshevik party was dominated by revolutionaries who largely followed the Westernizing ethos of the Russsian cultural tradition. Many of them had spent formidable periods of their pre-1917 lives abroad in Western Europe, and some had received their major (or continuing) education there. Furthermore, the basic ideology of the new political group in power was an imported entity—the whole terminology of Marxist philosophy and social policy in Russian was based on words borrowed from the German language. The new, 'bolshevik' change of a traditional society was being carried out, and the new leaders were often ill-prepared to handle many practical tasks of the organization of people's everyday life at which their despised enemies—'capitalists'—had been very skilful. As in many similar social changes, the bolshevik goals for the 'new Russia' were embedded in a revitalizing view of the ideal future for the country, with only meagre understanding of how, if at all, that ideal state of affairs could be reached.

All the social-political events that took place in Soviet society in the 1920s and early 1930s had their direct impact on the development of science in its different areas. The domain of science, however, was not one in which socio-political changes could have an immediate influence. Science in Russia had traditionally enjoyed a semi-autonomous status, especially in the framework of the Academy of Sciences. Among other goals, the establishment of control over the Academy was one that the new rulers set for themselves. The efforts by the Party to gain control of the Academy of Sciences throughout the 1920s have been well documented (see Graham, 1967). One of the major institutional efforts to reach that goal was the opening of alternative frameworks for pro-bolshevik scientists. The establishment of the 'Socialist Academy' as a centre of 'bolshevik science' in 1918, and its increasingly prominent role after 1923 (under the new name 'Communist Academy') was directly aimed at creating a counterforce among the pro-bolshevik intelligentsia to the 'bourgeois' ways of thinking of the older generations of scientists, who gathered in and around the Academy of Sciences.

Life in the young Soviet Russia was anything but peaceful in the early 1920s. People who happened to be associated with political groupings that were at a given time considered to be the 'enemies' of the bolsheviks faced persecution in its different forms—ranging from execution or prison sentences to forced internal or external exile. Such persecution was the fate of many scientists, literary figures, and philosophers. To name just a few: the Russian poet Nikolai Gumilev was executed in 1921; the later world-famous sociologist Pitirim Sorokin was sentenced to death in 1922 and waited for six weeks to be executed—until his death sentence was transmuted into exile from Russia (see Zimmerman, 1968, p. 21). A number of leading intellectuals were expelled from Soviet Russia at that time. Pavlov himself threatened to emigrate—but was denied a permit and offered especially favourable working conditions instead, despite his continuing disagreement with bolshevik philosophies (see Joravsky, 1985). All these experiences of different scientists living in a society where revolutionary ferment raged, set the stage for a complicated growth of science. On the one hand a number of novel ideas and their applications were contemplated and expressed, often under poor conditions for research that were not surprising after the civil war. On the other, the issues of political conflict did influence scientists' lives in adverse ways. For scientists, the period from 1920 to the early 1930s in the Soviet Union was not one of pure youthful creativity inspired by new possibilities granted by the imagery of the future 'new society'. Instead their endeavours were framed by the social events of the day that practically prepared for society's transition to the Stalinist era.

Children in the USSR and the reorganization of the education system

The practical context for the advancement of Soviet developmental psychology was the introduction of new social policies on education. In the conditions of the Soviet Union in the early 1920s, educational issues were highly complex. First, the majority of the population, especially in rural areas, was illiterate. Secondly the civil war had led to many children becoming homeless. Bands of such children roamed around the country, usually living by theft and robbery. Thirdly, the new political regime had its own social goals which could be worked towards only via reorganization of the educational system, which was staffed by teachers and administrators with no widespread sympathy with the new regime. Finally, different groupings within the regime had vastly differing opinions of how to reorganize the educational system. These opinions were in perpetual state of friction with one another, which led to different experiments with the educational system all throughout the 1920s.

The paradoxes of treating the problem of *besprizorniki* (homeless children) became obvious in the 1920s. The estimated number of homeless children was 7 million in post-civil war Russia. Juvenile delinquency was rampant among these children— 80–90% of lawbreaking juveniles were *besprizorniki* (Juviler, 1985, p. 264). The new political power was unprepared to deal with the problem. On the one hand, the *besprizorniki* were considered to be 'victims' of the old regime. According to that perspective, they should improve their behaviour immediately once given 'normal' humane living conditions by the new regime, which advertised itself as the saviour of the oppressed people. These normal living conditions obviously included efforts towards re-education of the children. Both of the two major organizations that took care of street children's rehabilitation efforts in the 1920s—the Comissariat (Ministry) of Education (led by Anatoli Lunacharskii) and the state secret police OGPU (led by Felix Dzherzinskii)—conceptualized the street children as re-educable 'victims' of the past, rather than irreversibly socialized juvenile delinquents of the present. Both of these organizations established boarding schools ('communes') for captured street children, where the rehabilitation of the children along the lines of socialist ideas was to take place. The best-known of such communes was that led by Anton Makarenko (cf. Kumarin, 1976), who originally worked in the Commissariat of Education, and switched over to a commune managed by the OGPU in 1927–28 (after serious disagreement on educational methods with his superiors at the former Commissariat).

On the other hand, the street children's society in Soviet Russia was a subculture on its own, and for some children the socialization within its frame prepared them well for the life of *besprizornik* soceity. Such children, when captured and sent to communes, would escape and resume their street life. Such incidents obviously disqualified the idea that juvenile delinquency was the direct result of the previous 'oppressive environment', the effects of which can be easily reversed by changes in the children's surroundings. The rival concepts of child delinquents as 'innocent victims of society' and 'criminal personalities' in Russia were in many ways similar to the ethos of environmental versus organismic determinism of psyche in other countries.

However, the majority of children in Soviet Russia were not homeless and delinquents, but ordinary children mostly of semi-illiterate parents. One of the widespread issues emerging in the early 1920s was the question of how to reorganize the educational system in the USSR in general. Given the utopian nature of the contrast of the 'new' as opposed to the 'old' society, the educational system was to be constructed in ways fitting the 'new' and abandoning the 'old'. However, in reality, educational reform was not at all easy to carry through, and the organizers of that reform were far from being of one opinion in what direction the educational system should develop (see Fitzpatrick, 1979).

One of the important issues in educational reform in the USSR was the issue of 'affirmative action', concerning the access of the previously underprivileged class (proletariat) which was now advertised as the class in power, to education at all levels. The provision of easy access to education for children or adults of working-class origin was coupled with limitation of such access to representatives of those classes (bourgeoisie, intelligentsia) who had previously been overwhelmingly represented among the educated part of the population. Such 'affirmative action' was directly related to the efforts of the Party to raise new, 'proletarian intelligentsia' that would take over the key positions in different specialities from the 'old' specialists who were always distrusted as possessors of more knowledge than was available to the Party and that was largely uncontrollable by it.

The Soviet Ministry of Education (*Narkompros*) introduced a number of experiments into the educational system in the 1920s. Instead of the earlier classroom situation with the teacher fully in control of the pupils, new complex themes were to be studied by the 'work method'—where pupils themselves discover knowledge by working on the relevant materials. This method obviously relies on the activity of children themselves, rather than on the role of the teacher as the conveyor of information to the pupils. Many schools in Soviet Russia lacked the necessary materials and instructions for organizing classes in the new ways, and teachers were often at least sceptical of such reforms 'from above' that did not fit their own ways of teaching nor the realities of the schools. The turmoil in the educational system was somewhat curbed when the Commissariat of Education introduced its first compulsory teaching plans and timetable in 1927. This new wave in Soviet education included a special (compulsory) social studies programme meant to teach the new Soviet ideology in a more consistent, and often in a more catechizing, way (cf. Fitzpatrick, 1979, pp. 38–9). The central role of the teacher was partially reinstated, especially in the realm of social studies. Different kinds of experiment in Soviet schools continued into the early 1930s, ending with the 1936 Decree on Paedology.

The variety of experiments in the Soviet educational system during the 1920s was quite understandable, as the whole society was overwhelmed with efforts to rebuild itself along 'new' lines which had not existed before. However, as is usually the case, the 'new' often constituted a direct refusal to make use of anything 'old'. At other times, some 'old' forms of organizing social life could emphatically be relabelled 'new'. Last (but not least), the new Soviet society was led by the Communist Party whose explicit aim was to preserve political power, and that could easily be challenged under the conditions of a highly heterogeneous society.

The young Soviet state and its policy on science

The contemporary Soviet perspective on the development of Soviet science normatively emphasizes the 'liberator's' role that the bolshevik revolution of 1917 is said to have played in the lives of scientists and other intelligentsia. This view may be adequate to those scientists who sided with the bolsheviks in the political struggle, or at least to those who were sympathetic to them. However, it would be grossly inaccurate to consider *all* scientists and intelligentsia as the trusted bolshevik think-tank to whom the construction of the 'new society' was delegated. The issue of the Bolshevik Party's 'trust' of different intellectuals emerged first of all in philosophy

The basic events 'on the philosophical front' (to use the symptomatic bolshevik use of military metaphors always carried over to social life in Soviet discourse) in the 1920s and early 1930s had three basic stages. The first involved the 'fight' for 'militant materialism', that was instigated by Lenin in 1922 as part of a campaign for the 'defence' of 'materialism and Marxism' that became the role of the newly established journal *Pod znamenem Marksizma*. Lenin's article 'On the meaning of militant materialism' was published in that journal in March 1922 (Lenin, 1970).

That article is considered an important milestone in the development of Soviet society by the official position in the USSR, which is represented by schoolbooks and university courses on the history of the Soviet Communist Party. Its publication coincided with the beginning of increased ideologization of philosophy and the social sciences. In a way, Lenin's thinking about relationships between communists and scientists in different disciplines laid the foundation for the emergence of the Sovietophilic and nationalistic concept of the 'Science of the Fatherland' (*otechestvennaia nauka*). This concept has served as an ideological organizing means for most of Soviet science, including psychology and other social sciences since the early 1930s onwards.

A careful reading of the article reveals Lenin's utilization of different social-psychological mechanisms in his message. Thus he relies on ingroup-outgroup status separation (contrasting 'our', i.e. 'socialist' science to the 'bourgeois' one), paired with the idea of Russian superiority over other countries (particularly Europe) in understanding the world. It is important not to forget that the combination of these two mechanisms was used widely in the social discourse of Russia under the ethos of communist utopia, and is not limited to the particular article here considered in greater detail. Furthermore, the idea of *being attacked* by 'enemies' on the 'philosophical front' was clearly a basis of Lenin's message. Such 'fortress mentality' is not surprising after a society has been torn apart by a civil war. However, what is noteworthy is that it continued to be fostered after the war had ended, and came to be used as a means of pre-emptive attacking of any direct or potential ideological opponents of the power-holding group. The successful militant bolsheviks had learned an important lesson—in order to hold power, opposition should not be provided with opportunities to increase its power. Lenin's leadership role in manoeuvring his faction of the Party into a domineering position was substantial in the pre-1917 years, and continued the same after the October revolution.

Lenin's political shrewdness can be seen not in the success of taking power in the 1917 October revolution, but in his extremely purposive efforts first to retain it when challenged (sometimes via compromises that were temporarily disastrous), and later by his pre-emptive eradication of possible future opposition to his line.

In his article, Lenin calls for the 'defence of materialism and Marxism', expressing his conviction that 'Russia, fortunately, has a solid materialist tradition' among the 'progressive' representatives of social thought (Lenin, 1970, p. 24). This tradition (exemplified by reference to social thinkers G. Plekhanov and N. Chernyshevskii of the nineteenth century) was contrasted favourably with some of Lenin's contemporary ideological opponents, who had 'regressed', often in their quest for 'modern reactionary philosophical teachings', which were considered '"the latest word" of European science' (Lenin, 1970, p. 24). Lenin here attempts to make use of the Russian Slavophilic sentiment of his contemporary readers (contrasting the positive value attached to Russian nineteenth-century materialists with the negatively valued following of European 'fashions' of thought among his opponents). However, simply contrasting these was not enough for Lenin—he attributed the 'danger' of following such European 'fashions' to his opponents' inability to understand the background of different forms of 'servitude to the bourgeoisie' that is supposedly hidden behind these ideas.

The ghost of the 'bourgeoisie' that could be projected to lie 'behind' any philosophical position of any thinker who at the time differs in opinion with the Party has been a standard tool in the arsenal of Soviet propaganda. The possibilities that such a system affords in flexibility of social discourse are formidable. In principle, *any* idea can be declared to be generated by an 'enemy' if it does not suit the goals of the declarer at the time, and by such promoted association its effect on the people (who are already kept alert by the 'fortress mentality') can be effectively curbed. The ingroup-outgroup separation, together with the perception among the ingroup that they are under siege, creates the psychological basis for the rejection of ideas associated with the outgroup, and facilitates the social construction and acceptance of the ingroup's own ideas—on a very wide scale at some times (cf. Festinger, Riecken & Schachter, 1956).

Lenin's political tactic in different situations was to compromise with some groups who were not directly opposing his party, neutralize others, and under these conditions attack the 'enemy' on any 'front' or location. His article on militant materialism called for efforts to get Russia's 'non-communist, but materialist' scientists on to the side of Marxist emphasis on materialism—'in the fight with the philosophical reactionaries and philosophical superstitions of the so-called "educated society"' (Lenin, 1970, p. 24). In such a 'fight' the leading role is allotted to the *ideological* basis for natural sciences that, Lenin declared, must be Marxism.

The social events in the USSR in the first half of the 1920s were leading in the direction of establishing the grounds for 'Marxist' viewpoints in different sciences, mostly along the line of emphasis on the materialistic side of Marxism. The second stage entailed the emphasis by different groups within philosophy (for example, Deborin's group) and sciences to introduce dialectics into these disciplines, especially from around 1925. Finally, after militant infighting with much verbal abuse and loose (and variable) fuzzy ideas that qualified as 'dialectics', the third stage of centralized Party control over the ideas used in different sciences became established by mid-1931. This last (and final) stage in the communist 'fight for science and philosophy' was an outgrowth of the previous two stages, which effectively paved the way for it. It was at the third stage that *partiinost'* became the unquestionable basis for 'Soviet science'. *Partiinost'* is a key concept, the understanding of which is necessary for making sense of life in the Soviet Union at large. Its importance to understanding the history of developmental ideas in Soviet psychology is likewise substantial, for ever since the beginning of the 1930s this concept has determined the fate of many developmental ideas, allowing some to flourish, and eliminating others from psychologists' discourse.

'Partiinost'' and its meaning in Soviet science

One of the few key innovations that the Soviet system has introduced as means to its own ends is the concept of 'partiinost'' (partisan or party nature) as the criterion for all 'true knowledge'. The authorship of this innovation can be credited to Lenin, although the concept has its analogies in the theological past of Europe, and in the social norms of 'good citizenship' that Catherine II introduced in Russia in the eighteenth century (see Chapter II).

The function of 'partiinost" is to homogenize different world views within a group of human beings. Every person views the world from a slightly different angle, depending on his/her goals and position. Based on these perspectives, different persons act in their objectively similar environments in individually different ways.

Such difference of perspectives can be treated differently—by stating the equality of all different perspectives, or by establishing the prevalence of one over the others. Lenin's politically clever idea is evident at exactly this point—from the relativity of different perspectives he arrived at the conclusion about the necessity that *one* perspective gain dominance over the others. But which one? The dominant position of a perspective can be established by different means. However, the goal of a party (in this case Lenin's own party) was considered the means to establish that position. Besides, the truthfulness of this way of establishing the 'party line' was to be internalized by the holders of divergent viewpoints. Thus, 'partiinost" constitutes an enthusiastic acceptance of the perspective that the party in power provides, by people who may originally have had different viewpoints. Gurian has explained the role of 'partiinost":

Partiinost' does not consist in a set of fixed rules, from which one ought not to deviate, or a stock of principles. True, some basic slogans are always quoted such as dialectical materialism, anti-idealism, rejection of a religious outlook, mechanicism; others are added in particular epochs, such as emphasis upon love for the motherland and rejection of cosmopolitanism. But these slogan-principles are so general and ambiguous that they permit interpretation and application according to the changing situations and policies. A classic example of this flexibility was given by those decisions of Party authorities which condemned the originally accepted satirical treatment of Russia's Christianization and, on the contrary, proclaimed that this Christianization corresponded to a cultural progress.

The *partiinost'* which originally seemed to be based on the belief that there was an all-embracing true doctrine represented and developed by the Party moves in the direction of a decisionism. That means: What the Party, that is, the Party leadership, decides to be true, must be true and accepted as such, and what the Party, that is, the Party leadership, decides to be wrong and therefore condemns must be regarded as wrong and condemned. But the pretense of knowing the absolute truth, based on the right scientific knowledge, remains. It must remain because the Party does not pretend to be based on a revelation of some sort, but to correspond to reason and science, which it alone correctly expresses and directs. The reason and science of the Party are not static-fixed, but dynamic-evolutionary. (Gurian, 1955, p. 304)

Thus, *partiinost'* is an organizing concept that legitimizes *any* possible decision or viewpoint, once it is certified by the Party. The successful introduction of that concept in Soviet society in the 1920s resulted in the interesting pattern of the development of different theoretical perspectives (all self-confessed Marxists!) that were competing with one another for the symbolic approval of the Party, thus becoming 'the true Marxist' psychology. The concept of *partiinost'*, while serving the function of governing the hierarchically organized society 'from above', has its incentives for those who want to succeed in such society, working 'from below'. In the latter case, the winning of official approval by the Party—ahead of competitors who could be better declared 'non-Marxist' (while they try to attach the same label to the claimant)—would establish the truthfulness of the given psychological system of a seeker.

It is in respect to 'partiinost'' that evaluation of particular ideas expressed by psychologists in the Soviet Union has often been conducted. Any viewpoint or theoretical system in psychology today labelled 'X' may tomorrow be labelled exactly the opposite. This change of evaluation can then be explained nicely by reference to the label of 'dialectical negation' borrowed from the basics of dialectical philosophy, or by reference to an equally spurious 'the need of time' borrowed from the political lexicon. As applied to scientific discourse in the USSR, the 'partiinost'' of the evaluation of science takes the form of 'diagnosis' of different kinds of 'errors'. The status of the ultimately true scientific meta-theory is by definition based on the dialectical materialism of all sciences, and on historical materialism in all social sciences. From this axiomatic perspective, every possible theory or empirical investigation is evaluated in terms of its 'true' or 'erring' nature.

McLeish (1975, pp. 133–49), analyzing the connection of Soviet psychological thought with its ideological predecessor (that of the Russian Orthodox Church) has distinguished different errors widely used in Soviet psychological discourse: 'idealism', 'mechanical materialism', 'abstract human essence', 'reductionism', 'dualism', and 'electicism'. All these labels have been used actively in Soviet psychological discourse. The exact meanings of the terms are fluid, since they are redefinable in accordance with the political needs as stated by the Party at any given time. The negative connotation of these terms within the context of Soviet society is the basis for the functional use of these labels. By attaching one (or more!) of these labels to one's opponent in a dispute between psychologists of different opinions, the invoker of the labels brings the 'higher authority' of the political Party into the discourse through the mere semantic network of the labels' meaning.

The history of Soviet psychology in the 1920s

What, then, happened in psychology in Russia in the 1920s and early 1930s, and how did developmental ideas fare in the course of that period? According to Soviet views on the history of psychology at that time, it was characterized by a 'fight' for new, 'Marxist psychology' (Iaroshevskii, 1966, 1985; Petrovskii, 1967; Smirnov, 1975). The history of psychology in Soviet Russia in the 1920s is an interesting case of science-society relationships. On the one hand, that historical period illustrates the developmental course by which the ideology of the ruling communist party gradually came to play a part in events that took place in Soviet psychology. On the other hand, it also reveals how a number of younger-generation enthusiastic psychologists tried to build up new and different systems of psychological science, borrowing some ideas from the proclaimed philsophical basis of the ideology—Marxist dialectics. In the end, of course, it was the political-administrative officialdom of psychology that reached its goal of centralized ideological control over psychology, as well as of all other areas of intellectual life in Soviet society. The fate of the different psychological systems that emerged *en route* has been variable, and fully dependent upon the decisions by the state at any given time. Some of these systems were first suppressed and later glorified (for example Vygotsky's thinking—see Chapter IV; also Pavlov's reflex-based views of higher psychological functions). Others (for example, Bekhterev, or Basov—see Chapter V) likewise disappeared from psychologists' minds and writings, and have not had the luck to be resurrected on a wider scale in the USSR up to the present time.

As observed above, the social-political environment in Soviet Russia from the beginning to the end of the 1920s was characterized by continuing militant 'fights' for, and against, different objectives, social and political factions in society, and the handling of economics. The military style of that 'fight' was kept away from psychology for a while, which allowed the relatively free resumption of activities by psychologists of different perspectives in the early 1920s (see Kozulin, 1984, pp. 11–12). However, that situation began to change as the decade progressed. The process of change was systemic in character—it included administrative efforts to promote the change (on behalf of the bolshevik Party), and simultaneously different psychologists' individual initiative to use Marxist philosophy in their work, or in its public promotion. In the latter, individuals with strong wills eventually conflicted with others in their effort to dominate the emerging Soviet psychology. The crushing of the institutions and rules of the old society had created a condition of anarchistic freedom of expression, in which psychological disputes could easily escalate to their extremes and transform into inter-personal verbal fights in which the scientific substance could be easily lost.

In that atmosphere of anarchistic and militant discussions, two tendencies in the organization of early Soviet psychology are significant. First (and characteristically for the 1920s), the use of *large conventions, conferences, and congresses* of psychologists during which psychological issues were solved by establishing (or failing to establish) some agreement among the majority of the participants. No doubt that enthusiasm about organizing a number of such conventions between 1923 and 1931 on the initiative of different groupings in Soviet psychology largely mimicked the use of such conventions to regulate other areas of social life—from the Party to different kinds of workers', peasants', etc. 'congresses', 'conventions', 'meetings' and so on. Such meetings also had their predecessor in the discourse of psychologists and educationalists in pre-1917 Russia. Secondly, the *attribution of opponents to some outgroup of negative connotation*, paired obviously with claiming the 'ingroup' ('true') status for oneself, constituted an accepted method of dispute. Such attribution-based interaction in a field of science certainly goes beyond psychology in the context of the Soviet Union of the 1920s. Recurrent contemporary attribution of 'soft' (as opposed to 'hard') scientific status by one group of psychologists to another group, in psychologies, of Western countries is another version of the same social-psychological mechanism of the institutional organization of psychology. The way in which this general mechanism was used from the very beginning of Soviet psychology, however, has two features that set it apart from the academic lifestyle of Western countries. First, it was characterized by open and little-constrained fierce verbal attacks on one's opponents. Second, in those attacks, appeals to extra-scientific authority (i.e., institutions of political power) surfaced from time to time. It is in this latter respect that Kuhn's description of the rules of scientific discourse (see Chapter I) can be seen as specific ideal that fits European and North-American traditions of the social organization of scientific discourse.

An example of the fierceness and appeal to extra-scientific authority in settling disputes in psychology is informative:

At the Communist Academy in March 1930, Kornilov repeated his previous criticisms of Pavlov's doctrine and virtually called for the old man's arrest: 'His recent political speeches have been *clearly counterrevolutionary*, requiring *intervention by the appropriate organs.*' But Zalkind rebuked Kornilov *for diverging from the Central Committee's policy*: political struggle with Pavlov, but support for his important scientific work. (Joravsky 1978, p. 126, emphases added)

It is noteworthy that *both* the assailant on Pavlov (Kornilov) and the defender (Zalkind) use similar extra-scientific arguments in their dispute. In the atmosphere of a society where the Party was claiming to 'unmask', 'attack', and 'defeat' its 'enemies' in a multitude of versions, it is not surprising that extra-scientific arguments became widely used in psychologists' disputes. Furthermore, the openly fierce disputes among psychologists in the Soviet Union of the 1920s often took place in highly public settings—huge national and regional conferences that were organized in great quantities at that time.

The role of mass meetings in early Soviet psychology

When the inter-group struggle of Soviet psychologists was going on with the help of attributional name-calling, a necessary step for any side in this fight was to establish his perspective as the 'right' one. One way to accomplish that task that was originally used in Soviet psychology was to use the voting by 'masses' of psychologists at the above mentioned large meetings. This function of these large 'all union' conventions may have been of the highest priority to their organizers: assemble a convention that is sufficiently well prepared to vote in support of the ideas put forward by the organizers themselves. In the 1920s, that goal was not always easy to attain, as the opponents of the conference organizers often ended up being more successful in turning the 'masses' of gathered specialists in their favour (for example, the First All-Russian Congress on Psychoneurology ended up supporting Kornilov's 'Marxist' standpoint against the 'idealist' one espoused by one of the major conveners of the Congress, Chelpanov). As time went by and society changed in the 1930s, such 'surprises' to the organizers of conventions became extinct, as the political ritual system of the Soviet Union changed into the tradition of large public gatherings which were planned to endorse a certain statement put forward by the organizers indeed do that— and with remarkably absolute majority of votes!

Another means to the same end of establishing the prominence of one's psychological theoretical system in Soviet psychology was to prove that it was 'the most Marxist' among its competitors. As the Party established increasing control over different sciences and aspects of cultural life, this method became dominant in Soviet psychology around the beginning of the 1930s. No longer was demonstration of the 'support of the masses' in the form of convention voting relevant, or sufficient. Instead, it was the support of the Party in its different versions that counted towards social-professional upward mobility of a psychological perspective (and its author). This could be achieved either by organizing explicit Party support for the given theory (in the form of *Pravda* articles in favour of it, or an invited speech by a Party leader stating his praise of it), or by proxy. In the latter case, the psychologist competing for the status of 'true Marxist' thinker in psychology would align himself with the work of some Marxist philosopher of the time who was believed to have the Party's approval. For example, the philosophical writings of Deborin and Bukharin were used by different psychologists at that time—only to lead to the downfall of their psychological theories together with the philosophical ones of these Party philosophers! Such efforts by psychologists to fit into the social-ideological belief structure at any given time served as simple raw material in the political power games in Soviet society that became the rule by the beginning of the 1930s.

The period of large organizational meetings of Soviet

psychology began with the First All-Russian Congress on Psychoneurology (10–15 January, 1923, including about 160 presentations), at which psychologists, psychiatrists and neurologists met under very different social conditions. It was convened along the lines of pre-1917 all-Russian conventions on educational psychology, and mimicked their structure (Petrovskii, 1967, p. 53). However, the conditions for simple continuity with the pre-1917 ways of holding conventions were already too different. The interest of the political power-holding group in the meeting on psychoneurology was evident in different forms. The Commissar (Minister) on Public Education, in his inaugural speech, expressed the hope that 'wide masses of the workers will find in the work of the Congress scientific answers to questions that excite them at the present time' (cited in Petrovskii, 1967, p. 54). Selected information from the Congress was published in the newspaper *Izvestia*—including summaries of some leading participants (Bekhterev, Kornilov), but not of others (Chelpanov, on whose initiative the Congress was organized).

The background for the attention paid by *Izvestia* to the self-proclaimed 'Marxist opposition' present at the Congress reflects the fight for dominance in the emerging Soviet psychological establishment between Chelpanov (the founder and Director of the Moscow Psychological Institute, from its beginning in 1912), and Kornilov. The latter's call for explicitly 'Marxist psychology' along the lines of behaviouristic 'reactology' (Kornilov, 1923a, 1923b, 1924) was part of the overthrow of the 'old' by the young. That administrative power struggle ended in the latter's favour—and on 15 November 1923 Chelpanov was forced to transfer the directorship of his Psychological Institute to Kornilov.

The resuscitated tradition of grandiose congresses (also modelled after the communist Party congresses) on psychology was continued in January 1924 (3rd–10th) when the second All-Russian Congress on Psychoneurology took place in Petrograd. It included about 1000 participants and 420 presentations (divided between nine sections). The second congress received more direct coverage from the main Party newspaper *Pravda* on the last day of the convention (in the form of a front-page article by Aron Zalkind, a psychologist with Marxist orientation and close contact with the Party).

In the official Soviet version of history, the congress was

described as providing further support to Kornilov's line in building 'materialist' and 'dialectical' psychology—in opposition to 'idealist' and 'empiricist' trends in the discipline. What these ideologically flavoured descriptions really reflected was a continuation of infighting among different schools of psychology, each now claiming to be more Marxist than the others (cf. Davydov & Radzikhovskii, 1981, p. 67). Beside such ideological infights, however, some highly creative theoretical and empirical research was performed, especially along the behaviouristic lines that became accepted as Marxist given their explicitly materialistic basis in the elementary reflexes of the nervous system.

It may be interesting to draw a parallel between the first and second Congresses on Psychoneurology in the USSR on the one hand, and the American advent of behaviourism around 1913. In both countries, emphases on the 'objectivity' of behaviour became a new basis for psychology. However, the Russian behaviourism of the 1920s was characteristically divided into a number of 'schools' (Bekhterev's 'reflexology'; Kornilov's 'reactology'; and Pavlov's and Blonski's brands of emphasis on the study of behaviour and the nervous system). Furthermore, Russian behaviourism was generally more directly related to the actual physiological activity of the brain (following the traditions of European neuro-physiology which had its influence on Sechenov and Pavlov), than its 'mind-' and 'brain-free' American counterpart of Watson and Thorndike. A brief description of the major Soviet behaviouristic 'schools' is of interest here, as it enables us to make sense of Soviet psychological discourse of the 1920s and early 1930s.

Kornilov's 'reactology'

Kornilov's 'reactology' (which was first comprehensively presented in his book, *Study of human reactions* (1921) was originally a highly empirical discipline, based firmly on experimental psychology. Traditionally, the research in psychology on the reactions of organisms has been fairly free of sophisticated philosophical background, and Kornilov's early work was no exception. However, only a couple of years later (at the 1923 and 1924 congresses on psychoneurology) Kornilov became involved in inserting Marxist philosophy into his reactology at a vast pace (e.g., Kornilov, 1925). His major English-language publication (Kornilov, 1930) reflects the results of this newly-found philosophy on his behaviouristic empirical science. His chapter is in effect an overview of the basic tenets of the dialectical thinking of Marx, Engels and Lenin, interpreted by Kornilov in accordance with the ethos of his time and his country. In style, it is more similar to the ways Soviet psychologists have written since 1931, including the heavy emphasis on Marxist authorities (which, for instance, is next to absent in the writings of Vygotsky, Luria, and their colleagues, who at the time were working in the Institute of which Kornilov was then Director). Kornilov's way of integrating his emphasis on 'reactions' with Marxist dialectics is of interest as a case study of how the new philosophy could be made to fit a brand of blatant behaviourism. He considered '*reactions* as the responses of the living organism to the stimuli of its surroundings,' and all psychology became thus 'reactology', 'that is, the science of the reactions of the individual' (Kornilov, 1930, p. 268). He went on to explain:

Reactions are a *biosociological* conception, under which it is possible to group all the phenomena of the living organism, from the simplest to the more complicated forms of human behaviour in the conditions of social life. The reactions of man in connection with his social relations acquire a social signifiance. In this we observe the main distinction between psychology and physiology. The latter also studies the reactions of man, but studies them without any reference to his social relations, while in psychology these relations constitute the principal context of the reactions studied. This is why we regard psychology as a social science rather than as a branch of natural science.

We regard the conception of reactions as the basis of the analytical study of psychology, and we prefer it to the purely physiological conception, deprived of every subjective content, of *reflexes*, with which only extreme reflexologists and objectivists operate, and to the narrow psychological (separated from all objective mechanism) conception of *emotions*, on which the subjectivists work. The conception of reactions seems to us more acceptable since it includes, with the biological and formal quantitative elements inherent to the reflex, the whole wealth of qualitative ideological content, foreign to the conception of the reflex. (Kornilov, 1930, p. 268)

Kornilov made it clear that his brand of psychology is qualitatively different from Bekhterev's 'reflexology' and Pavlov's physiology. This was accomplished by emphasizing the 'ideological content' of reactions, while retaining the objective-behavioural nature of the reactions as observable behaviours, as is evident in this quote. Among the formal-quantitative elements of reaction, Kornilov outlined *rate* (at which the reaction takes place—from the moment of stimulus appearance until response), *intensity* (the force with which the responsive movement proceeds), and *the form of the reaction* (the path traversed by the stimulated organ). In addition to this combination of quantitative and qualitative aspects of reaction, he inserts the social aspect:

Besides the formal quantitative elements inherent to reaction there are also *interior contents*—its *social significance*—which are expressed, for instance, when a person writes a letter to inform someone of his coming, or of the death of a relative or friend. From this we may conclude that the *behaviour of a person taken as a whole, as well as every separate reaction of a person, represents unity of form and content of qualitative and quantitative elements and of biological and social significance.* (Kornilov, 1930, p. 269)

Kornilov's theoretical combination of social and biological, as well as quantitative and qualitative, sides of his favourite concept 'reaction' constituted an interesting background for the work of other investigators in his Institute—particularly, that of Alexander Luria and Lev Vygotsky. However, in contrast to Kornilov's direct and declarative combination of the social and the behavioural under the label of their 'dialectical unity', Vygotsky (see Chapter IV) and Luria (e.g., 1925, 1930) proceeded to develop a system of thought in which the *development* of any such 'unity' is observed and explained. Kornilov's own theoretical system, although its author attached the fashionable Marxist terminology to it, remained basically non-developmental in emphasis. Only some of its features imply consideration of development as an issue worth investigation.

Perhaps the most interesting issue of relevance to developmental psychology in Kornilov's propagation of Marxist dialectics is his treatment of the *interdependence of qualitative and quantitative change*. The background of this idea is directly that of Marxist emphasis on qualitative breaking-points in otherwise quantitative change ('The Law of Transition of Quantity into Quality, and vice versa'). Kornilov tried to relate it to psychological phenomena:

Much of [man's behaviour as a whole] will become comprehensible to us if it is examined from a dialectic point of view, that is, according to the principle of leaping development. Why is it that important facts often pass without leaving any trace, while some scrap of casual conversation, a fleeting encounter, or a passing remark calls out a sharp reaction, changing our behaviour entirely? This is determined to a considerable extent by the weakness of man at the definite 'juncture,' where only the slightest additional weight is necessary, in order to get an effect out of all proportion to the external influence, qualitatively changing entirely the behaviour of man. (Kornilov, 1930, p. 255)

The recognition of development as leading to a qualitatively new state of the organism is a key feature in Marxist dialectics. Kornilov called for the reorganization of psychology's methodology to make it more sensitive to analyses of unexpected outcomes of laboratory studies (Kornilov, 1927, p. 203). In line with Marxist dialectics, he also called for the study of relationships of the behaviour and cognition of subjects. Kornilov's co-workers at the Institute of Psychology—Luria, Vygotsky, Rybnikov and others—proceeded to work in that direction along developmental lines.

Pavel Blonski's behaviourism

It was Pavel Blonski (also transliterated as Blonsky) who was the most direct developmentalist among Russian behaviourists of the early 1920s. At the same time, his role in the advancement of psychology in the framework of the Soviet utopian thought of the time is noteworthy (see Kozulin, 1984, Ch. 6). The influence of Blonski's thinking on Vygotsky will be analyzed later (Chapter IV). Blonski's books *Reforma nauki* ('The reform of science'; 1920) and *Ocherki nauchnoi psikhologii* ('Essays on scientific psychology'; 1921) carried the message of behaviourism and developmentalism. According to Blonski, the only scientific psychology conceivable is developmental and comparative in scope (1921, p. 28). The tradition of Soviet psychology in emphasizing the developmental nature of *all* psychology, in all of its areas or branches, originates in Blonski's enthusiastic writings of the early 1920s. Perhaps it was particularly fortunate that Blonski did not form a competing 'school' of psychology the ardent followers of which could have made his ideas the centre of some aggressive infighting at some psychoneurological convention—with the likely outcome of being deposed as 'erring' against the dialectically changing official perspectives. Instead, Blonski became active in a social fight of another kind—that for improvement in the educational system to make it more closely linked to real-life work. This caused him to be associated with the 'camp of paedology' (see Petrovskii, 1964), resulting in the public disappearance of his works together with the elimination of paedology in 1936. Blonski's behaviouristic emphasis declined over the years, as he was active in writing curriculum plans for schools while at the same time leading the collection of data on children's cognitive processes. His last major work (1935) provides a survey of empirical findings of the ways of thinking of pre-adolescents and adolescents. His data are in some ways parallel to Piaget's interest in children's knowledge and processes of thinking, and have very little in common with his excessive behaviouristic slogans of the early 1920s.

The 'Bekhterev school' of reflexology in the 1920s

The fate of Bekhterev's tradition of 'reflexology' within the social turmoil of Soviet psychology of the 1920s is quite different from that of Blonski, although the emphasis on objective psychology in the form of study of behaviour was similar. After the 1917 revolution, Bekhterev's thinking moved towards greater emphasis on the total reflexological study of man. This involved the extension of the 'associative reflex' as an explanatory concept into a wide range of psychological areas, including collective psychology (Bekhterev, 1921). Marxist philosophy seemed to Bekhterev a world view only slightly different from the energetistic concepts that underlay his reflexology. Furthermore, Bekhterev had already in 1904 considered organisms to be active organizers of their environments (Bekhterev, 1904)—a view in harmony with the Marxist thesis that philosophers must begin to alter the world to make it better.

The liaison of reflexology with Marxist philosophy also led to an emphasis on the study of the development of organism-environment relationships (Bekhterev & Dubrovskii, 1926). Within Bekhterev's eclectic system of reflexology, issues of child development were included alongside other research targets. This research orientation continued Bekhterev's interest in developmental issues of pre-1917 times. In 1922, two research units on developmental study of behaviour were established on Bekhterev's initiative. First, a special branch of reflexology (with an infancy ward) was established at the Petrograd Paedological Institute. That branch was co-directed by Nikolai Shchelovanov, and included a number of other investigators (N. Figurin and M. Denisova) whose contribution to child development research in the USSR has been substantial (Bekhterev & Shchelovanov, 1969; Denisova &

Figurin, 1969; Figurin & Denisova, 1969; Shchelovanov, 1969). The research in this laboratory included description of behavioural differentiation in infancy and the development of complex behavioural acts as a result of synthesis of the elementary reflexes. Secondly, a laboratory on the study of childhood was established in Bekhterev's Institute of the Brain. These two laboratories carried on two lines of research that were directly relevant to developmental psychology. First, the division of 'age reflexology' (led by V. N. Osipova) included empirical research on correlated reflex activity of normal school-age children (Osipova, 1926, 1927, 1929). Issues of the typology of children, formation of associated reflex-activity, and the use of associated-reflex therapy were dealt with. Under the leadership of V. N. Miasishchev, the integration of external stimuli of the human organism and its internal psychoneurological structure came under investigation (Miasishchev, 1925, 1930). That line of research proceeded along the lines of differential psychology, and involved experimental analysis of the individual–typological characteristics of the coordinative activity of the nervous system (e.g., Beliaiev & Lukina, 1932; Feodorov & Nikol'skii, 1930; Kanicheva, 1930; Miliavskaia, 1932 and others). Miasishchev's emphasis on the typology of individuals, based on the functioning of the nervous system, emerged in the context of Bekhterevian reflexology. However, in conjunction with the decreasing popularity of reflexology, Miasishchev started to rely more directly on Pavlov's typology of the nervous system in his writings (see Miasishchev, 1932).

The division of 'genetic reflexology' at the Brain Institute (also under the leadership of Shchelovanov) studied the early ontogeny of reflex activity in humans and in animal species. The ontogeny of sleep patterns was also studied in comparative vein, and the successful raising of animal puppies with early local brain damage is listed among the successes of this division. The 'experiments by Nature' that result in developmental anomalies were studied in the division in order to explain the normal course of development. The development of motor functions in the course of childhood constituted another area of empirical research in the laboratory (Iarmolenko, 1930; Iarmolenko & Belikova, 1930; Osipova, 1928, Zhukovskaia, 1930; for information available in English see Schniermann, 1930 p. 235).

The two reflex-based schools of thinking—that of Kornilov in

Moscow, and of Bekhterev's disciples (after his death in 1927) in Leningrad—both of which were sufficiently eclectic in their theoretical sphere and eager to integrate Marxist philosophy into their systems, eventually ended their existence under the social conditions of the 'cultural revolution' and constant political re-evaluation of different Marxist standpoints in society. The end of Bekhterev's reflexology came in the course of a number of 'discussions' after his death—first at the First All-Russia Paedological Congress (December 1927–January 1928), then among Leningrad psychoneurologists (4 May–10 June, 1929), and later at the First All-Union Congress on the Study of Human Behaviour (25 January–2 February, 1930). These discussions led to changes in the theoretical positions of many leading reflexologists, although their intellecutal indebtedness to Bekhterev's thinking became difficult to recognize in their later work. The ideological fervent of 'Marxist' psychoneurology was characteristic of these discussions. Earlier work of reflexologists (e.g., that of Ivanov-Smolenskii) was labelled 'mechanistic' and 'anti-dialectical', and the requirement for viewing human psychology from a 'class perspective' was aired unabashedly (see Kurazov, 1930). A number of major disciples of Bekhterev, who had been active in reflexological research after his death, expressed their intentions to reform Bekhterev's reflexology in the direction of the study of socio-historical formation of human consciousness (Ananiev, 1930a; Schnierman, 1930b). In the case of Ananiev (who started his work with Bekhterev, and later became influential as the 'leader' of the 'Leningrad school' of Soviet psychology) the reform effort of reflexologists became the basis for the unique developmental course of contemporary psychology at Leningrad University (see Chapter 9).

It can also be argued that the introduction of Pavlovian terminology as the obligatory language of Soviet psychology in the 1950s was facilitated by Bekhterev's heritage. Pavlov, whose relationships with psychology as a discipline, and with many psychologists of his time, were less than ideal, was not a very influential figure in psychologists' thinking before 1950. Bekhterev's reflexology which was close in its ideas to Pavlov's, was in the 1920s vastly popular among psychologists (cf. Schniermann, 1928) and, more importanly, among educationalists. The commonsense nature of many of Bekhterev's ideas (for example, the explanation of almost anything in individual and social psychology by attribution to the 'associative' reflexes and their combinations) may have been the cultural basis for the widespread dissemination of Bekhterev's popularity. Nevertheless, in the late 1920s Bekhterev's version of 'objective' and 'materialistic' psychology became the next target of the social infights of Soviet psychologists. Thus reversal of the status of Bekhterev's (and Kornilov's) brands of behaviourism in the Soviet psychology establishment of the late 1920s was interdependent with oscillations of viewpoints in other areas of cultural life—literature (see Ermolaev, 1963), and the social sciences. It was in the field of philosophy that intellectual and social-political aspects of Soviet society became intertwined in the most complex way, leading to the 'great break' with the past. The change in Soviet philosophy had a profound effect on Soviet psychology. Furthermore, a careful analysis of the way in which the change in philosophy took place would make it possible for us to understand how Soviet psychology changed in the early 1930s.

The 'great break' in Soviet social sciences and its mechanism

What, then, had changed by the time that the previously hailed materialist reflexology came under attack in the late 1920s? The socio-political situation during the 1920s had changed rapidly, and the rules of psychologists' game in Marxist dialectics had been redefined accordingly. The strong devotion to *partiinost'* among the Russians participating in psychological discourse facilitated changes in the direction that moved psychology closer to ideology. The emphasis on the 'objectivity' of reflexes or reactions was redefined as an error, rather than a good example of Marxist science. Of course, there were good reasons to rethink the self-declared 'objectivity' of Russian behaviouristic researchers. The reflexes or reactions used by them (and their counterparts in American behaviourism) to explain behaviour were as 'material' as a unicorn. However, the most important force that led Soviet psychologists of the second half of the 1920s to re-evaluate behaviouristic 'materialism' was extra-psychological—a turn from the simple 'materialistic' emphasis of Soviet philosophy to the introduction of *dialectics* to that thought. The philosophical change towards emphasizing the *unity* of the material and the ideal (rather than their equivalence) paved the way towards restoration of the role of the subjective side of psychology (e.g., issues of consciousness) among the viable research questions in psychology.

The change from the previous emphasis on the material substrate of the psychological phenomena (reflexes or reactions) to the new unity of the material and ideal sides of the psyche was not at all a matter of conflict between mutually opposed ideas within the psychologists' professional community in the USSR. As opposed to previous years in the 1920s, the 'leading role' of the version of political ideology that was currently 'in' with the Party came to be increasingly influential in the field of psychology. The mechanism of how that 'leading role' became manifested involved both efforts to guide psychologists' work 'from above' (calls by Party officials for a greater practical role for scientists in building the 'new society'), and the use by different in-fighting groups of specialists of ideologically-flavoured accusations against one another. This double-channel ('vertical', i.e. from higher administrative levels downward; and 'horizontal'—control by peers of one another by virtue of mutual watchfulness and criticism) social control system became widespread in the USSR far beyond the issues of governing the activities of scientists (Valsiner, 1981). The alignment of the content material used in the 'horizontal' channel with that in the 'vertical' one, by scientists' own initiative, was building on the rich traditions in Russian history of defining freedom of action by individuals as their obligation to act in the expected manner, as defined by the state.

The consolidation of ideological control within psychology in the USSR took place via the intermediary discipline of philosophy. This is a natural sequence of transition of control over psychology in a society where the political ideology of the rulers aspires towards a fundamentalistic central role in the whole of society. The political power group would in the first place extend its control to the scientific discipline closest to its ideology—which is philosophy. As long as psychology is closely intertwined with philosophy, the transformation of the latter is likely to infiltrate the former, by some explicit plan, or through carry-over of ideas from the prevailing philosophical ethos to psychology.

A turnaround in Soviet philosophy

The transition in Soviet psychology of the 1920s from a fight between 'idealism' (of Chelpanov's brand) and the 'materialism' of Kornilov and Bekhterev occured in parallel with a similar 'fight' for 'materialism' in philosophy. Likewise, the views of Bekhterev and Kornilov came under attack in psychology at the same time as a 'fight for dialectics' as opposed to the reign of 'mechanistic materialism' became the event of the day in Soviet philosophy (see Joravsky, 1961, Chs. 6–8). That 'fight' was led by Abram Deborin, whose role in propagating Hegel's, Marx's, Engel's, and Lenin's thinking about dialectics in the 1920s is noteworthy. Deborin formed a tightly organized 'school' of his followers around him, among whom was Mark Mitin, a young and militant Marxist philosopher who later deposed Deborin as 'leader' of Soviet Marxist philosophy. The course of events in that change 'on the philosophical front', to use the militant bolshevik terminology widely applied at the time, constitutes an empirical example of the 'double-channel' process of social control. The 'horizontal channel' in that process involved infighting between different groups of philosophers. First, Deborin's group was fighting the 'mechanist' groups with the aim of establishing the dominance of dialectical views. However, in that process some sub-dominant members of the 'Deborinites' began to prepare for their own ascent to the leadership of the Soviet philosophy establishment.

The 'vertical channel' in the process of change in Soviet philosophy at the turn of the twenties/thirties involved a small number of appearances by Stalin at philosophers' gatherings. The first of those took place in December 1929 at a conference of agrarian economists. The emphasis in Stalin's presentation was on making theoretical perspectives of Marxism serve 'practical needs'. The latter, of course, were defined by Party policy and involved the orchestration of 'the great break' (*velikii perelom*) prescribed for the year 1929 in the Soviet Union in industry, agriculture and human culture.

This provision of the direction for further action by philosophers became the basis for discussions along the prescribed lines of emphasizing 'practical needs'. It is through the 'horizontal channel' that these discussions led to the first challenges to Deborin from his disciples. It is symptomatic of the work of this 'horizontal channel' in Soviet life that it leads either to regaining control by the previously dominant figure (and the repentance of critics), or to self-criticism by that figure (which is a step towards his being 'on his way out', but still with some hopes for survival). If the latter outcome occurs, then the critics of the dominant figure may (a) not accept the self-criticism and continue their attack; (b) require more extreme self-criticism from him; or (c) be satisfied with it and let the figure retain his position. Obviously, the option (c) retains the *status quo*, whereas (a) and (b) may lead to further disequilibrium of the peer-group structure, and may result in a change of leader.

It is interesting to note the wide use of the [DIRECTION PROVISION ---> (CRITICISM <===> SELF-CRITICISM)] mechanism in organizing the activities of social groups. Its use in children's collectives (see Mead & Calas, 1955), and the Soviet efforts after 1917 to gain control over child socialization in families (Valsiner, 1981) is very similar to the ways in which philosophers' and psychologists' peer-interaction in the Soviet Union takes place. The inclusion of self-criticism in that mechanism is the aspect that differs greatly from inter-individual social interaction in West-European and North-American secular life, although similar phenomena can be found in the religious histories of Western countries.

The actual course of the 'break' in Soviet philosophy illustrates the ways in which action within the 'horizontal' and 'vertical' channels was used intermittently. The sequence of events (see Joravsky, 1961, Ch. 17) in the 'break' in philosophy unfolded within the 'horizontal channel' after Stalin's directive in December 1929. In the following months, Deborin was criticized by his dissenting disciples along the lines of the 'need for practical applications.' In April 1930, at a planning meeting for a philosophical conference at the Communist Academy, Deborin himself suggested a resolution accepting the failure of philosophers to be 'closer to reality'. However, that compromise did not satisfy young militant critics of Deborin's line, led by Mitin, and they pressed for more active self-criticism, but this was voted down by the meeting. After this defeat in the 'horizontal channel' of communication, Mitin and his supporters turned for help to the 'vertical' one—by sending a complaint to the Party's official newspaper *Pravda*. The publication of their article on 7 June 1930 in that official newspaper (Mitin, Ral'tsevich, & Iudin, 1930), together with an explicit statement of the agreement of the editors with Mitin's perspective, was the second stage of the 'message' in the 'vertical' communication channel in the 'break in philosophy'. The article by Mitin and his colleagues called for greater *partiinost'* in philosophy, as well as for criticism and self-criticism by philosophers.

Following this step, the criticism of Deborin and of the 'old' Marxist philosophy that assumed a position separate from the social-political issues of the day continued. It was Mitin who called for centralized organization of the 'theoretical' and 'philosophical front' (Joravsky, 1961, p. 258)—on his own, and *before* the Party administrative organs indicated that they indeed would take over that organizing role. This nuance of the infights in philosophy is significant as it illustrates how peer interaction via the 'horizontal' channel of communication *that took the direction given in the 'vertical' channel* could escalate and produce results which were expected 'at the top'.

The next intervention through the 'vertical channel' took place in September 1930, at the meeting of the Presidium of the Communist Academy, at which a number of people who belonged both to social sciences and to Party establishments provided key addresses. Although Deborin was given the chance to respond to his critics, his response was suppressed by militant accusations against him on the grounds of his political past. In October, at the conference at the Communist Academy, the peer-infighting among philosophers of Deborin's and Mitin's groups escalated in the ferocity of mutual recrimination and personal-political accusations, leading Mitin to call the participants to 'lending an ear' to the 'signal that the Party is giving' (Joravsky, 1961, p. 260)—an explicit turn to the extra-scientific authorities with the aim of winning the 'battle'. Deborin, as his final word, switched to a strategy of self-criticism, mixed with efforts to prove the adequacy of at least some of his ideas. This change of strategy did not help. The resolution passed at the conference took an anti-Deborin stand.

A number of administrative events followed. First, the main Marxist philosophical journal *Pod znamenem Marksizma* (edited by Deborin) temporarily ceased publication. On 9 December 1930, a group of young 'bolshevizers' of philosophy (Mitin's group) met with Stalin who gave his support to their line (already by the mere fact of meeting with them). In addition, Stalin made public calls for a fight against 'menshevizing idealism' (a label coined to describe Deborin and his followers) in the intellectual life of Soviet society. This was followed by the decree of the Central Committee of the Party from 26 January 1931 about the *Pod znamenem Marksizma* which led to the social-political takeover of power in Soviet philosophy by the Mitin group.

The new group in power in the Soviet philosophy establishment did not leave its militant role behind with its ascent. From the dominant position it continued its 'fight' for *partiinost'* in Soviet philosophy and other social sciences. The role of *practice*—defined as the practical needs of the building of socialist society—became the declared cornerstone of Soviet social sciences (Mitin, 1931). Furthermore, the philosophers who were publicly labelled as belonging to the 'menshevizing idealism' traditions were called on to display self-criticism. Some of them did so on their own initiative, others were coerced by these calls, and very few could stand on their own under the fire of fierce criticism. The style of Soviet philosophical discourse changed to one that afforded both public witch-hunting of 'menshevizing idealists', and their 'self-criticism' in the form of denouncement of their own previous work, and the 'disclosure' of the 'hidden' flaws in the thinking and writings of their peers.

The social-psychological mechanism by which the 'great break' in Marxist philosophy took place in 1929–31 in the USSR is not unique in social life. It fits the time-honoured political practice of 'divide and rule', when viewed from the perspective of the Party leaders. They, at different times, would provide different hints about their current needs for philosophers' knowhow. These hints lead to the formation of groups of philosophers, each of which is based on a slightly different version of the general (in this case, Marxist) philosophy. Each group may find it most productive to consolidate by attacking other groups. Such inter-group conflict could be maintained by the provision of occasional and partial support to one or another group—either by plan, or by the leadership's lack of interest (and no common line) in the issues of the given area (philosophy). The infighting between groups then created a situation where the Party could select one of the rival groupings (obviously the one most suitable at the time) and declare its support for it. That declared support 'from above' could tilt the situation in the power struggle within philosophy circles in favour of the selected group, which would defeat its 'enemies' by its own effort. As a result, the Party gains a loyal group who is in power in the given discipline, while retaining the possibility of shifting its support to another group (currently in a sub-dominant position) when necessary. That group could then come to power by its own effort, but helped by support 'from above', and would then become another loyal dominant group.

A 'great break' similar to that in Soviet philosophy also took place in Soviet psychology in the early 1930s. In fact, the change in psychology was closely connected to that in philosophy. Similar terminology (e.g., 'menshevizing idealism') was used for similar purposes (efforts to eliminate opponents), and with similar calls for the increasing importance of applied social problems ('practice of socialist construction') in the determination of the advancement in psychology.

Psychology and attacks on 'menshevizing idealism'

In parallel with the 'fight' in philosophy against Abram Deborin's dialectical viewpoint under the ideologically explicit label of eradication of the 'menshevizing idealism', psychology became the battleground for a wide witch-hunt and punishment of similar 'idealists' among psychologists. Many Soviet psychologists of the time were working towards developing their versions of Marxist or dialectical psychologies. Kornilov's 'reactology' and its Marxist-dialectical conceptual context (which also constituted the environment of the work of Lev Vygotsky and Alexander Luria at Kornilov's Institute of Psychology) became one target of a 'break' in psychology.

The removal of Kornilov's 'reactology' from its influential position in Soviet psychology occurred quite directly by the efforts of a group of young militant psychologists who belonged to the Party. At the start of 1931, the Communist Party organization of Kornilov's own Psychological Institute initiated a series of 'discussions' of Kornilov's views, the aim of which was to remove his ideas from their leading role in Soviet psychology.

History seemed to repeat itself—if in 1923 Kornilov himself challenged his mentor Chelpanov and ended by taking over his position, then at the beginning of 1931 Kornilov's younger disciples challenged his position in Soviet psychology, and his directorship at the Institute. Still, something very important had changed in these eight years. No longer was a huge convention of psychologists necessary to settle internal matters of the discipline by majority opinion. Instead, the explicit link of the young challengers of Kornilov to the Party, and their calls for following the Party line (similarly to Mitin's group in philosophy), were now used to settle theoretical issues in psychology. Later Soviet accounts of the discussions in Kornilov's Institute in early 1931 (e.g., Petrovskii, 1967; Smirnov, 1975) have presented the establishment of the direct guiding role of the Party in matters of psychology as another progressive step in the development of Soviet psychology. In the official Soviet descriptions of these 'discussions', it is openly stated that the young attackers of Kornilov (K. Anson, A. Talankin, F. Shemiakin, T. Kogan, A. Vedenov and others)

... emphasized in their speeches that *the new stage* in the development of philosophy *requires* from psychologists *the fulfillment of the task of the study of the Leninist heritage*, and that only by mastering Marxist methodology could psychologists *join in* with the practice of socialist construction. (Petrovskii, 1967, p. 122, emphasis added)

It is evident from this short description of these 'discussions' that what was being discussed was the 'sin' of the reactologists (and, especially, of Kornilov) who were supposedly 'lagging behind' the 'always progressive' Marxist philosophy that was constantly changing under the Party's practical leadership and the declared needs of any given time, and which set no limits on its future progress. The social function of these meetings, together with their style of dispute, was very similar to the Mitin-Deborin conflict in philosophy. The 'disputes' about reactology were no internal matter of the Psychological Institute either. The 'reactological discussion' in the Psychological Institute coincided with open attacks (in the form of critical articles) in psychological journals, not only against Kornilov (who was explicitly grouped together with Deborin's philosophy—see Zalkind, 1931a, p. 5), but also against other psychologists who were accused for their alleged 'theoretical mistakes'. The list of such psychologists included, amongst many others, Blonski (Gel'mont, 1931), Vygotsky (Feofanov, 1932), Basov (Feofanov, 1931), and Zalkind (by his own 'self-criticism'—see Zalkind, 1931b, 1932).

The nature of the wave of criticism had also changed, since the late 1920s. Instead of analyses of the theoretical ideas or empirical work of the criticized authors that was largely the rule in the 1920s, critics at the start of the 1930s were all too happy to attach ideologically symbolic negative labels to the authors they took to task. The style of criticism became increasingly declarative, and the connection of the critical arguments with the actual work of the targets of the criticism became loose. It is in the context of the wave of criticism (and self-criticism) in the early 1930s that psychology in the USSR practically turned into an ideologically distinctive 'Soviet psychology'. As such, the prevailing discourse style of 'Soviet psychology' became detached from the tradition of scientific discussion in international psychology that had played an important part in the advancement of psychology in the 1920s in the USSR.

What, then, were the crucial aspects of Soviet society that became reflected in psychologists' writings around 1931? The ascending wave of militant criticism of other psychologists (as well as oneself) in leading child psychology journals coincided with an emphasis on the necessity of building a psychology that would take the 'specifics' of the 'new socialist society' into account. These 'specifics' concentrated on the issue of a *social class-based* view of psychological issues, since the political ideology of the time accepted the thesis of *continuing* class struggle in the developing socialist society. That led to the need for psychologists to make 'practical input' to that struggle. They were expected to participate in it—certainly on the 'right side' (as defined by *partiinost'*), following the political goals set by the Party. Different areas of natural and social sciences, including psychology, were successfully brought into the service of the political system of society in which the rhetoric about its 'new' status was intensified as it actually turned back to the centralized and hierarchical state exemplified by the pre-1917 years.

Lenin's social-political goals, expressed in his article on militant materialism, were attained in this 'new society'. The leading role of the 'old' (i.e., pre-1917 educated) intellectuals in social sciences was lessened by the number of 'young cadres' from a working-class background entering academia. The 'new cadres' were already in a position to take control over the scientific establishments, overriding the 'olds' both in number and in 'revolutionary militancy'. The relative, although violent and Party-supervised, democracy in psychology during the 1920s was over, never to return. What emerged instead was a wave of Slavophilic, anti-cosmopolitan and ideological quasi-philosophical writings that proceeded to dominate Soviet psychological discourse in the course of the next three decades at least. That 'Soviet psychology' was certainly not homogeneous in its theoretical and empirical domains. It continued to have its own conflicts between personalities and groupings, and changes in fashions for ideas over time. In contrast to the earlier decade, *partiinost'* became the accepted central criterion of the 'truthfulness' of a psychological idea, or a psychologist's presentation. The battleground of conflict between different groupings of psychologists became more abstract and philosophy-bound from the beginning of the 1930s. All of these changes were strictly channelled by the political ideology of the Party, supported by the initiative of the psychologists themselves. The majority of Soviet psychologists of the 1930s seemed to follow the historical rules of 'good citizenship' that Catherine II had introduced in Russia a century and a half earlier, and that they had internalized in the course of their lives.

Soviet society and science, 1930s–1950s

Raymond Bauer has characterized the nature of the social changes in the USSR of the 1930s in a way that shows the difficulty that many a Western observer of events in a non-Western society encounters:

The main idea behind the social changes of the mid-thirties seems to have been the decision to bring all possible facilities of society to bear on the problem of *training* and *controlling* its *individual* citizens. It is only in the light of such a decision that it is possible to understand the changes which took place in education, and thereby in psychology. (Bauer, 1952, p. 123, emphases added)

The difficulty here is in projecting the Anglo-American concept of the *individual person* to a society whose cultural history has given rise to the concept of an individual as *inevitably interdependent* with other people and with society at large. The projection into Russian conditions of the idea that the individual is *originally independent* of other people, and that his independence may be *suppressed* under some conditions by *training* in order to establish *control* over them has led Westerners to recurrent and widespread misunderstanding of Soviet society and of the ways in which Soviet citizens act in different situations (Lefebvre, 1980; Valsiner, 1984c).

Bauer's description, expressed above, also overlooks the *process* by which society in the USSR became more organized in a hierarchical way. Not only were individual citizens brought under state control, but the ideology on which that control was based was also internalized by the majority of these individual citizens. That internalized ideology provided the basis for self-control, the achievement of which became an explicitly stated goal of the Soviet educational system. Anton Makarenko, who in the 1930s was made a celebrity of Soviet pedagogy, expressed the importance of internalized self-control very clearly. According to him, the 'Soviet citizen'

is expected not only to appreciate to what end and why it is necessary for him to carry out this or that command, but also actively to endeavour to carry it out to the best of his ability. Yet that is still not everything. Our citizens are expected *to do their duty at any moment of their lives without waiting for instructions or orders*, they are expected to be ready to take the initiative and be possessed of creative will ... it is always expected of our citizens that they never be bounded by the narrow horizon of their own personal affairs ... but be able to see beyond to the concerns of people around them, their lives and behaviour and be able to come to the help of their fellow-men, not only in word but also in deed, *even if their own personal tranquility has to be sacrificed in the process.* In respect of our common enemies it is demanded of every individual that he resolutely obstruct their activities and be constantly vigilant whatever unpleasantness and dangers might ensue. (Kumarin, 1976, pp. 245–6)

These goals of Soviet education, expressed in Makarenko's writings in the 1930s, even if they seem foreign from the perspective of contemporary Western psychologies, may actually reflect some basic psychological socialization goals present in many religious systems across the world. The Soviet social system has emerged along the lines of reconstruction of a hierarchical structure that in some aspects may be similar to pre-1917 Russia, but in others displays sufficiently remarkable novelty. The Party's monopolization of ideological influence, and the concentration of centralized power took place in a society that was infested with a mixture of Slavophilic (now Sovietophilic) and messianic ideas. In Soviet discourse, that reorganization of society in Sovietophilic ways amounted to a 'cultural revolution' (see Fitzpatrick, 1979). It is during this historical period that the separation of 'Soviet science' from its international and cosmopolitan roots became dominant (see Medvedev, 1979). Scientists were expected to consider seriously the matter of emotional loyalties to the *otechestvennaia nauka* ('science of the fatherland'). That included unquestionably following the Sovetophilic style in science, publishing its results, and discussing its progress and contributions to society.

It would be a gross sociological simplification to attribute the changes that took place in Soviet society, as it moved from the 1920s to the 1930s, to the actions of only the Party leadership, or to an individual leader of the Party. Although the Party leadership, and its leader, worked towards their social-political goals, the end product of any social process is determined jointly by all the people interlocked in the particular social system. In this respect any effort by the Party to provoke people to act in a certain way had to be supported by the people's actual readiness to act in that way. Once they actually execute the actions expected by the Party, feedback from these actions is likely to strengthen their readiness to act in a similar fashion in the future. This simple social-psychological mechanism has been widely used to win followers by different social groups, in any society. It could be considered a trans-culturally universal mechanism, to be evoked when the cohesiveness of any social group is a desired goal.

It is in the context of efforts towards socializing people in the belief in internalized acceptance of *partiinost'* that the changes in Soviet society can be understood. The relations of people to different ideological and scientific viewpoints became both the testing ground of their character as 'Soviet people', and the mechanism by which Party control of the life in society was promoted. The infallible role that *partiinost'* unquestioningly attributes to the Party makes it possible for the latter to change its course without the loss of any credibility in the eyes of the believers who have internalized that concept. Loyalty to the ideology-setting institution (Party) is taken to be of primary relevance, and the adequacy of this loyal position to reality is of secondary importance. Furthermore, such loyalty is not of the passive kind, characteristic of slaves, but constitutes *active* loyalty to the ideology. That active loyalty involves discipline that is internalized by people ('conscious discipline', as it is called in Soviet education—cf. Kumarin, 1976; Mead & Calas, 1955). It can be evoked by people themselves in situations where no external disciplining force is present, but where the nature of the situation calls for loyal action. Psychologically, the phenomena of 'conscious discipline' play the role of mediating devices (see Chapter IV) in a person's individual psychology, in the environmental contexts perceived as requiring the 'right action'. A person whose loyalty to a certain belief system is strongly internalized does not need external guidelines of action, his (or her) *own* thinking leads to acting in the socialized way.

External factors of social life were actively used by the Soviet authorities to play a role in the promotion of loyalty of individual citizens of the Soviet Union. All through the 1930s, the Soviet people were kept terrified of the advent of fascism in Europe. The waves of Stalinist purges during which innocent citizens ended as declared 'spies' of imperialism or fascism in the repertoire of Soviet internal propaganda increased the feeling of being besieged to those who were guided to take that propaganda at its face value. When overwhelmed by the 'fortress mentality', the supposed 'discovery' of hordes of 'foreign spies' among neighbours and co-workers could have intensified the loyalty of many people to the Soviet system (rather than undermined it). In the 1940s, the Second World War forced people in the USSR to bear significant losses in actual war—which served as a consolidating force of the loyalty to the social system. The promotion of Stalin's 'personality cult' by the Party bureaucracy over these decades only fortified the fundamentalism of Soviet ideology already internalized by the wide population of the USSR. Of course, no socialization system works in a 'flawless' manner—at any time in the history of the USSR there have been people in whose case the socialization system had not worked in the expected way and who could see through the picture of the USSR painted by the Soviet communication system. However, the presence of such 'dissidents' at different times does not eliminate the remarkable efficiency that the Soviet internal system has had in the promotion of loyalty to the state and the Party.

The same socializing forces that were widespread in Soviet society as a whole were naturally important within science. An interesting parallel between biological and psychological thought in the Soviet Union illustrates this. This history of science has been enriched by the case of Trofim D. Lysenko—a Soviet agrobiologist whose activities in the 1930s and 1940s led to the temporary extinction of most of Soviet genetics (which, at the time, was in many of its areas highly progressive). The story of the 'Lysenko phenomenon' is usually told as a case in which persons, rather than their transaction with their environments, play the central role. In reality, the advent of Lysenko's 'agrobiology' not only was a product of his personal scheming and political power-struggle, but was also facilitated by the social conditions of the whole of Soviet society.

The 'Lysenko phenomenon' and Soviet psychology: exaggeration of the idea of changeability

The social situation within which the phenomenon of Lysenko could occur in 'Soviet biology' was catalyzed by increasing xenophobia and Sovietophilic utopianism in social discourse about science in the USSR. Back in 1955, Dobzhansky described the changes in the style of work acceptable in 'Soviet science':

> The lengths reached by nationalism in Soviet science are almost unbelievable. Some twenty years ago it became unpatriotic for Soviet scientists to publish any of their works in international scientific periodicals. Then, the periodicals published in the U.S.S.R. lost articles printed in foreign languages. Next, the summaries, tables of contents, and the names of the periodicals themselves were printed only in Russian. Finally the point was reached when most authors considered it prudent to avoid references to foreign works. The result was that the periodicals became totally useless to anybody who is not at home in the Russian language. This may be flattering to national pride, but certainly is not conducive to appreciation of the attainments of Russian scientists by colleagues throughout the world. (Dobzhansky, 1955, p. 344)

The case of the 'Michurinist biology' of Trofim D. Lysenko and its social background is instrumental in illustrating how the increasing self-isolation of Soviet biology from international science, together with excessive references to Russian patriotism, *partiinost'*, ingroup/outgroup separation and conflict, and infighting between different groupings in biology, led to the 'Lysenko phenomenon' as it has been widely known all around the world (see Joravsky, 1961, 1970; Medvedev, 1969).

Understanding the social mechanisms that produced the 'Lysenko phenomenon' is of interest to anybody trying to make sense of the history of Soviet psychology. Lysenko's thinking about the environmental modifiability of agricultural species has its conceptual basis, which happened to be shared with much of child psychology in the USSR. The roots of both 'Michurinist biology' and 'Soviet developmental psychology' may be located in the social-utopian ideas widespread in the Soviet society in the 1920s (see also Roll-Hansen, 1985). However, while Lysenko's 'biology' took these ideas to an absurd extreme using social-political means and the support of Soviet agricultural bureaucracy, Soviet developmental psychology made productive use of Marxist emphasis on development in the theoretical realm.

The idea on which Lysenko later built his ideology—*that of unlimited possibilities for biological change under rearrangement of the environment*—was already present in Russian/Soviet social discourse in the 1920s, in conjunction with the proclaimed goals of raising the qualitatively 'new man' through establishment of the 'new society'. It is via the ideology of building the 'new society' that Lysenko's agrobiology and Soviet developmental psychology are distant relatives. In the 1930s and 1940s, Lysenko, working under social conditions of increased emphasis on the isolated and self-indulgent Sovietophilia, transposed the idea of unlimited possibilities from the sphere of society to that of biology. His ardent followers carried it to extremes—which, eventually, made the absurdity of Lysenko's biology blatantly evident. In other sciences, music, literature, and art, similar but smaller-scale 'Lysenko phenomena' may have been less evident to Western observers, but nevertheless were as influential in the Soviet context.

The history of the idea of 'unlimited developmental potential' in psychology, starting from the same background, was different. In the 1920s the majority of leading young psychologists were reluctant to take the idea of environmental modifiability of development to its absolute extreme. Borrowing from the same social ethos, Vygotsky and many of his contemporary psychologists were fascinated by the possibilities open to growing children, provided their development is assisted by social conditions which help them to reach qualitatively new levels of psychological development. Vygotsky did not try to advance this developmental idea to its ultimate conclusion, always reminding himself and his listeners (readers) of the limited nature of that modifiability. However, some of his disciples (such as A.N. Leont'ev) had no difficulty in agreeing with Lysenko's basic ideas in developmental psychology at the height of Lysenkoism at the end of the 1940s (see Bauer, 1949). The evangelistic social ethos of the utopian 'new society' inhabited by 'new man' whose active impact on the environment is always progressive when carried out under the wise leadership of the Party, made it only too natural for both Lysenkoites and Soviet psychologists to speculate on the topic of modifiability of development in nature and psychology. But in the case of Lysenko, the application of the idea in agricultural practice produced a miserable effect on Soviet agriculture quite soon. In contrast, the talk of psychologists of the time, emphasizing similar advancements, was not tested in the reality of school education on a wider scale. This may be attributed to the limited access of psychologists to the educational practices on any wide scale.

Soviet psychology in the 1930s and 1940s: emphasis on consciousness

The change around 1931 in the accepted ways of psychologists' discourse continued all through the 1930s and coincided with social changes: waves of Slavlophilia orchestrated by Stalinist purges and accusations against the purged; the changing world situation; the development of Marxist philosophy in conjunction with that of Stalin's personality cult. A number of important administrative changes relevant to psychology took place at this time. First, almost all psychological and especially child study (paedological) periodicals that had started to appear around 1928 ceased publication by 1932. Secondly, the decree by the Party's Central Committee on 4 July 1936 'On paedological perversions in the system of the People's Commissariat of Education' effectively ended any wide-scale empirical work on psychological research in the Soviet school system.

The decree eliminated paedology from the Soviet school system, and made it impossible for paedologists to carry out research or applied work within the system. Psychological testing practices by paedologists who used the test results for placement of children in special schools was explicitly ridiculed in the decree (see text in Wortis, 1950, pp. 242–3). Furthermore, the decree declared paedology 'pseudo-scientific' on the grounds of its misfit with the needs of Soviet society as defined by the Party at the time. The wording of the decree left little hope for the survival of paedology,

and of many paedologists, in the Soviet Union of the latter half of
the 1930s:

> The Central Committee of the CPSU considers that both the theory and practice
> of so-called paedalogy represent pseudo-scientific and anti-Marxist positions.
> These positions are based first of all, on the main 'law' of contemporary
> paedology—the 'law' of the dependence of children's development on biological
> and social factors, on the influence of heredity and some sort of unchanging
> environment. This deeply reactionary 'law' is in complete contradiction to
> Marxism and to its practice of socialist construction, which is now successfully
> re-educating people in the spirit of socialism and liquidating the remnants of
> capitalism in the economics and consciousness of the people. The CC of CPSU
> resolves that such a theory could have appeared only as a result of the uncritical
> transference into Soviet paedagogy of the views and principles of anti-scientific
> bourgeois paedology which has as its aim the preservation of a ruling class and
> which therefore undertakes to prove that special talents and special rights justify
> the existence of exploiting classes and 'higher races', while on the other hand it
> has the task of proving that the working class or 'lower races' are doomed to
> physical and emotional failure. Such a transference of the anti-scientific principles
> of bourgeois science into Soviet science is all the more harmful because it is
> concealed by 'Marxist' phraseology. (Wortis, 1950, pp. 244–5)

This quote from the decree is noteworthy in different respects.
First, it demonstrates how the Soviet Communist Party had taken
on itself the role of the arbiter in scientific matters, making
decisions about which approaches in a science are, or are not,
'scientific'. The criterion for that decision was how the given
approach fits Marxist philosophy *as it was viewed from the
political standpoint of the day*. Secondly, the reference to the use of
Marxist phraseology as a 'masking device' of an 'anti-Marxist' view
as *more* harmful than openly non-Marxist viewpoints paved the
way for potential accusations against *anybody*. Rival groupings of
psychologists claiming adherence to Marxism thus became
vulnerable, as old infights would easily lead to 'unmasking' the
'enemy' in one's colleague or opponent.

The change of 'fashion' in the topics of investigation in Soviet
psychology that resulted from the wave of 'criticisms' and 'self-
criticisms' of 1931–32 led to the emergence of new psychologists as
the 'leaders' of their psychology. Given the ethos of the time, no
empirically oriented or non-Marxist theoretician could be put into
such a 'leadership' position. Furthermore, psychologists' own peer
consensus about the importance of one or another psychologist's
work was no longer sufficient for anyone to become such an

established 'leader'. As the matters of social sciences in general became more controlled by the centralized Party organization, the establishment of 'leadership' became determined by one or another symbolic event that could be interpreted by the public as endorsement of a given psychologist in the leading role.

Sergei L. Rubinshtein (1889–1960), a German-educated Russian-Jewish philosophical psychologist, emerged in the course of the second half of the 1930s to become a leader among Soviet psychologists of the early 1940s. A number of conditions facilitated his ascendance to that role. First, Rubinshtein was well educated in philosophy (under the supervision of neo-Kantian philosophers Hermann Cohen and Paul Natorp in Marburg, before the First World War). Therefore he could develop a good and thorough analytic grasp of the original work in the 'classics' of Marxism, a self-evident necessity for psychologists in the 1930s. Secondly, Rubinshtein did not participate in the confrontations of different groups of psychologists in the late 1920s and early 1930s.

A thorough overview of Rubinshtein's role in Soviet psychology is available elsewhere (Payne, 1968), so the present coverage concerns only the most general issues of his role, together with his relevance to isues of developmental psychology. Rubinshtein's first publication, which has been highly valued in Soviet accounts of the history of their psychology, was an article published in 1934 (Rubinshtein, 1934; see English translation—Rubinshtein, 1987), titled 'Problems of psychology in the works of Karl Marx'. This was followed in 1935 by the book *Foundations of psychology*, a forerunner to his major work (meant as a textbook, as well as a theoretical work in its own right) in 1940. For his *Foundations of general psychology* (Rubinshtein, 1940) the author was awarded the second highest prize in the USSR—the Stalin Prize (after 1956 renamed the 'State Prize') in 1941. This official recognition turned Rubinshtein into the 'leader' of Soviet psychology in the 1940s, until his views came under a wave of criticism towards the end of that decade, after the publication of the second edition of his *Foundations...* (Rubinshtein, 1946).

Rubinshtein's major interest in issues of consciousness was explicitly developmental, although it remained fully in the area of theory. He was interested in revealing the process by which consciousness emerges through coordinated functions of analytic and synthetic psychological processes. His emphasis on the *unity* of activity and consciousness made him well suited to the psychological ambience of the 1930s and 1940s. His remarkable philosophical erudition led him towards highly philosophical rather than empirical work in psychology which was also very appropriate to the time.

Rubinshtein's officially sanctioned status as a winner of the 'Stalin Prize' made it possible for him to chart the course of development for Soviet psychology in the early 1940s. Not surprisingly, his own ideas happen to constitute the core of these suggestions. The question of development is clearly as relevant in that scheme as it was in the thinking of his predecessors of the 1920s:

Above all particular problems [of psychology] ... rise the key issues of psychological science—the problem of consciousness, its structure and development, the interaction of the social and personal in it, of ideology and psychology. (Rubinshtein, 1943, p. 48)

The emphasis on the development of consciousness in Rubinshtein's article is all the more noteworthy since the task of the article was to overview Soviet psychology during wartime. Practical applications of psychology were obviously more important at that time than philosophical declarations. It was during the First World War that psychometric testing movement in USA got its boost due to the military needs of personnel selection and placement. A similar task was important to the Soviet Army during the war. Nevertheless, Rubinshtein argued *against* a return to the use of standardized tests (which were eliminated from the Soviet educational system in 1936). His advice against the use of tests was based on clear understanding that the *outcomes* of psychological processes covered by tests tell the investigator little about the processes by which the outcomes were reached. If more elementary psychological processes were important for military selection purposes, then experimental psychophysical procedures could be sufficient. However, more complex psychological characteristics

... are variable, they are transformed in the process of instruction [*obuchenie*] and should be studied in the course of a more or less extensive period of their formation and development, in the course of rationally organized instruction. In order to find out about people's suitability for one or another work, including one or another military speciality, they [i.e. people] must be *studied while instructing them, and instructed while they are being studied.* (Rubinshtein, 1943, p. 52)

The emphasis on an interactive teaching and learning (instruction) process as the tool for both research and practical application here continues the line of Vygotsky's and Luria's earlier calls for the study of development in the process of instruction (see Chapter 4). It also outlines another issue—it was not only as a result of the Party decree of 1936 that Soviet psychologists abandoned the use of psychological tests. For many psychologists in the USSR, both before and after Rubinshtein wrote these lines, the rejection of standardized tests followed naturally from their theoretical thinking (cf. Brožek, 1972). If the psychological processes that participate in development are the object of study, then the use of standardized tests that can at best locate the subject's performance outcomes relative to other people is an inappropriate method for serious research.

The end of the war left the USSR in the winner's position, yet the damage from the war had been considerable. So had been the help from the Western allies, whose social order was considered inferior (and historically regressing) in the Soviet world view. Increased contacts with Western countries during the war—both with allies and with enemies—served as alternative information sources for Soviet citizens. In the Soviet totalitarian social system, the loss of the 'fortress mentality' that was so carefully cultivated before the war could have threatened the social system. The advent of 'cold war' made it possible to restart the build-up of Soviet citizens' socialization in distrusting things and ideas foreign to Russian/Soviet society. It was under these general conditions that another social witch-hunt of 'cosmopolitan' and 'foreign' influences began. Rubinshtein's work became one of the targets in that wave of criticism. The particular style used by his critics (see Chernakov, 1948; English trans. in Wortis, 1950, pp. 261–85) was characteristic of the discourse style of the time. Rubinshtein was found 'guilty' of studying human consciousness as that of an undefined person, rather than that of the 'Soviet new man'. His intellectual indebtedness to Western psychologists was 'unmasked'. Rubinshtein's leading position in Soviet psychology began to evaporate.

The wave of criticism not only of Rubinshtein but also of other consciousness-oriented Soviet psychologists (e.g., Leontiev—see Maslina, 1947; Wortis, 1950) was part of the social campaign for *partiinost'* in different areas of Soviet life. Aside from calling for anti-cosmopolitan and Sovietophilic acting and thinking by Soviet psychologists, the campaign also had directly West-bashing goals including the denunciation of Western (especially American) psychology (e.g., Iaroshevskii, 1947). These 'social purification' events of the late 1940s prepared the conditions for the introduction of neo-Pavlovian ideas as the univeral and required theoretical system of Soviet psychology a couple of years later.

Rubinshtein's theoretical system

Rubinshtein's theoretical system included a persistent emphasis on the relevance of the ideas of development and historicity for psychology as a whole. In this he continued the traditions of Blonski, Vygotsky, Basov, and others of the 1920s, whose names were no longer mentioned in the Soviet psychological discourse of Rubinshtein's time. Furthermore, Rubinshtein continued the emphasis on the unity of analysis and synthesis in the location of 'psychological units' evident in Basov's work (see Chapter V). He also called for the study of psychological processes rather than outcomes—an idea that was at the core of Vygotsky's developmental view, as well as of that of Western developmental psychologists (e.g., Heinz Werner). This perspective has led to an interesting tradition in contemporary research on adults' thinking processes, both in the Soviet Union (Brushlinskii, 1968, 1979, 1983, 1984) and in the West (Markova, 1982).

Rubinshtein's contribution to the promotion and maintenance of developmental ideas in Soviet psychology is noteworthy, particularly as his main interest was in the theory of general psychology. His most important theoretical work, *Being and consciousness* (Rubinshtein, 1957), summarizes the relevance of developmental ideas for *all* psychology. This book, published after two decades of Sovietophilic and anti-international intellectual atmosphere that dominated social life, is highly internationally oriented in its coverage. During the years when Soviet psychologists were discouraged from keeping themselves informed about the thinking of 'bourgeois' psychology and philosophy, Rubinshtein's analysis of psychological issues in 1957 was performed in a manner recognizing the international nature of psychology as science. Furthermore, based on his theoretical thesis that the subjective side of the human psyche is objective *because it it is a reflection of objective conditions* of the person's life, Rubinshtein argued against the existence of 'the Soviet man'. His insistence upon the 'cosmopolitan' idea (cf. Rubinstein, 1957, p. 239) that had previously served as a target for his critics shows that Rubinshtein's own intellectual connection with world philosophy and theoretical psychology had survived the Stalinist decades, despite the ups and downs in his position in the Soviet psychological establishment. Furthermore, his philosophical psychology has had a demonstrable effect on the development of 'critical psychology' in Germany, and of the school of 'dialectical psychology' in the United States (Van IJzendoorn & Van der Veer, 1984).

'Pavlovization' of Soviet psychology

Pavlovian neurophysiology became the major fashion of Soviet physiology and psychology in the 1950s as a result of social processes at the end of 1940s which, among other things, established Lysenko's 'school of agrobiology' as the single accepted brand of 'Soviet biology', and declared Joseph Stalin the innovator of linguistics. The roots of the process of 'Pavlovization' of Soviet psychology can be found in the transformation of Sovet society in the post-war years, rather than in the development of Soviet psychology itself.

The highly patriotic and anti-cosmopolitan campaign that was aimed at making Pavlov the Russian indigenous hero of 'Soviet science' began first in physiology, from where it was taken further into the institutions of Soviet psychology. The 'Pavlovian Session', or the United Scientific Session of the Academies of Science and Medicine of the USSR for the discussion of Pavlov's contribution to physiology and related sciences took place in Moscow between 28 June and 4 July 1950. Its main result was the establishment of the interpretation of Pavlov's ideas by some of his disciples (particularly A. Ivanov-Smolenskii) as the accepted version of physiological theory. A number of physiologists (Beritashvili, Orbeli, Anokhin) were 'proven wrong' in their ideas, to which derogatory labels were attached with the ease that was so characteristic of the time.

A number of auxiliary factors seemed to have prepared the stage for such institutionalized emergence of Pavlovian ideas as the core of Soviet neurophysiology. First, the construction of the personality cult of Stalin had its counterparts in lower levels of society, and in different professions. Already in the 1930s, during the last years of Pavlov's life, his disciples tended to establish a local personality cult within the domain of his laboratory, competing with one another for his attention and approval. In the decade after Pavlov's death his numerous disciples made their careers in different institutions all over the Soviet Union. Of course, these disciples were far from monolithic in their interpretations of Pavlov, and became involved in clashes for establishing the role of the dominant (equal to 'the right') view in Soviet neo-Pavlovian physiology. As in the infights of psychologists in the 1920s, the mechanisms of which were analyzed above, Pavlov's disciples promoted the name of their revered teacher in order to improve their own status in the physiology establishment of the USSR.

Secondly, the Slavophilic ethos of the Soviet society of the time could accept as the official 'hero' of physiology a well-known *Russian* scientist who was also known to be a patriot of the 'fatherland', and who had been critical of his colleagues outside the USSR. Pavlov fitted that slot reasonably well. Although his actual attitude towards the Soviet power had been quite hostile all through the 1920s, it became more accepting in the last years of his life. However, Pavlov had had highly patriotic feelings towards Russia in general. His active critical style of opposing scientists whose work he did not value was also well known. He was fiercely critical of schools of thought in other countries (e.g., Gestalt psychology, Sherrington's physiology). His criticism could easily be presented to the Soviet public as evidence for the 'superiority' of Pavlov's ideas over anybody else's. Thirdly, the Soviet Marxist philosophical orthodoxy had by the 1930s embraced Lenin's phrase that the psyche is the property of highly organized matter—the brain. This phrase became accepted as the 'Marxist-Leninist' definition of psychological phenomena. Pavlov, above all, emphasized the relevance of understanding how the brain works, all through his scientific career. While Soviet Marxist philosophy arrived at the necessity of emphasizing the role of the brain from the point of view of philosophy, Pavlov insisted upon it from the perspective of biological science. The conceptual basis for

Pavlovization of Soviet psychology was emerging all through the 1930s (e.g., Kolbanovskii, 1939, Kurazov, 1930), and was supported in the second half of the 1940s by the wave of Slavophilic and anti-Western sentiments to which Pavlov's Russian patriotism was well suited.

Finally, in 1949, the centennial of Pavlov's birth was celebrated, and that symbolic occasion included the decoration of some of his disciples with high prizes. For instance, A. Ivanov-Smolenskii received the Stalin Prize in 1949 for his book *Essays on the patho-physiology of the higher nervous activity* (translated into English—Ivanov-Smolenskii, 1954).

The propagation of neo-Pavlovianism in Soviet physiology starting from the 'Pavlovian session' may actually be less orthodoxly Pavlovian than the multitude of declarations at the time, and later, imply. In neurophysiological research in the USSR, the disciples of Pavlov and Bekhterev of the first decades of the century were not very distinctly separated, despite certain animosity between Pavlov and Bekhterev. Some collaborators of Bekhterev later became associated with Pavlov's ideas. For example, Viktor Protopopov, who in 1909 published a work on associated motor reflexes that was conducted in Bekhterev's laboratory (Protopopov, 1909) and who in the 1920s propagated Bekhterev's ideas and role in neurobehavioural sciences (Proto-popov, 1928), turned to research using Pavlov's ideas (Protopopov, 1950) and to writing about Pavlov (Protopopov, 1948). At the same time, his suggestions concerning clinical practice in the treatment of schizophrenia resemble the calls for inter-disciplinary and multi-faceted approach *à la* Bekhterev far more than the experimental thinking of Pavlov (Protopopov, 1946).

The similarity of Pavlov's and Bekhterev's ideas created a situation in which physicians and physiologists educated in the wide system of institutes organized by Bekhterev at various times switch easily over to the use of Pavlovian terminology. The reverse switch was also possible. Some of Pavlov's collaborators increasingly became interested in the reflex activity of humans, including children. Just as Pavlov's own laboratory always remained oriented towards animal experimentation, the in-stitutions in St Petersburg (and later Leningrad) were associated with Bekhterev's ideas and organizational activities. Of researchers associated with *both* Pavlov's and Bekhterev's areas of activity,

Anatoli Ivanov-Smolenskii is noteworthy. He was one of the two leaders of the neo-Pavlovian group that gained dominance at the 'Pavlovian session' of 1950. He graduated from the Military Medical Academy in 1917, and started to work in 1919 on psychiatric research under the supervision of Bekhterev. Only in 1921 did he start to work in Pavlov's laboratory in parallel to his continued work in psychiatry at Bekhterev's institute. This was natural for any physiologist or psychiatrist of the 1920s in Leningrad who was interested in both animal and human studies of the activities of the nervous system. He could end up working in conjunction with Bekhterev on human-related topics, and with Pavlov depending on how he fitted in with the work done in Pavlov's laboratory at the time. In the case of Ivanov-Smolenskii, his first publications represent his research on humans and were published in journals edited by Bekhterev and his colleagues, whereas his animal work appeared in Pavlov's laboratory publications (see Kvasov & Fedorova-Grot, 1967, pp. 117–18). However, much of his research over the 1920s and early 1930s was devoted to the study of neurodynamic phenomena in humans (Ivanov-Smolenskii, 1933, 1934), including in children (Ivanov-Smolenskii, 1935). In 1930, he was criticized during the First All-Union Congress of the Study of Behaviour as one of the most active 'vulgar materialists' and 'mechanical materialists' who refused to confess (Kurazov, 1930). During the 'Pavlovian session' of 1950, Ivanov-Smolenskii advocated the acceptance of Pavlov's approach in neurophysiology and psychology. At the same time, he explicitly acknowledged his indebtedness to Bekhterev in his prize-winning book (1954). This is not surprising although Bekhter-ev's reflexology disappeared from Soviet *psychology* at the end of 1920s, his *physiological* work continued to be recognized in medicine and was referenced and acknowledged.

Given the closeness of Bekhterev's and Pavlov's emphases on acquired reflexes, it is interesting to hypothesize that the introduction of Pavlov's ideas as the leading theory of Soviet neurophysiology at the 1950 session has Bekhterevian nuances to it. Many of the physiologists who welcomed the new fashion for Pavlov were not strictly following his experimental puritanism that was distrustful of wide applications of ideas, but were closer in their nature to Bekhterev's propagation of similar associationistic ideas. This is particularly probable in the application of neo-

Pavlovian ideas to humans, and to children in particular. If the merging of Bekhterev's and Pavlov's ideas under the disguise of neo-Pavlovian terminology is an accurate description of the events of the 1950s, then it is not the first time that Bekhterev's ideas have been taken over under Pavlovian labels in the history of psychology. As much as American behaviourism has had input from Russian reflexologies of the beginning of the century, Bekhterev's line of thinking has had a closer affinity with it.

The 'Pavlovian session' set the stage for the enforced importation of Pavlov's terminology into Soviety psychology, which had rejected similar ideas at the end of the 1920s. However, this time the introduction of 'Pavlovianism' took place by directions from above and outside (i.e., originating in physiology), rather than by psychologists' own initiative. The process by which the new fashion for Pavlov became part of psychology was not quick, and involved relatively active hidden opposition (cf. McLeish, 1975, pp. 216–230). First and foremost, Soviet psychologists of the time lacked knowledge of both the theoretical and experimental sides of Pavlov's work. Two 'sessions' of psychologists, in 1952 and in 1953, included discussions on the role of Pavlovian theory in psychology (Petrovskii, 1953a). The external nature of the introduction of Pavlovian ideas into Soviet psychology was also evident in the discussion that the Soviet philosophy journal *Voprosy filosofii* started at the beginning of 1952. In the first article published in the context of that discussion (Mansurov, 1952), the names of Pavlov and Stalin occur intermittently and are allotted almost equal praise, in opposition to 'bourgeois' or 'demonic' (*mrakobes*) psychologies of the West. The articles that followed (Boiko, 1952; Lehtman, 1953; Petrovskii, 1953b; Rozov, 1953; Simonov, 1953) in the same journal indicated that the acceptance of Pavlovian ideas by Soviet psychologists was rather their assimilation into the pre-existing theoretical systems than their wholesale acceptance of them. What emerged was a mixture of philosophical, pedagogical and neo-Pavlovian aspects in psychologists' writing style. Superficial and overextended use of Pavlovian terms became widespread, paired with little change in what psychologists had been doing before, namely, philosophizing. Empirical evidence, had become of little importance at the beginning of 1930s, and continued to play a low-key role. The area in which 'Pavlovization' was perhaps most strongly influential was the content of psychology textbooks. According to Razran's (1957, p. 1101) analysis, psychology textbooks published in the USSR prior to 1950 included only 0.9 to 3.9% of mentions of Pavlov in their reference lists. In the case of textbooks published after 1950, the extent of references to Pavlov was substantially higher (22.9 to 41.7% in different books).

Fortunately the social conditions that led to 'Pavlovization' of Soviet psychology in 1950 changed—first with the death of Stalin in 1953, followed by Khrustschev's campaign to eradicate Stalin's 'personality cult' in 1956 and to open Soviet society to some interaction with the West. In the second half of the 1950s, Soviet psychology began to re-establish itself in the conditions of post-Stalinist society. The first specifically psychological journal *Problems of psychology* was started in 1955, ending the 23-year long absence of any psychology journal in the USSR. The work of some psychologists (Vygotsky, Blonski) who had been active in the 1920s came to be known again thanks to the reissue of some of their work. Psychology slowly moved farther away from philosophy again and established a number of empirical areas in which research began to be carried out. Psychology in the USSR gradually became less 'Soviet' in nature, and slowly established contact with its international counterpart. However, even in the slow re-emergence of a non-national science of psychology, the old Russian opposition of 'Slavophilic' and 'Westernizing' tendencies is evident. Soviet psychology has never been, nor will it ever become, a discipline free of the social context in which it is embedded. In that, the history of Soviet psychology is no different to psychologies in any other country in the industrialized West, nor the Third World. Psychologies in those countries can be as much interdependent with the social-political events as Soviet psychology has been. Only in the Soviet case, the ups and downs of psychology as a discipline have been more openly visible to outsiders, and more often the centre of attention of observers in the rest of the world.

Conclusions: ideas of development and the turmoils of history

The concept of development became important in the thinking of a few Russian scientists in the pre-1917 era. Some of them continued their activities after the 1917 revolution. The acceptance of developmental ideas in science was facilitated by political belief systems in Soviet society. When the advent of the utopian society did not take place, social ideology became defended by the political system. This defence kept alive the interest in the concept of development in psychology, albeit mostly in the theoretical sphere.

The contemporary state of affairs in developmental psychology of the USSR is deeply rooted in the stormy past of Soviet society and psychology. All different 'schools' of contemporary developmental research in the USSR (see Chapter IX) have their ties with the past. Many of the contemporary theoretical disputes (for example the squabbles of 'Vygotskians' and 'Rubinshteinians'; or between the Moscow and Leningrad 'schools' of psychology) have their pre-history in the past. Without an analytic overview of the past, events in contemporary developmental psychology in the USSR are difficult to follow, and the ideas expressed by Soviet psychologists hard to understand. The history of Soviet society has had its socializing effect on psychologists for whom integration in the wider social system is an accepted part of reality. By trying to help to build 'the new man' in the USSR they have actually rebuilt their own way of thinking. Vygotsky's idea of internalization of external experience, for example, is applicable to the thinking of Soviet psychologists as much as it is to the explanation of children's cognitive development. Ideas that have surrounded psychologists in society of their time have become internalized by them, and used in their theorizing. The ethos of change and development of a society (the construction of Soviet society) has facilitated the making of Soviet psychology along explicitly developmental lines, despite the weird turns the history of Soviet psychology has at times taken.

IV L. S. Vygotsky and Contemporary Developmental Psychology

In recent years Vygotsky has attracted the interest of American psychologists and philosophers, making him one of the best-known Soviet behavioral scientists. This is in itself a kind of mystery. Vygotsky's works are loaded with philosophical issues, literary images, and the once-topical arguments of European scholars. What could be more remote from the mainstream American thought? But perhaps it is precisely these 'remote' ideas that are needed now.

Alex Kozulin, *Psychology in utopia*, 1984, p. 102

Present-day psychologists' interest in Vygotsky's thinking is indeed paradoxical. On the one hand, his writings seem increasingly popular among developmental psychologists in Europe and North America. On the other hand, however, careful analyses and thorough understanding of the background of Vygotsky's ideas is rare (see Kozulin, 1984, 1986; van IJzendoorn & van der Veer, 1984; van der Veer, 1983, 1984, 1986; Wertsch, 1985). Vygotsky seems to be increasingly well known in international psychology, while remaining little understood. The roots of his thinking in international philosophical and psychological discourse remain largely hidden. His ideas have rarely been developed further, along either theoretical or empirical lines.

In the present chapter, following a short history of Vygotsky's research programme in the web of emerging Soviet Marxist psychology, some ideas stemming from his work that are considered of principal importance for contemporary developmental psychology are analyzed. The emphasis in that analysis will be on the potential usefulness of these ideas, rather than on an overview of how these ideas have been further developed. The latter is an impossible task, since the particular ideas analyzed here have not in fact developed further in any significant way.

The cultural-historical beginnings of Vygotsky's role in Soviet psychology

Little is known about Vygotsky's academic life prior to his entry into the young Soviet psychology (see Levitin, 1982; Wozniak, 1983). In 1924 he was invited to Moscow from Gomel, to work in Alexander Luria's department in the Institute of Psychology, the directorship of which was taken over by Kornilov in late 1923. The collective of the institute included a number of other young psychologists who were enthusiastic about the building of a 'new' psychology along Marxist lines.

Vygotsky's erudition, together with his intelligent rhetoric (which is reflected in his written works) made him a suitable candidate for a leadership role in the public discussions of psychologists of those times. His emergence as the unofficial leader of the group of young psychologists (whose formal leader at that time was Alexander Luria) at the Institute of Psychology created a unique situation in the history of science where a novice in the discipline (as Vygotsky definitely was in 1924) became the leader of the attempts by more experienced colleagues to construct new ways of scientific research (see Radzikhovsky & Homskaya, 1981). Such a situation could emerge only under the conditions of a basic reorganization of society as a whole, where the old social-administrative hierarchies of a profession were broken down and had not yet established their new structure. In other words, Vygotsky was fortunate to enter the scene of the development of Soviet psychology at a particularly appropriate historical moment. It was then that his 'novice' status in psychology could be appreciated by psychologists who tried to revolutionize psychology. Had Vygotsky been born a couple of decades earlier in pre-1917 Russia, he might never have been invited to become a leader in the 'new' psychology, because there might have been no such psychology. Had he been born a couple of decades later, he might have found the state of affairs in Soviet psychology to be of little interest for a person of serious humanitarian education. Vygotsky and psychology were united at the rare historical moment during which the latter needed the former, and the former—particularly because of his *lack* of formal training in psychology—was in a position to enrich the latter.

The timing of Vygotsky's activities in psychology made him

rush the introduction of his thinking to many areas of psychology, and he had no time to develop his theoretical system to a state of completion. However, it is only rarely that the incompleteness of his theoretical system is recognized (Iaroshevskii & Gurgenidze, 1981).

In some ways, the creative thinking of a theorist and a completed theory can be thought of as a 'contradiction in terms'. A theory that is considered to be 'completed' cannot develop any further. This is particularly the case for a dialectical thinker who made it his aim to advance a developmental theory of psychology. Perhaps it is precisely the unfinished (therefore open) nature of Vygotsky's theoretical system that makes different component ideas of his thinking valuable. In order to understand it better, the system's intellectual roots must be analyzed.

European roots of Vygotsky's ideas and his constructive thinking

It was Vygotsky's literary scholarship and his wide knowledge of philosophy that made it possible for him to generate ideas that were genuinely new for psychology as a whole and developmental psychology in particular. His rhetoric—remaining largely Russian in its stylistic features—was based on a deep knowledge of European and American philosophy and literature. Among other philosophies, it included a thoughtful understanding of Marxist philosophy irrespective of its many socially fashionable interpretations that were present in Soviet society in the 1920s.

Vygotsky, together with his colleagues Luria and Leontiev, began their efforts to build a new psychology on Marxist grounds from a critical review of all psychology. This review (see Vygotsky, 1982a) resulted in both an extensive understanding of the epistemological problems of contemporaneous psychological systems, and in a (Marxism-based) view of how to overcome psychology's 'crisis' through an emphasis on the *development* of the *higher psychological processes*—in both the history of mankind and the ontogeny of children.

Vygotsky was definitely a continental-European kind of thinker. His erudition as a literary analyst and philosopher, before he was invited into psychology, was extensive. In this sense, he represents an example of a cosmopolitan ('Westernizing') thinker of which there had been many in the history of Russian culture before him.

It is exactly in connection with Vygotsky's cosmopolitan thinking that his ideas came under active declarative criticism especially from the side of 'Sovietophilic' activists in Soviet psychology in the early 1930s (on those attacks see Radzikhovsky, 1979). For example, Vygotsky was accused of being a 'bourgeois psychologist' who was classified together with others 'of the kind'—which included such 'Western bourgeois' scientists as Levy-Bruhl, Piaget and Durkheim (Razmyslov, 1934; cited in Petrovskii, 1967, pp. 245–6). Vygotsky was also criticized for his 'mechanicist-idealist' position because of his reliance on James Mark Baldwin's emphasis on evolution and involution in development (Feofanov, 1932). In a curious way, Vygotsky and his colleagues—founders of the 'cultural-historical' view in developmental psychology—were also criticized for *not* taking 'historical factors' of development into account and reducing all development to biological transformations of form (Abel'skaia & Neopikhonova, 1932). All these criticisms carried anti-cosmopolitian undertones that became characteristic of Soviet psychological discourse in the 1930s. Vygotsky's Jewish background made him an immediate target of attacks on the grounds of his 'cosmopolitan' views, which indeed were very evident in his writings and oral presentations.

Vygotsky's theoretical connection with the thinking of his contemporary European and American psychologists was direct and substantial. That connection served as the basis for developing *his own* solutions to the 'crisis of psychology', rather than resulting in his following any of these schools of thought in a dogmatic way. Some of these schools of thought, while well-known to Vygotsky, he set aside as in principle useless in his effort to construct a new psychology in which issues of higher psychological processes occupied the central part. Thus, behaviouristic ideas of both American and Russian scientists were omitted from Vygotsky's synthesis of new psychology. His witty irony at the expense of reflexological reductionism of his time was quite biting:

The concept of reflex, in the sense in which it is used among us [in Soviet psychology], is very much like the story of Kannitfershtan [as actually in Dutch: *kan niet verstaan*], whose name a poor foreigner heard in Holland every time in response to his questions: who is being buried, whose is this house ... and so on. In his naiveté he thought that everything in that country is accomplished by Kannitfershtan, at the same time as that word meant only that the Dutchmen he met did not understand his questions. (Fam Min Hak & Radzikhovsky, 1977, p. 12; cf. also Vygotsky, 1979a, p. 10)

In contrast to Vygotsky's outright rejection of American and Russian behaviouristic thinking, his positive contribution to psychology was clearly rooted in the continental-European psychology of his time. German Gestalt psychology was well known to Russian psychologists, and had a strong influence on Vygotsky. For instance, his experimental method of 'double stimulation' (e.g., Levina, 1968; Vigotsky, 1934) constituted an elaboration of Köhler's experimental problem-solving tasks with apes, also mediated by the experimental research traditions with children of Mikhail Basov's group in Leningrad (more specifically—the work of Shapiro and Gerke, 1930). The other major source of input into the development of the 'double stimulation' method of Vygotsky's can be traced to the work of Narciss Ach on concept formation (Sakharov, 1930). On numerous occasions Vygotsky based his thinking (albeit not without criticism) on Koffka's work. Kurt Lewin's field theory surfaces in appropriate places in Vygotsky's writings. Likewise, his connection with the work of the 'Leipzig school' of psychological thinking (represented by the work of Volkelt and Krueger) occupies a central position in his writings. His roots in continental-European psychological traditions are of course deeper, also including the contributions of K. and Ch. Bühler, Hetzer, W. Stern, Werner, and Ach. Vygotsky's connection with European thinking also includes reliance on French-language psychology. He develops further Binet's work on memory (see Vygotsky, 1929a), criticizes and follows Piaget (Vygotsky, 1956), Paulhan (e.g. borrowing the distinction 'meaning'/'sense' from him—see Paulhan, 1928; Vigotsky, 1939, p. 47; Vygotsky, 1956, pp. 359–60; Vygotsky, 1962, p. 146) and Claparède. Vygotsky and his colleagues, particularly Luria, were likewise open to the important ideas that Freud and other psychoanalytic thinkers had explicated (psychoanalysis was rather widespread in the USSR of the 1920s—see Miller, 1986; Sapir, 1926). Vygotsky depended greatly on Pierre Janet's work, and frequently referred to it. Last but not least, he explicitly recognized the relevance of James Mark Baldwin's contribution to understanding psychological development. This is evidenced in his writing in different ways. First, he pointed to the connection between Baldwin's and Piaget's ideas in different key places (e.g., while analyzing Piaget's thinking directly—Piaget, 1926; 1932; Vygotsky, 1956, p. 95; 1960, p. 192). He also integrated the idea of imitation into his own theoretical framework (Vygotsky, 1960, p. 179), and emphasized the relevance of viewing evolution as intimately tied to involution.

Vygotsky's integration of different theoretical ideas into his holistic theoretical system did not stop with psychology, psychopathology, and evolutionary theory. He also used knowledge from contemporary cultural anthropology (especially the works of Thrunwald and Levy-Bruhl).

Vygotsky's connection with Western psychology was an outgrowth of his European-type philosophical and literary education. It is not surprising that he was highly knowledgeable both of the history and of the contemporary situation in European and American philosophy and psychology. All the major writings of European and American science, philosophy and psychology were available in translation in pre-1917 Russia, and were widely known among psychologists. For example, six volumes by Alfred Binet and his colleagues were published in Russian translation in the period 1899–1911; James Mark Baldwin's *Mental development of the individual child and the human race* appeared in translation in 1911, followed the next year by the *second* Russian edition of his *Introduction to psychology*. Karl Groos' book on the soul of the child appeared in St Petersburg in 1906, Edouard Claparède's *Psychology of child and experimental pedagogics* in 1916 (see Nikol'skaia, 1975). The Russian (often Jewish, like Vygotsky) intellectuals of that period received a very good education that made it easy for them to excel in different areas of science and the humanities.

It was such cultural-historical background that helped Vygotsky to reach a remarkable general erudition, which in its turn made it possible for him to analyze the state of affairs of contemporary psychology at a very quick pace, and to set the stage for the first empirical efforts of his new kind of psychology. The distinction between 'explaining' (*Erklären*) and 'understanding' (*Verstehen*) psychologies that laid the framework for Vygotsky's analysis of psychology has its explicit roots in the German scientific philosophies of the nineteenth century (Wilhelm Dilthey). And, of course, an important role in Vygotsky's thinking was played by the German dialectical and materialistic philosophies of Hegel, Feuerbach, Marx and Engels.

Aside from having definite deep roots in continental-European thinking, Vygotsky was in no way opposed to the thinking of other Russian Marxist philosophers and empirically-oriented psychologists of his time. In his crucial emphasis on the central role of the developmental approach in all psychology he explicity followed Pavel Blonski (see Kozulin, 1984, Ch. 6 for a description of Blonski's role in Soviet psychology). In developing his thinking about the unit of analysis in psychology he was not alone in the psychological community of his time, as the anti-reductionist ideas which Vygotsky propagated were widely shared in contemporary psychology (see Baldwin, 1930; Basov, 1929; Köhler, 1928).

Pre-1917 Russian intellectual thought also provided Vygotsky with a rich intellectual heritage on to which he could add his new ideas. Again, it must be emphasized that this heritage was deeply rooted in the continental-European thinking of the nineteenth century. In this sense, even when relying upon Russian thinkers of the past, Vygotsky was in fact advancing ideas that *had originated internationally*, rather than in the isolation of an independent 'Russian genius'. Of course, Vygotsky was embedded in the Russian intellectual environment (which, as a whole, was tied to European cultures) of his time.

For instance, Vygotsky's background in evolutionary theory was mediated by the Russian pioneer of comparative psychology, Vagner, whose ideas on evolution penetrated Vygotsky's theoretical system in different ways. Vygotsky also made use of some aspects of the Pavlovian idea of 'conditional reflex'. In the domain of linguistics, Vygotsky relied on the ideas of the Russian linguist A. A. Potebnya. The conceptualization of words and tools as parallel psychological means is derived from Potebnya (Piskun and Tkachenko, 1981; also see Vygotsky, 1956, p. 195). Potebnya, writing in the middle and second half of the nineteenth century, based his thinking largely on German linguists and philosophers (Wilhelm von Humboldt, Heyman Steinthal, Hermann Lotze—cf. Potebnya, 1926). Also, Van der Veer (1983) has pointed to the direct connection of Vygotsky's thinking (especially considering words to be instrumental devices of control over oneself) with the philosophy of Spinoza (see also Vygotsky, 1970), albeit mediated via nineteenth-century Marxist philosophical thought.

To summarize: Vygotsky, being of Russian-Jewish origin, was an European thinker of philosophical and humanitarian orientation, whose entry on to the stage of emerging Soviet psychology took place at a time when his thinking could have high impact upon the developing discipline. Vygotsky's European connection is unfortunately difficult to trace in the first more widespread English-language translations of his major works on which most of Western present-day knowledge about him is based (Vygotsky, 1962, 1978). The current emerging fascination with Vygotsky's ideas in Anglo-American psychology is thus largely also fascination with continental-European thinking which, in different versions, has emphasized the structural and dynamic nature of phenomena of the world.

Vygotsky's thorough and erudite analysis of the existing psychology of his times was the basis for his active effort to create new ways of thinking in psychology. His new way of thinking made the developmental approach into the cornerstone of *all* psychology. This was undoubtedly facilitated by the prevailing ethos in the whole Soviet society of Vygotsky's time which emphasized the *construction* of a 'new society'. Knowledge of international psychology and enthusiasm for overcoming its 'crisis' motivated Vygotsky to work towards new solutions of psychology's problems.

Vygotsky's Marxism, and the study of development

Vygotsky placed the study of development—made possible by the genetic, or historical method of study—at the core of all psychology. Only if psychological phenomena are viewed in their process of change can they be analyzed in adequate ways. Vygotsky's emphasis on the historical view of psychological processes seemed to go against the common sense of his contemporaries, since Vygotsky himself felt compelled to clarify the concept of historical study quite emphatically:

Up to this time, many people are tempted to present the idea of historical psychology in wrong ways. They equate history with the past. For them, to study something historically immediately means to study one or another of the facts of the past. That is why there exists a naive understanding that there is an insurmountable boundary between the study of historical and present forms. According to this, historical study simply means the application of the category of development to the study of phenomena. To study something historically means to study it in its movement. That is the main requirement of the dialectical method. To grasp in investigation the process of development of something in all of its phases and changes—from its emergence to its end of existence—is the essence of revealing its nature, since 'it is only in movement that a body shows what it is'. Thus, the historical study of behaviour is not an addition to the theoretical study, instead it constitutes the core of the latter.

In this sense one can study historically both the present, existing, as well as previous forms. The historical understanding extends also to general psychology. P. Blonski expressed it in the general statement: 'Behaviour can be understood only as the history of behaviour'. This is the truly dialectical viewpoint in psychology .... (Vygotsky, 1960, p. 89)

As described in previous chapters, the historical approach to nature and society was already present in Russian intellectual thought at the end of the last century (Bogdanov), and was actively propagated by Blonski during the years following the 1917 revolutions. Vygotsky's following of Blonski's emphasis on the historical perspective in psychology was also influenced by the thinking of Heinz Werner. The application of the developmental (historical) view to psychological processes makes it possible for Vygotsky to retain the continuity between the past, present, and future of these processes. He relied seriously but intelligently on the Marxist philosophical background which considers human beings to be active participants in their interaction with the environment. Among the few, but selective and highly adequate references to different aspects of Marxist philosophy one can find discussions of Engels on the role of labour and the use of tools in their mediating roles in the anthropogenetic process (Vygotsky, 1960, pp. 80–1), and Marx's thesis on the active role of the human being's transformation of the nature that constitutes the foundation of human history (ibid., p. 112). Vygotsky's acceptance of Marxist philosophy was not that of an ardent follower. Instead, he was an active creator of Marxist psychology. This can be observed in his rare but appropriate use of Marxist philsophy. The demagogical use of Marxist-worded slogans in trying to solve issues facing Soviet psychology was conspicuously absent from Vygotsky's writings.

Criticism of psychology's experimental methodologies

The task of building a new psychology centred upon development required a basic reformation of 'the scientific method' in psychology. Vygotsky did not start from an empty basis in his efforts toward that goal. The emerging tradition of Gestalt psychology brought the insufficiency of the Baconian quantitative method to the attention of young Soviet psychologists. In reality the whole organismic school of thinking had created its own scientific method. It was shown to fit biological complexity better than any quantitative reductionistic viewpoint. The natural-philosophic scientific method serves as the forerunner of Vygotsky's methodological innovations (Jevons, 1873/1958; Williams, 1973). Vygotsky was certainly not the first person in the history of psychology to realize the inconsistency of developmental perspectives and the methods imported to psychology from the physical sciences. At the turn of the century, James Mark Baldwin moved away from quantitative methodology. In his autobiography, Baldwin explained:

To one to whom, however, the psychological problem was the central one, the interest in biological evolution was secondary to that in genetic psychology. In the latter, two great problems presented themselves; first, that of method: how can the development of the mental order of phenomena—or that of any other truly genetic order, involving progress—be fruitfully investigated? The Spencerian or quantitative method, brought over into psychology from the exact sciences, physics and chemistry, must be discarded; for its ideal consisted in reducing the more complex to the more simple, the whole to its parts, the later-evolved to the earlier-existent, thus *denying or eliminating just the factor which constituted or revealed what was truly genetic*. Newer modes of manifestation cannot be stated in atomic terms without doing violence to the more synthetic modes which observation reveals. The qualities of flower and fruit, for example, cannot be accounted for, much less predicted, from the chemical formulas of processes going on in the tissue of the fruit tree. (Baldwin, 1930, p. 7, emphases added)

Baldwin's understanding of the necessity of constructing a scientific method adequate for developmental phenomena was related to Piaget's revolutionary application of the clinical method to the study of the *processes* of solving cognitive problems. Vygotsky proceeded along similar lines. Although he was uncompromisingly critical of Piaget's theoretical foundations, particularly those related to the ideas of children's egocentrism in early speech (see Piaget, 1926; Vygotsky, 1956, 1982b), he described Piaget's methodological innovations in most laudatory terms:

J. Piaget was the first who, with the help of the elaborated clinical method of the study of child speech and thinking, that he introduced into science, has subjected characteristics of child logic to investigation from a completely new perspective, with unusual courage, depth, and width of the study .... (Vygotsky, 1982b, p. 23)

Vygotsky proceeds to quote Claparède's introduction to Piaget's 1926 edition of *The language and thought of the child*, emphasizing his agreement with Claparède's evaluation of Piaget's theoretical revolution in developmental psychology—concentrating on the transition from purely quantitative perspectives to child development to the qualitative standpoint. Claparède (Piaget, 1959, pp. xiii-viv) described Piaget's methodological innovation:

The method which in M. Piaget's hands has proved to be so prolific is also one of great originality. Its author has christened it 'the clinical method.' It is, in fact, that method of observation, which consists in letting the child talk and in noticing the manner in which his thought unfolds itself. The novelty consists in not being content simply to record the answers given by the child to the questions which have been put to him, but letting him talk of his own accord.

Vygotsky's view of Piaget's clinical method in the science of developmental psychology was basic and full of fascination. However, it did not stop him from being critical of Piaget's refusal to trace philosophical axioms behind the 'facts':

The acquisition of new facts and their golden glare by Piaget is due, first of all, to the new method which he introduced—*the clinical method*, the strength and uniqueness of which *advances that method to be one of the best methods of psychological investigation, and makes it an irreplaceable means in the study of complex, holistic formations in child thinking, and of their change and development* [emphasis added here]. That method gives the real unity to all of Piaget's various factual investigations, which result in a united, real-life clinical picture of the child's thinking. (Vygotsky, 1982b, p. 26)

Vygotsky's positive feelings towards Piaget's method are natural. Piaget, following Baldwin's earlier ideas and his own empirical experience in testing children, introduced the first developmental method to the study of child development. Vygotsky's criticism of Piaget's theoretical ideas did not prevent him from taking over the developmental method from Piaget and modifying it. The roots of the 'method of double stimulation' are in Piaget's clinical method, along with Köhler's problem-solving methodology, and aspects of behaviouristic traditions. It is therefore not surprising that the reception of *both* Piaget's and Vygotsky's experimentally oriented ideas in the context of quantitatively inclined positivistic views of 'the scientific method' in Western psychologies has either been dismissive, or has turned towards efforts of *quantitative standardization* of these methods or their descendants. The excessive emphasis on the quantified 'stimulus-response' approach in psychology has flourished in much of psychology parallel to, and after, Vygotsky's and Piaget's elaborate criticisms of that general methodological ethos as principally inapplicable to the empirical study of development.

Vygotsky's analysis of the 'stimulus-response' methodology

For Vygotsky, the need to develop a new methodology stemmed from the same source as it had for other developmentalists—notably Baldwin, Claparède and Piaget. It was based on the transition from a non-developmental standpoint to an explicitly developmental perspective. The dilemma for any developmental investigator who wants to use the non-developmental methodology of other sciences for the purposes of the scientific study of development is quite simple: the ethos of the methods (revealing the 'true' state of the status quo) simply does not fit the thinking about movement away from that status quo (development). Three ways of dealing with such a misfit are conceivable. First, an investigator may practically give up the study of development in order to stick to the use of existing, non-developmental methods. As a result, the empirical data do not reflect development—even if their constructor goes to great pains to persuade his readers that they do. Secondly, s/he may turn to a general-intuitive understanding of development that bypasses the method (for example, becoming a humanistic psychologist, or a philosopher). Finally, s/he may try to *construct a new method*. Vygotsky took the third path, whereas Baldwin chose to move away from empirical research on development into social-moral philosophy (cf. Baldwin, 1915).

How did Vygotsky attempt to construct the new method? He started from the *requirement that the method must afford analysis of the complex process by which human beings themselves construct their own higher psychological functions, with the assistance from their peers or parents*. This requirement necessarily involved an open-ended method, since the process of such construction can always lead to novel psychological phenomena.

Vygotsky started from the critique of the traditional experimental method (the stimulus-response method, or S-R method) that was (and has remained) dominant in psychology. He first demonstrated that the S-R method is insensitive to the possibility that the subject might be active in controlling his own behaviour. Such insensitivity is unacceptable in the light of the axiomatic acceptance of the *active* role of human beings. According to the Marxist perspective, people change their environments and through that also themselves. The active role of the subject renders the traditional S-R method of little use for psychology.

Vygotsky, however, did not eliminate the stimulus-response scheme in full, since the *general* scheme of S-R was accepted by him as the general, but not particular, principle of psychological experimentation (Vygotsky, 1960, p. 63). Instead of replacing the general idea of the S-R scheme, Vygotsky enriched it by introducing the distinction between two kinds of stimuli: 'stimulus-objects' (*stimul-obiekt*) and 'stimulus-means' (*stimul-sredstvo*—cf. Vygotsky, 1960, p. 228). The class of stimulus-objects includes the sub-class of potential stimulus-means, since all stimuli that can in principle become means to some end in the hands of an active individual are first present as stimuli which affect the individual. The active subject constructs novel means to some (experimentally) given end, using the resources (stimuli) that the experimenter has provided.

Vygotsky's innovation in psychological methodology included a basic shift in emphasis. Instead of treating the subject in an experiment as a passive responder to stimuli, he was provided with *possibilities* of utilizing some aspects of the experimental situation (some of the stimuli) as means towards the goal of solving the problems that the experiment posed for the subject. Given that the interest of Vygotsky and his colleagues was in the study of *higher* psychological functions (e.g., voluntary memory, attention, etc.), the behaviour of subjects in experimental situations could not be reduced to their elementary behaviours. Instead, its complexity had to be retained. However, the complexity could not be retained in its entirety, since this would preclude any rational analysis and would allow only full-but-particular description of the phenomena. The latter was the result of a behaviouristic attitude taken to its extreme. Alternatively a global 'understanding' of the phenomena could be attempted. Vygotsky never tired of criticizing both the behaviouristic reductionism and humanistic holism in psychology. He saw a direct way out of the problem of analysis—calling for the *analysis of complex structured processes into units*—'minimal gestalts' of these processes that retain the functional properties of the whole while abstracting from the original complexity (cf. Vygotsky, 1960, p. 119; 1982b, pp. 15–16; see also the discussion in Chapter 5 of the present book). This emphasis determined the kind of explanations that Vygotsky's theoretical system makes relevant for developmental investigators.

Requirements of the developmental method

Vygotsky outlined three major characteristics of his new experimental method. First, he emphasized *the distinction between the analysis of a thing and the analysis of a process*, definitely considering the latter the target of psychological investigation. In this emphasis, Vygotsky follows the lead of Kurt Koffka and Heinz Werner (Vygotsky, 1960, p. 132; compare also Werner, 1937, 1957; Werner & Kaplan, 1963). Vygotsky envisaged the possibility of experimentally creating the conditions for observing the process of some psychological functions in their development. It is easy to see how the requirement that the ongoing developmental processes be studied directly fits with the emphasis on the sequential unfolding of phenomena in Piaget's clinical method. The aspect in which Vygotsky modified Piaget's method involved the provision of structured conditions within which the child's psychological processes could unfold.

Secondly, Vygotsky emphasized the potential for explanation of psychological processes that historical analysis affords—he thus overcomes the separation of description and explanation that had haunted traditional psychology. In doing that, Vygotsky follows Kurt Lewin' s thinking about the separation of *conditional-genetic* and *phenotypical* sides of psychological phenomena (cf. Vygotsky, 1960, pp. 133–4). He explained:

The phenomenological, or descriptive, analysis accepts the given phenomenon as it is in its external, observed form. This approach stems from the naive presupposition that the external appearance of a thing and the actual causal-dynamic relation that lies at its basis, coincide. The conditional-genetic analysis stems from the discovery of the real relations which are hidden behind the external appearance of some process. That analysis asks questions about the emergence and disappearance, about causes and conditions, and about all these actual relations that underlie some phenomenon. In this sense we could, after K. Lewin, transfer into psychology the distinction between pheno- and genotypic viewpoints. We will mean by genetic analysis of an issue the discovery of its genesis, its causal-dynamic foundation. The phenotypic analysis is based on the immediately given characteristics of the external appearance of the object. (Vygotsky, 1960, pp. 134-5)

The roots of the emphasis on the conditional-genetic analysis of developmental phenomena go back further than Lewin, and can be traced to Marx and Hegel in nineteenth-century German philosophy. In our contemporary terms, Vygotsky's emphasis on the separation of the genotypic and phenotypic aspects in psychological research parallels the analogy versus homology distinction in evolutionary theory (Ghiselin, 1976). This parallel is wrought by the similarity of the contrast between non-developmental (phenotypic, analogical) and developmental (genotypic, homological) viewpoints in developmental psychology and evolutionary biology. For a non-developmental thinker the issue of explanation of a particular phenomenon may be limited to the comparison of its appearance to those of other—quite similar or very different—phenomena. The non-developmental empirical investigator need not ask questions about the history of the target phenomenon—how, under what conditions, the phenomenon has come into being. Such questions do not fit into the meta-theoretical system of non-developmental research. In contrast, the meta-theoretical background of the developmental investigator allows, and in fact compels, him to ask questions about the emergence and dissipation of the target phenomena. Such questions need not overlook the present status quo, as observable in the phenotype, but can *connect the phenotypic outcome to the description of how it has emerged*. Although Vygotsky did not explicitly state that the description of the developmental process constitutes the explanation of the phenotypic outcome, he came close to it:

The analysis ... is not limited to only the genetic viewpoint, but, if necessary, views the analyzed process *as a known set of possibilities*, which lead to the formation of a specific phenotype *only under a certain complex of conditions or in a specified situation*. Thus, the new perspective does not exclude or postpone the explanation of the phenotypic characteristics of the process, but sets those into a subordinate position in relation to their actual origin. (Vygotsky, 1960, p. 137, emphases added)

Vygotsky's emphasis on the treatment of the genetic process in terms of a *generator* of different phenotypic forms is important in two respects. First, it underlies his general position that empirical observations (even of the processes of development) cannot in principle provide the investigator with direct answers to the theoretical questions asked. In other words: Vygotsky rejected the extreme inductivist-empiricist position in science, *without denying the relevance of empirical observations to theory*. He emphasized the necessity to analyze concepts that are used in science, alongside the scrutiny of facts:

... if the concepts, as tools, were predetermined for [the analysis of] particular facts of experience, then all science would be superfluous. In that case, a thousand or so officials-registrators or statisticians-accountants would take the whole Universe to pieces and put those into [table] columns and categories. *Scientific cognition differs from the registration of the fact by the act of choice of the necessary concept*, that is, by the analysis of the fact *and* the analysis of the concept. (Vygotsky, 1982a, p. 316, emphases added)

Secondly, his rejection of the 'data-driven' empiricist ideas is built upon the *de facto* acceptance of the *conditional* and *situational* dependence of psychological development. Acceptance of the context-dependence of the developmental process (and, therefore, the recognition that the same process can lead to different outcomes, dependent upon circumstances) relates Vygotsky's theoretical perspective to that of systems theorists who emphasize the open-systems (i.e. context-dependent) nature of biological and social phenomena (e.g., Bertalanffy, 1981, Bogdanov, 1899, 1922). On the side of methodology, this recognition led Vygotsky to search for an adequate experimental method for psychology in ways that are, in principle, opposite to the prevailing view on experimentation. The latter excludes the subjects' efforts at *active construction* of their responses beyond the minimum required by the experimenter, as 'error'.

Thirdly, Vygotsky emphasizes the frequent presence of 'fossilized' phenomena in psychological observations. This emphasis follows from his developmental perspective—in the process of development, new psychological processes emerge and advance to their 'established' form, in which they perform certain functions for the organism. In their established form, these processes have become 'fossilized' in the sense that they retain only limited remnants of their developmental history. The analogy with palaeobiological reconstruction of the behaviour and habitats of 'fossilized' organisms is evident. Vygotsky accepted that psychological processes become 'fossilized' as a result of their long history:

These fossils of behaviour can most easily be discovered in so-called automatized or mechanicized psychological processes. These processes, which as a result of their long functioning are brought to action for already the millionth time, have become mechanical, have lost their original appearance and their present external appearance tells us nothing about their internal nature. It looks as if they lose all characteristics of their origin. Due to such automatization, immense difficulties appear on the way towards their psychological analysis. (Vygotsky, 1960, p. 137)

Fossilization of psychological processes is thus a clear obstacle in the way of psychological analysis if such analysis were to start solely from the phenotype and attempt to reconstruct the developmental course backwards from a present appearance to its history. Only the actual tracing of the history of the phenomenon can provide information about the developmental course.

Vygotsky's three requirements for adequate scientific method in psychology emphasize the dynamic and time-dependent nature of all psychological phenomena. The first requirement—the study of process—leads to experimentation with psychological phenomena that *do not yet exist, but can be brought into existence under appropriate experimental conditions.* This requirement validates the use of *teaching experiments* as an experimental direction in psychology. In order to understand a particular psychological process, the experimenter sets up conditions for the subject that require learning how to perform some task. The scientific inference about the process is then based on the dynamics of the teaching-learning process. This requirement relates empirical research on a particular topic with the practical promotion of that topic for the psychological functioning of the subjects *in the future.* The second requirement sets up the demand for looking at the generative processes that have given rise to present outcomes, or that can be used in future-oriented experimentation to give rise to new outcomes. Finally, the third requirement furnishes scientific method in psychology with the guidelines of tracing the organization of a phenomenon not *in* the presently observable phenotype, but in its history—taking into account the process of fossilization that has taken place. Thus, both past-oriented and future-oriented directions are required by Vygotsky to set up the foundation for the new experimental method in psychology— which he labelled 'the method of double stimulation.'

The 'method of double stimulation'

Vygotsky's new method was very simple. In an experimental setting, the subject is confronted with a complex pattern of stimuli. Some of those are the result of the work of the experimenter. Others are simply present as an inevitable part of the experimental setting. As the subject is active, s/he reorganizes the stimuli into two categories: stimulus-means and stimulus-objects. The former begin to serve as means to the transformation of the latter, in connection with the subject's goals.

Vygotsky did not create his method out of nothing. The roots of the 'method of double stimulation' can be traced back to the thinking of Pierre Janet (see Van der Veer & Valsiner, 1987 in press). In his clinical practice as a psychiatrist, Janet discovered a number of complex ways in which cultural ideas served as 'means' to the end of helping the patient to act (or not act—see Janet, 1921) often in peculiar ways. Furthermore, Janet explicitly discussed the role of memory in human psychological functioning. Vygotsky's (and his colleagues') use of the double stimulation method also started from experiments on children's memory. Vygotsky's interest in two kinds of memory—'natural' and 'artificial' (sign-mediated)—follows Binet's work (Vygotsky, 1929a, p. 422).

The 'method of double stimulation' (itself emerged also as an extension of Wolfgang Köhler's experimental studies of apes' use of objects to solve problems (Köhler, 1928, 1927/1973, 1971). The following remark by Köhler on the purposeful intervention by the experimenter comes close to Vygotsky's subsequent legitimation of 'teaching experiments' in developmental psychology:

Clever apes can even be 'taught.' By all possible means you may draw their attention to the colour of two boxes (or their difference) and you may show at the same time that inside the box of one colour there is nothing; whereas behind the walls of the other colour there is a banana. Whenever I proceeded so, *forgetting the rule that an experimenter shall not play any direct role in experiments with animals*, a striking increase of right choices used to be the immediate effect. *And why not forget that rule, provided our principal intention in the actual experiment is not the study of the most clumsy form of learning but to make the chimpanzee master his problem as fast as possible?* We teach our children this way, and only a bad teacher would not be able to verify afterwards if the result of learning is independent of himself. (Köhler, 1928, p. 152, emphases added)

Köhler, as is evident, used experimenter intervention while still trying to separate 'true' (i.e. independent) and instructed learning. Vygotsky changed that: the 'teacher' or experimenter is actively trying to attain the goal of the subject's learning a new task. In the process, the input and guidance provided by the 'helper' serves as a basis for stimulus input, of which some become used as stimulus-means to attain new goals.

The whole nature of the method of double stimulation is developmental—it creates the conditions under which the subject's course of action towards an experimentally given goal explicates the psychological processes involved. Vygotsky remarked:

... we find that this method tends in the course of the experiment to call into being the very process of formation of the highest forms of behavior, instead of investigating the function already formed in its developed stage .... When we connect the complicated internal activity with the external one, making the child choose and spread cards for the purpose of memorizing, and move about and distribute pieces, etc., for the purpose of creating concepts, we thereby create an objective series of reactions, functionally connected with the internal activity and serving as a starting point for objective investigation. In so doing we are acting in the same way as, for instance, one who wanted to investigate the path which the fish follows in the depths from the point where it sinks into water until it comes up again to the surface. We envelop the fish with a string loop and try to reconstruct the curve of its path by watching the movement of that end of the string which we hold in our hands. In our experiments we shall at all times also hold the outer thread of the internal process in our hands. (Vygotski, 1929a, p. 432)

Vygotsky's insistence on the dynamic nature of the experiment, in which subjects construct their solutions using the auxiliary means that are available to them, sets the whole issue of the experimental method in psychology into a new light. Possibly Vygotsky's answer to the meaning of experimentation could have satisfied Baldwin's concerns about the ways in which experimental methods were used in psychology at the beginning of the century.

The ethos of Vygotsky's reformulation of the experimental method parallels his emphasis on the active (rather than reactive) character of psychological processes (Sakharov, 1930). If these processes are oriented towards attaining future goals in development, they have to be studied by adequate methods that make these processes explicit as they work—and that is exactly what Vygotsky's methodological contribution to the experimental method in psychology entails.

Despite the simplicity of Vygotsky's new experimental methodology, examples of its use are not easy to come by in his own writings. Examples of the method appeared in the publications of his co-workers (e.g., Levina, 1968, 1979) and can be used to illustrate the method.

Levina studied the planning function of speech under Vygotsky's supervision. Two series of experiments were conducted in parallel. In one, problem-solving using an external object was observed. That series was similar to Köchler's experiments. The other series was devoted to the observation of the process of the emergence of the child's control over his own psychological processes. Here, the child's speech—commenting on what she is doing and why—is of importance. Levina's description of subjects' speech and action in the experimental situation reveals a basic characteristic of the method of double stimulation:

Anya T., 3 years 7 mo. Situation: a candy is on the cupboard. A stick is hanging on the wall. Reaches silently. 'It is very high (climbs onto couch, reaches). It is very high, I should call Lyuba, so that she'll get it (reaches). Can't get it, too high. (Grasps the stick, leans on it, but does not use it.) No way to get it, very high (holds the stick in one hand, reaches towards the candy with the other). My hand is tired ... Can't get it. We also have a high cupboard, papa put things on it and I couldn't get them (reaches). No, I can't reach it, I am still small. (Reaches. Stands on chair, swings the stick, aims at the candy.) Pah-pah. (Laughs, moves the stick forward. Looks quickly at the candy, smiling, gets it with the help of the stick.) See, I got it with the stick. I'll hang it up at home, and my cat will be reaching for it.' (Levina, 1968, pp. 107–108)

This brief excerpt from a protocol of an experiment illustrates the essence of Vygotsky's experimental method. The experimenter sets up the situation of the task, together with some possible means that can lead to the solution if the subject uses them. The subject, put into such a situation, is expected to *act constructively* in devising a way to reach a solution to the problem. That constructive action involves action along two lines: first, the use of an action-means to the end of solving the problem, and second, the use of verbal action to comment upon what is going on. *It is the observation of the process by which solution is reached that constitutes the Vygotskian equivalent of the 'dependent variable' in traditional psychological experimentation.* Instead of 'measuring' the outcomes of the subject's problem-solving efforts, Vygotsky concentrates on the description of the action sequence that leads to these outcomes. In this his method is similar not only to Köhler's, but also to Piaget's 'clinical method'. The original aspect of the method of double stimulation is introduced when the emphasis in the observations of the child's problem-solving efforts is put on the child's construction of new means that can help to solve the problem and that restructure the whole task situation once invented. Thus, when a child is asked to draw pictograms by the investigator, and indeed does that, with the result that the pictogram becomes a powerful memorizing device, the whole situation has been reconstructed by the child into a new form through such construction of a sign.

The emphasis on the construction of *new means* that can be used to reach some goal in the experimental situation is not part of any 'eclectic innovations' that Vygotsky may be thought of as making for the purposes of his new experimetal method. *It follows logically from the emphasis on the active role of the human being in reorganizing his environment, and through that—himself.* Furthermore, it is based on the idea of a dialectical relationship between the philosophical categories of *quality* and *quantity*— when quantitative aspects of a phenomenon accumulate, it leads to a qualitative change in the nature of the phenomenon (see the description of Kornilov's dialectical thinking, in Chapter III). Thus, Vygotsky devised his experimental method in psychology quite directly on the basis of dialectical philosophy, from which position he criticized the 'stimulus-response' (S-R) method of traditional (and especially behaviouristic) psychology.

Vygotsky's contribution to the theory of the experimental method in psychology is particularly important as it has made the process of construction of higher mental processes not only the object, but also a tool of investigation. A child who is put into an experimental problem-solving situation constructs a new way of solving it. On many occasions the child makes use of some stimuli from his enviroment, turning those into means-to-the-end ('stimulus-means'). However, as long as the ready-made stimuli are utilized for this purpose, the child *has not yet constructed a new means*. Nevertheless, under some experimental conditions the child may suddenly construct a new means to an end, from the materials available in the situation (physical environment), *or within his own internal structure of psychological processes*. Coordination of the construction of external means and internal psychological processes by the child assists in the developmental process. The experimenter, observing the child's active construction of novel means, makes inferences about how that construction was reached, and thus gains access to that process.

The development of the method of double stimulation itself constitutes an interesting case history of the emergence of a qualitatively new means to solve a new kind of scientific problem. The transition of its author's thinking from the realm of the traditional S-R method can be traced by looking at the history of how the stimuli-means became conceptualized. In earlier experiments on memory, children were given a set of predetermined stimulus-means—'the artificial series'. The nature of that series of stimuli did not afford the children more than the pairing of a stimulus from that series with another one in the series of 'target' (memorizable) stimuli. The child could thus select the ways in which stimuli in the 'artificial series' help to memorize the 'target' stimuli, but was limited by the sets of stimuli provided by the experimenter.

This practice changed soon. Vygotsky and his colleagues proceeded from the *selection from pre-given material* to letting the subject *construct these stimuli* from the very beginning. In the domain of memory experiments, starting in 1929 (see Luria, 1982, p. 38) the children (subjects) were asked to invent pictograms that would help them to memorize abstract words, rather than just select a stimulus from the set of given 'neutral' stimuli (see Vygotsky, 1978, p. 74). This transition in memory experiments of Vygotsky's group from greater limitation of children's constructive role to greater freedom of construction is well in line with Vygotsky's and Luria's analysis of anthropological materials (particularly familiar to Vygotsky through the work of Levy-Bruhl and Thurnwald) on construction of mnemo-techniques (Vygotsky

& Luria, 1930b, esp. Ch. 2). The emphasis in the 'method of double stimulation' on the subject's constructive role is also evident in experiments on concept formation that were conducted under Vygotsky's supervisions by his colleagues (Sakharov, 1930; Schiff, 1935). As is well-known, the 'Vygotsky-Sakharov' classifications method used for the study of concept formation constitutes a modification of the method previously used by Ach and his colleagues. The major difference that Vygotsky and Sakharov introduced into that method included *greater variability* in the stimulus materials that were given to the subjects. In this, the stimulus materials constitute a heterogeneous and only partially pre-organized field (in resemblance to the real-life conditions), on the basis of which the subjects' actions towards concept formation can be brought out from the depth of mind into the experimental setting (Sakharov, 1930).

To summarize, Vygotsky's major contribution to developmental psychology lies in his efforts to provide the discipline with a methodological strategy that would afford the empirical study of developmental phenomena. That strategy is developmental in its nature, and qualitative in the majority of its conceivable applications. It involves the empirical analysis of the process of development, either 'on-line' (i.e., through analyzing the dynamics of subjects' solving of the experimental problem within the setting and resources given), or 'off-line' (as in the case of the efforts to analyze the developmental process of already existing phenomena using the available information). Whatever concrete form Vygotsky's method might take in the hands of different empirical investigators, its emphasis on the *subject's active nature* in his/her relations with other people within the given (structured) environment remains the heart of the matter. As Vygotsky himself emphasized repeatedly, this new methodological scheme extends the boundaries of the traditional (S-R) methodology by making the subject an active and constructive participant in the experimental process. That latter active role, however, *is always limited*, and purposefully so—since Vygotsky's experimental method involves the experimenter's purposeful varying of the *structural task conditions* with the aim of revealing the set of these conditions that leads to the emergence of *new* developmental processes. The experimental method has been enriched by Vygotsky to become developmental at its core and therefore applicable to the study of psychological development. Not surprisingly, though, psychologists after Vygotsky have largely overlooked the fundamental implications of his revolutionary innovation in scientific method.

The process of internalization

In contemporary presentations of Vygotsky's ideas to an international readership (e.g., in Vygotsky, 1978), the issues of internalization are given adequate attention as the backbone of Vygotsky's thinking. The intellectual and cultural history of the idea is well outlined by James Wertsch (Wertsch, 1985; Wertsch & Stone, 1985). Here I intend to analyze the connections of the idea of internalization with other concepts used by Vygotsky to describe social development.

The background of the idea
Vygotsky's emphasis on internalization (interiorization) is another issue in which he relied constructively on the world psychology of his times. Its roots are embedded in the thinking of Janet, Baldwin, Stern and Piaget, and are analyzed in greater depth elsewhere (Van der Veer & Valsiner, 1987 in press; Valsiner & Van der Veer, 1987 in press). At the same time, the idea of internalization borrowed from other psychologists was considered by Vygotsky to develop further Marx's basic idea of human psychology as a system of social relationships. He conceptualized internalization as a 'set of social relationships, transposed inside and having become functions of personality and the forms of its structure' (Vygotsky, 1960, pp. 198–9). Again, in the domain of internalization it is possible to see how Vygotsky acted as an integrator of ideas expressed in psychology with Marx's idea on the social nature of human beings.

The issue of internalization gained prominence in Vygotsky's thinking in the course of his discussion of the relationships of speech and thought, largely in the context of his analysis of Piaget's research. In Chapter 2 of *Myshlenie i rech* (Thinking and Speech 1956; that chapter is a reprint of Vygotsky's introduction to the Russian edition of Piaget's *Rech i myshlenie rebenka*—Piaget, 1932, same as Piaget, 1959), Vygotsky summarizes his disagreement with Piaget on the issue of the direction of the development of children's thinking:

The actual course of the process of development of the child's thinking takes place not in the direction going from the individual to the socialized state, but starting from the social and proceeding to the individual—such is the main result of both theoretical as well as experimental investigation of the problem that interests us. (Vygotsky, 1956, p. 89)

Vygotsky's further analysis of the question of *how* children's thinking advances on the course from its social to its individual state illustrates his structural-dynamic approach to the issues of internalization:

The first function of speech is the function of message, social contact, influence on others—on behalf of both adults and children. Thus, the first speech of the child is purely social; to call it socialized would be inaccurate because that word implies something that was at first non-social and which becomes social only in the process of its change and development.

Only later, in the process of growth, does the social speech of the child, which is multifunctional, develop according to the principle of differentiation of separate functions, and at a certain age quite sharply becomes differentiated into egocentric and communicative forms of speech .... Both of these forms of speech are, from the perspective of our hypothesis, equally social, but oriented in different directions in their functions. Thus, the egocentric speech ... emerges on the basis of social forms of behaviour, forms of collective cooperation, that the child has transposed into the sphere of personal psychological functions in social ways.

This tendency of the child to use, in relation to himself, these forms of behaviour that were previously social forms of behaviour is well known to Piaget and used nicely in the present book [i.e., Piaget, 1932] in the explanation of the emergence, out of disputes, of the child's thinking by himself. Piaget demonstrated that the child's reasoning [*razmyshlenie*] emerges after the occurrence of a dispute ... in a children's collective, since only in dispute, discussion, do those functional moments emerge that provide the starting point for the development of thinking-by-oneself. (Vygotsky, 1956, pp. 86 7)

Thus, the empirical side of the idea of internalization was obtained from Piaget's research. However, the theoretical interpretation of Piaget's empirical facts took a different direction in Vygotsky's thinking. The idea of the role of children's dialogue as the basis for the children's thinking-by-themselves has its roots in James Mark Baldwin's work (1892, 1894, 1895), and was directly acknowledged by Vygotsky on appropriate occasions (e.g., Vygotsky, 1956, p. 449; 1960, p. 192). Janet's work on development by transposition of external experience into internal psychological processes was likewise directly relevant to Vygotsky's concept of internalization. Vygotsky himself remarked:

The history of the development of signs brings us, however, to a far more general law that directs the development of behaviour. Janet calls it the fundamental law in psychology. The essence of that law is that the child in the process of development begins to apply to himself the very same forms of behaviour which others applied to him prior to that. The child himself acquires social forms of behaviour and transposes those on to himself. In application to the domain of our interest, we could say that the truthfulness of that law is nowhere as evident as in the use of signs. The sign originally is always a means of social contact, means of influence upon others, and only subsequently does it find itself in the role of a means for influencing oneself. (Vygotsky, 1960, p. 192)

Vygotsky followed Janet's idea that words were originally commands for others, and later in history turned into means of regulating one's own self (cf. also Vygotsky, 1960, p. 194). This is one of Vygotsky's cornerstones in the explanation of the ontogeny of speech and thinking. It is on the basis of clearly documented relationships between Vygotsky's thinking and the earlier or contemporary ideas of Janet, Baldwin, Piaget, Bühler, Kretschmer, and Marx that Vygotsky's general formulation of the internalization process as the core of social development of cognition emerged. Vygotsky did not invent it—instead he creatively integrated different existing viewpoints into a new general principle, in the form of the following statement:

We could formulate the general genetic law of cultural development in the following way: every function in the cultural development of the child comes on to the stage twice, in two respects; first in the social, later in the psychological, first in relations between people as an interpsychological category, afterwards within the child as an intrapsychological category ....

All higher psychological functions are internalized relationships of the social kind, and constitute the social structure of personality. Their composition, genetic structure, ways of functioning, in one word all their nature is social. Even when they have become psychological processes, their nature remains quasi-social. The human being who is alone retains the function of interaction. (Vygotsky, 1960, pp. 197-8)

However, it would be inaccurate to place Vygotsky in the category of thinkers who explain away all cognitive phenomena as reflections of the influence of the environment. Vygotsky's thinking was *structural-dynamic*, involving an emphasis on the subject's interaction with the socially organized environment. The structural aspect of Vygotsky's thought was closely related to the ways in which Gestalt psychologists conceptualized psychological phenomena in the process of their empirical study. Although

Vygotsky disagreed with the theoretical assumptions of particular Gestalt psychologists, his own empirical efforts (as shown above) followed closely the experimental traditions of the Gestalt school. The idea of internalization of inter-individual social experience was analyzed by Vygotsky in different empirical contexts. This is illustrated first by the example of how infants develop internalized means of paying attention to something, beginning from the motor action of trying to grasp something, which is subsequently turned into a sign (pointing, or indicatory gesture) in interaction with others. Following the emergence of grasping, the child and his social others cooperate in the internalization process of the indicatory gesture:

When the mother comes to the aid of the child and comprehends his/her movement as an indicator, the situation changes in an essential way. The indicatory gesture becomes a gesture to others. In response to the child's unsuccessful grasping movement, a response emerges not on the part of the object, but on the part of another human. Thus, other people introduce the primary sense into this unsuccessful grasping movement. And only afterwards, owing to the fact that they have already connected the unsuccessful grasping movement with the whole objective situation, do children themselves begin to use the movement as an indication. The functions of the movement itself have undergone a change here: from a movement directed toward an object it has become a movement directed toward another human being. The grasping is converted into an indication. Thanks to this, the movement is reduced and abbreviated, and the form of the indicatory gesture is elaborated. We can now say that it is a gesture for oneself. However, this movement does not become a gesture for oneself except by first being an indication, i.e., functioning objectively as an indication and gesture to others, being comprehended and understood by surrounding people as an indicator. Thus, the child is the last to become conscious of his/her gesture. Its significance and functions are first created by the objective situation and then by the people surrounding the child. The indicatory gesture initially relies on a movement to point to what others understand and only later becomes an indicator for the child. (Vygotsky, 1981a, p. 16; original: Vygotsky, 1960, p. 196)

This example illustrates the dependence of the particular internalization process on the context of the child's relationship to the environment, which is regulated (through the adult caregiver's responding to child's effort, and later gesture) by the social others surrounding the child. Whereas the principle of internalization is general and abstract, its actualization always takes place in some concrete context. *Vygotsky integrated the concept of internalization with contexts of child development through the invention of the concept of the Zone of Proximal Development (zona blizaishego razvitia).* The latter concept refers to the connection of the child's previous knowledge with the new kinds of experience, that are not yet internalized but may become so—with assistance from social others.

The role of instruction in child development

The concept of the ZPD (zone of proximal development) which has gained some popularity in contemporary international psychology (Rogoff & Wertsch, 1984) long after Vygotsky devised it, is a theoretical concept which can be explained and made concrete in different ways. Its basis is the idea of internalization as it is *organized by the child's interaction with others* in different contexts. The organization of child development is, of course, in the hands of the more competent other people surrounding the child in settings where the child is expected to develop in a certain direction. Settings of formal education—schools—are obviously highly salient in this respect. Therefore, it is not surprising that Vygotsky introduced his concept of ZPD in the context of discourse on the role of instruction (*obuchenie* in Russian—see Rogoff & Wertsch, 1984, p. 3). Instruction involves the *participation* of the 'instructor' and the 'instructed' in goal-directed joint action of teaching/learning. The instructor (teacher, parent) may try to get the child to learn a new skill or meaning, but the child need not learn it. As a result, the issue of the 'readiness' of children of a particular age or background for learning one or another new skill is a frequent topic of discourse among educationalists and parents. The situation was similar in the USSR at the time when Vygotsky developed his psychological thinking— part of the ethos of constructing 'the new society' involved rethinking the old educational system, and a substantial number of the population was subjected to quick courses which aimed to teach the illiterate reading and writing skills. Thus, Vygotsky's efforts to conceptualize the *psychological functions of instruction* fitted the social interests of his time.

Given this social context, it is not surprising that Vygotsky introduced the concept of ZPD in connection (and contrast) with the psychometric (paedological) tradition of testing children's abilities. His introductory explanation of the ZPD as being 'the distance between the actual developmental level as determined by independent problem solving and the level of potential development as determined through problem solving under adult guidance or in collaboration with more capable peers' (Vygotsky, 1978, p. 86)—has become assimilated into contemporary psychological neo-Vygotskian discourse. However, for Vygotsky, the example of comparison of the child's actual and assisted performances on some test served only as a means to get across to his pedagogically-minded listeners (and readers) a more basic theoretical message. That basic message was the *interdependence of the process of child development and the socially provided resources for that development.* That interdependence was conceptualized by Vygotsky in structural-dynamic terms, following the lead of Gestalt psychology. Vygotsky gave credit to Koffka (see Vygotsky, 1960, pp. 440-1) for overcoming both the pre-formationist and environmentalist perspectives on the relationship of learning and instruction. The pre-formationist (hereditary, determinist) view on the issue reduced the relationship to the dominance of the biological development of the organism. The child was considered ready for instruction when the psychological processes (that were to be the object of instruction) were ready in their mature form. As Vygotsky characterized this perspective: 'instruction drags after development, development is always ahead of instruction' (Vygotsky, 1960, p. 439). Indeed, when causality in child development is fully attributed to maturational (genetically predetermined) course, then considering the role of instruction in that development would, by definition, be viewed as superfluous. The opposite of the maturationist view—the environmentalist perspective on child development—performed a similar (but opposite) extreme reduction of the issue to one of its sides. For an extreme environmentalist (of the Watsonian or Pavlovian kind), instruction (teaching) is equated with child development, and the child's contribution to it is reduced drastically. In this case, as Vygotsky figuratively remarked, 'development follows instruction, like the shadow follows the object of which it is a shadow' (Vygotsky, 1960, p. 440).

In contrast, Koffka's view of learning and instruction emphasized the interdependence of the two processes, linking development to the general influence of instruction that makes it possible for the organism to transfer what is learned in one setting into another one. Vygotsky's thinking, however, proceeded beyond that of Koffka—by asking the question *at which developmental stage of the emergence of some new psychological function would instruction be the most appropriate?* He answered that question by locating the most appropriate time for linking instruction with learning at the time when new functions are *beginning* to emerge, but have not yet unfolded. Otherwise, instruction would have no effect on learning if the new psychological function is beyond the current biological capacity of the organism. It is within the range between the 'already begun, but not yet developed' and 'fully developed' state of a function X when the instruction aimed at helping the child to learn X becomes integrated with (and assists) the child's learning efforts. Within these boundaries, the processes of development follow the processes of instruction, whereas outside them instruction for X either does not relate to the child's learning of X (inappropriately early beginning of the instruction), or is irrelevant to the learning of X (instruction for a function that is already acquired). Such dependence of the success of instruction upon its timing—introducing it when the learning of something is only beginning in the child—and guiding the child towards the mastery of the new function was formulated by Vygotsky as 'a general law' which unites the internalization process with the interdependence of instruction and learning. He stated:

... the crucial characteristic of instruction is the fact that instruction creates the zone of proximal development, i.e. elicits in the child, promotes, and brings to movement a number of internal developmental processes, which at the present time are available for the child only in the sphere of relations with the people around and in joint action with peers, but which later, undergoing internal course of development, become then the internal property of the child himself. (Vygotsky, 1960, p. 450)

It is clear how the ZPD concept is used by Vygotsky to integrate the guiding role of the child's social environment with the process of internalization of external experience by the child. The system suggested by Vygotsky is very simple—adults and children are always engaged in social relationships; the adults try to help the child to develop (by instructing the child), but the effectiveness of that instruction is dependent upon its timing *relative to the child's current state of action and thinking*, which in turn is a product of the child's previous development. Only if instruction is thus properly timed would it lead to the utilization of the social nature of child development—integration of the instructed function into the child's own action schemes, and the internalization of it into his cognitive schemata (making use of Piaget's [1970] terminology here).

Redundancy in children's life environments and the ZPD

Perhaps one aspect of the explanation of child development through the use of ZPD that Vygotsky was not very eager to emphasize is the presence of different means that lead to the same outcome. For example, a child who grows up in a cultural environment but receives no purposeful instruction that is neatly fitted into the ZPD, would end up internalizing sufficient cultural background to function adequately as a member of the culture. Instead of the formal instruction in the form of schooling that Vygotsky mostly discussed while talking about instruction/learning relationships, all human societies have a prevalence of conditions without formal schooling and purposeful teaching of children outside their family environment, over a long period in their histories. The informal education that has been of primary relevance usually involves a combination of learning by observation and teaching-by-example, while integrating the developing child into the family's subsistence activities. At times, explicit instruction certainly plays a part in this education, but it may be rare. The overwhelming tendency in human cultures has been *not* to worry about fitting child-rearing efforts neatly into the ZPDs of the children of particular ages to arrive at the best educational outcome.

It is important to emphasize that children's interaction with their world includes redundant ways of constructing the ZPD. The adult-dominated interaction is only one. Alternatively, the ZPD can be constructed not only by the purposeful efforts of the instructor of the child, but also by cultural structuring of the environment in such ways that the developing child at any time is guided by his/her environment to make use of the parts of that environment that are currently within the ZPD. In other words, not only instruction but also the individual learner can define the ZPD, given the culturally structured life environment that provides the 'stimulus-means' for the child's own construction of the ZPD and, by that, of the child's own future development. However, Vygotsky insisted that even in the case of the child's own construction of his development within the ZPD, it is the adults (culture) who provide the guidelines and conditions within which the child's self-development takes place.

Cultural organization of child development is redundant. It may provide explicit instruction to the child in social interaction, or can alternatively structure the child's environment in such ways that the child develops along cultural lines on his/her own. More importantly, both of these lines are usually present simultaneously and complement each other: where adults' active instruction is misapplied (i.e., does not lead to the given child's ZPD for the given function X), the environment surrounding the child may guide the child to constructing his ZPD for X without the assistance of adults or of any other person. However, even that individual construction of ZPD is social in its nature, since the resources on the basis of which the ZPD is constructed are culturally pre-structured, and their use may have been observed by the child on many occasions. For example, a child who grows up in a family environment full of books may acquire reading in his sixth year of life without any explicit instruction (Vytogsky, 1956, p. 437). That environment, however, is provided for the child by the parents, who may also provide children with models by their own actions in the given environment.

Vygotsky's reference to the child's development of a cultural function (reading) under conditions of availability of opportunities without explicit instruction constitutes an understanding of alternative routes to the same end—cultural development of the child. It coincides with Vygotsky's emphasis on the active role of the pre-school-age child who constructs new means for solving new problems, using the resources that the adults have made available, for example language. Finally, Vygotsky viewed the crucial role of children's play in its construction of the ZPD:

... play creates the zone of proximal development of the child. In play the child is always above his average age, above his usual everyday behaviour; in play he is as if head-high above himself. The play contains in a condensed way, as in the focus of a magnifying glass, all tendencies of development; in play it is as if the child tries to accomplish a jump above the level of his ordinary behaviour. (Vygotsky, 1966, p. 74)

As is evident, Vygotsky recognized the explicit possibility that the child too can create his own ZPD—in the context of play. This accords well with the general idea that the child is active in his environment. The play context is crucial to the understanding of redundancy in development: if an explicit context of instruction (involving the leading, but child-dependent role of the adult or older sibling) is present, the ZPD will be created in that context. If, however, there is no explicit instruction present in a situation, and the child is left on his own and becomes engaged in play—the child himself constructs his ZPD making use of the available environmental resources. *In either case, the cultural development of the child is guaranteed by the two ways of acting beyond the knowledge and skills the child already has at the moment—under instruction or in play.* This redundancy was understood by Vygotsky, despite the fact that in his writings and speeches he limited himself to an emphasis on one or the other of the two routes of development. In other words, the developing child is constantly in the process of constructing his own future development—sometimes by his own means (in play) and at other times with explicit assistance from others (under instruction). However, even when the child constructs his own development in play, the environment within which the play takes place is pre-structured culturally. In this sense, all child development is necessarily cultural in its nature—culture is constructed by the child within the limits specified by the child's 'social others'.

Temporary integration of developmental lines

Vygotsky's thinking was characterized by a relatively strict separation of different lines in development, the major ones—the 'lower' (biological) and the 'higher' (cultural)—having perhaps become the topic of most controversy in discussions of his theorizing ever since his time. Vygotsky's liking for separating different abstract developmental courses and tracing their divergence and convergence over time is also obvious in other respects. For instance, in the previous sections the lines of development and instruction were viewed as principally separate, only becoming integrated within the boundaries of the ZPD.

Vygotsky's emphasis on separate and temporarily integrated developmental lines borrows its basis from the comparative-psychological thinking of Vladimir Vagner (see Chapter III). Particularly, Vagner's distinction of 'pure' and 'combined' lines was of importance to him. A new psychological function emerges in evolution as a 'pure line' if it does not interfere with the set of already existing functions. In contrast, the evolution of a function as a 'combined line' results not so much from the emergence of a new function *per se*, but is a result of the whole structure of the previously formed psychological system of the animal (Vygotsky, 1960, p. 368).

For Vygotsky, the idea of 'combined lines' in human psychological ontogeny proved important. He viewed the higher psychological functions as emerging on the basis of a pre-viously existing structure, and acquiring a new quality in themselves; thus the 'lower' processes of *involuntary* attention, memory, and thinking are transformed into their *voluntary* (qualitatively different, 'higher') versions (Vygotsky, 1960, p. 370). This transformation of lower processes into higher forms *occurs at the intersection of the previously separate lines of development of the child's actions and speech.* The child, before the end of his second year, was alleged by Vygotsky to demonstrate *parallel* lines of development in the domains of action and speech. Only when these lines become *integrated* and speech acquires the controlling function over actions, do the higher psychological processes, which are characterized by their internal cognitive planning, emerge. Such integration of the two lines of development may disappear in time—as in the case of differentiation of speech into inner speech and social speech. The same general feature of Vygotsky's thinking appears here: from the perspective of development it is the periods of integration of different psychological systems that result in the emergence of a qualitatively new state of the organism.

Vygotsky's ideas and Western psychology

We have seen that Vygotsky's new ideas were based on the know-how of the international science of his time. Now we will analyze the process of reverse influence—that by Vygotsky on Western psychology. Vygotsky has had a profound effect on developmental psychology, both in the USSR and beyond its borders. The social-political history of the Soviet Union has affected the use, dissemination and advancement of his ideas in Soviet psychology. What, then, has influenced Vygotsky's role in international developmental psychology? An analysis of the dissemination of the understanding (and misunderstanding) of Vygotsky's ideas in Western psychology constitutes an interesting elaboration of the general model of scientific discourse that was introduced in Chapter 1.

Communication between psychologies: a general analysis

The process of communication between psychologies embedded in different cultural systems can be viewed as a case of active co-construction of understanding by both the 'donor' (Communicator) and the 'Recipient' psychological systems. The 'donor' may actively promote *its* version of a certain view, but the 'recipient' need not accept that in 'donor's' terms and will transform the view actively into a new form that fits in with its previous state. Both the communication and reception of messages is selective: only some ideas are transferred from the Communicator to the Recipient; of those, many are changed by the Recipient on the receiving end, or soon forgotten, or even rejected from the very beginning.

In inter-cultural scientific communication, certain kinds of information can be helpful in tracing the discovery, assimilation, and—ultimately—forgetting of a foreign idea imported into the 'recipient' culture. First, the presence of the idea in the 'donor' culture must be documented. That idea itself may have resulted from some previous importing of other ideas into the 'donor' culture. Vygotsky's ideas were based in the Western European thinking of his time. Secondly, the particular idea that is present in the 'donor' culture must find its way to the 'recipient' culture. This can happen in different ways. First, documenting the *history of translations* of texts that contain the idea into the language of the 'recipient' culture lets us know about the availability of this idea on a wider scale. This information, however, is by itself insufficient. Some scientists in the 'recipient' culture are able to access the idea in question without its being translated into the language. Thus, the first information source needs to be supplemented by a second—an *analysis of explicit use* of the idea in the 'recipient' culture. A citation analysis may be utilized here. However, this too provides only a limited angle on the assimilation of the idea in the 'recipient' culture. It affords an extensive, quantitative view on the *width* of dissemination of the idea. This has to be supplemented by another perspective—an intensive, qualitative analysis of the *transformation of the message* in the process of communication. In our case of scientific communication, it involves an analysis of alterations in the original meaning of ideas once these have become translated into another language, and used by psychologists in the 'recipient' culture(s). It is the patterns of the 'recipient' culture that guide any rearrangements in the translations.

What are the potential consequences for psychologists' work, from this inter-cultural selective diffusion of ideas? If substantial differences between the original psychological texts and their translations are traced, then a general analysis of references made by scientists within the 'recipient' culture to the originals and to the translations may provide us with some crude estimate of which ideas are, or are not, becoming assimilated in the culture. For example, let us assume that an original publication included a set of interconnected ideas (A-B-C), but the translation was abbreviated so that only part of the original (say, B-C) was retained. A psychologist (X) who makes use of the original text (containing A-B-C) is likely to use the ideas in it differently from another psychologist (Y) who has access only to the translated and abbreviated (B-C) version of the same text. Quite possibly, X and Y discover that they have difficulties communicating with each other. They may both think that they understand the same ideas in a similar way, but in reality they already start from different 'input complexes' of ideas, from which it may be very difficult to proceed to shared similar understanding. The abbreviated translation serves as a socially constructed frame for Y, that canalizes his understanding of the given set of ideas. This need not be a serious problem for science since the aim of the discipline is not to follow dutifully another scientist's ideas but rather to go beyond them, and an abbreviated version in a translation may be helpful rather than counterproductive. However, it is often the *connection* between ideas, the holistic structure (Gestalt) of a scientist's thinking that is necessary to understand the meanings of the elements as these make up the whole. In this sense, the problem with the translation is *not* with the missing idea (A), but *with the missing connection between it (A) and the rest (B-C)*. The scientists who are forced to, or prefer to, use such translation could easily fail to perceive the author's more subtle nuances of ideas.

Vygotsky's writings and their English translations
The case of Vygotsky's ideas in developmental psychology calls for

a documentation of these different aspects of the migration of ideas. First, his developmental ideas are interesting to developmental psychologists in any country, given the lack of developmental theories. Secondly, Vygotsky's ideas have become available to the international scientific community in different translations ranging over half a century. Some of his writings have been translated in a selective way.

The complexity involved in translating Vygotsky's writings into English has been influenced by the disappearance of his ideas from public consumption in Soviet psychology for two decades (from 1936 to 1956). Only after Vygotsky has become 'rehabilitated' in Soviet psychology since the latter part of 1950s, and by the efforts of his surviving colleagues, has it become realistic for Western psychologies to 'discover' his writings and get some of them translated. Interestingly, previously available translations of Vygotsky's work had had only a small impact before that time.

The history of how Vytogsky's ideas have reached the international psychological community is made easier given the limited availability of Vygotsky's writings in English translations, as well as the wide time-span of these available publications. Vygotsky's English-language translations cover the time from the mid-1920s (Vygotsky, 1925) to the present. In the course of that history, the first uncertainty of translation can be observed in the different versions of the transliteration of his last name (e.g., Vygotski, 1929a; Vigotsky, 1934, 1939; Vygotsky, 1962, 1967, 1971, 1977, 1978, 1979a, 1979b, 1981a, 1981b, 1981c).

In general terms, translations of different aspects of the writings by Vygotsky have appeared in two waves. The first ranges from the late 1920s until 1939, and the second from 1961 to the present. Many of the translations were largely initiated by Russian psychologists themselves who tried to reach out to the international scientific community. For example, Alexander Luria's was a member of the Editorial Board of the *Pedagogical Seminary and Journal of Genetic Psychology* from 1928 to 1952. During his tenure on the Board, Luria organized the translation and publication in that journal of a number of articles from Vygotsky's circle (Luria, 1928b; Vygotski, 1929a; Leontiev, 1932). He was also active in informing the international psychological community of new developments in psychology in the USSR (e.g., Luria, 1928a). In addition to Luria's editorial and promotional efforts, the active interest of international psychologists resulted in wide accessibility of the ideas of different 'schools' of thought in Soviet psychology in English translation. Thus, Carl Murchison organized the publication of a section on 'Russian psychologies' in his *Psychologies of 1930* which included overviews of different perspectives (Kornilov, 1930; Pavlov, 1930; Schniermann, 1930a). Other psychologists' writings were also available in English at the end of the 1920s (Basov, 1929; Blonski, 1928). The first wave of translations decreased in scope in the 1930s, practically ending with the translation of a chapter from Vygotsky's *Myshlenie i rech* in 1939 (Vigotsky, 1939).

Turning to particular ideas of Vygotsky's cultural-historical school of thought that were made available in English, a simple chronological account may provide a good picture. The first of these appeared in 1925 and was devoted to issues of the education of handicapped children (Vygotsky, 1925). The first actual exposure of the emerging Vygotskian perspective in psychology to English-language readers came in Luria's article 'The problem of the cultural behaviour of the child' (Luria, 1928b). In that article the basic issue for the new psychology—the investigation of laws that govern the development of cultural forms of adaptation—was outlined. In the same publication, the essence of the method of double stimulation was presented, its historical links with Claparède's and Köhler's experimental approaches were emphasized, and an example from the area of children's memory development was provided as an illustration of the new approach. This was followed by Vygotsky's own article (Vygotski, 1929a), in which the logic of the new developmental methodology was explained, again with examples from the area of memory research. Vygotsky's position and empirical data on the issue of egocentric speech was made available in English in the abstracts volume of the Ninth International Congress of Psychology (Vygotsky and Luria, 1930a). The next major appearance of results from Vygotsky's research group took place in 1932 when Leontiev's article on the development of voluntary attention was published (Leontiev, 1932). In 1934, a short article on the thinking of schizophrenics was published (Vigotsky, 1934) in which Vygotsky's idea of the use of artificial concept formation as an instrument to observe the thinking process was advanced. That was supplemented by the publication of Luria's studies of twins, which closely followed Vygotskian line of thought (Luria, 1936). Finally, the presentation of Vygotsky's thinking in English-language psychology literature ended its first wave five years after Vygotsky's death, with an article devoted to the relevance of meaning in the psychological organization of human beings (Vigotsky, 1939).

In general, all basic aspects of Vygotsky's cultural-historical approach to psychological issues—the instrumental method, the social function of egocentric speech, the importance of new quality emerging in psychological ontogeny as a result of the child's making of signs, and the relevance of the meanings of established signs—were available to the interested reader in the English language.

After a period of twenty-two years during which no new publications by Vygotsky appeared in English, the second wave of translations began in the early 1960s. It is interesting to note that this wave began from a re-issue of his translated chapter of 1939—in Sol Saporta's *Readings in psycholinguistics* in 1961. The interest in Vygotsky (and Piaget) among American psychologists was facilitated by the gradual re-establishment of cognitive interests among the legitimate issues of psychology as a science (cf. Bruner, 1983, 1984). This led first to the publication of Vygotsky's *Myshlenie i rech* (Thinking and speech) under the title of *Language and thought*, and in a substantially abbreviated version (153 pp. instead of the 318 pp. of the original—cf. Kozulin, 1984, p. 116). On the Soviet side, Alexander Luria was again active in promoting translations of Vygotsky's writings (Luria, 1961; Vygotsky, 1966, 1967). Vygotsky's *Psikhologiu iskusstva* (Psychology of art) appeared in English translation in 1971 (Vygotsky, 1971). Thanks to the efforts by Michael Cole and his colleagues to publicize Vygotsky's name among American psychologists, a potpourri of Vygotsky's ideas, collected together from different sources and linked in ways judged to fit the 'recipient' culture better than the original (cf. John-Steiner, Souberman, Cole, & Scribner, 1978, p. x) appeared in English, including in a paperback edition (Vygotsky, 1978). This was followed by a less widespread but close to the original translation of portions of Vygotsky's writings in the journal *Soviet psychology* (Vygotsky, 1977, 1979a, 1979b), and by James Wertsch in his volume *The concept of activity in Soviet psychology* (Vygotsky, 1981a, 1981b). The most recent times have led different investigators to efforts to analyze Vygotsky's contributions in depth (Van der Veer, 1984; Van IJzendoorn & Van der Veer, 1984; Wertsch, 1985; Wertsch & Stone, 1985). Also, a full translation of Vygotsky's *Thinking and speech* has recently appeared, still under the title *Thought and language* (Vygotsky, 1986a)—twenty-four years after the first (abbreviated) translation.

As will become evident in the next section, the efforts to popularize Vygotsky's name among English-speaking psychologists have succeeded to a great extent. However, success in understanding Vygotsky's actual conceptual system may be less extensive, since the popularity of a system of thought is often inversely related to the depth in which it is understood.

Vygotsky's writings in contemporary English-language psychologies

A frequency count of the number of times an author is cited is a largely superficial way of analyzing the impact of the author on others. A citation analysis is vulnerable to the social fashion and stylistic norms in science. For example, some very widely-known self-evident aspects of knowledge are *not* cited (for example, Aristotle would undoubtedly be the most cited author across all disciplines that make use of the conventional 2-valued logic in the thinking of scientists). Finally, any frequency count of citations depends on the base sample of texts on which the count is based. Since the representativeness of that sample (of the population it represents) cannot be guaranteed—especially across culture/ language boundaries—then absolute frequencies of citation are of limited value. However, the relative frequencies of citation of different publications (conveying the same basic idea in different contexts) may be useful in understanding how the particular idea(s) enter new cultural and scientific surroundings.

The present analysis of the frequency with which different writings by Vygotsky were cited follows the latter strategy. The analysis is based on the *Social Science Citation Index* compiled by the Institute of Scientific Information in Philadelphia. It includes relative frequences with which reference is made to Vygotsky's particular Russian *and* English-language publications in English-language psychological literature. The study covered the period between 1969 and 1984. The results of this quantitative analysis are presented in Table IV.

Table IV.1: Citation frequencies of Vygotsky's publications in English-language literature 1969–1984 (based on ISI's Social Science Citation Index)

Reference	Frequencies per year															
	1969	1970	1971	1972	1973	1974	1975	1976	1977	1978	1979	1980	1981	1982	1983	1984
1925 (Conference on the Education of the Deaf)	0	0	0	0	0	0	0	0	0	0	0	1	0	0	0	0
1929 (Journal of Genetic Psychology)	1	0	0	2	1	0	2	0	1	0	1	0	0	0	0	1
1930a (Proceedings of the 9th International Congress of Psychology)	0	0	0	1	0	0	0	0	0	0	0	0	0	0	0	2
1934 (Archives of Neurology and Psychiatry)	4	2	2	3	1	5	1	4	2	2	0	3	1	1	1	1
1939 (Psychiatry)	1	2	0	0	0	0	0	1	0	1	0	0	0	0	0	2
1961 (Saporta, ed., Psycholinguistics)	0	0	0	0	0	0	0	0	0	1	1	0	0	0	0	1
1962 (Thought and language)	39	40	43	37	27	50	54	55	57	51	77	102	70	108	63	78
1963 (B. & J. Simon, eds., Educational psychology in USSR)	0	0	0	0	1	0	0	0	0	1	0	0	2	1	0	0
1965 (Neuropsychologia)	0	0	1	0	0	0	1	3	0	0	2	1	1	1	0	0
1966 (A.N. Leontiev, A. Luria, & A. Smirnov, eds, Psychological research in USSR)	0	0	0	0	0	1	0	1	2	0	1	1	5	0	0	2
1967 (Soviet Psychology)	0	0	1	1	3	3	1	1	3	3	4	3	11	6	1	2
1971 (Psychology of art)	—	—	0	0	0	3	1	1	1	0	1	0	0	0	0	3
1974 (Human Development)	—	—	—	—	—	0	0	0	0	0	0	1	1	0	0	1
1976 (J. Bruner, A. Jolly & K. Sylva, eds, Play: its role in development and evolution)	—	—	—	—	—	—	0	0	0	0	2	0	4	6	2	5

Table IV.1 continued

Reference	Frequencies per year															
	1969	1970	1971	1972	1973	1974	1975	1976	1977	1978	1979	1980	1981	1982	1983	1984
1977 (Soviet Psychology)	—	—	—	—	—	—	—	—	0	0	0	0	0	0	1	0
1978 (Mind in society)	—	—	—	—	—	—	—	—	1	2	10	14	51	33	24	43
1979 (Soviet Psychology, vol. 18)	—	—	—	—	—	—	—	—	—	—	0	0	1	0	0	0
1981 (J. Wertsch, ed., *Concept of activity in Soviet psychology*)	—	—	—	—	—	—	—	—	—	—	—	—	0	2	2	1
Russian originals:																
1925 (Consciousness as a problem of behavioural psychology. *Psikhologia i marksizm*)	0	0	0	0	0	0	0	1	0	2	0	1	1	0	0	0
1929 (Developmental roots of thinking and speech. *Estestvoznanie i marksizm*)	0	0	0	0	0	0	0	0	0	0	0	1	0	0	0	0
1930b (Etiudy po istorii povedinia)	0	0	1	0	0	0	0	0	1	0	0	1	1	0	0	1
1934 (Myshlenie i rech)	2	1	0	4	3	4	0	2	1	5	1	1	1	0	0	1
1935 (Umstvennoie razvitie detei v protsesse obuchenia)	0	0	0	0	0	0	0	0	0	1	0	0	0	0	0	0
1935 (Umstvenno otstalyi rebenok)	0	0	0	0	0	0	0	0	0	0	0	1	0	0	0	0
1956 (Izbrannie psikhologicheskie issledovania/Myshlenie i rech)	1	1	1	1	0	4	0	1	2	2	1	6	0	4	1	1

Table IV.1 continued

Reference	1969	1970	1971	1972	1973	1974	1975	1976	1977	1978	1979	1980	1981	1982	1983	1984
								Frequencies per year								
1960 (Razvitie vyshikh psikhicheskih funktsii)	0	0	0	0	0	3	0	1	1	1	1	1	0	1	0	2
1965 (Psikhologia iskusstva)	0	0	0	0	0	0	0	0	0	1	0	0	0	0	0	0
1966 (Igra i ego rol' v psikhicheskom razvitii rebenka. Voprosy psikhologia)	0	0	0	0	1	0	0	0	0	0	0	0	0	0	0	0
1968 (Psikhologia grammatiki)	0	0	0	0	0	0	0	1	0	0	0	1	1	0	0	0
1970 (Spinoza i ego uchenie ob emotsiah... Voprosy filosofii)	—	0	0	0	0	0	0	0	0	1	0	0	0	0	0	0
1972 (Voprosy psikhologia)	—	—	0	0	1	0	0	0	0	0	0	1	0	0	2	0
1982 (Sobranie sochinenii, tom 1)	—	—	—	—	—	—	—	—	—	—	—	—	—	0	0	0
1983 (Sobranie sochinenii, tom 5)	—	—	—	—	—	—	—	—	—	—	—	—	—	—	0	1

This table is interesting in two respects. First, it illustrates the *canalized nature* of references to Vygotsky in English-language publications over the period covered. Summary frequencies of references are indicative of this—of a total of 1373 times that Vygotsky's work has been cited, 1129 (or 82.2%) of the references have been made to two book-format translations (*Thought and language*—Vygotsky, 1962 was cited 951 times; and *Mind in society*—Vygotsky, 1978 178 times), both of which are modified and abbreviated translations of the original work. In contrast, the only other English-language book by Vygotsky—*The psychology of art* (Vygotsky, 1971)—has been cited thrice over the thirteen-year period during which it has been available. The selective nature of references to Vygotsky is all the more dramatic since previously available (although partial) translations of the ideas expressed in these two books have rarely been cited. For example, Chapter 7 of Vygotsky's *Myshlenie i rech* had been available in English translation twice before it reappeared in *Thought and language* (1962). It first appeared in *Psychiatry* (Vigotsky, 1939), and as is clear from Table IV, this has been cited only seven times from 1969 to 1984. Secondly it was reprinted in Sol Saporta's *Psycholinguistics* (Vigotsky, 1961), which was cited three times during the period covered in the table. This contrasts quite dramatically with the number of references to the 1962 translation of *Thought and language*—951 citations in all!

Another good example of the availability of parallel translations from the same original text is that of Vygotsky's 1935 essay 'The problem of instruction and mental development in the school years' (Vygotsky, 1956, pp. 438–52). This particular text is important in contemporary developmental psychology because it is one of the four writings that reflect Vygotsky's theoretical background for introducing the concept of Zone of Proximal Development (*zona blizaishego razvitia*). Its full version was translated into English in 1963 (Vygotski, 1963). The Social Science Citation Index records only five citations of that paper over the period studied. At the same time, an abbreviated and compositionally re-arranged version of the same text appeared under the title 'Interaction between learning and development' as Chapter 6 of *Mind and society* (Vygotsky, 1978, pp. 79–91). The total number of citations of *Mind in society* between 1977 (a year before its publication) and 1984 is 178.

Of course, the two book-format translations of Vygotsky's writings include a greater number of different aspects of Vygotsky's thinking than do single articles. Therefore it is only natural to expect references to books to be more frequent than those to specific articles. The information included in a chapter is just one facet of the whole book, so the citation of the book cannot be interpreted as a clear sign of the dissemination of ideas expressed in a particular chapter.

A more adequate specific analysis of the citations should thus exclude the two overly popular books. The source in which the majority of full (i.e., unabbreviated) translations of Vygotsky's writings have appeared over a long time (from 1967 to the present) is the journal *Soviet psychology*. However, the share of citations of more specific translations published in that journal is only 3.3% of all references to Vygotsky, and 18.6% of references excluding those of the 1962 and 1978 books (45 out of 242).

The second kind of information available from Table 4 concerns the kinds of citations that could have, but have not, been observed in scientific literature in English. Namely, the translation of Vygotsky's first explicitly psychological and innovative paper 'Consciousness as a problem in the psychology of behaviour' (1925) was published in 1979 (Vygotsky, 1979a). No citations of that paper were recorded in the SSCI for the period 1979–84, although the relevance of the ideas expressed in it is obvious to an adequate understanding of why Vygotsky started to develop his psychological theory along the lines that resulted in *Myshlenie i rech*.

Finally, a look at the frequencies of reference to Russian language originals in English-language publications reveals the overwhelming dominance of the use of translations. Only 5.9% (N=8) of all citations were made to Russian-language originals, and many of these were due to translations of papers by present-day Soviet psychologists who referred to Vygotsky in Russian in their papers which were subsequently translated into English. This heavy dependence of the international scientific community on translations is undoubtedly a reflection of the language barrier—which merely emphasizes the importance of the availability of careful translations of the full versions of the original Russian texts of Vygotsky's writings. Fortunately, the careful translating of Vygotsky's original texts has recently begun (Vygotsky, 1986a).

Such translation, however, is not without its semantic difficulties, since Vygotsky used a number of Russian terms with semantic fields that make their translation into English psychological terminology a complicated task. In the next section, one particular case—that of *obuchenie*—is analyzed.

Semantic problems in translation: the case of 'obuchenie'

Vygotsky's theoretical approach, which often looks overly complicated to contemporary international readers, was based on his thinking in Russian-language terms that are used to indicate *interdependence* of issues that are thought about. A tradition of thinking about the interdependence of phenomena embedded in specific Russian terms used both by laypersons and psychologists may have guided Vygotsky towards viewing psychological development in ways that are difficult to capture in English. This 'mild' version of linguistic determinism (e.g., see Bertalanffy, 1955, also the discussion in Chapter I) may be illustrated by the difficulty that translators of Vygotsky's work have had in finding an adequate equivalent to the concept of *obuchenie*. What adds to the importance of the difficulty is that this concept is of central relevance to an understanding of the core of Vygotsky's thinking. For example, the ideas that led Vygotsky to advance the concept of Zone of Proximal Development and its relationships with internalization and play (see the section on the process of internalization, above) would remain quite obscure to an English-language reader unless some adequate term (and/or explanation) of 'obuchenie' can be found.

The translation problem of 'obuchenie' lies in the *reference to the interdependence of individuals involved in the learning process* that the Russian term implies. As was briefly mentioned above, 'obuchenie' transcends the exclusive teacher/learner separation that other terms carry. Consider the meanings of some other, related, Russian terms: 'uchenie' can be used both in the meaning of 'learning'—the activity of the individual who learns—and 'teaching'—the activity of the individual who teaches somebody else. The prefix 'ob', attached to 'uchenie' in the term 'obuchenie' introduces two nuances of meaning that 'uchenie' lacks. First, the 'teacher' and 'learner' are set up in an interdependent relationship in which one cannot exist without the other. Thus, the learner cannot learn without another person (instructor) who fulfils the teaching function. Likewise, the instructor cannot teach anything to the learner that the latter is not oriented towards accepting. The instructor and the learner are intertwined within a mutually dependent relationship, and the *process* side of that relationship is what 'obuchenie' means in Russian. The term is semantically distinct from 'uchenie' (translatable as either 'learning' or 'teaching', depending on context) and 'nauchenie' (teaching, instruction). The latter term is closer to 'obuchenie' as it implies the teacher's active teaching of the learner, but differently from 'obuchenie', it overlooks the active role of the learner in the process of being taught.

Historically, the translation of the term 'obuchenie' into English has posed constant problems for different translators of Vygotsky's writings. The earliest available translation of Vygotsky's paper 'The problem of learning ["obuchenie" in Russian] and mental development in school age' appeared in the volume *Educational psychology in the U.S.S.R.* (cf. Vygotski, 1963). In that publication, 'obuchenie' was translated on some occasions as 'learning' (e.g., in the English title of the paper), and at other times as 'teaching'. The following paragraph illustrates how the terminological difficulty becomes apparent (note also that in this paragraph the concept 'zona blizaishego razvitia' is translated as 'zone of *potential* development'):

Similar considerations [referring to earlier described conditions under which 'obuchenie' of mentally retarded children takes place] apply to the development of the normal child. Teaching ['obuchenie' in the original] which is oriented to an already accomplished stage of development is ineffective from the point of view of the child's general development, it does not lead the process of development but lags behind this process. The theory of the zone of potential development allows for a formula which directly contradicts the traditional approach: *the only good teaching* [*'obuchenie' in the original*] is that which outpaces development. (original italics, source: Vygotski, 1963, p. 31)

It is evident from this quotation that Vygotsky's original idea of the interdependence of learner and instructor that was coded in the meaning of 'obuchenie' becomes lost (or at least difficult to trace) in the translation. Here the situation is further complicated by the relatively greater dominance of the agent of 'obuchenie' (instructor) over the object (students at school) that makes the use of 'teaching' look quite reasonable in the translated version.

However, the idea that the 'teaching' is inevitably intertwined with 'learning' within its context—that of the 'zone of potential development'—is no longer evident in the quote.

The second available translation of exactly the same paragraph has used 'learning' as the equivalent of the Russian 'obuchenie', and with the following result:

> Similarly, in normal children, learning ['obuchenie' in the original] which is oriented toward developmental levels that have already been reached is ineffective from the viewpoint of a child's overall development. It does not aim for a new stage of the developmental process but rather lags behind this process. Thus, the notion of a zone of proximal development enables us to propound a new formula, namely, that the only 'good learning' ['obuchenie' in the original] is that which is in advance of development. (Vygotsky, 1978, p. 89)

Here the translation of 'obuchenie' has resulted in an emphasis on the learner, at the expense of the instructor. Considering each of these translated passages separately, the international reader may be ready to consider Vygotsky himself an inconsistent writer who 'jumps' between the concepts of learning and teaching just as it pleases him. The actual difficulty, however, is in the absence of an adequate English-language term. Both translations are perfectly adequate renderings of the original passage, save the opposite decisions made by the translators on the case of 'obuchenie'. However, due to the choices by the translators to use *either* the 'learning' or the 'teaching' components of the interdependence of the two that is covered by 'obuchenie', both translations are likely to lead to further misunderstanding of Vygotsky's systemic ideas—contrary to the very best hopes of the translators.

The translation difficulty involved in the case of 'obuchenie' is well recognized in contemporary neo-Vygotskian research literature. Wertsch and Rogoff (1984, p. 3) deal explicitly with the issue, explaining the meaning of 'obuchenie' as best described by the lengthy formulation of 'teaching-learning process' and suggesting 'instruction' as a convenient (but not perfect) English equivalent. Meanwhile, however, the previous translations of the particular passage used here, and many others where similar inter-language differences are crucial, continue to add to international readers' difficulties in understanding what 'Vygotsky really meant' while writing his interesting treatises which are nevertheless difficult to understand.

Conclusions: Vygotsky and contemporary developmental psychology

Vygotsky's contribution to psychology was profound. He made all psychology developmental by his concentration on the *process* of individual-environment interaction by which development takes place. His emphasis on the person's *active construction* of his/her own 'higher' psychological functions made it possible for psychology to conceptualize the emergence of new psychological phenomena in the people's lives.

Vygotsky's ideas, however, were based on European intellectual traditions. He was not an independent 'Russian/Soviet thinker' as he may at times be presented—both by non-Russians who are fascinated by his work, and by Sovietophilic Soviet psychological officialdom. He integrated different ideas of his predecessors and contemporaries into a new theoretical system of developmental psychology. He devised a new scientific methodology for the empirical study of developmental processes. The social environment of the USSR in the 1920s canalized his and his colleagues' efforts in the direction of searching for explanations of ways in which individual-environment relationships *today* participate in the construction of the person's psychological functions *in the future*. However, Vygotsky and his colleagues in the 'cultural-historical school' of Soviet psychology were not the only intellectual school with such aims and successes in revolutionizing psychology. In the next chapter the work of Mikhail Basov is analyzed. Basov was Vygotsky's contemporary who, unlike Vygotsky, has remained little known among developmental psychologists in the USSR up to the present time. As a consequence, his work is also unknown to the international readership—undeservedly, as I hope will be found out.

V Mikhail Basov and the Structural-dynamic Perspective on Child Development

The first, the clearest theory of the new form of analysis is created by Basov, who in the framework of the method of structural analysis tries to unite two lines of investigation—the line of analysis and the line of holistic approach to personality.

L.S. Vygotsky, 1960, p. 129

Who was Basov and what was his contribution to innovation in developmental psychology which was so highly valued by Vygotsky? For international readers this question may look quite new, although a serious reader in the area of older literature on child development may have discovered an English-language overview of Basov's major theoretical contribution to the issues of analysis in psychology (Basov, 1929), or the prominent role attributed to him in an early overview of Russian psychology (Luria, 1928a). Basov's contributions to developmental psychology also seem to have remained beyond the sphere of interest of contemporary editors and translators, who have taken great care in making both older and newer psychological contributions in Russia available to English-language readers. The Social Science Citation Index reveals only seventeen references to Basov in the fifteen years between 1969 and 1984, out of which only two appeared outside the USSR. This is quite a contrast with the wide popularity of references to Vygotsky, as was observed above (Chapter IV).

Furthermore, even to the majority of contemporary Soviet psychologists Basov is not a household name. For a number of decades, his work was not reissued in the Soviet Union. This situation is very similar to the fate of Vygotsky's writings, which likewise ceased to be available, and his ideas unused, in the period following the waves of ideological criticism of 1931 and subsequent years (see Chapter III). In Basov's case, the period of lack of interest in him by Soviet psychologists has been even more extensive —his works were reissued only in mid 1970s (Basov, 1975) for the first time since 1931 (Basov, 1931a). Even then only a limited selection of his writings was reissued. In the same year, his role in the history of Soviet psychology was restored, albeit in a way that was little representative of his actual contribution to the discipline (cf. Smirnov, 1975, pp. 158–68). Some areas of Basov's work (for example, his initiative in studying children's understanding of social institutions—cf. Chapter VII in this book) have remained beyond the coverage of historical writings on Soviet psychology both in the USSR and in the West.

Prior to the mid-1970s, Basov's work was only rarely mentioned in Soviet psychological literature. Efforts to bring it back into the focus of interest of psychologists were made by some of his former colleagues (Merlin, 1965) as well as by historians and philosophers of psychology (Budilova, 1972; Iaroshevskii, 1971). Other historical accounts of Soviet psychology passed by Basov's name, mentioning his pedagogical activities (Bodalev, 1967) or quickly passing over his theoretical contributions (Bozhovich & Slavina, 1967). It is only in the 1980s that Basov's leading role in Soviet developmental psychology seems to have become acknowledged again (e.g., Iaroshevskii, 1985, p. 495).

The long-lasting oversight of Basov's work in the USSR is not a chance event. During his professional life, Basov was closely connected with the paedology movement. So was Vygotsky. Unlike Vygotsky, however, Basov left behind no substantial group of followers to rise to positions allowing them to restate his relevance to developmental psychology once social circumstances after 1956 again made this possible. In contrast, both Soviet and world psychology owe their re-'discovery' of Vygotsky to the latter's disciples—Luria, Leont'ev, and others—who emerged in the post-1950s era as leading administrators in Soviet psychology, thus enabling an earlier and wider propagation of Vygotsky's ideas. In comparison, the contemporary Soviet psychologists who were active in reissuing Basov's work in the 1970s (V. Miasishchev, V. Merlin) were located in relatively peripheral positions in the Soviet psychological establishment.

However, it is becoming evident that the substantial role that Basov in emerging Soviet psychology is in many ways comparable to that of Vygotsky in the theoretical realm, and may be considered to surpass him in the careful emphasis on empirical detail.

In the present I am attempting to spell out Basov's theoretical solution to psychology's 'crisis'—the same 'crisis' that motivated

Vygotsky to integrate approaches and findings from philosophy and different social sciences into his own cultural-historical theory (Vygotsky, 1982a). Basov's perspective on overcoming the 'crisis' in psychology stemmed from his own intellectual life history on the basis of which he synthesized his unique theory of development.

Basov's life and activities

Mikhail Basov was born in 1892 in a peasant family near Pskov. After finishing his secondary education, he entered the St Petersburg Psychoneurology Institute in 1909. It was in St Petersburg that he became a student of A. F. Lazurskii who was on the faculty of the institute at that time, together with a number of other Russian thinkers of the time who were active in the advancement of the biological and social sciences (V. Bekhterev, V. Vagner, P. Lesgaft and others). Basov collaborated extensively with Lazurskii and his colleagues on research (Basov & Nadol'skaia, 1913), and was continuously associated with the institutional settings of psychoneurological research that Bekhterev organized in Leningrad. The simultaneous presence of the personality-oriented (Lazurskii) and behaviouristic (Bekhterev) perspectives in Basov's education may have led him to the continuous effort to integrate the two, instead of separating them from one another. Basov's interest in the subjective side of human psychological processes culminated in his book on volition (Basov, 1922).

In 1920 Basov began to work in the Brain Research Institute that Bekhterev had organized, where his work brought him into contact with a number of other investigators whose role in further advancement of developmental psychology in the USSR turned out to be substantial (N. Shchelovanov, M. Denisova, N. Figurin). In 1921 Basov continued his work in the Psychology Division of the Psychoneurological Academy—another institution organized by Bekhterev. During that period he turned more actively away from the traditions of subjective psychology and towards increased emphasis on the study of behaviour. However, he never became a 'true' behaviourist/reflexologist, as he insisted upon the active role of the behaving organism in its relations with the environment.

Furthermore, while becoming interested in behaviour Basov did not abandon his interest in the internal, subjective side of psychological phenomena. In this his development as a psychologist parallels Vygotsky's emphasis on the relevance of the study of consciousness. Basov, like Vygotsky, saw the solution to the 'crisis' in psychology in the *integration* of behavioural and cognitive-affective aspects of psychological phenomena (Basov, 1929b).

Basov's work at the Psychoneurological Academy resulted in a manual for observational studies of child development in naturalistic settings (Basov, 1923). The emphasis on the richness of empirical observational details together with theoretically thoughtful and careful analysis of the issues of generalizations based on observational data that characterizes this book remains unsurpassed up to the present time in all of Soviet psychology, and in most international research that uses observational methods to study child development. He was active in organizing the empirical research of his co-workers which produced very interesting results. The topics of research of Basov's collaborators included issues of perception in pre-school-age children (Filosofova, 1924; Nekliudova, 1924), the use of free play in pre-schoolers (Zeiliger & Levina, 1924, 1930), and methodological questions of observation of children's behaviour in kindergarten settings (Shapiro & Gerke, 1930; Nekliudova & Vol'berg, 1930), together with the issue of the importance of those questions in educational practice (Basov, 1924b; Basov, 1925b; Basov & Gerke, 1924; Levina, 1925; Zeiliger, 1925).

In 1924, Basov became one of the founders of the State Institute of Scientific Pedagogics (GINP: Gosudarstvennyi Institut Nauchnoi Pedagogiki). It was at this institute that the research programme for the study of children's social world views was started at Basov's initiative (Merlin & Khriakova, 1930). Apart from his research activities, in 1925 he became a professor at the A. I. Herzen State Pedagogical Institute in Leningrad. His major theoretical contribution also appeared during that period—the Russian publication of *General foundations of paedology (Obshchie osnovy pedologii)* (Basov, 1928; 2nd edn Basov 1931a). Basov's only English-language publication during his lifetime (and up to the present) expressed his theoretical views (Basov, 1929a). A preliminary version of this article was made available to a Soviet audience in the newly established journal *Paedologia* in 1928 (Basov, 1928b).

Basov's objectivistic and non-partisan (although dialectically oriented) approach in psychology did not remain outside the wave of ideologically filled criticism of the early 1930s. Partly that was related to the programme for the study of children's world views (see Chapter 7 for a detailed overview), which made the research of his group a target of lively dispute during the 'Behavioural congress' of Soviet psychologists in January/February 1930. The major wave of criticism that Basov had to face started in April 1931, initiated by 'a brigade of post-doctoral students' (cf. Levina & El'konin, 1931, p. 29) of his own department at Leningrad Pedagogical Institute. The wave of criticism of Basov's theoretical position in 1931 was directly linked with the turn towards an aggressive 'partiinost''-based style of discourse in Soviet social sciences (as described in Chapter III). Basov's system of developmental psychology was labelled 'the most dangerous anti-proletarian theory which gives output into purely menshevistic practices' (Levina & El'konin, 1931, p. 39). Basov was accused of 'formalism' in his thinking (Feofanov, 1931). The meaning of the term 'formalism' in such accusations was based on Basov's reluctance to look at psychological development from an ideologically flavoured and aggressive 'class position'. Even in his reply to these accusations (which was written a couple of months before, but published only after his death), Basov retained his analytic and ideologically low-key style, just as the framework for his reply was declared to be one of 'self-criticism' (Basov, 1931b). Basov died unexpectedly in October 1931 of general blood poisoning (Basov, 1975, pp. 400–3; also the announcement in *Paedologia*, 1931, No. 4).

Basov's theoretical system

Basov, like Vygotsky, synthesized ideas from many different sources into his general theory of development. His thinking was closely related with both the European philosophical and psychological traditions, as well as with the ideas of his contemporaries and mentors.

Basov's emphasis on the active role of the individual within the environment is close to Bekhterev's similar announcements (Bekhterev, 1904). More specifically, the influence of A. Lazurskii can be traced in Basov's thinking. The emphasis on ecologically valid experimentation in developmental psychology that Basov proclaimed (Basov, 1931a, p. 262) is rooted in Lazurskii's similar thinking. The emphasis on integration of internal and external lines of stimulation likewise benefitted from Lazurskii's work (Lazurskii, 1906), but was also close to the ideas of the German psychologist Carl Stumpf (see Basov, 1920, p. 226). Furthermore, Basov's effort to transcend associationistic thinking in favour of linking the idea of apperception with his structural-dynamic theoretical view is traceable to Lazurskii's mediation of German psychological thought (Basov, 1920).

Basov's intellectual indebtedness to European psychology is very obvious. First, his methodological emphasis on the structural nature of psychological phenomena was directly related to Gestalt psychology—particularly that of Wolfgang Köhler (see below). In his developmental perspective, Basov relied (again like Vygotsky) on the views of Claparède and Piaget—particularly on the issue of cognitive internalization of action difficulties (Claparède) and in respect of Piaget's views on the constructive nature of psychological processes (Basov, 1975, pp. 228–9).

Like Vygotsky, Luria, and the majority of other psychologists working in the USSR in the 1920s, Basov's theoretical background led to a synthesis of European philosophical and psychological traditions with the social context in Russia of the 1920s. That context, as seen above, was essentially the first phase of a social utopian ideology that put strong emphasis on the issues of the *development* of *qualitatively novel* forms of society, personality, and ways of behaving through *social* means. Not surprisingly these theses became centrally relevant in Soviet psychology, and in this respect Basov's contribution is noteworthy for its careful emphasis on the connection of observational data with theoretical generalizations.

The social and developmental nature of human personality
Basov's original interest in problems of personality emerges from his joint work with Lazurskii (Basov, 1920). Like Vygotsky, Basov emphasized the qualitative distinction between the psychological processes of humans and other animal species. However, as an

investigator interested in personality issues, Basov addresses the issue of how the *individual* and *social* aspects are intertwined in the *development* of personality:

The personality grows on the basis of social experience common to all human beings. But at the same time it continues that experience, brings into it something new, peculiar. As a unique individuality, every personality gets some work done in his life, and that work cannot be substituted for by anybody else. In this respect there is no difference between a genius and mediocrity, as the difference between them exists only in the degree of what they provide to the present and the future of mankind. But as long as every individual personality has a part of himself, his own soul, in the trans-personal experience that nourishes the upcoming generations, and as the individual personality finds its continuation in it—to that extent it [personality] is immortal. (Basov, 1923, p. 243)

Basov gave a very materialistic and psychological reformulation of personality in the context of *inter-personal and inter-generational shared experiences* of people. Basov's view on personality was developmental and transactional—personality develops within the individual-environment interdependence relationship. That central theme led Basov to the development of his structural-dynamic psychology.

Basov's emphasis on the developmental nature of human personality is rooted in the emphasis on the distinction between the 'higher' and 'lower' mental processes, where this distinction is located at the borderline of non-human and human species in evolutionary history. Basov emphasizes that child development takes place as a result of the child's acting within the environment, changing that environment into a new state and, by doing that, changing himself. This position fits well with both the Marxist dialectical emphasis on the relationships between the active person with his environment, and with Piaget's emphasis on the active role of the child in relations with the environment. According to Basov, the human being develops through *actional cognition* (*deistvennoe poznanie*—cognition-by-acting) of the environment. Basov explained:

This internal sense ['actional cognition'] remains the same however unimportant the aspect of cognized reality—and, consequently, the aspect of development—is. Can the person understand the characteristics of some distinguishable object, that make it possible to act with that object in accordance with its nature; can he learn to grow plants the harvest from which he uses for food; does he notice the organization in sequences of natural phenomena in connection with which he arranges his own life? On the other hand—can a young child understand the concept of number and elementary operations with numbers that make it possible for him to establish his relations with environment on the basis of exact measurement? Can he know the organization of the surrounding world or the history of his society?—in all these cases, and cases like them, the penetration of the human being into reality and its mastery via its cognition lies at the basis. In this case, we deal with real stages on the path of the development of the human being *as the actor within the environment*, i.e. of psychological development. In this sense, by its nature the path of psychological development is infinite, like the world. This distinguishes it from the biological development of the organism: the latter has a finite task—to create an organism of a certain kind, and once that result is achieved, so the development ends. Psychological development itself can proceed to the infinity of the universe. However, it does not exist outside of the organism and therefore also becomes practically limited. That limitation takes place not only on the side of time, i.e., not by the limits of the lifetime of a human organism, but also in content. Every organism processes a limited and at the same time determinate set of characteristics that make him fit for penetration into some domains of reality and unfit for others. A child born deaf will never become active in the world of sounds, and a blind child is for ever denied the possibility to rely in his activity (and, therefore, development) on those characteristics of the world that are available only to vision. (Basov, 1975, p. 252, emphasis in original)

The *active organism—fitting environment* relationship is central to Basov's understanding of the developmental nature of human personality. The temporal nature of that relationship—the understanding that development is possibly only over time—is important in Basov's theoretical thinking. Not only is the person active in his/her environment, but that activity ('penetration' of the person into the environment) changes its form over time. This theoretical background led Basov to conceptualize the structural organization of the developmental process.

Basov and Vygotsky: two approaches to the 'analysis into units'

This chapter started with an indication of Vygotsky's high regard for Basov's theoretical analysis. What, then, was the basis for this high evaluation of Basov's contribution to psychology? First, the theme that is clearly evident in Vygotsky's writings and for which Basov is credited is the *principle of analysis into units, rather than elements*. As was indicated in the previous chapter, Vygotsky reiterates that idea in different contexts in his writings, not always taking care to add a reference to Basov. However, in some cases (see Vygotsky, 1960, p. 129) he claims to follow Basov in the emphasis on the analysis into units—the 'minimal gestalts' that preserve the systemic functioning nature of the whole from which the unit is derived, while abstracting from many concrete aspects of the original phenomenon. Secondly, Vygotsky and Basov shared the perspective of viewing child development as a social-constructive phenomenon. In the ways in which they conteptualized that process they took different paths, but there was basic agreement in principle.

The question of the appropriate 'units of anaysis' was of high priority among social and biological scientists of the 1920s. Its relevance was expressed in the disputes of Gestalt and associationistic psychological traditions, and was of importance in the discussions on evolutionary theory (Agol, 1928).

It is in the context of the issue of units of psychological analysis that Vygotsky followed Basov's lead in advancing the idea of 'analysis into units' instead of 'elements' (Vygotsky, 1960, p. 129). Vygotsky's description of Basov's structurally oriented approach is interesting since it included a misunderstanding of a relevant aspect of Basov's conceptualization. Vygotsky described Basov's ideas in the following way:

Basov distinguishes real objective elements that are constituents of a given process, and only later differentiates these elements. He envisages these phenomena as being original, existing by themselves; but looks for their component parts so that every one of these parts would nevertheless preserve the characteristics of the whole. Thus, in an analysis of water the molecule H_2O would be an objective real element of water, although infinitely small by size, but homogeneous by its content. Therefore, particles of water must, in accordance with this distinction, be considered basic elements of that substance. (Vygotsky, 1960, p. 129)

Actually, the way in which the 'real elements' were defined by Basov is different. Basov, following Wolfgang Köhler, distinguished two kinds of 'structural elements' that can be observed in physical or psychological phenomena:

In what sense may we speak about *structural elements* of a formation such as the process of behaviour? Before answering this question, we must recall to mind the discrimination between elements which Köhler (1925) establishes when speaking of 'real, objective elements' and 'differential elements'. While the former are self-existent primary phenomena, inherent in the essence of things and ever abiding with them, the latter are caused by purely quantitative modifications of a given phenomenon and are the same as this phenomenon but only on a limited scale. So, when we analyze water into its elements, H_2 and O are the objective, the real elements, while some particle of water, infinitesimal but homogeneous as to its constitution, must, according to this discrimination, be considered as a differential element. When speaking of the elements of the process of behaviour, with reference to the first problem of structural analysis, we consider mainly the elements of the first species. Still, in some cases, in the course of the structural analysis of man's activity, the conception of 'element' may undergo variations which cause the second meaning of this concept to obtain some practical value. Of course, any confusion is to be carefully avoided; still, the discrimination of the two meanings presented above when applying them in practice does not offer great difficulties. (Basov, 1929, p. 270)

As is evident from a comparison of these two quotes. Vygotsky overlooked the *structural-qualitative* nature of Basov's separation of (and preference for) the 'real, objective elements' (components) of psychological processes. Instead, Vygotsky considered the 'differential elements' (water molecules—infinitesimally small in size, and homogeneous in content) to be 'real elments', and reiterates Basov's call for structural analysis of the relationships of these elements in dynamically organized processes. However, *it is very evident that Basov emphasized the use of exactly the opposite kinds of unit—those of qualitatively different sub-components like oxygen and hydrogen which make up molecules of water as a qualitatively new structure.* These are the 'real' or 'objective' units whose *relationship* gives rise to new quality. The relevance of 'differential' elements of the structure—the 'minimal quantities' of the substance (as a single molecule of water would be, relative to quantities of water that contain many similarly structured molecules)—was limited in Basov's view, as the above quote illustrates.

Basov's separation of the 'real' and 'differential' elements of the structure was borrowed directly and openly from Wolfgang Köhler's thinking. Köhler (1928) introduced it in connection with an implicit reference to the previously widespread idea that 'units' in psychology can be separated in a psychophysical experiment with the help of establishing 'just noticeable differences' by a subject:

Let us take an instance from the physical world. If we want to study the air which surrounds us in this room, we also shall feel inclined to analyze it. We may do that in different ways. Either our attention picks out a 'differential' of this volume of air, i.e., an extremely small volume which may be regarded as homogeneous in density, temperature, etc.; or we concentrate our attention on one molecule, say O_2. In the first case, everybody knows that we are not dealing wth a *real* element of the air. We know that the differential is not defined by objective physical properties, as if its interior were kept together somehow, while there is no such holding together beyond the limits of the differential, between *different* differentials. We know, therefore, that the limits of the differential exist in thought only. On the other hand, if we take the molecule as the final product of our analysis, we mean an element of the other kind. It is well defined physically as a real unit; mutual inner forces which keep the interior of it together do not, in comparable degree, unite parts of one molecule with those of another. In order to get differentials, we imagine arbitrary separations in the medium; where a molecule is, begins, and ends is a matter which nature has decided. The molecule is an *objective* unit. (Köhler, 1971, pp. 41–2)

It is easy to see that Basov followed Köhler's separation of 'real' and 'differential' elements, whereas Vygotsky mixed the two kinds up by displacing the meaning of the latter (differential units) as if it belonged to the former (real units). Two arguments are buried in this misunderstanding. First, Köhler and Basov argued against using unnatural units (e.g., results of introspective studies of units of consciousness derived through just noticeable differences), taking for granted that any analysis is of Gestalt/structural kind. However, for Vygotsky the issue of analysis was framed by the contrast between *any* atomistic as compared to Gestalt perspective on phenomena. In their emphasis on the holistic nature of phenomena, Basov and Vygotsky coincide. However, they differ greatly in the ways in which they conceptualize the analysis of the holistic phenomena.

It is an interesting historical question in what ways Vygotsky's misrepresentation of Basov's idea on this issue affected his conceptualization of analysis in psychology's 'analysis into units' as an alternative to the 'analysis into elements'. There are two possible directions that conceptualization of 'units' can take. One involves *structural-dynamic* study of the components and their relationships that make up the holistic phenomenon. This route is pursued by Basov and Köhler, who emphasize the structural connections of units that make up the qualitatively different whole which is not the sum of its component units. The other direction— pursued by Vygotsky—involves the search for the 'minimal whole'—the unit becomes defined as the 'minimal Gestalt' that preserves the quality of the whole. The first direction deals simultaneously with analysis (distinction of components in the whole) and synthesis (describing the nature of the connection of the components that create the super-componential new quality of the whole). The second direction analyzes more complex into less complex wholes, calling the latter units, without proceeding to describe how these units function.

In his writings where the issue of 'analysis into units' surfaces, Vygotsky is keen to use the idea that lies behind his misrepresentation of Basov's example. For instance, Vygotsky uses the same example in his *Thinking and speech* (Vygotsky, 1982b, pp. 13–14):

The first kind of psychological analysis can be called separation of complex psychological wholes into elements. That can be compared with the chemical analysis of water, which separates it into oxygen and hydrogen. The crucial feature of such analysis is that as its result products are obtained which are alien to the analyzed whole—elements that do not contain in them characteristics of the whole, and include a number of new characteristics which can never be discovered in that whole. What happens with an investigator who tries to separate speech and thinking is the same that would take place with any person who, while searching for scientific explanation of some characteristics of water—for example, why does water put out fire and why Archimedes' law is applicable to water— would use the separation of water into hydrogen and oxygen as a means for explanation of water's characteristics. He would be surprised to discover that hydrogen itself is inflammable, and that oxygen supports fire, and could never explain the character of the whole through the characteristics of these elements. Exactly the same is the case with psychology which separates speech-based thinking [*rechevoi myshlenie*] into elements in the search for explanation of the crucial features that belong to it as the whole...

Again, Vygotsky emphasized the idea of the nature of the whole (using the familiar example of the water molecule) that cannot be studied by analytic separation into its composite elements (which, while losing some characteristics of the whole may obtain some other features that are not present in the whole). He replaces the anaysis of a whole into its *elementary* constituents by the analysis of the *minimal wholes* of the phenomenon by finding out what these units have in common:

... the chemical formula of water, that relates equally to all of its characteristics, equally applies in general to all of its kinds, to an equal degree to the Pacific Ocean as well as a raindrop. That is why the analysis of water into its elements cannot serve as the way that brings us the explanation of its concrete characteristics .... (Vygotsky, 1982b, p. 14)

This quite obviously is an emphasis on the 'different element' aspect of phenomena in Köhler's terminology, which Basov accepted, but which kinds of element he considered to be of secondary relevance in psychological explanation. Basov's idea of the analysis of psychological phenomena involved the discovery of the 'real' (instead of artificial, subjective) components of the whole, which *do not* preserve the quality of the whole in and by themselves separately, but whose systemic relatedness gives rise to that quality. Basov would proceed to observe that relatedness as it functions (or emerges) over time, keeping track of both the components and their relations at the same time. This approach, similarly to that of Vygotsky, denies the usefulness of the associationist ethos of sub-dividing phenomena into their elements. However, unlike Vygotsky, Basov accepts the analysis of the whole into its components *so that the synthesis of the quality of the whole can be observed in the course of keeping track of the relationships of the components of the system.* Vygotsky, instead, would not proceed to analyze the units by looking at the components and their relations, but would rather advocate the observation of the behaviour of the units over time and conditions:

We think that a decisive and revolutionary moment in the study of thinking and speech is the transition from this analysis [into elements] to another kind of analysis. That latter we could describe as analysis that divides a complex whole into its units. By unit we mean such product of analysis that, differently from elements, possesses *all basic properties of the whole* and which cannot be further divided into living parts of that unity. Not the chemical formula of water but the study of molecules and their movement are the key to the understanding of the properties of the water. Likewise, the living cell that possesses the basic properties of life characteristic of living organism, is the real unit of biological analysis. (Vygotsky, 1982b, pp. 15–16, emphasis in original)

As is evident from this statement, Vygotsky's main concern when discussing the issue of units was *how to avoid the analysis of complex phenomena into their elements that consequently would lose the character of the holistic system.* He did not address the issue of how the *components* of the wholes are related with one another so that the systemic properties of the whole emerge. In contrast, Basov's emphasis in the case of units went beyond Vygotsky's in that latter sense. Basov both recognized that the complex whole is not the sum of its elements, and that these elements (components) still exist separably (but interdependently) with one another. He accepted the necessity for reconstructing the process of how the interdependence of components of a whole gives rise to the new qualitative characteristics of that whole— those characteristics that cannot be reduced to the sum of the parts in the whole. Not only would Basov (like Vygotsky) reduce a complex phenomenon to its 'minimal Gestalt' state, but (unlike Vygotsky) he would proceed to analyze that 'minimal Gestalt' into its components and *observe how these components work together* in order to explain the nature of the systemic 'minimal Gestalt'. In this respect, Basov's ideas surpassed those of Vygotsky.

The reasons why Basov's and Vygotsky's ways of analyzing complex phenomena took different paths after starting off from common ground may be grounded in Basov's basic education as a personality psychologist who at the same time was a pioneer in the area of observational methodology in psychology. It is exactly in the context of elaborate observations of children's behaviour *from which Basov devised generalized personality descriptions* that the necessity arises of explaining how more elementary levels of observed behaviour become integrated into the more abstract whole of personality descriptions of the children observed. Basov took great care in his manuals on the observational method (e.g. Basov, 1923, pp. 206–7; 1975, pp. 183–9) to point out that the holistic nature of personality should become known on the basis of careful analysis of behaviour and environment. For Basov, the task of working towards *connecting* the levels of elements of behaviour and holistic structures of personality was the centrally relevant one. In contrast, Vygotsky entered psychology from the basis of humanitarian and philosophical traditions of thought in which sensitivity of observation of holistic qualities (for example, in literary criticism) is highly relevant, but within which the question of element-whole relations is of secondary importance.

Stimuli and the behaviour of the organism within the environment

Basov's interest in personality in conjunction with his observations of children's behaviour created the intellectual basis for an effort to overcome both the reductionistic ethos of behaviourism and reflexology on the one hand, and the traditions of subjective-speculative personology on the other. Given such a background,

Basov's thinking moved towards a systemic and interactional perspective in the study of behaviour.

Basov's emphasis on personality-within-the-environment led him to a clear critical understanding of the limits of the psychological approaches of his (and the present) time:

The problem of stimuli of behaviour is one of the most important ones in the study of child personality, as well as of all human psychology. The meaning of that problem is always reduced to clarification of what triggers one or another expression of personality, what is the source of these expressions, or on what grounds these expressions could emerge. Very often, if not always, *psychology has not considered the relation of personality with the surrounding enviroment. It has not realized that only this relationship feeds personality, gives it the possibility to develop, and forms it to a certain extent.* Very often the person was (and is) studied by psychology as if he were separated from all usual conditions of his life, as some kind of self-contained entity which can be understood and studied outside of any conditions of space and time. (Basov, 1975, pp. 59–60, emphasis added)

This view—that at the present time may find the label 'transactional' attached to it—guided Basov to advance a highly elaborate conceptualization of stimuli in psychology. In his promotion of observational methods for empirical research in psychology, Basov required that simultaneously with the study of children's behaviour psychologists must describe the children's environment—both contemporaneous and that of the child's past. This demand upon investigators leads to the limitations of the observational methodology, as the account of children's (especially past) background remains beyond the immediately observable behaviour. Basov understood that limitation very clearly:

It is not possible to understand fully any of the child's more-or-less complex expressions if we do not know which objective conditions, of biological and social environment, the particular child is the product of, in general. When we observe him during a lesson or play in the children's home, in the kindergarten, at home or at school, we never accurately understand the results of our observations unless we can know and take into account the environment that surrounds (or has surrounded) the child at home or everywhere, where he comes before and where he goes after the lessons. The reverse is also true—while observing the child at home, we must know that he reflects in his personality a wider social environment with which he has to interact, and we should also take that into account. (Basov, 1975, p. 61)

The personal life history of the child renders inference from observations of behaviour difficult, since the child is neither exclusively controlled by the immediate external stimuli in a situation, nor is he fully independent of such stimulation. In every observable situation, the child may be seen acting as a seemingly independent personality, whereas in reality s/he may be considering the situational demands in some implicit ways. Furthermore, the child who has just been acting in a seemingly independent way, may move into an episode of joint action with a peer or adult at the next moment, and back to the mode of independent acting later. The child integrates *external* and *internal* stimuli into a complex whole of acting in a given situation. It often happens that the external stimuli reflect only the occasional effects of the given situation that temporarily penetrate the child's developmentally emerged (and developing) action scheme. Basov recognized that children develop as self-organized systems who develop internal control over their action in the course of their individual life histories of acting-within-environments. Similarly to Vygotsky, Basov views the class of internal stimuli as a developmental result of the process of internalization:

It is necessary to bear in mind that a close relationship exists between external stimuli—which affect the child from the environment—and internal stimuli of the child's past experience. That relationship exists in the sense that *every external stimulus after its first action, and to one or another degree, becomes the property of the given individual and can subsequently affect his behaviour as an internal stimulus of the child's previous experience.* Furthermore, quite often an external stimulus influencing the individual for the first time triggers no behavioural reaction, but at the same time does not pass fully without a trace. The latter can be observed later when reactions to exactly the same stimulus can be observed—but now already as the internal stimulus of past experience. In these cases it must be accepted that the stimulus reached the organism and was perceived by it, but the reaction to it was temporarily delayed. (Basov, 1975, pp. 63–4, emphasis added)

This description of internalization of external stimuli bears a resemblance to Vygotsky's thinking on internalization, but includes aspects that go beyond Vygotsky. First, Basov's description of internalization of external stimuli is more directly tied to empirical observatons than Vygotsky's treatment of the concept. Basov's empirical experience (his own 'external stimuli'!) was obtained in the course of his extensive programme of observations of the activities of kindergarten children in their 'natural habitats' (Basov,

1923, 1924a, 1925a, 1931a). In contrast, Vygotsky's empirical basis mostly entailed experimental probes with children of different ages. Secondly, *Basov emphasizes that internalization can take place without any observable direct effects of the influence of the originally external stimuli.* The child's observable external action with some stimulus material need not be the only vehicle that leads to the internalization of the particular psychological processes. As an alternative route, the effects of external stimulus situations can become internalized by the child's *internal action* that cannot be observed in behaviour when it is becoming internalized, but becomes explicit after it has become internalized. Thus, Köhler's 'insight learning' and children's delayed imitation (of earlier externally presented models) can be explained as belonging to the class of such an 'internally proceeding' internalization process. At the same time, Basov's formulation also recognizes the 'externally proceeding' internalization (emphasized by Vygotsky as the primary mechanism of cultural development) in which the child's externally observable actions are gradually carried over into the internal sphere of the child's mind. Basov's 'general scheme of development' involves both aspects of internalization:

When we speak of the structure of organization of stimuli, their differences can be divided along two lines. First, by the line of the change of *the degree of complexity of the structure* of the given stimulus, which the latter projects on to the process of behaviour of the person. Second, [it may occur] by the way of change of the *quality of content* of the stimuli. Both these lines are related to each other, as the form is always related to the content. The changes along the first line probably proceed by constant increasing of the degree of complexity of the structure, and we can distinguish no stages in it. By way of the second line stimuli change by proceeding via certain qualitative categories that have developmental meaning. The primary and fundamental category here consists of the stimuli of the external environment in its natural form. From here, one line of development leads to the transposition of the external to the internal, and the other leads to the formation of special forms of stimuli that are created in cultural development *by the social environment.* These latter are transposed from the external sphere into the internal sphere as well. (Basov, 1931a, pp. 290–1).

This quote, albeit phrased in a complicated way, summarizes Basov's conceptualization of the process of internalization. It is the structure of the environment that provides the developing child with the basis (background) for constructing new experiences by acting within it. The structural complexity of the environment may vary on its own. However, it is also changed by the acting agent, who turns the natural environment into a culturally organized one. In this process the agent internalizes experienced input along two lines. First the 'natural' external stimuli are internalized while the agent is changing them, turning some of them into new, cultural objects. These newly constructed objects serve as the cultural external stimuli, which become transposed into the internal sphere of the personality as well.

Basov's developmental scheme is thus quite simple in its kernel. The person is an active agent in the structured environment. By being active, he transforms the environmental structure into a new state, while changing his own psychological constitution in the process. The latter change takes place as internalization of the experience with external stimuli, and leads to the formation of the psychological structures ('internal stimuli') that proceed to serve as the basis for the person's further encounters with new structured environments. The internal and external stimuli become integrated in the course of action in a variety of ways, some of which are highly complex. In Basov's scheme, the developing person is neither the puppet of the environmental structure, nor an egocentric actor, but a person who reflects the environment in his psychology while actively transforming it.

Basov's understanding of different complex integrative relationships between the lines of internal and external stimulation is evident in his descriptions of children's activities:

It very often happens that a reaction that is immediately triggered by a certain stimulus, is actually brought into action only due to the fact that the stimulus affected the child in the presence of a certain situation, in the full system of which it plays only a minor part. In such cases it would be a clear mistake to attribute the whole reaction to the effect of that single immediate stimulus. On the other hand, there exist occasions on which a child in a certain situation proceeds with some activity, working from beginning to end seemingly outside the influence of the surroundings. No immediate external stimuli can be observed, all behaviour proceeds as if it were exclusively regulated by internal stimuli, and so to say, emerged from itself. In reality very often the key to the understanding of the child's behaviour is still hidden in the surrounding situation: the child may be infected, for instance, by the general working atmosphere that has become established at the given time in the children's collective, that atmosphere provides him with a single general push, under the influence of which he proceeds in a certain direction. Under such conditions the internal stimulation which seems to be the only one determining the child's behaviour, actually only complements and deepens the most general external stimulation. Besides, the effects of the internal stimulation can occur only when certain external conditions are present. (Basov, 1975, pp. 61–2)

Basov's emphasis on the 'hidden' role of the 'social atmosphere' of the children's collective as the condition under which the child's internal system of stimulation guides the child to acting in a seemingly self-oriented way matches the interest of his contemporaries who studied collective psychology (Bekhterev, Zaluzhnyi—see Chapters III and VII). Like the research of those investigators, Basov's emphasis antedates the emphasis of 'social group climates' that became an important topic in social psychology due to the fertilization of that discipline by Kurt Lewin's theoretical thinking (Lewin, Lippitt, & White, 1939). It should be emphasized that Basov's own thinking developed in clear connection with that of Lewin and his disciples in Berlin in the course of the 1920s (particularly Ovsiankina). More importantly, Basov emphasized the relevance of *interdependence* of the *systems* of internal and external stimuli in the determination of child's actions *at every moment in time*. In this sense, Basov actually suggested a field-theoretical approach in ways parallel to Lewin's. However, Basov's theoretical account was explicitly developmental from the start, whereas Lewin's account remained largely non-developmental in the study of ontogeny.

Furthermore, Basov's account of the internalization of external stimulation and the integration of the two proceeded in parallel with, and sometimes chronologically ahead of, Vygotsky's developing theoretical views. Basov's view emphasized the internal-external integration of stimulus systems, whereas Vygotsky proceeded to the analysis of how internal signs are constructed under conditions of external demands. Basov also viewed the internal stimulus system as a structure that includes mediated stimuli:

It is well known that sometimes a minute stimulus, some kind of just noticeable change in the facial expression of a person, can elicit in another person a most complex reaction.... A small match, as is said, can lead to a big fire....' In all such cases we deal with the preparation of the given reaction by *mediated stimuli*, which play the decisive part in that reaction, whereas the immediate stimulus is just the last drop that fills the cup. It is the condition, an external push, that brings into action the prepared energies... (Basov, 1975, p. 297, emphasis in original)

Basov and Vygotsky proceeded along parallel lines in their thinking. Vygotsky put a greater stress on the constructive activity of the child in making up mediating devices to solve problems.

Although he did not deny the relevance of the cultural knowledge that the child has acquired and internalized prior to the new task, his concern was explicitly on the question of *how* the child proceeds to act in solving the problem by devising novel means and changing his own existence through it. For example, Vygotsky's discussion of the 'zone of proximal development' (see Chapter IV) concentrates on the analysis of the child's future development. Issues of the child's actions at the present developmental level, or below it, were of no special importance in Vygotsky's thinking. He did not analyze the 'zone of actual development' or 'zone of past development' (Ignjatovic-Savic *et al.*, 1985) other than by reference to the psychometric intelligence testing tradition. In contrast, Basov's major concern was *how the novel external stimulation becomes integrated with the already existing internal stimulus structure*. In this emphasis on child development, Basov stands somewhere between Vygotsky and Piaget—looking at the structural change of the internal stimulus system under the input of external stimulus systems by the child who is conceptualized as being active within his environment (an aspect that makes Basov close to Piaget), but whose activity within his environment is socially and culturally regulated (the point shared by Vygotsky).

Basov was also concerned with the dynamics of the relationship between internal and external stimulus systems in the course of time. This interest was clearly related to his observations of pre-schoolers' play in peer groups and under adult supervision. His observations revealed a picture that would be familiar to anybody who has observed children's actions from toddlerhood onwards— the child acts with some objects sequentially, and when the child is immersed in acting with a certain object it can be very difficult for an outsider to influence that process. However, when the child's interest in the particular object wanes, s/he may become more open to outside influences. Basov recognized the 'temporarily vulnerable' nature of the child's play very clearly, when he suggested that external stimulation becomes influential only at some 'node points' (*uzlovyie tochki*) in the temporal structure of children's action (Basov, 1975, p. 68). A child who is immersed in an individual action sequence with some objects may be viewed as generating self-stimulation by acting with these objects. Only when the individual self-stimulating action system reaches a certain 'node' would it become open, to outside influence (external stimulation). The child regulates the openness-closedness of the system of his action with objects to outside (socially introduced) influences. The self-organizing and context-related nature of child development is very clearly understood by Basov, together with the idea of periodic regulation of the extent of immediate context-dependency of action.

Basov, behaviouristic theorizing, and the issue of consciousness

The relationship between Basov's theorizing and that of different brands of behaviouristic thought in Russia and abroad is an interesting topic in itself—all the more since his frequent use of the terms 'stimulus' and 'reaction' may lead the reader to assign him to one of the 'schools' of Russian behaviourism of the 1920s. Undoubtedly there are aspects in which Basov's thinking is indebted to some aspects of the work of researchers associated with Bekhterev (see Shchelovanov, 1969), and, after all, Basov's own education as a psychologist took place in the Psychoneurology Institute of St Petersburg which was organized by Bekhterev. However, Basov's intellectual ties can be seen to extend more towards Russian evolutionary thought (Severtsov) and zoo-psychology (Vagner), than as fixed in the Pavlovian or Bekhterevian 'schools' of reflexology of the 1920s. Even more interestingly, Basov was quite adamant in his opposition to reflexologists' efforts to eradicate psychological terminology from psychological research. It is not without certain irony that Basov described Pavlov's lonely fight against psychological terms:

It is known that academician I. P. Pavlov fines his associates for the use of psychological terminology in his laboratory. Under the influence of such a strong stimulus, it would seem, all the reflexes that may be involved should become inhibited. Nevertheless, while reading his book on the 20-year long efforts in that direction [i.e., Pavlov, 1928], we often come across feelings of delight, fascination, and other experiences in it, which its author went through in his creative activity. I think that here the issue is not an improper way of expression. (Basov, 1924b, p. 17)

Basov's criticism of behaviouristic thinking went far beyond this little irony about Pavlov's training of his laboratory personnel. He analyzed the biological and organismic reductionism of con-temporary American behaviourism (of Watson and Lashley—

Basov, 1931a, pp. 265–8). At the same time, he did not deny the relevance of the conditional reflexes in the organization of organism-environment relationships, which he considered to be the basis onto which the real, more complex, structures of acting in the environment are built (Basov, 1941a, p. 298).

Aside from accepting the relevant contribution from reflexology, Basov did not proceed to eliminate consciousness from the legitimate topics of psychology. Instead, he found an appropriate location for it in his analytic-synthetic theory. Basov emphasized the relevance of consciousness in the organization of internal psychological functions. In fact, for him, consciousness has a very important role to play in the personality structure:

The main relevance of consciousness is in the fact that it subsumes under the organism's control not only the moments of immediate contact with the external world, but also those internal forms of activity of our thinking, our imagination, etc. that emerge outside of that immediate contact. If we imagine all those forms without the quality of consciousness, then they become void of any sense or meaning. The immediate influence of the external world on the organism can trigger one or another response reaction from him, which in this way reflects the relationship of the organism with the external world independently of whether he possesses the quality of consciousness or not. However, the internal forms of the organism's activity establish that relationship only by making themselves conscious. Without the latter, these forms cease to have any relevance for the organism's relationships with the environment. Thus, without the quality of consciousness, we would be unable to act towards goals other than the most immediate ones, and to act on the basis of an idea or by an earlier made plan. (Basov, 1931a, p. 251)

Consciousness, for Basov, thus plays the role of a regulator of the integration of the external and internal structures of stimulation, making it possible for the person to act in goal-directed and abstracted idea-based ways. Consciousness itself, of course, is a product of the organisms' active relationships with their environments. It is the capability of organisms to move from associationistic acting to the construction of goals and moving towards them that cardinally separates Basov's theory of development from the majority of other perspectives. Basov, like Vygotsky, tried to study the functioning of consciousness in its complexity, rather than reduce it to some more elementary constituents for the sake of 'objectivity', as claimed by behaviouristic thinkers of different brands. However, he differed from Vygotsky cardinally in *how* to study consciousness in adequate ways. Basov's path was to try to analyze *and* then re-synthesize observable events in the course of active agents' (mostly children's) interaction with their environments. He accomplished this by analysis of different forms of psychological structure.

Basov's dynamic structuralism

Basov's systemic view of the child-environment interaction as it takes place in structurally organized ways over time guided him to the necessity of providing a descriptive account of how the structure of behaviour can be analyzed, and how that structure develops. It is this latter part of Basov's contribution to developmental psychology that can be valuable nowadays when it is gradually becoming obvious that the fashion of strictly quantitative measurements—a legacy of behaviourism—is passing, and the structural complexity of developmental phenomena is at times becoming evident to some psychologists. In the domain of structuralistic perspectives on child development, very little has been offered in the sense of empirical methodology and theoretical views since Basov's times. Perhaps the only persistent dynamic-structuralist view of development that has been present (and mostly misunderstood) in child psychology for decades has been the equilibration theory of Piaget (Piaget, 1970, 1977). As mentioned earlier, Basov's ideas (like those of Vygotsky) were directly influenced by Piaget's thinking in the 1920s. At least on the side of understanding structurally organized dynamic relationships between the developing child and his environment, Basov's structuralistic accounts may look fresh and new—due to the standstill in developmental psychology over the years that separate us from Basov's writings.

Basic psychological structures
Our analysis of Basov's structuralism starts from an outline of his three forms of structural organization of behaviour. The overview is based on the relatively abbreviated synopsis of Basov's work available in English (Basov, 1929), and the full-length accounts of his original ideas (Basov, 1931a, pp. 278–347; also: Basov, 1975, pp. 320–51).

Basov's structural analysis of behaviour follows his general notion of the *unity of analysis of the whole into components and synthesis of the components into the whole*. Basov, who took the foundations of his structuralistic emphasis from contemporary Gestalt psychology, advanced *his* brand of Gestalt viewpoint far beyond his predecessors in ways that led to a developmental view on psychological structures. *Basov's contribution to developmental psychology constitutes the most elaborate developmental perspective within the small family of structuralistic psychologies.* Even Piaget's well-known dynamic structuralism—which has had about fifty years since the time of Basov to become more concrete—is relatively schematic as compared to Basov's (also somewhat schematic) descriptions of structures.

Basov's developmentally-oriented idea of 'structure' becomes clearer in the following explanation:

We must take into account that the idea of the 'whole' does not exist without the idea of 'part', and, equally, the concept of 'structure' is inseparably connected with the concept of 'elements' which the given structure consists of. Therefore it would be wrong to emphasize one and not to see or reject the other. 'Structure' or 'whole' should be understood not only as they are, but by viewing the whole complexity of their content, the differences within them. Without these differences the structures cannot exist—they would not be holistic structures but simple homogeneous masses. Further, it is necessary to understand every whole in the course of the process of its emergence and formation. Structures do not exist as always ready givens, but are constructed and dissipate in our full view, under the conditions of organism-environment transaction. (Basov, 1975, p. 274)

Basov's emphasis on the developmental (constructive and dissipative) nature of structures makes him transcend the static view of structures that traditional Gestalt psychology espoused. Basov pointed to the fact that the beginnings of Gestalt psychological thinking were embedded in the study of perception—where it is particularly easy to think of structures as rigidly given, and where any conceptualization of structural dynamics is easily thought of as a movement towards the 'true' or 'good' form. In contrast, developmental psychologists 'are present at the birth of structures and have the opportunity to follow their development, step-by-step' (Basov, 1975, p. 275).

Basov's structuralism transcends the individual and includes the environment. Like the individual, the environment too is conceptualized as a dynamic structure, related to the individual who is acting within it (Basov, 1931a, p. 68–77). The relationships between the structured environment and the holistic (structured) personality who is active within that environment, transforms its structure, and develops by that activity, is at the core of Basov's structuralism.

Types of structure

Basov starts his description of different types of psychological process structures by moving from the simpler to the more complex cases. The simplest structural form is *the simple temporal chain of acts* (prostaia vremennaia tshep' aktov). This simplest form can be found when a process of behaviour proceeds over time with no relations between the adjacent events. For example, a person can be forced to answer a series of unrelated questions in a row. After answering the first question, the person turns to the second one, then to the third one, and so on. It is easy to see how this temporal organization of behaviour exemplifies the ideal of psychologists' tests, or consecutive trials in some psychophysics experiments, where the experimenter hopes that the previous trial is answered by the subject without interference with the next one. Graphically, Basov suggested a way of describing the temporal structure of the simplest form; this is presented in Figure V.1.

Figure V.1: Basov's graphic representation of the simple
temporal chain of acts

Source: Basov (1929a) p. 282

Ontogenetically, Basov claimed that this simplest structual form can be observed in the behaviour of the young infant. Since the infant is assumed to have very little experience with the environment, it is assumed to be 'at the mercy' of external stimulation. The incoming stimuli are responded to by separate reactions, which do not recognize connections between stimuli and are not united in any organized action sequence. Of course, as the simple temporal form characterizes infant-environment relationships it is becoming prepared for the transformation into the second type of structure—which Basov called the *associatively determined process.* This type of process structure is the simplest form of *organized* process which is characterized by associative relations between the antecedent and consequent units in the temporal sequence. For example, if there exists an associatively determined process in the form of a symbol sequence: A---B---C---D, then A is connected by its contents with B, which in its turn is somehow connected with C, which in its turn is connected with D. However, no connection is present between A and C, A and D, and B and D. In the present-day terminology of psychologists Basov's associatively determined process is equivalent to a Markovian process. Any contemporary analysis of temporal associations between adjacent behavioural events—often using conditional frequencies of transitions from antecedents to consequents which are interpreted as probabilities—constructs psychological data that fit Basov's simple organized associatively determined process type.

Basov was not very inspired by the level of organization in the associatively determined processes. He described the organization of that type in following terms:

the process of that kind does not possess a definite direction and develops fully due to these associative-reflectory links which at the given moment happen to be in maximum readiness .... The unorganized and occasional path of the chain [see Figure V.2] crudely symbolizes the lack of definite directionality in the given process .... (Basov, 1975, p. 328)

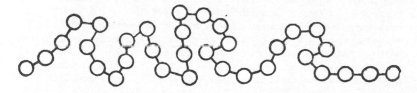

Figure V.2: Basov's graphic representation of the associatively-determined process

Source: Basov (1929a) p. 282.

Basov's recognition of the contributions of research traditions phrased in terms of the associationist world view (i.e., reflexology) is related particularly with this structural form. The members in the sequence are related by association-based ties, where the next member in the sequence is triggered by the previous one. However, this associationistic picture of psychological phenomena does not take the actor's goal-oriented activity into account. A psychological process of the associatively determined type moves ahead in time on the basis of whatever associations each following member of the sequence happens to lead to.

It is exactly the issue of *future-oriented directionality* that for Basov marks the highest structural form of psychological processes. Such directionality is an inevitable part of the organism's active effort to solve problems that emerge in its interaction with the environment. However, not every aspect of human life is free of associatively-determined behavioural structures. Instead, Basov saw in the combination of goal-directed and associatively determined processes the key to explanation of human psychological functioning within environments. He wrote:

The environment at any given moment surrounds the adult person with such conditions that his activity must be directed towards solving some problems, reaching some goals, towards *planned satisfaction of the need to exist*. None of this can be realized in the course of activity that does not have a defined direction, and which is regulated along its course by chaining reactions by chance. However, at the same time one can't say that the associatively-determined process ... is in general alien to the activity of an adult person. If not in external activity which is more strictly dependent upon the surrounding environment, then in the internal processes of behaviour we can at times observe [examples of associatively-determined processes] .... We go out for a walk in the evening, exhausted after a hard day at work. The problems that we had been trying to solve during the day disappear from our mind, we take a rest from that goal-directedness that keeps us in a state of constant strain. And what can we observe in our mind? A multitude of images and remote reminiscences suddenly take over our minds for some reason. These change from one to another without our active participation in it, tending in a haphazard way towards an unknown direction .... (Basov, 1975, p. 329, emphasis added)

Nevertheless, Basov considered the goal-directed structures of behavioural processes to be of the 'highest' kind in human psychology. This emphasis parallels the important role of 'higher psychological processes' in Vygotsky's writing and thinking. This parallel is not surprising if we recollect that Basov's background in the volitional aspect of human personality (Basov, 1922) could serve as a natural intellectual stepping stone for his conceptualization of the behavioural description of the human being as an actor-within-the-environment. The idea of the subject's *activity* relative to his environment became shared by Vygotsky and Basov—who were themselves actors within the social environment of the Soviet psychology of the 1920s that was embedded in the Marxist philosophical ethos.

Basov's third structural form of behavioural process was labelled the *apperceptively-determined process*. Basov explains its nature and distinctive features with a strong emphasis on integration of the structure of behaviour around a goal:

> The main distinctive feature in the determination of that process ... is, that its major determining factor is the basic stimulus that usually enters the process as a certain task or goal. *That stimulus directs the whole process along a certain path in such a way that every part of the process, every separate act, takes place under its [stimulus'] immediate influence.* At the same time the reflector-associative mechanism retains all of its relevance in the process. Separate acts of the process follow one another in a sequence, being regulated by that mechanism. Every antecedent act here demands its successor—as in the real associatively determined process. *The crucial difference, however, lies in the circumstance that every successive act here is coordinated not only with its preceding stimulus, but also with the basic stimulus of the whole process, with its goal or task.* That circumstance is the organizing basis that directs the whole process along a strictly determined path. The basic stimulus, when determining the process, closes some paths to it, leaving other paths open. Thus, if in the associatively determined process one could find relationships between elements of only one kind— associative ties of each following element with its predecessor—then in the process that we analyze now we have to accept the existence of double links. The first of these remain similar to the previous case [of the associatively determined process] (we call them local links), but others are characteristic of only this new process. The latter constitute the central links of every separate act with the basic stimulus. (Basov, 1975, pp. 331-2, emphasis added)

Basov tried to convey the meaning of the linkages in the appreceptively-determined process through schematic pictures. Unfortunately, the difficulty of introducing the time domain into these schemes may render these not at all easy to comprehend. In Figure V.3, Basov's original scheme (from Basov, 1929a) is reproduced.

Despite Basov's efforts to emphasize the relevance of the central organization of behaviour by the basic stimulus (goal) in this figure, the meaning of the process he was explaining seems to have become lost due to the circular two-dimensional nature of the scheme in Figure V.3. Basov himself seemed to recognize this, calling the scheme 'rather imperfect' in his paper and adding a clarifying footnote saying that 'the apperceptively determined process does not, at its close, revert to its beginning, as is

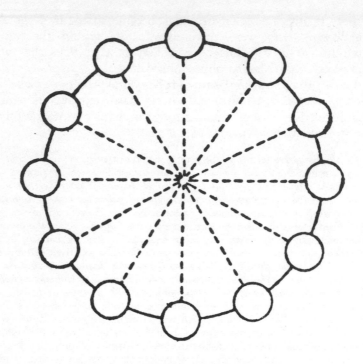

Figure V.3: Basov's graphic representation of the
apperceptively-determined process

Source: Basov (1929a) p. 283

represented on our scheme ...' (Basov, 1929a, p. 284). In the
second edition of his major book on paedology (Basov, 1931a) he
introduced a modified two-part figure to better convey the open-
ended, developmental nature of the apperceptively determined
structural form of behaviour (see Figure V.4).

Even this scheme did not satisfy Basov, as he recognized that in
the spiral description of the process (Figure V.4.b) 'the double
links in the process are not shown as clearly...' (Basov, 1975, p. 333)
as in the first part of the figure.

The value of Basov's conceptualization for developmental
psychology in the twentieth century lies in his purposeful effort to
find structural descriptions of psychological processes that
adequately represent all the complexity of external (behavioural)

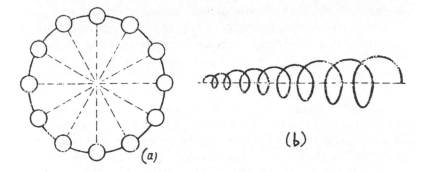

Figure V.4: Basov's extended graphic representation of the apperceptively-determined process

Source: Basov (1975) p. 332

and internal (cognitive, emotional) psychological phenomena in the individual-environment interaction. Furthermore, Basov went beyond the structuralistic, non-developmental traditions in psychology and other social sciences where structures have usually been conceptualized as static and immutable entities (or, at most, entities that strive towards some static equilibrium state if pushed away from a balanced state). Basov's structuralism is developmental in its nature—structures of psychological processes emerge in the individual's active dealing with his environment, and lead to the emergence of new structures. The 'higher' structural forms are built upon the 'lower' forms—they are integrated into the new hierarchically organized behavioural structure. That process takes place in its most characteristic form in the course of children's development, and it goes through different transitional structural forms.

The development of structures and their transitional forms
The reality of child development is by far more complex than the simple schematic forms of behaviour that Basov outlined. Basov explicitly recognized this. The case of child development includes not only the development of new structural forms in child-environment relationships (which would come close to Piaget's dynamic structuralism), but is purposefully organized by adults so that it would lead to the emergence of new structures. This latter point again illustrates the closeness of Basov's thinking to that of

Vygotsky in the realm of theory. On the side of empirical studies, however, Basov went beyond Vygotsky in his efforts to document the emergence of different structural forms in the social interaction of children. Together with his colleagues, Basov observed the presence or absence of different forms within play in children's peer groups between ages of three and eight years (Basov, 1924a, 1924b, 1930; Zeiliger, 1925; Zeiliger and Levina, 1924, 1930). The development of children from the simpler (simple temporal chain of acts) to the most complex version of apperceptively-determined processes includes the intermediate emergence of various transitional forms alongside the 'pure' forms. The progression to the apperceptively-determined process, however, need not always proceed through the associatively-determined state of affairs. Basov (1931a, p. 330) allowed for the possibility of a direct transition from the type of the simple temporal chain of acts to the apperceptively-determined process. His three types of process structures do not constitute a rigid 'stage theory' *à la* Piaget, but are related with one another in an open-ended way.

Let us briefly describe some of the transitions between Basov's structural types. The first major transition involves the progression from the simple temporal chain of acts to the associatively-determined process. Basov's description of that transition integrates *two directions* in the temporal relationship between stimuli in the temporal structure. The first of these directions entails the *forward association* from an antecedent to the subsequent act. Basov illustrated that direction graphically (see Basov, 1929a, p. 284). The second direction involves the *backward association* between adjacent acts in a chain. The following scheme may convey Basov's meaning of these two kinds of association more adequately than his own efforts to represent them.

Basov's description of the combining of forward and backward associations represents a structuralistic reformulation of the idea of conditional reflex (in Pavlov's terminology). The flow of time—the irreversible dimension within which the simple temporal chain of acts is located—leads to the establishment of forward-oriented associations between adjacent acts in the chain. On the other hand, the openness of the chain to environmental input leads to the insertion of the backward-oriented associations into the emerging associative process. The combination of the two directions is reflected in Figure V.5, where the transition A-->B can be

STARTING CONDITION:

| A | B | | C | | D | | E |

FORWARD ASSOCIATION: BACKWARD ASSOCIATION:

A ---> B---> C ---> D --->E   A <--- B < ---C <--- D <--- E

COMBINATION OF TWO DIRECTIONS OF ASSOCIATIONS:
A ---> B <--- C ---> D---> E

Note: A, B, C, D and E are acts in the stimulus sequence

Figure V.5: Transition from the simple temporal chain of acts to the associatively-determined process

interpreted as an example of continuation along the line of internal associative chain of stimuli, which at the next step comes under the influence of the external stimulus C that becomes integrated into the structure. Basov himself provided an example of a child's drawing to illustrate this transitional form:

There is nothing more usual for the little painter than such a kind of drawing in which the plot of the drawing develops not from inside (i.e., from the antecedent to the subsequent), but under external influences that gradually become layered on one another, forming a more or less connected whole. In that process, of course, not every new external stimulus can link with the previous process and be assimilated by it; obviously only some stimuli which the child selects out of the many others are capable of that. The remaining stimuli do not affect the course of the process at all .... (Basov, 1975, p. 334)

Basov's example of the child's drawing relates the particular transitional structural form (from the simple temporal chain of acts to the associatively determined process) to his general idea of integration of internal and external lines of stimuli that the child encounters over time. The given transitional form is particularly interesting for developmental psychology because it explains the structure of the *process* by which the child develops from a dissociated temporal conglomerate of acts into an integrated (reflectory-associative) organized process. Contrary to the mind-set of behaviouristic or reflexological reductionism of complexity to elementary reflexes, Basov retains a systemic organismic view on the developmental process. For him, the development of the child is neither determined solely by external environmental influences that work out reflexes of different kinds, nor by any internal mystique of 'soul' or 'character' of the child that develops along a predetermined (maturational) course. While insisting—very similarly to the contemporary 'interactionist' or 'transactionist' perspectives—that both person and environment participate in the process of child development, Basov proceeded to the effort to describe how these two become integrated with one another *in the course of time*, and how that integration itself leads to new forms of the process.

The second transitional form that Basov emphasized involves the progression from the associatively-determined to the apperceptively-determined process. This transition constitutes the process of development of goal-directed action and qualities related to it (intentionality, volition). Basov emphasizes the *emerging nature* of the apperceptively-determined process—it emerges from the associatively determined one through inclusion of temporal relationships between acts beyond the predecent-consequent association. Figure V.6 illustrates Basov's idea of that transition.

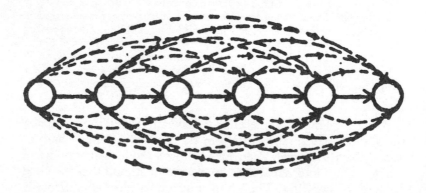

Figure V.6: Basov's graphic representation of the transition from an associatively-determined state of a process into an apperceptively-determined state

Source: Basov (1929a) p. 286

As can be seen, forward-orienting influences ('messages') from every act in the process lead to every other subsequent act. In our contemporary terminology we could assume that the emergence of goal-orientation in that transition process is connected with the use of *feed-forward* messages in the system. The child's concentration on an explicit goal ('basic stimulus' in Basov's terminology) does not emerge unexpectedly in child development, but is prepared by the child's *prediction* of his own possible acts in the future, given the circumstances. It is again perhaps the limited meaning of Basov's diagrams that have obscured his dynamic-structural ideas. For instance, his readers may have a hard time trying to imagine how to proceed from the intermediate state (Figure V.6) to the developed version of the apperceptively-determined process (Figures V.3 and V.4), and how the internal and external stimulus lines are integrated in the case of this transition.

Basov's example of the process of a child's movement into constructive play in the context of a children's playgroup may illustrate the transition. Here, it is important to note that the *goal* ('basic stimulus') *emerges* in the process of the child's acting:

We have a playing child in front of us. We find him being in the process of rather random and unorganized following of the external stimuli of the environment. The child goes from one object to another, talks to peers, tries to intervene in their play, but does not stop and get involved more persistently and does not demonstrate the presence of any organized process yet. But now his glance falls on a box with building material. The child approaches the box, takes the blocks, and begins to combine some configurations out of them. He does not set for himself any goal or task yet, but the very first successful configuration that the child makes inserts meaningfulness and goal-directedness into the construction process in the associative way. The child now takes the constructed configuration as the foundation of a house, and then develops that further, so that finally something like a house indeed becomes constructed. (Basov, 1931a, p. 327)

The structure of the child's play is in this example transformed (by the child himself) first from the simple temporal chain of acts (walking around, episodic action with objects or in relation to peers) to the associatively determined process (constructing *something* without a clear plan, merely on the basis of associations that guide the 'what to do now?' at every step). Secondly, the apperceptively determined process emerges in the web of the child's play in the association-based play with the building materials—the child, at a certain moment, decides to build a house (for example, by declaring 'I am going to build a house'), and subsequently accomplishes that task. The setting of the goal of the building process is a stimulus (in Basov's terminology) that is a number of steps ahead of the child at the time when it is set up. As it emerges, it immediately narrows down the child's actions with the building blocks, providing a constraining model to which the child's actions need to conform if the task is to be accomplished. Basov's analysis of the transition from associatively determined to the apperceptively determined structure of psychological processes parallels Vygotsky's emphasis on the making of signs to organize the person's thinking and acting. Basov's 'basic stimulus' (goal), similarly to Vygotsky's idea of signs, establishes the forward-oriented control over the person's own actions. Of course, there remains a basic difference between Vygotsky and Basov— compared with the generality and relatively context-free nature of signs, the goals as analyzed by Basov are always part of the given structure of individual-environment relationships, and are therefore ephemeral and transitory.

The transition from the associatively determined process to the apperceptively determined structural form need not be as spontaneous as the example with a child's building play seems to lead us to believe. On the contrary, that transition is organized by the demands set forth by the organization of the environment. The goal for the child's actions may be given to the child from outside—by a teacher, for instance, who makes children solve a mathematics problem in class. The child starts to plan a strategy of solution, but may end up at a dead-end. In order to try again, s/he begins from the beginning again, going forward in a certain direction in a semi-planned manner, where the associative processes from one step to the next in the solving process are guided by the solution goal. Nevertheless, the solution process may fail, and the child starts again, trying not to miss the path that can lead to solution (Basov, 1931a, pp. 328–9). For Basov, as a developmental psychologist, the process of transition from one structural form to another, as well as the presence of intermediate (mixed) forms, was of greater interest than the presence or absence of the 'pure' forms. Furthermore, the development of the structures of action within the environment is guided by the organization of that environment.

Environmental guidance of psychological development

Environmental conditions set the stage for transitions between different structural forms. Furthermore, the experience of the developing child in recurrent action settings within environments lead the child on the way towards establishing his/her action structures. Basov viewed the environment as providing structural schemes for the actions of the child:

The environment that surrounds the child gives him a multitude of ready forms and different complex structures that relate to static objects as well as to various dynamic phenomena. All these contents of environment become stored in his experience in the form of certain 'schemes' (schemes of objects and schemes of actions), which he subsequently represents in his activity. Each such 'scheme', as it lays the foundation of the process of activity, directs it towards a certain course and mediates the planfulness of its development. Depending on the state of the 'scheme', on how complete, exact, well-defined etc. it is, is the character of the developing process, its structure. Among the multiplicity of 'schemes' that are present in the child's experience, some can be old in origin and fortified on many occasions of the child's activity, whereas others are very new, uncertain, and easily changeable in their basic form. The objects that the child has contact with on a daily basis, actions that he is used to performing always in one and the same way, form the steady and persistent 'schemes' in his experience. The activity that develops on the basis of such schemes includes in it to the full extent features of goal-directedness and planfulness, but at the same time it is fully automatized in its nature (i.e., proceeds like a simple reflectory-associative process). (Basov, 1931a, pp. 331–2)

The environment, guiding the development of children's action structures by its 'schemes', leads to the fossilization (to use Vygotsky's term here—see Chapter IV) and automatization of goal-oriented action. On the other hand, it is the provision of *new* problems to the person by the environment that triggers the need for active efforts to solve these. Conversely, when the environmental conditions do not require the person's operation at the higher (apperceptively determined) manner, the person (adult or child) can 'get by' through acting at a lower level of organization of the psychological processes involved. In respect to different action domains, the same person can perform a task with the help of different structural forms—a parallel to *décalage* in Piaget's view of children's cognition.

Environmental challenges can further lead to the differentiation of the structural form of action, especially at the highest (apperceptively determined) level. That takes the form of establishment of a hierarchical goal *structure* that includes goals of different generality in the same structure. A more general goal can be set up, from which a number of less general sub-goals can be derived, and reached in action one after the other, en route to the general goal. The presence of such complex action structures is largely the prerogative of adults, whereas through childhood the environment directs developing children towards the capability of setting such goals and reaching them.

Empirical evidence: presence of different structures in children's play

Basov and his colleagues (Zeiliger and Levina, 1930) undertook the analysis of frequencies of different structural forms—'pure' and 'transitional'—in the play of children between two and eight years of age. The study resulted in percentage distributions of the observed forms for each of the three age groups that are presented in Table V.1.

Table V.1: Distributions of different structural forms observed in play (in % total N=127)

No. Structure	Age group		
	2–4 years	4–6 years	6–8 years
1. Simple temporal chain	38.5	14.3	6.2
2. Associatively-determined processes	16.9	21.9	6.9
3. Apperceptively-determined processes	19.4	27.3	44.3
4. Transitional forms:			
(a) from 1 to 2	1.4	2.4	—
(b) from 2 to 3	18.0	22.9	34.2
5. Externally given forms:	2.4	8.7	6.6
6. Unclear forms	3.4	2.5	1.8
Total	100.0	100.0	100.0

Source: Zeiliger and Levina (1930), p. 55

As is evident from this table, the relative frequency of unorganized forms in play (simple temporal chains) declines substantially from the 2–4 year age group to that of 6–8 years. The associatively-determined forms observed in play are predominant in the middle (4–6 years) age group, and later decline. The apperceptively-determined forms (as well as transitional forms between the associatively and apperceptively determined ones) are observed to become dominant in the older age group. Of course, these data illustrate only the populational side of how children's play changes over age. Basov himself actively promoted the search for individual developmental processes, but did not proceed far along that line. At the same time, his studies revealed considerable inter-individual variability in the distributions of different structural forms of play in all age groups.

Basov's efforts to define and analyze dynamic structures in child-environment relations constituted a direction in developmental psychology that could satisfy both the theoretically-minded investigators and empirical purists. Aside from making the Gestalt approach applicable to the study of children's development, the depth of Basov's methodological thinking led him to conceptualize the relationships between different methods—observational and introspective—in one general framework.

Methodological integration: retrospective unity of extro- and introspection

Basov's interests in the inferential problems of empirical research methods were deep throughout all his work as a psychologist. His own empirical work involved the use of both observational methodology (usually in the 'natural habitats' of children—in kindergarten class, during group walks, etc.)—and the clinical interview (mostly for research on children's social knowledge; see Chapter VII). Undoubtedly, for Basov, the observational method constituted the core of the scientific method of developmental psychology, from which other methods can be derived by adding and subtracting conditions under which observations are carried out. Thus, by adding variation of specific conditions to the children's environments, the method of natural experiment is derived. Likewise, the observation paired with explicit questioning of the child who is performing some tasks, results in the 'clinical interview' along the lines of Piaget. Each of these versions of research methods, derived from observation, fits the research objectives in its own way. Thus guiding the subject to provide introspective evidence to the experimenter may be very appropriate for the study of the subject's ideas, but not for an adequate view of actions. Contrary to the prevailing fashion among his contemporary reflexologist colleagues, Basov did not intend to eliminate the introspective method from the instrumentarium of scientific psychology; he tried to put it to work in the context of research problems, and other adjacent methods.

Basov recognized the basic similarity between introspection and observation of behaviour of others (extrospection). First, both introspection and extrospection are *retrospective* in their nature— by the mere impossibility of reflecting upon an event (internal or external) at *exactly* the same moment as it takes place (i.e., it always takes place with some latency—see Basov, 1931a, p. 260). That retrospective unity of introspection and extrospection raises a number of problems of inference from the empirical data which involve the role of the investigator's conscious goals and readiness for more (or less) elaborate immediate description of the extrospectively observed or introspectively experienced events. Much of Basov's energy was spent on analysis of the processes by which different observers record data of children's behaviour (Basov, 1923, 1924a, 1925a). The research on children's social cognition that was carried out under his supervision (Merlin & Khriakova, 1930) led him to address the issues of children's thinking as revealed by introspection guided by interview. Methodological concerns about empirical research were always of high relevance in Basov's thinking.

Summary: Basov's relevance in developmental psychology

The present chapter serves the function of bringing Basov's theoretical ideas and empirical-methodological notions to the attention of contemporary developmental psychologists who may be interested in what can be learned from Soviet psychology of the 1920s. The picture that emerges here is very different from Western psychology's oversight of Basov's work in the past— despite its general availability (Basov, 1929a)—and from its active promotion (see Luria, 1928a, 1930b), as well as from the (few) glimpses that contemporary Soviet psychological officialdom (e.g., Smirnov, 1975) provides of Basov. Contrary to the rare Western evaluations, Basov was neither a 'native Russian forebear' of Soviet psychology, as Bauer (1952, p. 155) tried to present him, nor a simple follower of Soviet reflexological behaviourism (Wozniak, 1975, p. 25). Instead, his thinking would be close to systems-theory oriented developmental psychologists of the present time who tend to label themselves 'interactionists' or 'transactionists'. In his structuralistic emphasis Basov was close to (and influenced by) Piaget. He, however, surpassed Piaget in his more explicit treatment of the dynamic structural forms, and the conceptualization of how the internal and external stimulus structures become integrated. He also surpassed Piaget in an emphasis on the social nature of children's personality development. In that latter aspect he was close to Vygotsky in essence, only using slightly different (more behaviourally oriented) terminology and emphasizing the observational method as the key to developmental knowledge (whereas Vygotsky revolutionized the experimental method at the same time). Basov's structuralism was a step in the direction of developing a new theoretical perspective on child development adequate to the empirical phenomenology available to investigators in observations.

Basov's contribution to developmental psychology is comparable to that of Vygotsky. This is not surprising, as both of them developed their psychological ideas in the conditions of the Soviet Union of the 1920s which was highly conducive to the advancement of developmental ideas in any area of social science. The decades since Basov's death have seen the overlooking of his contributions in different ways—in the USSR his paedology-related writings have been unavailable for a long time, and among the international psychological community very few investigators search through old journal volumes of the 1920s for reasons other than historical curiosity. Fortunately, neglect of a highly creative Soviet developmental psychologist seems to be nearing an end. Basov's contribution has become explicitly mentioned more often in contemporary Soviet psychology, and his pioneering role in developmental psychology seems to have become recognized. Indeed, Basov had innovative answers to a number of questions that worry developmental psychologists at the present time. For example, his account of structural forms of behavioural processes overcomes the methodological difficulties that investigators using conditional probability-based Markovian methods for the study of behavioural chains in adult-infant or child-child interactions are currently facing. His advice about methods to investigators planning on observing pre-school children in their natural surroundings, but worry about minimizing the effect of the observers on the children, is likewise a part of Basov's valuable heritage which contemporary developmental psychology may need to resurrect in order to progress. Like Vygotsky, Basov did not leave a fully completed theoretical system, but what he did leave is worth serious study.

VI Studies on the Development of Children's Action, Cognition and Perception

Issues of perception and action have been of interest to Soviet psychologists for many decades. Likewise, problems of consciousness, exemplified in psychology in the form of studies of reasoning, decision-making, and their development (both in its microgenetic and ontogenetic aspects), are prominent in Soviet psychology. Interest in these themes has traditionally covered the whole range from infancy to adolescence and adulthood.

It is usual for Soviet developmentalists interested in the development of cognition to see it as being interdependent with action. Furthermore, the social nature of the organization of children's action is kept in mind with remarkable persistency in Soviet developmentalist's research. Quite often, the Soviet action-based perspective on cognitive development is contrasted with Piaget's views, and an emphasis is placed on his egocentric-to-socialized sequence in the development of children's thinking. This emphasis can be traced historically to Vygotsky's criticism of Piaget in the early 1930s, which Soviet psychologists have echoed on numerous occasions. On the other hand, Piaget's constructive interactionism and attribution of causality for cognitive development to children's actions upon objects in their environments has made him a close ally of Soviet psychologists' developmental views.

The emphasis on children's acting-upon-environments as the major source of children's cognitive development is an outgrowth of the whole history of Soviet psychology. It is based on the Marxist thesis of human capability of changing their world by acting upon it. That thesis was embedded, in different forms, in the thinking of Basov, Kornilov, Vygotsky, Rubinshtein and other theoretically-oriented psychologists in the USSR. It was further advanced under the social conditions of the 1930s (which were reflected in the thinking of the 'Kharkov School' of psychology; see below), and has reached the interest of contemporary psychologists in the context of the 'activity theory' of A.N. Leontiev, as well as other theories that emphasize the active role of the subject (see Brushlinskii, 1984; Matiushkin, 1983; Rubinshtein, 1957; Wertsch, 1981).

A number of aspects of action development can be encountered in the studies of Soviet psychologists, ranging from issues of relationships of acting and perceiving (e.g., Venger, 1969; Zaporozhets, Venger, Zinchenko, & Ruzskaia, 1967) to the organization of motor action (Bernshtein, 1947, 1966) and its comparative ontogeny of relations with cognition (Fabri, 1978; Ladygina-Kots, 1935; Novoselova, 1978). The development of the voluntary nature of children's action (e.g., Zaporozhets, 1960) has been an important aspect of research in the tradition of the study of 'higher psychological functions' (see Chapter IV). The role of the work of the 'Kharkov School' of Soviet psychology— consisting of a group of psychologists who worked in the Ukrainian town Kharkov in the 1930s—is formidable in the history of the contemporary research on children's action and cognition.

The 'Kharkov school' and research on cognitive development

The group of Soviet psychologists that has acquired the label the 'Kharkov school' included part of the group of people that had concentrated around Vygotsky at the turn of the 1920s/1930s (A.N. Leontiev, A. Luria, A. Zaporozhets, L. Bozhovich) who moved to Kharkov (then the capital city of the Ukraine) in the early 1930s and based their research activities at the Ukrainian Psychoneurological Institute and Kharkov Paedagogical Institute. A number of Ukrainian psychologists organized their research on the basis of the ideas of the leaders of the 'Kharkov school' (V. Asnin, G. Lukov, P. Zinchenko, P. Gal'perin).

The roots of the ideas of the 'Kharkov school' were deeply grounded in Vygotsky's 'cultural-historical' perspective. However, the direction in which Vygotsky's ideas were developed further by the 'Kharkov school' was different from the primary emphasis on the meaning in developing consciousness that Vygotsky began to be interested in by the final years of his life. In contrast with that line, the 'Kharkov school' advanced another, less directly

'Vygotskian', idea of the relationship of developing psychological processes with actions upon objects, in conjunction with goal-directed social guidance (instruction) of these actions (A. A. Leontiev, 1983, p. 11). However, in line with the criticism of Vygotsky's views which was gathering momentum in the course of the 1930s, the 'Kharkov school' publicly declared themselves separate from the Vygotskian tradition (traces of this can be seen in P. I. Zinchenko, 1983–84). This, however, did not make the 'Kharkov School' any less indebted to its Vygotskian heritage.

The general credo of the 'Kharkov school' in the study of cognitive development was expressed succinctly by Zaporozhets in his introductory comments to a symposium in 1941, at a Ukrainian conference on psychology and pedagogy (English translation: Zaporozhets, 1979–80):

We are interested not so much in analyzing the different forms of thinking in childhood, drawing on the descriptions that already exist in child psychology, as in determining the conditions under which changes in these forms occur ... The question arises as to how children, who at birth have no concepts or ideas about reality, come to acquire a knowledge of reality, i.e., what the conditions are that give rise to thought and its development in childhood. (Zaporozhets, 1979–80, p. 9)

The emphasis on *conditions* under which development takes place is given central relevance by Zaporozhets, as is evident in the quote. These conditions in general are of three kinds. First, conditions for development are directed by the child's actions with objects. Secondly, interaction with others serves as a condition for development. A special status is here given to adults who instruct the child in a purposeful manner in the process of interaction. Finally, the child's own, newly developed, reflection about his own actions and thinking process (in contemporary terminology this may pass under the label of 'metacognition') constitutes a condition for his further psychological development.

All these three kinds of conditions of development were studied by psychologists of the 'Kharkov school'. Zaporozhets' own work in the 1930s addressed the issue of action with objects and speech as conditions for cognitive development. The results of that research were published in relatively inaccessible places, and were made more widely available only decades later (English translation, Zaporozhets & Lukov, 1979–80; in Russian, Zaporozhets, 1980).

Using the clinical interview connected with experimental manipulation of objects that is characteristic of Piaget's work, Zaporozhets and Lukov demonstrated the dependence of children's thinking on their practical experience with the objects involved. However, the latter do not determine the thinking process in a simple manner. Rather, the child's thinking sets up hypotheses (triggered by the experimenter's questions) which are subsequently proved (or disproved) by his manipulation of the objects. The child's cognitive response to cases of disproof of a hypothesis was found not to be determined by the reality in all cases. Rather, the child could retain his hypothesis, even if the latter was proven wrong by the object manipulation. Zaporozhets and Lukov found that some children made efforts not to accept disconfirmatory evidence:

In the course of our study, a child aged five years, six months, came to the conclusion that iron sank. Then the child was shown a tin box, and asked 'What is this box made of?' The child took the box in his hands, examined it, and said 'It is made of iron'.

'What will happen to it,' asked the experimenter, 'if it is put in water?'

'It will sink,' said the child.

'Why?'

'Because it is made of iron.'

The child was told to put the box in the vessel containing water. He did so, quickly turned around and said 'It sank.' (The box was floating).

The experimenter suggested the child should take a look and see that the box had sunk, but the child did not want to and, turning away from the vessel containing the water, said that the box had sunk.

When the child was asked once again to take a look at the floating box, he said: 'The box is floating.'

'Then why did you say that the box had sunk?'

'I was guessing,' answered the child, 'that it had sunk.'

The child, of course, did not think that the box had sunk. He quite clearly saw that the box was floating, and turned away in order to be able to reconcile his forecasting judgement with his confirming judgement. This innocent bit of trickery unquestionably shows that children sense the contradictoriness in their judgements. (Zaporozhets & Lukov, 1979–80, pp. 60–1)

Although Zaporozhets' general aim in peforming Piagetian experiments of this kind was to prove the relevance of practical activity in the development of children's thinking, his empirical data, like the case reported here, reveal a far more complicated interplay between acting upon objects and the child's personal history of thinking and speech. The complex interplay of action, speech and cognition made Vygotsky interested in studying children with abnormalities. A 'natural experiment' that takes the form of some biological abnormality was also used by Zaporozhets in the study of the normal development of cognition. Zaporozhets (1980) used children (4–9 years olds) with impaired hearing and articulatory functions, from whose development the role of speech in its ordinary (acoustic) form was excluded. Using a task similar to those of Gestalt psychology (use of a lever for getting an object), Zaporozhets was interested in the development of generalization in the children who could not use speech to help in that task. The experimenter's role was to hint and direct the child's action with the lever towards arrival at a solution, after which another task was presented to the child. The critical phenomenon which was of interest to the experimenter was the transfer by the child of the ways of acting developed in one situation to another. A picture of limited transfer of problem-solving skills appeared to characterize the 'deaf-and-mute' children. The limits on these children's communication with others set constraints on their development of thinking. In contrast, the speech of a normal child becomes integrated with his problem-solving activity, facilitating particularly the transfer of skills from one situation to another.

The issue of transfer of cognitive skills from one situation to another was studied by representatives of the 'Kharkov school'. Particularly the work of V. Asnin (1979–80) revealed an interesting general pattern: children who could cognitively generalize their knowledge up to a higher (abstract) level had a wider range of transfer of action skills across a range of tasks, as well as better performance on the tasks. The role of thinking at different levels of abstractness was also the object of study of Kharkov psychologists (e.g., visual-imagic thought—Khomenko, 1979–80; children's use of metaphors—Khomenko, 1980; acquisition of school knowledge—Bozhovich & Zinchenko, 1979–80). Asnin's other research revealed that personal understanding of the experimental situation by older children may inhibit their problem-solving activity, leading them to *not* use strategies that could solve the problem even when they are fully aware of the existence of such strategies (Asnin, 1980–81; Leontiev, 1975, pp. 286–9). In other words, a person's *orienting activity* in any new situation involves the formation of a psychological 'model' of the situation (and tasks to be performed in it), which further directs the subject's actions in that situation. Likewise, the question of use of tools as compared with auxiliary means for action (Gal'perin, 1980) and the role of social guidance in problem-solving (Asnin, 1980–81) was addressed by the Kharkovians. The thinking of the group of young psychologists in Kharkov in the 1930s, even if it did not result in a substantial number of publications during that decade, had nevertheless very substantial implications for the further development of Soviet research on cognitive development. It integrated thinking about activity and consciousness into one feedback-based system that follows dialectical (helical) view of development. Child development depends on the child's action with objects, which leads to the emergence of visual- and linguistic symbolic processes in consciousness, which in their turn start guiding the child's further actions within the environment.

The importance of the 'Kharkov school' to developmental research in the USSR is fundamental. The major theoretical traditions of the 'Moscow schools' of Soviet developmental psychology of the 1960s and 1970s are, to a greater or lesser degree, outgrowths from the activities of the 'Kharkov school'. Thus, Gal'perin's 'theory of step-by-step formation of mental actions' (see Gal'perin, 1968, 1969, 1982), Zaporozhets' and Venger's research on 'sensory education' and abilities (Venger, 1982; Zaporozhets, 1960, 1977a, 1977b; Zaporozhets & El'konin, 1971), Bozhovich's views on personality development (Bozhovich, 1978, 1979a, 1979b, and P. Zinchenko's work on involuntary memory (Zinchenko, 1961, 1983–84) all stem from the traditions of thought of the psychologists working in Kharkov in the 1930s.

Formation of children's cognitive processes

Most of the research in the USSR on cognitive development has over the past decades extended ideas that were present in their preliminary form in the 1930s. That continuity was wrought by the continued research activities of different members of the 'Kharkov school', among whom Piotr Gal'perin and Alexander Zaporozhets were perhaps the most influential for Soviet development psychology.

Piotr Gal'perin's work on the socially directed formation of children's cognitive processes is one of the major outgrowths from the 'Kharkov school'. Gal'perin received his degree at Kharkov in

1937 (Gal'perin, 1980). His 'theory of step-by-step formation of mental operations' emerged over the latter decades, actually reaching a better-known status thanks to publications by Gal'perin and his disciples in the 1960s (Gal'perin, 1959, 1966, 1968; Gal'perin & Georgiev, 1960a, 1960b, 1960c, 1960d, 1961; Gal'perin & Talyzina, 1968; Gal'perin & Danilova, 1980).

Gal'perin's experimental method of formation of mental operations is an extension of Vygotsky's emphasis on 'teaching experiments' as the major research tool for developmental psychology. It starts from orienting the child in the field of materials that are to be used for the formation of new cognitive operations. As a second step, the child is instructed to act with the materials (stage of materialized action). Thirdly, the child is required to express what he is doing verbally when the action takes place ('the audible stage'), after which the child is instructed to 'think aloud' without acting (the stage of externalized speech). Finally, the formed mental operation becomes internalized in full, showing no external signs of its proceeding.

It is easy to see Gal'perin's indebtedness to both Vygotsky and the 'Kharkov school' in his method. The process of internalization is here facilitated by the goal-directed guidance of the experimenter (the Vygotskian emphasis), and further supported by stepwise movement from acting upon objects to combining this with speech (along the lines of Zaporozhets, Leontiev, and Luria), and later to 'dropping out' the action while leading to further internalization of the formed cognitive operation (a Vygotskian feature again). Reviews of Gal'perin's work are available in English (Gal'perin, 1968, 1969, 1982) and need not be reviewed in greater detail here. Just one aspect of his research is important to point out—the relationship of contemporary Piagetian research in the USSR to that of the Gal'perin tradition. Piaget's demonstrations of the *presence* of qualitatively different cognitive operations at different stages of cognitive development is complemented by Gal'perin's emphasis on the *formation* of these operations in the process of instruction. A number of contemporary cognitive developmentalists combine the Piagetian and Soviet perspectives in their empirical research, giving primacy to the latter (e.g., Kaloshina & Kharicheva, 1975; Nikolaeva, 1979; Podgoretskaia, 1974, 1977; Sokhina, 1968).

The line of research promoted by Zaporozhets after the 1930s shows continuity with the topics and approach described above. After subjecting the traditions of mental testing to strong and justified criticism in his youth (Zaporozhets, 1930, see also Chapter 8), Zaporozhets proceeded to study the qualitative developmental progress in children's cognitive development. He viewed intellectual development as the enrichment of the content (rather than logical form—in opposition to Piaget) of the child's mental operations. In the course of this qualitative development of the content side of the mind, new means of cognitive activity emerge in ontogeny, which in their turn participate in further development of the child. The problem of age stages is thus closely related with the *functional* aspects of children's cognition at different stages—the functional development of cognition proceeds differently at different developmental stages (Zaporozhets, 1978). The series of stages in cognitive development that Zaporozhets and his co-workers have defined includes: (1) practical (visual-motor) reasoning; (2) the visual-figurative stage of thinking; and (3) the verbal-logical plan of thinking (cf. Zaporozhets & El'konin, 1971, pp. 227–31). This ontogenetic stage series is also a series of progression from 'lower' to 'higher' psychological processes. It is interesting to note that this stage account seems to bear marks of the 'Pavlovization' of Soviet psychology in the 1950s: the second and third stages in development parallel the Pavlovian distinction of 'primary' and 'secondary' signalling systems that were imported into psychology at that time. The general ethos of Zaporozhets' account, though, remains Vygotskian and true to his own work in Kharkov in the 1930s.

For dialectically-minded developmental psychologists, it is the process of transition from one cognitive stage to the next that is of special importance. Zaporozhets and other Soviet psychologists (El'konin, 1960; Poddiakov, 1977) have taken interest in both transitions—from the visual-motor to visual-figurative; and from the latter to the verbal-logical form of thought. Pre-schoolers' transition from visual-motor to visual-figurative stage takes place through their mastery of actions of substitution, imitation, modelling in play. Efforts have been made to construct empirical research methods that could be used to diagnose children's cognitive development within the stage-framework of Zaporozhets (Slobodchikov, 1982; Venger, 1974; Venger & Kholmovskaia,

1978). The role of sensory models (*sensornyie etalony*) that help the child to act in conjunction with tasks he is confronted with has been considered of special importance (Poddiakov, 1977; Venger, 1983; Zaporozhets, 1967). The role of the young child's actions in the process of development is emphasized in their various forms (Novoselova, 1978; Zaporozhets, Venger, Zinchenko, & Ruzskaia, 1967). Following the lines charted by Vygotsky (1966), the role of children's play in their development has been studied in Soviet developmental psychology (El'konin, 1978; Fabri, 1982; Fradkina, 1949; Vol'tsis, 1974).

The second transition—from the visual-figurative to the verbal-logical form of thinking—is intertwined with the goals of education in the thinking of Soviet developmental psychologists (e.g., Bodalev, Lomov, & Matiushkin, 1984; Davydov, 1983). As the educational goals are those of adults' guidance of the formation of new psychological functions in the child, the development of the 'internal sphere' of cognition (verbal-logical thinking) involves active efforts on behalf of educators (Davydov, 1972; El'konin, 1974). This education-centredness covers more than just school age children—the beginnings of educational efforts are present in the formation of cognition of pre-schoolers and kindergarten children, aside from schoolchildren (Davydov, 1957, 1969, 1972; Davydov & Andronov, 1979; Korneeva, 1978; Maksimov, 1979; Sal'mina & Kolmogorova, 1980; Zak, 1978). Again, the issues of voluntary psychological functions ('higher psychological functions' as termed by Vygotsky) are studied in their particular forms (Istomina, 1948; Smirnov, 1967). The transition of psychological functions, especially under guidance from others, into the intra-personal sphere *in conjunction with* the development of control over these functions is the single main theme in Soviet developmental research.

Aside from interest in the processes of transition from one cognitive stage to another, the issues of functioning (maintenance) of cognitive functions within a given stage is of interest to some contemporary developmentalists in the USSR. Poddiakov's interest in the role of activity as the context in which a child's cognitive functions are maintained (outside the context of efforts oriented towards formation of some new functions—cf. Poddiakov, 1981) is a new aspect of developmental research in the USSR. Poddiakov views cognitive functions at any stage of development as a systemic entity that includes both stable (images, axiomatic knowledge) and labile (emerging new psychological functions) parts, the functioning of which is regulated within the same whole. The issue of maintenance of cognitive functions by activity is also addressed in the framework of contemporary cultural-historical research (Tamm & Tulviste, 1980; Tulviste, 1984a). Further advancement of Vygotsky's ideas on the typology of verbal-logical thinking is likewise present today (Tulviste, 1981c). Perhaps the new tendency in Soviet cognitive development research in the 1980s is its openness to new ideas about how activity can relate to cognitive processes. This goes beyond the tradition of exaggerated emphases on the prime importance of activity for next to everything in psychological development that was characteristic of much of Soviet psychology in the 1970s.

Issues of cognitive development and Leontiev's 'activity theory'

Many an empirical study of action development in contemporary Soviet psychology stems from A. N. Leontiev's activity theory (Leontiev, 1972a, 1972b, 1975; van Rappard & van der Sijde, 1982; Wertsch, 1981). Historically this line of thought emerged from the 'Kharkov school' (see Cole, 1979–80; Kozulin, 1984, 1986; A. A. Leontiev, 1983, and below) that linked Vygotsky's 'cultural-historical' school of thought with contemporary Soviet psychology. The 'Kharkov school', unlike Vygotsky, emphasized the role of the child's practical relations with the environment, hence the relevance of children's actions to development and the construction of Leontiev's philosophically-minded activity theory.

For Leontiev, 'activity' plays the most important function in the person's psychological development and existence. The structure of activity is defined through organism-environment relations:

All activity has a looplike structure: afferentation ---> effector processes, which make contact with the object environment ---> correction and enrichment, with the help of feedback to the initial afferent image. The looplike nature of the processes that effect the organism's interaction with the environment is now generally accepted and quite well described. However, the key point is the looplike structure itself: what is crucial is that mental reflection of the object world is not produced directly by external influences (including 'reverse' influences), but by processes through which the subject enters into practical contact with the object world. These processes are therefore necessarily subordinated to the world's independent properties, connections, and relations. This means that the 'afferent agent' that directs activity is *primarily* the object itself, and only *secondarily* its image as a *subjective product* of activity that fixes, stabilizes, and assimilates its object content. In other words, a twofold transition takes place: the transition from object to the process of activity, and the transition from activity to subjective product of activity. (Leontiev, 1981, p. 49)

The 'twofold transition' mentioned by Leontiev is the focus of many research efforts on children's cognitive development. On the one hand, the 'transition from object to the process of activity' has been studied by numerous investigators who have concentrated on the analysis of children's visual-motor actions (Novoselova, 1978; Zaporozhets *et al.*, 1967). The 'transition from activity to its subjective product' has been studied by investigators of cognitive processes in conjunction with subjects' actions (Gal'perin, 1959; Gal'perin & Talyzina, 1968; Gal'perin & Kabyl'nitskaia, 1974; Talyzina, 1969). The role of *organized* social environment in the role of transition from activity to cognitive processes has been studied in the context of educational psychology (Davydov, 1972).

Leontiev's activity theory was systematically presented by its author only in the 1970s (Leontiev, 1972a, 1972b, 1974a, 1974b, 1975; in English: Leontiev, 1981). Nevertheless, the development of that theoretical system covers the whole lifetime of its author (see A. A. Leontiev, 1983). Besides upholding the principle of development in his theory, Leontiev was also involved in different empirical issues (Leontiev, 1931, 1932, 1944, 1946, 1950, 1980; Leontiev & Gal'perin, 1964).

Leontiev's theory of activity (*deiatel 'nost'*) involves a different use of the terms. Different activities (forms of human relationships with the object-world, distinguished and guided by their motives) include actions (*deistvie*: processes that are guided by conscious goals). Leontiev explicitly defines actions as 'the process that is subservient to the representation of the result that must be reached, i.e., the process that is subservient to a conscious goal' (Leontiev, 1975, p. 103). Actions, in their turn, consist of operations (behaviours that are immediately dependent upon the context of attainment of concrete goals). Leontiev explains his use of the term 'operations' in the following way:

Every goal—even those such as like 'reach point N'—exists objectively in some object-related [environmental] situation. Of course, for the subject's consciousness the goal may be in the form of an abstraction from that situation, but his *action* cannot be abstracted from it. That is the reason why, aside from the intentional aspect (*what* must be accomplished) action also includes its operational aspect (*how*, in what way it can be accomplished), which is determined not by the goal in itself, but by the objective object-related [environmental] conditions of its accomplishment. In other words, the *action that is being carried out* matches the task; the task—that is the goal which is given under certain circumstances. That is why action has a special character that in special ways 'creates it—the ways by which it is carried out. I call these ways of accomplishment of action *operations*. (Leontiev, 1975, p. 107)

Leontiev's theory is founded on his understanding of motives as the results of individual-environment interaction. Motives, for Leontiev, constitute the object (which either exists in reality, or is constructed in the ideal sphere of a person) that directs the activity of the person towards him/herself. Leontiev posits the absolute existence of motives—according to him, 'non-motivated' activity cannot exist (if it seems to exist, it represents a case with hidden motives—cf. Leontiev, 1975, p. 102).

The human consciousness, according to Leontiev, emerges in ontogeny at the intersection of meanings of concepts in language that become internalized by persons in the course of activity. For Leontiev, the contrast between cultural meanings and their subjectivised counterparts, called 'personal senses' (*lichnostnyi smysl*, direct translation: 'personality-bound sense') largely parallels Vygotsky's emphasis on meaning vs. sense separation. However, there are two distinctions between Leontiev's view and that of Vygotsky. First, the development of meaning and sense in ontogeny is subsumed under the primacy of activity. Secondly, Leontiev explicitly bases his concept of 'personal sense' on Marx's writings, rather than those of Vygotsky (who in his turn borrowed it from Paulhan).

Leontiev explained his separation of *lichnostnyi smysl* from meaning on the basis of a school example:

all pupils of higher forms, of course, understand the meaning of examination results and their consequences very well. Nevertheless, one and the same grade may appear in the consciousness of each of them in different ways: say, as a step towards (or obstacle to) the choice of a profession, or as a means for actualizing one's self in the eyes of others, or perhaps in another way. That feature makes it necessary for psychology to separate the cognized objective meaning and the meaning-for-the-person. In order to avoid the doubling of the term, I prefer in the latter case to use the term *personal sense* (*lichnostnyi smysl*). In this case, our example can be expressed as follows: the meaning of a grade can acquire different personal senses in the consciousness of different pupils. (Leontiev, 1975, p. 145)

Leontiev emphasizes the relevance of the process of internalization in ontogeny as the mechanism by which individual consciousness emerges. The role of activity is of central importance in that process. Although Leontiev himself left the question of internalization largely unstudied, it has been the object of empirical study by another 'school' of Soviet psychological thought—that of Gal'perin (see Gal'perin, 1982).

The widespread use of Leontiev's theoretical system by other Soviet psychologists, particularly in the 1970s, was partly related to Leontiev's administrative position as the Dean of the Psychology Faculty at Moscow University. As a result, more than usual lip-service has been paid to Leontiev's theory by more empirically oriented researchers, which has not advanced the theory (although because of this Leontiev's theory has become well known in the USSR and internationally). However, in the last decade, efforts to advance Leontiev's activity theory further in a serious way have been undertaken (Asmolov & Petrovskii, 1978; Asmolov *et al.*, 1979).

'Neo-Leontievian' perspectives in contemporary Soviet psychology
The direction in which Leontiev's activity theory is being advanced by his younger-generation disciples is orthogonal to Leontiev's own emphasis on the structure of action. Asmolov and Petrovskii (1978, p. 70) have characterized that traditional view of activity as the *morphological paradigm* (which includes the analysis of activity structure described above), which they constrast with their *dynamic paradigm* in activity research. In the framework of the dynamic paradigm.

the analysis of activity involves the discovery of the specific nature of those moments which represent the dynamic side of activity and its structural components. The units that characterize the movement of activity, are: *set* [*ustanovka*] that is considered as the stabilizer of movement in the field of the starting situation of the unfolding activity, and *supersituative activity*. (Asmolov & Petrovskii, 1978, p. 72)

The concept of set that Asmolov and Petrovskii introduce into the dynamic view of the activity theory is related to Uznadze's

(1966b) respective concept, but is carefully distinguished by its authors from similar concepts of other Soviet psychologists ('relationship', as used by Miasishchev, 'meaningful experiences' by Bassin). The stabilizing role of set in the process of activity (Asmolov, 1977, 1979; Asmolov & Petrovskii, 1978) is observed in the continuity in the direction of activity under conditions of changing environmental demands. Three hierarchically organized levels of set are posited by Asmolov and Petrovskii. The highest level is conceptualized as *senseful set (smyslovaia ustanovka)*. It is an outgrowth from Leontiev's emphasis on *lichnostnyi smysl* that was described above. It involves the readiness of the personality for a certain activity in general. The next (lower) level of set is *goal set (tselevaia ustanovka)* that is present in cases where goals of actions can be demonstrated to be present in a person's behaviour. The condition in which the goal set can be studied is a situation where a subject's action is blocked from reaching towards goals. Finally, at the lowest level, Asmolov and Petrovskii (1978, p. 74) consider the *operational set (operatsional'naia ustanovka)* that is defined as 'the readiness for execution of a certain kind of action that emerges in the problem-solving situation on the basis of situational conditions and probabilistic prediction of the change of these conditions on the basis of previous experience' (Asmolov & Petrovskii, 1978. p. 74). The reflection of Leontiev's basic ACTIVITY-ACTION-OPERATION scheme is evident in the definition of the three levels of set.

V. A. Petrovskii's contribution to the innovation of Leontiev's activity theory concentrates on the concept of *suprasituative activity [nadsituativnaia aktivnost']*. The idea of suprasituative activity stems from Petrovskii's experimental work on pragmatically unmotivated risk-taking by subjects in experimental situations (Petrovskii, 1975). In the most general form, the term 'suprasituative activity' refers to the feature of activity that leads people to go beyond the 'optimal' (most pragmatic) ways of acting in any given situation. Relative to the demands of a situation, a person acts in it in ways that do not maximize gains through minimal efforts, but rather in ways that involve surplus of actions. The 'suprasituative activity' includes a wide variety of psychological phenomena: risk-taking, altruistic behaviour, emotional identification with social groups, emergence of cognitive motivation, and phenomena of exaggerated emphasis on the use of social norms in group activity situations.

The dynamic paradigm of activity theory has become popular among a number of psychologists of different areas and generations, all linked with Moscow University. In an article that served the function of a programmatic 'position statement' for future research (Asmolov *et al.*, 1979), both older-generation (e.g., Zeigarnik) and younger psychologists (Petrovskii, Asmolov) were united in their conviction that the dynamic paradigm in activity theory will move Leontiev's theory forward from the a stalemate it was perceived to have reached by the mid-1970s. This programmatic statement sets its goal as the study of the development of personality in a dialectical way, emphasizing the role of contradictions in development:

Anomalous, disharmonious development of personality, or, its opposite, normal, harmonious development do not differ from each other in that in the first case contradictions are present and in the second one absent. In both cases the contradictions remain the moving force. Only in the first case these contradictions, e.g., the contradiction between operational-technical and motivational sides of activity, become 'malignant' one way or another, are transformed into internal conflicts that are solved by inadequate ways, or alternatively, masked in the form of one or another form of 'psychological defence'. This only leads to the escalation of the emerging disharmony.

In the second case the contradictions appear in qualitatively variable forms. They appear as sufficiently conscious, clearly addressable in connection with the past and future of the subject, coordinated with general sense-generating aspirations and moral ideals of the person, i.e., they are in harmony with all of the development of the person in a general way. (Asmolov *et al.*, 1979, p. 39)

The emphasis on a holistic and dialectical study of personality in the context of neo-Leontievian activity theory has become widely popular among psychologists at Moscow University, where a number of investigators have switched from their previous interests in more narrowly defined research questions to the study of personality (e.g., Bratus', 1977a, 1977b; Gippenreiter, 1983; Viljunas, 1976). Undoubtedly this interest in personality is primarily general-psychological in nature, which is very appropriate given the history of activity theory from Vygotsky to the 'Kharkov school' of Leontiev and others, to Asmolov and Petrovskii in contemporary Soviet psychology. The emphasis on *developmental processes* within personality—both in their ontogenetic and especially microgenetic aspects—remain the core of the advancements of Leontiev's activity theory, whatever particular forms these advancements may end up taking.

Piagetian studies and Soviet cognitive-developmental psychology

Developmental cognitive psychology in the USSR historically is closely related to Piaget's work. Piaget's version of the 'clinical method' was taken over and put to innovative use by Basov, Vygotsky, Blonski, and others in the 1920s and 1930s. It constituted an important input to the thinking of the 'Kharkov school' of psychology who developed their own empirical methodology from its basis, remaining critical of a number of aspects in Piaget's theory (see Asnin, 1979–80, 1980–81; Zaporozhets & Lukov, 1979–80). It was very natural that the side of Piaget's thinking that psychologists in the USSR from the time of Vygotsky to the present have consistently rejected was that of individual-centred emphasis on development and lack of coverage of the social nature of children's environments. On the other hand, Piaget's interactionist view on child-object relationships as the vehicle for development made his thinking an ally of the emerging action-theoretic frameworks of Leontiev, Zaporozhets, Rubinshtein and Gal'perin.

Piaget's 'public fate' in Soviet psychology bears a resemblance to that of Vygotsky and Basov. After the 'great break' of the early 1930s, his theoretical and empirical work ceased to be translated, and he was rarely mentioned in approving terms. Piaget's theory became one of the many examples of the 'flaws' of non-Soviet ideas that had had the misfortune of emerging on 'bourgeois' grounds and were therefore useless for Soviet psychology. The attitude towards Piaget changed back to positive-but-critical only by the mid-1950s, when Piaget performed a role in re-opening contacts between Soviet psychologists and the international psychology community (see Piaget, 1956). That happened in the social context which allowed the reappearance of Vygotsky's name in the public discourse of Soviet psychologists. A number of new Russian translations of Piaget's own work (Piaget, 1969; Piaget & Inhelder, 1963) and of books about Piaget (Flavell, 1967) appeared.

In recent decades, a number of empirical studies in the USSR have been conducted in ways explicitly connected with Piaget's clever methods, or with his general methodology (Burmenskaia, 1978; Liders, 1978a, 1980a; Podgoretskaia, 1977; Subbotskii, 1984). Analyses of Piaget's methods and thinking have likewise become more frequent (Bil'chugov, 1978; Burmenskaia, 1978; Kaidanovskaia, 1984; Liders, 1978b; Obukhova, 1972). On the other hand, Vygotsky's tradition of linking interaction of children with others causally to their cognitive development (Rubtsov, 1980) provides the framework for utilizing Piagetian techniques.

Moral cognition and personality development

Issues of moral cognition are obviously very interesting subject matter for psychologists in any country. They acquire a special focus in the case of the USSR, where the prevailing cultural-political ideology has usually put much emphasis on the 'right' moral 'upbringing' of the 'new generation' (Tudge, 1983). A special issue of *Soviet psychology* (1983, 22, No. 1) on the topic of moral development gives the interested reader an exposure to Soviet psychologists' writing on that subject matter. A modern expression of the traditional sentiments accepted in Soviet society concerning the ideals of morality illustrates its particular relevance in society:

In the Soviet Union, moral education encompasses the fundamental aspects of the personality—the cognitive, emotional, and volitional facets. It seeks to forge them into a unity that is manifest in all the basic functional spheres of life (work, the acquisition of knowledge, social interaction, daily life, recreation) and that is embodied in the development of a consistent tendency to evaluate conduct (one's own or that of others) in light of communist morality—to experience an emotionally positive response to anything found to concur with those principles and, conversely, to respond negatively to all that runs counter to them. (Bodalev, 1983, p. 13)

This quote sets contemporary research on moral development in an appropriate light—it is perhaps impossible in any country to study the topic outside the society's definition of morality. In other words—the study of moral development of children is guided by the social definition of 'morality' in the culture of the investigators. In the context of Soviet psychology, issues of moral development are largely fused with the notion of personality. This is not surprising, since the moral side is the most important side of the Soviet ideal of harmoniously-developed personality.

Aside from many highly fluent writings by Soviet psychologists on moral development, some recent studies of children's moral thinking and its development have addressed the issues in a more concrete and empirical way (Iakobson, 1979; Iakobson & Pocherevina, 1982; Karpova & Petrushina, 1981; Subbotskii, 1977, 1978b, 1979, 1981b, 1983). Karpova and Petrushina (1981) address the issue of contextual embeddedness of the development of pre-schoolers' moral cognition. The context for that development—children's games and role-play—illustrates the social nature of moral-cognitive development. Subbotskii's and Iakobson's research concentrates on the coordination of pre-schoolers' action and reasoning about moral issues. On the other hand, the question of the purposeful formation of children's moral reasoning patterns has been of continued interest for Soviet psychologists. Thus, Shakirova (1981) demonstrated the influence of moral rules embedded in literature texts in the 5th-grade curriculum, on the children's ways of moral reasoning. Lipkina (1980) addressed the issue of the relationship of schoolchildren's moral cognition to the problems of formation of the 'communist world view'. This line of research continues the traditions of Soviet pedagogical psychology of the previous decades (Kairov & Bogdanova, 1979; Krasnobaev, 1960; Menchinskaia, 1975, 1978).

Issues of motivation, the relationships of needs and actions, and the problem of intentionality of children's actions are likewise continuous topics of research in Soviet child psychology. That interest is rooted in the connection with German motivation psychology (Narciss Ach in the first decades of the century, Kurt Lewin in the 1920s—see Bakanov, 1977; Bibrikh, 1978; Patiaeva, 1983), and has been maintained by Soviet authors' own interest in the general-psychological view of personality (Antsyferova, 1981; Gippenreiter, 1983; Leontiev, 1975; Lomov, 1981; Petrovskii, 1981a, 1981b; Petrovskii & Petrovskii, 1982), and a multi-faceted systemic view of human beings (Ananiev, 1965, 1966a, 1980). It is therefore not surprising to find Soviet views of motivation intertwined with other aspects of personality (Nepomniashchaia *et al.*, 1980), cultural history (Tulviste, 1981c), activity and its social guidance (Markova, 1979, 1980, 1986; Morgun, 1976), and situation (Patiaeva, 1983). Discussions on the inclusion of motives in Leontiev's activity theory (e.g., Kovalev, 1981) seem to keep the interest in motivation at the centre of attention in Soviet psychology.

The personality theory of Lidia Bozhovich (1968, 1978, 1979a, 1979b) is perhaps the most directly developmental view on personality among other conceptualizations of that complex issue by Soviet psychologists. It is noteworthy in at least two particular aspects. First, it is a surviving historical connection between Vygotsky's original views, through the 'Kharkov school', and present-day Soviet research on personality. Secondly, Bozhovich builds her system of personality development on the concept of children's needs, in relation with the organizing role of child development by society (on education, see Bozhovich, 1969). In line with the dialectical idea of 'controversy' of opposites that is overcome in the process of development, Bozhovich outlines four basic 'crisis periods' in the development of children's personality: at the age of one, three and seven years, and at adolescence. The Vygotskian line in Bozhovich's personality theory involves the increasing role of developing consciousness in the further development of personality. The first year of a child's life mostly concerns the child's immediate relationship with the environment. In the second year of life, a new kind of psychological structure— 'motivating representations' (*motiviruiushchie predstavlenia*)— constitutes a first step towards the establishment of more efficient mediating devices (e.g., speech) in personality organization. These 'motivating representations' enable the child to regulate his internal impulses, and constitute the result of the first synthesis of cognitive and affective components of his psychological processes. The child can 'go beyond' the immediate situation s/he is currently in, with the help of the 'motivating representations', which generate the child's decision to act according to his internal reasons (for example, the 'protest' of a child when his actions are blocked by circumstances).

At the three-years' crisis period, Bozhovich sees the differentiation of the child as subject from the field of objects. At this change period, the child already cognizes his 'I' and demands opportunities for self-activity ('I want to do it myself'). This transition moves the child further away from the influence of the immediate situation, and generates his tendency to *actively change the situation*, transforming it for the purpose of satisfying his needs and wishes.

The 'crisis' at the age of seven is viewed by Bozhovich at the intersection of the child's own needs and the social conditions for their satisfaction. In this sense, the 'social I' develops in the child's personality—the child tries to participate in the social system, which in Bozhovich's case (given the Soviet educational system) means a transition into school activities and environment.

Finally, at adolescence the child develops self-consciousness in the fullest sense of that term—s/he can direct the cognitive processes on to the study of her/himself, and can generate new self-perceptions in highly creative ways. The 'adolescent crisis' ends, according to Bozhovich, in that the young person's self-representation becomes stabilized and placed in an appropriate locus in the social matrix of society. New, socially appropriate goals are being set by adults, whereas in the adolescent period the person demonstrated strength of will, paired with 'weakness' (i.e., from the perspective of adults and society) of goals.

The importance given to the period of adolescence in Bozhovich's theory of personality development is matched by increasing interest in the study of different psychological issues of adolescence in contemporary Soviet developmental psychology (Fel'dshtein, 1982; Safin, 1982; Zakharov, 1982). At the Institute of General and Pedagogical Psychology of the Academy of Pedagogical Sciences in Moscow, the research laboratory of Pedagogics of Adolescence has made the issues of adolescents' personality development the major object of investigation (Fel'dshtein, 1983). The major focus of the research—integration of adolescents' activity and thinking with 'socially useful activity' (Fel'dshtein, 1980, 1982)—illustrates the root of the psychological problem of adolescence in contemporary Soviet society. If, in the 1920s, the soliciting of young people to transform the 'old' society (of the parents' generation) into 'new' made use of the psychology of adolescents (see Chapters III and VII), then by the 1980s it is the adolescents' potential search for 'self' that is to be formed in accordance with the rules and ideals of their parents. The educational relevance—the formation of personality of adolescents—is again the major direction of research, as in the rest of Soviet cognitive and personality research.

Development of speech and its functions in psychological development

The question of how children acquire language is usually one of the most interesting topics for child psychologists of any country and language background. Soviet developmental psychology is no exception. Interest in children's language development has been prominent in it over decades (Gvozdev, 1927, 1948; Kol'tsova, 1958; Luria & Iudovich, 1956; Rozengart-Pupko, 1948; Rybnikov, 1926, 1927; Vigotsky, 1934). However, there is a particular way of viewing the process of language acquisition by the majority of Soviet developmental psychologists that has been under-represented in international research on developmental psycholinguistics. In one version it involves the *study of the function of the developing speech of the child in further organization of the child's development*. In other incarnations, the particular standpoint involves *systemic* analysis of the acquisition of language in the context of other psychological processes (for example, in 'higher nervous activity').

The role of speech in control of psychological functions

The interest in the role of speech in organization of higher psychological processes that emerged in the context of Vygotsky's cultural-historical paradigm (see Chapter IV) has continued to be prominent in Soviet developmental psychology over the decades since Vygotsky's death (see overviews by Wilder, 1975–76; Wozniak, 1972). The advancement of this angle of approach to speech is largely the result of the activity of Alexander Luria, who has paid special interest to the issues of speech, whichever area of psychology he happened to work in, at different times during his professional career. Luria's interest in the role of speech functions in the organization of psychological processes dates back to the 1920s (see Luria, 1982, p.94), and it was further facilitated by Vygotsky's emphasis on the role of semiotic systems as mediating higher psychological processes (Luria, 1928d). In the late 1920s and early 1930s, Luria conducted empirical studies on the linguistic environments of children of different social backgrounds (Luria, 1978a), and on the development of writing in ontogeny (Luria, 1978b). Likewise, Luria's research on cognitive processes in twins (Luria, 1936) included an emphasis on the use of language by the child for regulation of cognition (more particularly, for memorizing). Furthermore, during Luria's association with the Medical-Genetic Institute in Moscow in the 1930s he could gain access to twins with delays in language development attributable to the 'twin situation' (in which interaction between the twins was sufficient, and hindered further advancement of either of the children towards adult-like speech). Luria's experimental-clinical intervention with such twins was to provide them with separate new environments where advancement of language skills was made necessary by planned scheduling of teachers' demands for appropriate language use. Together with the improvement of language skills, the twins' actions in play became more complex, and the newly improved speech forms became integrated into play (activity), and likewise into the thinking processes of the twins. The study illustrated the relevance of the connection of interaction and cognition as studied through 'teaching experiment' methodology advocated by Vygotsky (see Luria & Iudovich, 1956).

From the early 1950s onward, Luria's research with mentally retarded and normal children resulted in his well-known experimentation on the excitation/inhibition of speech and motor systems (Luria, 1956, 1958, 1960; Luria & Vinogradova, 1959). His interest in speech and language in the context of his neuropsychological investigations is very widely known and appreciated (Luria, 1966, 1976b). Finally, Luria's life-long interest in developmental aspects of speech is reflected in the publication of his lecture course on *Language and consciousness* (Luria, 1979).

Aside from the Vygotsky-Luria tradition of viewing the development of speech in the context of cognitive organization of the person, different researchers in the USSR have addressed other issues of children's development of speech (see El'konin, 1971 for an overview). One of the research orientations that deserves a short overview is the study of the development of infant babbling, and of the emergence of speech from babbling.

Development of infants' babbling
Interest in the development of infants' vocal play (babbling) was already present in the early years of Soviet developmental psychology (Goer & Goer, 1927). However, the most notable and thorough research programme on the development of babbling is that of Vladimir I. Bel'tiukov at the Institute of Defectology of the

Academy of Pedagogical Sciences in Moscow (Bel'tiukov, 1964, 1977; Bel'tiukov & Salakhova, 1973, 1975).

In a careful longitudinal study of five infants, Bel'tiukov and Salakhova (1973) revealed that the acoustic content of babbling is much more varied than the language environment available in the speech of adults around the child. Babbling, therefore, cannot be considered a product of imitation of the speech by the infant, but is rather a result of the unfolding of a speech-motor programme that generates an excess of produced sounds of highly varied kinds, out of which the interaction experience with adults further forms the phonological repertoire of the child's mother-tongue speech. Furthermore, research by Bel'tiukov and his colleagues has revealed particular sequences of sounds that appear, are maintained, and disappear in the course of babbling as the infant develops (Bel'tiukov, 1977; Bel'tiukov & Salakhova, 1975). The unfolding vocal programme of the babbling infant has a set of inbuilt articulatory constraints that provide for a margin of variability in the development of individual infants' babbling, while still demonstrating some universal sequences in development of sounds. They also demonstrated that the frequency of use of different sounds has no effect on the sequence of their appearance in the developmental sequence of speech sounds (Bel'tiukov & Salakhova, 1975, p. 77). Instead, new sounds can appear on the basis of the already existing sound structure of an infant's babbling, under the guidance of adults within the zone of proximal development (Bel'tiukov & Salakhova, 1973, p. 110). In the context of social interaction of infants with adults, the speech-sound system develops along lines of differentiation and integration, thus exemplifying the 'analysis by synthesis' principle (Bel'tiukov, 1977, p. 105). That principle has been emphasized constantly by different developmental theorists (Basov, Rubinshtein) in Soviet psychology over the past decades.

Development of visual-motor actions and perception in infancy

The tradition of psychological thinking in the Soviet Union that has guided investigators towards empirical studies of child development is the emphasis on the *active nature* of the organism relative to its environment. Emerging originally in Soviet psychology in conjunction with the acceptance of Marxist philosophy as its basis, this emphasis laid the foundation for a number of empirical efforts by psychologists to study the active nature of basic psychological processes both in adults (e.g., Zinchenko & Vergiles, 1969), and in children (Zaporozhets *et al.*, 1967).

Contemporary research on issues of development in infancy by psychologists working in the Soviet Union has emerged from two historical traditions. Traditions of Russian reflexology in its different forms (Pavlovian, Bekhterevian, etc.) form the basis of some of the contemporary efforts to understand infants' behavioural physiology. This tradition is linked with contemporary research efforts by the intermediaries who in the past have extended reflexological approaches to infancy (Kasatkin, 1935, 1948, 1951; Shchelovanov, 1948) or in a wider phylogenetic context (Ladygina-Kots, 1935; Tihh, 1966, 1970; Troshikhina, 1973). It is also related to the mechanisms of the orienting reflex that have been of interest to Soviet physiologists and psychologists.

The study of infants' development of behavioural and physiologically governed relationships with the environment has become a topic of investigation for a number of researchers (Beteleva, Dubrovinskaya, & Farber, 1977; Fonarev, 1977; Gizatullina, 1974; Kozlova, 1978; Mit'kin, 1981; Mit'kin & Yamshchikov, 1978; Mit'kin, Sergienko & Yamshchikov, 1978; 1979; Mit'kin, Kozlova, Sergienko & Yamshchikov, 1978; Polikanina, 1966; Sergienko, 1981; Varjun, 1981). The study of infant development is of interest to Soviet psychologists less as an object in itself, than as a preliminary stage for further development.

A.M. Fonarev's research on infants' visual-orienting reactions

The work on infancy by Alexander M. Fonarev spans a long period of time (since the late 1950s), but has over these decades remained largely unpublished. The major published results of his long-term research efforts are available in a little book titled *The development of orienting reactions in children* (Fonarev, 1977).

Fonarev's interest in newborns' visual reactions stems from his theoretical thinking about the adaptation of the developing organism to the new environment in which vision becomes the major channel by which the organism is stimulated by its surroundings. Fonarev has studied newborns' visual reactions to the presentation of a spheric object (a ball, 4 cm in diameter, in which a battery-operated electric light was mounted). One side of the sphere was transparent and was used as the stimulus for the newborn, the other side did not let light through and thus did not expose the investigator. The sphere was moved on an arc at 40 cm from the eyes of the newborn. Its presentation triggered in all children (N=5, maximum age 10 hours) a defensive reaction of eyelid movements, which, however, did not occur in all trials (e.g., Fonarev, 1977, p. 21 reports data on the basis of which we can calculate that this reaction occurred on 14.5% of trials—summed over 4 newborns—19 responses to 131 trials). Together with eyelid movements, Fonarev could observe the turning of the eyeballs as a response to stimulation in 2 out of 5 under-10-hour old newborns. By the fourth day of life all 5 children demonstrated the presence of oculomotor responses to the stimulus presentation, which still fell short of visual pursuit of the stimulus. At 8 days, 4 out of 5 children did demonstrate visual following of the moving stimulus, in conjunction with head movements, but with relative inhibition of the movements of the rest of the body. The reaction to the stimulus remained relatively infrequent, taking place on 20% of trials (Fonarev, 1977, p. 22).

The size of the functional visual field for triggering eye movements among newborns

In order to reveal the developmental process by which inborn visual-motor behaviour is transferred into the visual-orienting response, Fonarev was faced with the task of finding out what areas of the newborns' retinae are sensitive to visual stimulation which leads to oculomotor response. He modified the situation of perimetry for the use with infants. The infant subject was facing a spheric visual environment within which along two axes (horizontal and vertical) a light spot could be moved. At the beginning of each trial, a light spot was presented in the middle of the infant's visual field. One second later, another light spot appeared in a special location on either the horizontal or vertical axis of the sphere and started moving in the direction opposite to the centre of the child's visual field. In Fonarev's cross-sectional study (of 24 infants within the age range 13 days to 6 months 29 days) the 'receptor zone' of the oculomotor reflex was found to increase from 5 to 42 degrees along the horizontal axis, and from 1 to 31 degrees on the vertical axis (cf. data table in Fonarev, 1977, pp. 53 and 55).

Fonarev's theoretical goal is to go beyond the simple view of the orienting reaction as a simple transformation of an unconditioned reflex into a conditional one. Instead, he provides the following description of the structure of the orienting reactions:

They [i.e., orienting reactions] only externally appear as if they are elementary reactions to novelty. In reality these reactions have a three-phase structure. During the first phase, the reaction indeed is 'released' by the external agent as *reaction*; but it continues (second phase) as action, as active search, of course— not for the novelty itself (how can one look for something that is not known?)— but for the known meaning in the indeterminate signal. In the process of that search unexpected characteristics may be revealed, but those are represented already in the personal contact with the object and associated with it only by that contact. During the third phase, when the signal has been recognized, the orienting actions stops. In other words, the orienting search lasts until (within a limited time frame) a realistic result of this sensor/motor action is reached. The result of the action functions also at the same time as feedback ('reverse afferentation' in P.K. Anokhin's terminology) that blocks the activity of muscles that serve the receptive process. (Fonarev, 1977, p. 80)

Fonarev does not suggest any new mechanism to explain the development of the orienting response itself over time. His account of how, starting from the reflexive following of stimuli by eye movements, infants develop more complex forms of orienting activity resolves the issue by attributing that development to conditional reflex formation (Fonarev, 1977, p. 80). He does not analyze the actual process of that development theoretically, although empirical reflection of it is embedded in his longitudinal study of the early ontogeny of visual reactions of newborns during their stay in the maternity hospital.

Research on infants' eye movements by A.A. Mit'kin and his colleagues

The research group on early ontogeny of infant vision emerged within the institutional framework of the Institute of Psychology of the Academy of Sciences in Moscow around the mid-1970s, as a result of young psychologists concentrating around A.A. Mit'kin who previously had become known as a specialist in electro-oculography. The research group included a number of young investigators whose dissertations were devoted to the study of different aspects of the study of infants' eye movements, using the techniques of oculography (Y. Sergienko, Y. Kozlova, A. Yamshchikov). As a rule, the empirical studies conducted by members of this group take place in 'children's homes'—child-care centres in which infants live, either permanently (e.g., after being given up by their mothers when they were born) or temporarily (e.g., students giving their infants over to the care of the centre for some time during which they are involved with their studies).

A number of interesting empirical research results have emerged from the work of Mit'kin's group since its beginning. Among the few groups in contemporary developmental psychology in the USSR which have studied infancy, this group is by far the most interrelated in its ideas and research practices with similar research done in other countries.

Infants' eye movements in response to stationary and moving stimuli

As the first theme of studies that have emanated from their work, *the development of eye movements in infancy* should be mentioned (Kozlova & Mit'kin, 1977; Mit'kin, Sergienko, & Yamshchikov, 1978). In order to study infants' (2–16 weeks of age) eye movements in response to moving stimuli, different stimuli (lights, toys) were moved at the distance of 50cm from the bridge of the child's nose, in the radius of 50 degrees and at speeds of 12 and 24 degrees. The infants were kept in the horizontal (supine) position in the course of the experiments. The stimulus object was moved horizontally in their visual field at the given speed and within the 50-degree radius. In the stationary stimulus conditions, the infants were faced with an arc with 9 holes (each 5 degrees apart, at 40cm from the child, with the fixation point at the centre of the 40-degree arc). In 8 of these holes (the 9th being the fixation point) stimuli (lights, or lighted objects) could appear and disappear in any order.

The first noteworthy finding reported by Mit'kin, Sergienko and Yamshchikov (1978, pp. 174 and 176) pertains to the *unity of movement and stimulus form* in the triggering of infants' eye movements. Already at the age of 3–4 weeks a moving doll captivates the infants' visual following much more than a simple moving light stimulus. The same was observed in the experimental condition with stationary stimuli the location of which was altered on the perimeter arc to trigger eye movements—among 8-week-old infants the alteration of the location of *objects* as stimuli triggered eye movement responses 2.5 times more frequently than the relocation of a simple light stimulus on the same arc. These results can be viewed as indicating that for young infants responding to form of stimulus and its movement is not functionally separate—infants respond to 'moving forms' (objects in motion) rather than to the characteristics of movement and form as separate from one another. Traditional research on infant vision has often separated these two characteristics from one another, largely by the habit of experimenting with these characteristics separately in studies of adult vision. Mit'kin *et al.*'s (1978) results in this respect are relevant to current international literature on infants' visual-oculomotor or visual-manual actions which demonstrates the presence of response to moving objects in early infancy.

The development of visual pursuit of moving stimuli in infants was found to proceed in the following way. At first, in the very early ontogeny, the infant moves his eyes from one fixation point to a new one through a series of saccades which are separated from one another by fixating pauses. As the infants develop further, the amplitude of the saccades decreases, together with a decrease in the length of fixations in between these saccades. This leads to increasingly smooth pursuit movements of the infants' eyes following a moving object. As Mit'kin *et al.* (1978, p. 176) indicate, the development of the smoothness of infants' visual pursuit includes the decrease of intra-individual variability of the saccade amplitudes over time—from the age of 6-weeks where the coefficients of variation of saccade amplitudes of individual children ranged from 45 to 33%, to those at 14 weeks where they ranged between 26 and 20%. It must be emphasized that the development seems to be a reconstruction based on cross-sections of infants of different ages—in any case the authors do not provide specific information about the longitudinal nature of the observations.

Extension of movement: infants' responses to opto-kinetic stimulation

Sergienko's work (1981) has been devoted to the study of infants' (three age groups: 4–6, 8–16, and 24 weeks) eye movements in response to conditions of simultaneous (and conflicting) movement of two stimuli. This research originated directly in the study of the question of opto-kinetic nystagmus in adults. The infants—again in the supine position—were presented (at 40 cm distance) with the background of vertically placed black and white bands (each 6 degrees wide). This background could be moved at constant speed (either 12 or 24 degs.) to the left, or right. On the black-and-white background, a red 12-degrees wide square as the stimulus could likewise be moved horizontally to the left or right. As can be seen, this experimental situation is a modification of the one described above, with the addition of movement of the homogeneous but structured background of the moving object. The oculographic registration of eye movements afforded the registration of both the visual following of the stimulus and the opto-kinetic nystagmus in response to the moving background.

Cross-sectional comparison of the visual responses to the moving stimulus/background relationship conditions revealed a tendency towards decrease of the percentage of opto-kinetic nystagmus (out of all eye movements) from 57% at 4–6 weeks to around 25% by 24 weeks of age. At the same time, the percentage of visual pursuit movements increased from under 20% to over 65% of the total number of movements observed (and accumulated over individual infants—cf. Sergienko, 1981, p. 58, Fig. 2). A basic qualitative change in infants' eye movements was observed at the 8–16 weeks age, where full-scale (i.e., following the object's movement to the maximal state of their sidewise movement) visual pursuit was observed in the form of smooth (as opposed to the earlier, saccadic) movements. By the age of 24 weeks infants developed preference for visual pursuit of the stimulus object and could follow it despite the interference that the moving stripe pattern of the background created.

Visual-vestibular interaction in infancy

Investigations of infants by Mit'kin's group have likewise studied the other side of movement of the background of the stimulus—the movement of the 'background' of the perceiving visual system, i.e., the body. The issue of interaction between vestibular and visual systems has definitely been an understudied topic in contemporary international developmental psychology, despite its underlying reality in the history of childcare, as illustrated by the example of cradles, and the use of waterbeds in the care of premature infants (e.g. see Korner, 1979).

Mit'kin's (1981) investigation of how the vestibular and visual system of 2–16-week-old infants are coordinated involves an experiment which recreates a 'cradle' situation for the infant whose eye movements are oculographically studied under the conditions of vestibular stimulation (rocking of the cradle around the axis coinciding with that of the infant's body in supine position). Infants' eye movements were triggered by using two types of stimuli. The first type—the 'coordinated' condition—consisted of a stimulus moving in unison with the cradle (attached to the moving cradle—on a screen at 20–25cm from the eyes). The second type—the 'conflict' condition—involved a stimulus 'moving' in the direction opposite to the cradle movement. The latter 'movement' was due to the stimulus being attached to the side of the stationary infant crib into which the experimental cradle was put. So, for instance, when the infant in the cradle was moved in one direction (e.g., to the left), the stimulus (which was attached to the right side of the stationary crib structure) was replaced ('moved') to the opposite direction (right) in the visual field of the infant (cf. Mit'kin, 1981, p. 69, Fig. 1).

Infants' eye movements under the condition of vestibular stimulation in the cradle were studied both when the infants were asleep and when they were awake. In the sleep state—more specifically in the beginning stage of sleep during which retinal afferent stimulation is minimized while the REM-stage has not yet been reached—more or less 'pure' influences of the vestibular stimulation on infants' eye movements can be studied. It was found that in sleeping infants of the 2–16-week age range the registered compensatory eye movements were of *smooth tonic* nature at all frequencies of vestibular stimulation provided. These movements afford the study of the neuro-motor coordination of the vestibular and visual-motor systems under conditions of no visual input. In contrast, the *anti-compensatory saccadic* eye movements (ACSs) violate that pattern of smoothness in the infants' visual-motor response to vestibular stimulation while sleeping. These movements involve quick saccades *in the direction of the movement of the cradle*, rather than in the opposite (compensatory) direction. As Mit'kin argues (1981, p. 73), the presence of the ACSs in the visual-motor activity of a sleeping infant can be considered an indicator of the active character of the infant's relation to the environment. The proportion of ACSs in the total visual-motor activity of sleeping infants increases dramatically with age. In fact, the ACSs may illustrate the relative conventionality of the separation of 'sleep' and 'wakefulness' states in infancy: up to 2 months of age in infants even in the 'awake' condition and under conditions of visual stimulation *the vestibular input constitutes the dominating force in their oculo-motor activity*. This is empirically indicated by infrequent presence and low amplitude of ACSs in the oculographic recordings. They do not violate the smooth, sinusoidal pattern of vestibular effects on the eye movements. The period between 2 and 4 months of life is characterized by a dramatic increase in the number of ACSs in infants' eye movements that also occur at frequencies different to those of the vestibular stimulation provided.

The visual stimuli that the infant encounters while awake begin to introduce irregularities to the eye movements that are otherwise controlled by the vestibular input. Mit'kin had already observed the occurrence of this at the end of the first month of age. The results of the experimental procedure where the visual and vestibular inputs could be varied in different combinations revealed a reciprocal functional relationship in the work of these two psychological systems: the activation of the visual input channel attenuated the effect of the vestibulum on the eye movement, and the increase in the vestibular input leads to the lessening of the effectiveness of the retinal input (Mit'kin, 1981, p. 75). The vestibulo-oculomotoric system can be considered to be a phylogenetically ancient mechanism that emerges hetero-chronically in ontogeny.

The research in Mit'kin's group in Moscow has been devoted to the study of oculomotoric behaviour in infancy, together with different factors that influence that behaviour. The emphasis of the theoretical ideas that have underlain the research of this group is explicitly developmental and physiological, as the oculomotoric system in its physiological organization is the target of the study. In the empirical realm, Mit'kin's group has demonstrated careful and meticulous efforts to describe the oculomotor behavior of infants in detail which, of course, is made possible by the use of electro-oculographic techniques widely used on adult subjects. In general, it would be fair to say that the work of Mit'kin's group serves as one of the best examples of new contemporary scientific tendencies in developmental psychology in the USSR, as it has moved from Soviet psychology's rich traditions of the study of eye movements of adults to the study of the same function in infants.

Summary: interdependence of action, cognition and perception

The ways in which Soviet psychologists have viewed children's cognitive and personality development throughout childhood have proceeded in directions that are quite different from mainstream psychology in Western Europe and North America. The major issue embedded in almost every publication by a Soviet developmental psychologist on these topics is that of the emergence of qualitatively new psychological phenomena in the process of development of action and congition. Consequently, the analysis of empirical phenomena in the writings of less theoretically and more empirically oriented researchers is qualitative-structural, rather than quantitative. It is easy to connect this style of data presentation with events in the history of Soviet psychology (see Chapter III), particularly in the 1930s. However, the easy attribution of causality for the qualitative emphasis of Soviet cognitive and action research to the effects of administrative-political elimination of paedology from Soviet society would be an oversimplification. The 1936 decree outlawing paedology on educational-political grounds was only an external mediator in the development of Soviet cognitive-developmental research, which independently had already moved away from excessive quantification. The work of psychologists who have given Soviet developmental psychology its characteristic form (Vygotsky, Basov, Leontiev, Zaporozhets, Gal'perin, Bozhovich, and others) was, prior to the 1936 decree, already oriented in the qualitative direction.

All the different approaches to cognitive development in the USSR share a number of general features, even if the authors of these approaches may be in recurrent disagreement with one another. These features are: (1) a qualitative-structural, rather than quantitative perspective on cognitive phenomena; (2) the view that development results from the child's *active* influence on the environment, and the feedback of the latter on the child; (3) the emergence of cognitive processes in the context of action; and (4) the active formation of the cognitive functions of the child by purposeful educators (adults). Finally (5), children's speech development has been viewed in Soviet developmental psychology as the highest mediator (organizer) of other psychological processes. This perspective emerges from different standpoints— whether Vygotskian, Luria's, or neo-Pavlovian (Bekhterevian).

If the first three aspects make Soviet traditions in cognitive development similar to Piaget's research programme, then the fourth and the fifth set up a basic distinction which Soviet psychologists have actively used to separate themselves from Piaget. The roots of that distinction can be traced to the cultural history of Russia as compared to Western Europe (cf. Chapter II). What is characteristic of developmental cognitive research in the USSR may stem on the one hand from the cultural-cognitive axiom that posits relatedness of a person with others (their interdependence), and from futuristic goal-orientation (exemplified by the hope of formation of a new kind of person in the web of Soviet society) on the other. It need not be an overstatement to claim that most of Soviet cognitive-developmental research is closely intertwined with problems of social development, and vice versa.

VII Social Organization of Child Development

The social nature of the development of individual-psychological functions has been the basis for all Soviet psychology, from the times of Vygotsky and Basov to the present day. Besides active declarative statements by many Soviet psychologists who never seem to get tired of talking about the social nature of human development, some investigators have tried to study it empirically. These studies have covered almost the whole range of childhood ages. In line with the major characteristic of Soviet traditions in psychology, researchers have emphasized interdependence of the social and cognitive lines of development rather that studying these topics separately.

Research on children's social development in Soviet psychology has two historical 'peak' periods: the 1920s, and from the 1970s to the present time. A number of general topics of research have recurred in Soviet developmental psychology in the area of children's social development. First, the establishment and dynamics of *children's relationships with others* (teachers, parents, peers) has become widespread in recent decades. Secondly, the principles of the establishment, maintenance, and dissipation of *children's social groups and collectives* have been actively studied. Besides these recurrent themes, other topics were actively studied by Soviet psychologists in the 1920s, but interest in these remains rare in the present day. These include: the study of the effects of children's social class background, and their urban versus rural life environments on children's relationships and psychological development; the nature of children's world view and understanding of society and its institutions; the development of children's relationships with labour in different environmental conditions. These topics were of high importance in the social context of the 1920s, but no longer in the 1970s.

The goal of this chapter is to provide an overview of a number of directions of research on children's social development, covering

240

the whole age range from infancy to adolescence. The overview is purposefully selective, concentrating on those ideas and empirical studies that are closest to basic issues of child development research, rather than those which are of local relevance to the Soviet educational system.

Research on social interaction

Both in the 1920s and again in the 1970s, two lines of approach to the study of interaction (*obshchenie*: the meaning of the English term 'interaction' is not exactly equivalent) have been present in Soviet psychology. The first of them is rooted in the work of Bekhterev (see Chapter 3) and advances further some of the ideas expressed in his *Collective reflexology* (e.g., Lomov, 1980). The second line has its original basis in Vygotsky's theory, modified by A. N. Leontiev's activity theory and expressed in the work of his son (A. A. Leontiev, 1974). The major difference between these approaches as they are represented in contemporary Soviet psychological literature is in their relationship to empirical investigation. The 'Bekhterev-Lomov paradigm' mainly uses experimental methodology to determine in what ways interaction between persons ('subject'—'subject' relationship) has an effect on their individual performance in some problem-solving task ('subject'—'object' relationship: Lomov, 1975, 1976). Experimental evidence of this kind has been obtained outside developmental psychology (e.g., Nosulenko, 1979; Zabrodin & Nosulenko, 1979), with the aim of proving that interaction as a condition for individuals' work can facilitate their individual performance. The question of *how* interaction works while influencing individuals' actions largely remains beyond the scope of interest of this approach. In contrast, the action-theoretic approach to interaction (A. A. Leontiev, 1974) is by far less directly related to empirical investigation. If it addresses empirical issues, these are studied mostly by observational and rarely by experimental means, and usually by investigators for whom the action-theoretic perspective is in addition to their personal or humanitarian interest in practical issues concerning children (e.g., Lisina's research). Furthermore, the socio-geographical side of these two approaches is also disjunct—the Bekhterev-Lomov approach has developed mostly in Leningrad and has only in the last decade established its grounds in Moscow (at the Institute of Psychology of the Academy of Sciences), whereas the action-theoretic perspective has disseminated in Moscow in institutions where disciples of A.N. Leontiev work.

Of course, the dividing line between these two approaches is not strict, neither are they at present in exclusive conflict with each other. Rather, both benefit from the wave of interest in interaction and interpersonal relationships that became popular in Soviet psychology during the 1970s. Like fads and fashions in Western psychology, the overwhelming appeal that the word *obshchenie* has for Soviet developmental psychologists generates more vocally voluminous interest than direct active research. Fortunately, there are exceptions. The most notable research group devoted to the study of children's interaction is that of Maia Lisina in Moscow.

Studies of interaction in infancy: M.I. Lisina and her laboratory

The work by numerous investigators of social interaction in infancy that from the beginning of the 1970s emerged within the framework of the Laboratory of the Psychology of Children of Toddler and Preschool Age at the Institute of General and Pedagogical Psychology in Moscow is fortunately available to international readers in the form of a review article written by the instigator of most of this research—Maia I. Lisina (Lisina, 1982a). As the name of Lisina's laboratory implies, the research activity of its members goes beyond infancy and covers children's social development across the whole pre-school age range (0–7 years). In this chapter, however, only the theoretical bases of Lisina's thinking and her, as well as her colleagues', work on infancy are considered. The present author limits his treatment of the infancy-related work by Lisina and her colleagues to two major issues that may require explanation: the theoretical background of Lisina's research programme, and the role of the empirical data in it.

Lisina's theoretical background
Lisina has not enriched psychology with a new theory of early interaction, nor is it easy to ascribe her work to a tendency towards

following any particular Soviet psychologist. It is true that Lisina herself tried to make explicit her following of A.N. Leontiev's activity theory (Lisina, 1974a, 1974b, 1978a, 1982a, 1982b). She can also be observed to refer to Vygotsky's heritage of the study of 'higher psychological processes'. However, this declaration of theoretical roots seems to be determined largely by the fashion of Soviet psychologists in Moscow to claim allegiance to Leontiev's meta-theory of activity. Lisina's empirical studies bear little relation to Leontiev's thinking about activity, actions and operations, and instead reflect a close connection with the earlier systemic thinking of Bekhterevian paediatricians Nikolai Shchelovanov and his colleagues (Shchelovanov, 1938; Shchelovanov & Aksarina, 1939) who were interested in complex analysis of behavioural development in infancy with a particular emphasis on child development in institutions. She also follows the traditions of N. Figurin and M. Denisova, whose earlier studies on infant development are repeatedly cited in Lisina's writings (Figurin & Denisova, 1949). In many ways, Lisina's interest in the role of social interaction in the lives of institution-reared infants makes her related to the Western psychological tradition of John Bowlby—whose work Lisina has known well for decades (Lisina, 1961), but whose theoretical background she has consistently rejected in favour of Russian thinkers of the past. Lisina's theoretical roots—whatever they are—remain thoroughly embedded in the Soviet psychology of the post-Vygotsky era.

Lisina described her definition of interaction ('*obshchenie*') as:

... the process of mutual action of people, which is directed towards coordination and unification of their energy with the goal of reaching a common result. It is necessary to take into account that the concept of interaction is not equal in its meaning to the concept of activity—interaction usually makes up only one side of such activity. Two characteristics are specific to the act of interaction: its object is another person (partner); and that both participants in interaction are active, so that each of them alternates between being the object and the subject of activity. (Lisina, 1974b, p. 5)

Lisina's effort to talk about interaction as an aspect of activity may illustrate her inconsistency in following the prevailing fashion of her day which wanted to reduce all interaction to activity. In the same paper in which Lisina at first refuses to reduce interaction to activity (1974b, p. 5), some pages later (pp. 8–13) she agrees to equate interaction with activity. She insists upon considering interaction *a special kind of activity—communicative activity* (see also: Lisina, 1980, p. 3; 1982a, p. 134). Such theoretical eclecticism illustrates Lisina's role as an empirically minded child psychologist who cares much for the social life conditions of infants' environments, but who also tries to present herself as a theorist in the philosophically-oriented scene of contemporary Soviet psychology.

Lisina's empirical orientation and the way it is coupled with theoretical electicism is also affected by a theoretical feature of her interpretation of the activity theory of A.N. Leontiev—the empirically 'hidden' nature of the needs. Lisina illustrated that feature in her effort to analyze the process of activity and its study:

Activity—that is the need *that is already weighted by matter and words, expectations, and memories.* When we say that the subject experiences a need, *we usually prove it by references to the subsequent activity, that he later develops. When we say that the subject is cognitively active, we list the states that are not yet activity, but which already give evidence about the readiness for it* (signs of interest, attention, signals of preparation for the beginning of the work). (Lisina, 1982b, p. 22)

This quote reflects the theoretically fuzzy issue that Lisina has to deal with. On the one hand, 'needs' are considered to be psychological phenomena that provide 'energy' for the emergence of activity. However, since they are influential in the 'pre-activity' phase of empirical observations, the investigator is faced with a serious inferential difficulty for inductive analysis of needs that result in activity. However, the empiricist and child-oriented social humanist part of Lisina's thinking compels her to accomplish such inductive inference, the exact logic of which is often hidden deep in her writings.

Perhaps the concept mode indigenously reflective of Lisina's implicit theoretical basis is 'need in interaction' (*'potrebnost' v obshchenii'*—also translated as 'communicative need' and 'need for interaction'—see Lisina, 1982a, pp. 136-7). The experiential basis for this concept can be found both in the web of Russian cultural history (which is characterized by the tradition of collective discourse), and in Lisina's consistent interest in the psychological welfare of infants and children who grow up in institutional settings (children's homes). Thus, it is not surprising that Lisina introduces the theme of 'need in interaction' in the following way:

In searching for the best way to define the need for communication, we have proceeded from the observation that communication is a distinctive form of individual adaptation marked by coordination of one's actions with the actions of others in the process of affecting the surrounding world. Such functions suggest the vitally important need of man to communicate. For effective joint activity, it is necessary for the members of a group to *correctly understand and evaluate both themselves and their comrades.* This circumstance, in fact, *determines the emergence of the need for knowledge and evaluation of self and others.* The need for interaction is consciously experienced in suffering from loneliness, interest in other people, and the desire to talk to someone about oneself. (Lisina, 1982a, pp. 136–7, emphases added).

This quote reveals the social-cognitive core of Lisina's concept of 'need in interaction': the evaluation of self and others is considered a result of interaction that is of crucial relevance for human psychological functioning. In another paper Lisina (1974b, p. 10) emphatically states that '*the need in interaction is the aspiration towards evaluation and self-evaluation—towards evaluation of the other person, towards revelation by that person of his/her personality and actions, and towards self-evaluation*' (emphasis in original). The result of interaction is the *image of another person*, as well as the interactor's *image of himself.*

For obvious reasons, Lisina's conceptualization of the need in interaction is as it is expressed in infants' behaviour is a far cry from the adults' tendency towards understanding of others and themselves as a result of interaction. Surely it is impossible to think of an infant as an evaluator of the adult partner in complex cognitive ways. However, the beginning of this cognitive evaluative/self-evaluative process is laid in the social interaction of infants—the need in interaction develops through a series of stages, as Lisina has emphasized. First (in the course of the first 6 months) the infant's need in interaction is expressed by the *need for attention and positive relations from the side of the adults.* Between the second half of the first year and approximately 2–2.5 years of age the second stage in the development of need in interaction is present. That stage is expressed by the infant/toddler's *need for cooperation* with the adult, in the context of children's manipulation of objects in their environments. On the basis of such cooperation children are assumed to develop a 'more adequate image of the adult, which, though, is characterized by maximum situational nature ...' (Lisina, 1974b, p. 15). At the third stage (at early pre-school age), children add the *need for respect* to the needs for attention and cooperation from adults. This addition takes place already not in the context of 'practical' (material) but 'spiritual' (*dukhovnyi*) interaction between adults and pre-schoolers. According to Lisina (1974b, p. 15), 'the relation of adults to the child's cognitive interests as something really *important*, allows the widening of the knowledge of children, their accumulation of new data and the making of the existing ones more precise' (emphasis in original). Finally, at the fourth stage, the child develops to include the *need for mutual understanding* or *mutual empathy* (*soperezhivanie*) among the different incarnations of the need in interaction. A similar but parallel stage account is advanced by Lisina for the development of motives of interaction, where in early infancy the personal-contact (*lichnostnyi*) motives leads into the partnership (*delovoi*) motive (until 2.5 years), after which the cognitive (*poznavatel'nyi*—until 5 years) motive becomes dominant. The developmental sequence is ended by another stage of personal-contact motive dominant at the end of the pre-school period.

As stated before, Lisina's theoretical allegiance seems to be hidden in ideas on to which Leontiev's activity theory is superimposed. The central issue in her thinking seems to be the development of self- and other-evaluation, with the explicit recognition that these evaluation processes are linked. The major thrust in her thinking is related to the well-being of infants and children—in other words, the adults' understanding of the particular versions of the need in interaction can be satisfied better if knowledge of the development of interaction needs in ontogeny is obtained from child psychology. Empirical research in Lisina's laboratory has been devoted to the study of different issues of behaviour in infant-adult (and recently infant-peer) interaction. An analysis of what qualifies as empirical data in Lisina's scientific and social-humanistic discourse could reveal what in particular is meant by her discourse about the need in interaction and its development.

The nature of the empirical data on infancy obtained in Lisina's laboratory

One of the major areas of misunderstanding for psychologists who are outsiders to Soviet psychology is the role of empirical data in Soviet psychology in all of their aspects. It is usually difficult to find out from reading papers in Russian (or their often abbreviated translations) where the data are, and how they are used in theoretical discourse. Empirical research that has been conducted in Lisina's laboratory over the past two decades is in some ways a good example of this difficulty. Partly this may be caused by pressures towards publishing empirical papers in a small and limited space (which has also had an adverse effect on international psychology). However, even in publications where space limitations are clearly not present (e.g., Lisina, 1974a), the presentation of empirical data is embedded in the text in ways that make it difficult to make sense of it.

Most of the empirical studies conducted in Lisina's laboratory— at least in the course of the last decade—have been conducted by junior researchers and post-graduate students under Lisina's directive supervision (for example, see Lisina, 1982a, p. 133 footnote for a list of investigators). Thus, empirical data that are published often appear under different names of authors who in reality did collect and analyze these data; but the general design for data collection has been coordinated by Lisina herself (see also Lisina, 1985).

The basic analytic concept that has been used in Lisina's laboratory in the study of interaction in infancy is the 'complex of animation'—abbreviated COA (*kompleks ozhivlenia*). This term was originally introduced by Nikolai Shchelovanov to denote the holistic behaviour of an infant in response to some positive stimulation source. The COA begins to appear in infant's behaviour around the second month of life in conjunction with the appearance of externally triggered smiling. Apart from smiling, vocalization, visual concentration, and motor behaviour are construed as components of the COA (see Lisina, 1974a). Lisina has developed two ways of measuring the COA: first, its individual components (except vocalizations) are evaluated in a system of ratings assigned by the investigator to the infant in an experimental trial. The length of elicited vocalization is measured in seconds; secondly, the ratings (and length of vocalization) are combined into a summary index of COA using an arbitrary weighting system (which, for example, gives greater prominence to vocalizations than to other components—see Lisina, 1974a). Because of the artificial weight-assignment, it is very difficult to reconstruct the reality of infants' actions behind the reported summary scores of COA. The situation is less complicated when the data on individual components of the COA are provided (e.g., Meshcheryakova, 1975a, 1975b). Nevertheless the rating nature of these measurements leaves them open to the possibility that the investigator's common sense or knowledge of the tested hypotheses could influence the results—especially if the data are summarized into averages over infants studied who, among other things, often differ in their age.

Assuming (although it is impossible to verify this) that the latter concerns about the validity of the data are of little relevance, what then are the positive results in the study of interaction in infancy that have come out of Lisina's laboratory on the basis of empirical data?

Infants' discrimination of persons and objects in interaction

One of the key issues in the beginning of infants' social interaction with others that is relevant from Lisina's perspective is the *differentiation* of these others from non-social objects in the infant's world. Such differentiation, if present early in life, would make it possible to claim that the infant-adult interaction has started to emerge as a special activity—'communicative activity' as Lisina has termed it. If, in contrast, infants react similarly to persons and non-persons, that reaction cannot qualify as part of social interaction. Thus, in order to prove the correctness of Lisina's idea that social interaction begins early in infancy, differentiation by infants (based on behaviour) of these categories of objects needed to be demonstrated.

That task was undertaken by Lisina's co-worker Meshcheryakova (1975a, 1975b) who used the COA as the measure by which the differentiation was investigated. She demonstrated that infants indeed responded to objects in ways that differ from their responses to humans. This result paralleled similar findings in international research literature of the time (Brazelton, Koslowski, & Main, 1974). The theoretical relevance of this demonstration from Lisina's perspective lies in its stage-setting function for the study of how interaction influences the cognitive activity of infants and children.

Effects of interaction on cognition

Lisina's interest in the effects of interaction on infants' and children's cognitive activity has its origins in the psychoanalytic interpretations of children's development under adverse environmental conditions. This is not to say that Lisina is a 'secret proponent' of psychoanalysis, which has effectively been wiped out of the scene of Soviet psychology since the beginning of the 1930s. Rather, Lisina has analized the clinical data on the hospitalism syndrome (Spitz) and other ideas on how impoverished living conditions affect child development. Starting from these data (Lisina, 1961), she has tried to give them a different interpretation. The role of the adult in social interaction with an infant (or child) is considered to be that of an elicitor of the cognitive activity of the infant. In her experiments conducted in the late 1960s (cf. Lisina, 1982b, p. 24), Lisina compared an experimental group of 8 infants under 6 months of age who lived in a children's home and with whom thirty 8-minute long episodes of interaction with an adult were organized, with a control group (N=20) of similar age and life conditions. A number of measures were obtained from both groups before the start, after the 15th, and after the final (30th) session conducted, with the experimental group infants treated individually. Lisina found that in 38% (66) of the behavioural measures used, the experimental group performed better than the control group. More specifically, the infants in the experimental group were observed to (1) be engaged with toys longer; (2) show emotions more frequently; (3) display a greater number of orienting reactions; (4) show extended eye-hand-mouth exploration of objects; and (5) get rid of impulsive movements more quickly and develop goal-directed movements sooner, than the control group taken as a whole (Lisina, 1982b, p. 25).

Lisina's conceptualization of different qualitative ways by which the empirically observed effect of social interaction with adults could take place involves three possible process models. First, interaction can affect the state of the infant in a general, non-specific way. Such increase in the child's 'general tonus' (activity state) may continue in his individual action after the interactive episode with the adult is over. Secondly, interaction can facilitate the *transfer* of methods of orienting-exploratory activity from social interaction to situations in which the child interacts with physical objects alone. Third, the effects of interaction can be viewed 'as the primary push that the infant receives from the adult and which moves the infant out of the state of inactivity that characterizes the newborn who is overwhelmed by its internal sensations' (Lisina, 1982b, p. 25). Lisina considers infants to be intially in an 'introvert' phase that interaction with adults violates and turns the infant into an 'extrovert' state.

Effect of pre-schoolers' interaction with adults on their activity
Lisina's general goal has been to map out the effects of interaction with adults and peers on cognitive activity across the whole age range of Soviet pre-school years. Therefore it is not surprising that different researchers in Lisina's laboratory have extended the study of child-adult interaction beyond the first year of children's lives (see Lisina, 1985). The general idea implicit in these studies remains the same as in the case of infancy. Interaction with adults is expected to make the children more alert in general (first of all emotionally), which then is considered to have a positive effect upon the children's individual cognitive processes involved in their interaction with all of their environment. Godovikova (1974) argued, as a result of her study of 16 children (4–5 year olds), that interaction with adults influences children's cognitive activity in different ways. It was found that the content of interaction rather than its intensity related to children's cognitive activity. That influence could obviously take different forms, depending upon where in the process of problem-solving the child was. First, interaction with an adult was said to create *the emotional relation of the child to the problem*. Secondly, the *orientation towards the possible solution* appears as a result of that interaction. Thirdly, the interaction may lead the child to executing a *search* for the solution in an active way. Finally, the child's *feeling of satisfaction* when the solution is found is guided by the interaction.

Along similar lines, Smirnova (1974) has investigated the effects of 3–6 years olds' interaction with adults on their memory functions (retention). Different children were observed to relate to the adult in different ways: some considered her a play partner, others the teacher, while a third type of relations was labelled 'affective-personal' (including high trust of the adult, increased imitation of her actions, emotional reaction to the adult's remarks). Smirnova concluded that the case of treating the adult as teacher served as the most beneficial way of defining interaction, from the perspective of the retention outcomes.

Other empirical investigations conducted in Lisina's laboratory have addressed other issues of the effects of interaction on child development. Ruzskaya (1974) has investigated the effect of interaction in the acquisition of first words. Elagina (1974, 1975) likewise has studied issues of language development in conjunction with environmental contexts organized by an adult. Bedel'baeva (Lisina & Bedel'baeva, 1974) revealed some effects of interaction on children's exploration. Whichever particular empirical aspect has been tackled by different investigators in Lisina's laboratory (see overview in Lisina, 1982a), the guiding idea has been that, although different children display their affectedness by interaction with adults in different ways, in general the effect of the adults is of a positive nature. It is assumed that it enhances children's progression along their developmental course, whatever that may be. The empirical data used to support these claims are often reported in published form without any detailed analysis, which makes it quite complicated to compare them with the theoretically plausible claims.

Reflexology and activity theory in Lisina's research
Lisina's and her colleagues' variety of empirical work is an interesting phenomenon in the scene of Soviet developmental psychology over the last two decades. On the one hand, its theoretical basis and research methodology constitute a continuation of reflexological traditions of the 1920s (e.g., see Bekhterev & Shchelovanov, 1969; Denisova & Figurin, 1969; Figurin & Denisova, 1969). Like reflexologists of these earlier times, Lisina's emphasis on the observation of the transformation of behaviour complexes (COA) enriches the knowledge base on the study of early interaction. On the other hand, Lisina's own theoretical perspective is set up in ways that accommodate to A.N. Leontiev's activity theory, which otherwise remains very far from direct empirical research on child development. In any case, Lisina's research programme on early social interaction, and the activities of the group of her colleagues working within that programme, make her research the most systematic contribution to understanding social development in contemporary Soviet developmental psychology.

Social class and child development in Soviet psychology

Research on psychological phenomena which are tied to the social class status and environments of subjects is perhaps the area in psychology where social-political processes in a society are most closely intertwined with psychological investigations. This seems to be the case in any country at any period in history. For instance, the inclusion of social class (i.e., socio-economic status) comparisons in empirical research in American child psychology happens to be conducted from the perspective that American middle-class (i.e., majority) values and ways of acting constitute the normative basis against which children from other social strata (usually lower—Socio Economic Status, rather than higher—SES!), or race, are compared. A similar normative emphasis on a selected social class has been present in Soviet developmental psychology. However, the kinds of class selected for this purpose have been different from those in Western psychology. In the 1920s, when the social contrast between the working class and other classes (peasants, intelligentsia, bourgeoisie) was highlighted in the Soviet socio-political process, these class contrasts also became the usual basis for child psychologists' work. Later, the Soviet socio-political system declared that differences between those classes have been 'overcome' as a result of the 'victory of the proletariat' and the disappearance of differences between 'town and country' life. The dissemination of the declared emergence of 'Soviet people' as a homogeneous social class (said to be led, of course, by the proletariat, in accordance with Marxist belief) made the study of social–class comparison an irrelevant issue for research in Soviet psychology. Thus, both an emphasis on social class factors in child development, and its disappearance from psychologists' research activities, were directly guided by the socio-political changes.

There is, however, one particular feature of Soviet research on social class issues in child development that sets it apart from similar social canalization of research in other countries. Namely, in the Soviet context of the 1920s it was the previously (i.e., pre-1917 era) disadvantaged social class (working class and peasants) that became the 'leading creator' of the 'new society', and thus an ideal for other classes. The animosity between the new class in power and the toppled 'old' one (of bourgeoisie) was maintained at a high level in the 1920s, and further enhanced in the context of events in the 1930s. Under these conditions, psychologists' research on social–class issues in child development was not neutral by any means. Likewise, the response by others to the results of such research was far from being limited to the scientific and intellectual sides of social discourse.

Social formation of children's world views

The primacy of social interaction and relationships with practical activity that has been the core of Soviet psychology makes it natural that the development of children's world views (Russian: *mirovozrenie*, German: *Weltanschauung*) is viewed as closely tied to patterns of action and interaction. Towards the end of the 1920s, the issues of children's world-view development became a widespread topic in Soviet paedology. That research was actively promoted by Basov's research group (see Chapter V; Merlin & Khriakova, 1930). A number of interesting but subsequently (purposefully) neglected empirical findings came out of that short-lived research tradition. The reasons for each subsequent neglect are obvious from the list of themes studied, the majority of which gained socially a 'taboo' status as subject matters that did not fit in with the promoted perception of Soviet society. These themes included children's understanding of religion (Rives, 1929), politics of class relations (Gel'mont, 1929), reasoning about poverty and affluence (Lozinskii, 1929) and social justice (Merlin, 1929). The wide dissemination of studies of children's world view in paedology also brought this research topic into the centre of a social controversy (Leventuev, 1931) that eventually led to its disappearance from the scene of Soviet psychology.

Research on children's world views: basic methodology
Methods used in paedological studies of children's world views have been remarkably simple (hence the possibility of their wide use!). The influence of Piaget's work is explicit in the construction of interview schedules and story-texts used for that purpose (Basov, 1931a, p. 745; Merlin, 1929, p. 542). The use of Piaget's clinical interview technique was propagated by Basov as the leading investigator of children's world view. However,

paedologists who rushed to study these issues often did not follow the requirement for the complex interview, and substituted it with short and superficial questionnaires (cf. Leventuev, 1931).

The influence of Piaget's work on children's understanding of causality and animism is clearly evident in the interview schedule that Basov (1931a) suggested as a general guideline for the study of children's world view in the context of the clinical interview. It consists of two parts, the first of which bears a resemblance to Piaget's work, and the second illustrates the issues that Basov considered important to address in the context of contemporary Soviet society. The translation of the full programme of the clinical interview that was suggested for the study of children's social knowledge (Basov, 1931a, pp. 747–50) is given in Appendix A.

A careful reading of the interview schedule reveals why no mention has been made of Basov's and his colleagues' work on children's social knowledge in contemporary Soviet psychology. Basov's programme is highly comprehensive, and covers almost all important aspects of children's possible relationships with society in the conditions of the USSR at the end of the 1920s. These included 'socially sensitive' topics like religion (Part I, Section IV), class society and conflict between classes (Part II, Section II and III), political parties (Part II, Section IV), understanding of inter-ethnic relations (Part II, Section V), and power of state institutions (Part II, Section VI). In a way, Basov's interview schedule could reveal aspects of children's knowledge that were divergent from the goals towards which the state-controlled education system was working. It would subsequently depend on the consumer of such information—the information can be used to improve the efforts to reach one's goals, or it can be purposefully overlooked since it may upset some major tenets of the educational ideology. In the Soviet Union of the 1930s, the latter way of dealing with information came to prevail. Basov's efforts to study children's changing social knowledge under the conditions of a speedily changing society were caught in the middle of social controversies of that society.

Empirical data on children's understanding of social phenomena
Aside from empirical data on children's understanding of causality and animistic thinking, a number of findings by Basov and his

colleagues (Merlin, Khriakova, Zeiliger, Gershenson) in the context of children in Leningrad at the end of 1920s are noteworthy. First, the research carried out by Merlin and Khriakova (1930) involved 7-11 year old schoolchildren, studied in two schools of Leningrad in the 1927–28 school year. It was revealed that the structure of children's social knowledge reflected the structure of their major activity (play—which in its turn reflected the social environment of children). Furthermore, Merlin and Khriakova (1930, p. 124) concluded that the development of children's social understanding is more closely related with the children's school grade than their age— thus implying that their social understanding is guided by their school experiences.

However, children's understanding of social issues was not found to be a mere passive reflection of the social reality that surrounds them. In their thinking, children could attempt to devise their own explanations of issues, thus 'going beyond the reality'. The integration of religious beliefs into children's world views deserves special treatment, given its fundamental significance in developmental psychology. Basov outlined the theoretical importance of this question:

Idealism and religion are inseparably related with each other in the development of adults' world view. In children's consciousness that relationship is reflected in a special way, but it also here retains its basis. This is the result of the fact that the child's consciousness reflects in this case his environment, and, consequently, that relationship is not of his own creation. *In the experience of children, irrational and mystical explanations could emerge in situations where rational, natural understanding of phenomena is impossible for them.* Such is also the general law not only for a child, but for the whole of mankind. *The supernatural is used for explanation of the natural in cases where the latter cannot be understood by itself, while that understanding is of practical necessity.* It is usual that the child, with his weak strength and limited experience, comes across unfamiliar and mysterious phenomena in his environment at every step. (Basov, 1931a, p. 764)

Basov saw the process by which children's supernatural explanations are constructed in the context of solving environment-given problems. When a problem posed is difficult, but necessary, children often try to avoid it. Hence the large number of 'don't know' types of answer, or efforts to redefine the question, in most Piagetian clinical interviews. However, if the child is not given an opportunity to leave the question unanswered, he may try to construct an explanation by a creative combining of different aspects of his practical knowledge, rather than by references to irrational or supernatural powers. *However, if the child's social environment is given meaning, by the people around the child, that is of a supernatural or irrational nature, it is then that the child may devise explanations that the investigator is likely to label 'supernatural' or 'irrational'.* The roots of religiosity in the minds of developing children are thus in the ways that the structure of their environment is semantisized (made meaningful) by his 'social others', who share the given culture. For the child, that religiosity is embedded in the immediate experience with the environment in such cases.

Basov's co-workers, E. Zeiliger and E. Gershenson, studied 1,250 schoolchildren in Leningrad in the year 1929, revealing a wide distribution of children in the five levels of religious thought that were devised for their analysis. The levels were defined on the continuum from 'atheistic' to 'religious' forms of thought:

LEVEL 5 ('atheists'); these children deny the existence of God, while at the same time they reveal the consistent nature of their materialistic world view. They claim that 'all is created by nature' or 'everything emerged by itself', they deny various elements of religion (traditions, objects, existence of the Devil or 'unclean forces'). These children know that religious people exist, and identify themselves with other atheists.

LEVEL 4: At this level, basic but inconsistent atheism in children's world views can be observed. For example: while denying the existence of God, the child may consider the human soul a 'special' substance, or is not sure about the existence of the Devil, house spirits, etc.

LEVEL 3: Children at this level reveal contradictory views of religion. No general relationship to either religious or atheistic world view is present here, but the issue of religion is psychologically salient for the child, who can argue both against and for religious ideas.

LEVEL 2: At this level, children reveal basic, but inconsistent religiosity of their world view. Their world view, while remaining religious, has occasional relapses to natural or physical explanations of phenomena in selected domains.

LEVEL 1: Children at this level have strong and consistent beliefs and approve of all elements of religion. They believe in the existence of God, His influence on the fate of the world and people, insist on the necessity of religious observances, prefer religious people to non-religious ones, believe in the existence and immortality of the human soul, and believe in the 'unclean forces'.

The data obtained by Zeiliger and Gershenson speak to the gradual decrease in the percentage of the LEVEL 1 (deeply religious) world views across the cross-sectional sample of lower school age in all social class groups (workers, employees, other), while the percentages of LEVEL 5 (atheist) children are higher from lower to higher grade levels. For example, children of workers in Grade 1 were distributed into the atheistic end of the continuum (Levels 4 and 5) in 49.7% of the sample, and into the religious end (Levels 1 and 2) in 37.6%. In Grade 5, the respective distribution for working-class children was 64.8% and 22.1% (Basov, 1931a, p. 766). Basov was tempted to attribute the difference in distributions of atheism vs. religiosity levels across grades to the effect of atheistic education carried out in school. However, his conclusions on that matter remain hypothetical due to the cross-sectional nature of the study. The actual developmental process of the development of atheistic or religious world views in child–environment interaction remained largely beyond the collected data. These data, however, revealed the interesting issue of the presence of children with a religious world view among the Young Pioneer troops, although the difference between 'atheistic' and 'religious' world views among Pioneers was greater (78.8% 'atheistic', 9.1% 'religious') than among children who were not Pioneers (61.8% vs. 18.3% respectively; see Basov, 1931a, p. 767). The difference between Pioneers and non-Pioneers in these data is perhaps less relevant than Basov thought; what is more noteworthy is that some children with 'religious' world views happened to be members of the Young Pioneer Organization in Leningrad in 1929.

As is usual, the general-statistical information presented above is of little relevance to understanding the psychological processes behind the numerical data. Zeiliger's and Gershenson's qualitative observations reveal a more interesting story about children's world views. The images of God or the Devil that children with religious world views were shown to have were largely realistic-materialistic (anthropomorphic) in nature. Children of Grades 1–5 seemed unable to think of these religious figures outside the context of real-life experiences (with clergymen, or religious objects). The actual influence of cultural input to children in the school context (i.e., atheistic education) could be traced in the children's original reconstructions. For instance, some children expressed the idea that God existed earlier, before the October Revolution, and that workers expelled him together with the czar.

For that reason, God was declared as not existing in the USSR, but children could claim His continued existence in other (i.e.. 'bourgeois') countries.

A slightly different appraoch to the study of children's religiosity was reflected in the work of S.M. Rives (1929), who presented children with specifically constructed dilemmas ('collisions' of viewpoints) involving conflict of religious and secular ways of acting or thinking. The following dilemma with content taken from the school environment was one example:

The Wall-newspaper Found Out
In the school's wall-newspaper an article was published, dealing with the fact that a teacher, Anton Kuzmich, goes to church. The article demanded that a 'school trial' be organized to condemn the teacher. Among the pupils, arguments arose at a meeting.

Some were indignant: 'How can it be the business of the wall-newspaper whether a teacher goes or does not go to church? In his home he has the right to do what he wants. That is his personal matter.'

Others disagreed and said: 'In the Soviet school, the teacher must educate the children in the communist spirit. How can such a teacher, who goes to church, do it? Such a teacher must be fired from a Soviet school.'

The people in a third group said: 'True, the teacher in the Soviet school must not be religious. But there are still many religious teachers. Anton Kuzmich teaches his subject well, and he should not be tried.'

What would you say, if you were to speak at that meeting? Why would you say that? (Rives, 1929, p. 579)

The socio-politically active role of Rives' work is reflected in his description of his levels of children's religiosity. Using a 5-level categorization scheme, similar to that of Basov and his co-workers, Rives described the most 'atheistic' (5th) level of children's religiosity in rather militant terms:

This is a very clear, principally explicit attitude involving understanding of the necessity for incessant fight with religion as 'opium for the people', as with the force that is an enemy of the proletariat, as with the serious obstacle to the building of socialism. This is the right, class-conscious approach to religion, in which case religion does not remain a personal matter but is a social evil, with which all workers must fight. At that approach, there is no place for indecisiveness or 'retreats' .... In the believing teacher these children would see not a 'poor old man' who has been raised under old conditions and who can be pitied, but ... a serious threat not only to the new generation, but to all of the cultural revolution. Therefore, they are relentless towards him. (Rives, 1929, pp. 581–2)

In Rives' data, obtained from Grades 4–7 (total N = 1175) in early 1929, 25.7% of pupils were classified, on the basis of their written responses to the above-mentioned 'collision', as belonging to the highest 'atheistic' level. For other dilemmas used by Rives, the distributions of response categories revealed relatively high situation (dilemma)-specificity of answers. The lowest percentage of high-atheistic responses occurred in a dilemma in which three daughters were persuaded to go to church for Passover by their mother, in obvious 'collision' with the atheistic eduction in school. Rives' interpretation of his quantitative data concentrated on the 'negative' (i.e., religious) views, and he thus lamented the high (63.5%) pro-religious response rate to the Passover Dilemma as depending on the strength of religious rituals in the socialization of children's world view.

Other aspects of Rives' data reveal a high variety of patterns of atheistic vs. religious views across grade levels (4–7) in different schools in the study. He also found that females dominated over males in the percentage of pro-religious answers in all four dilemmas used, and that a small percentage of Young Pioneers (from 1.5 to 4.7% in different social class groups) were religious at the highest level. The results were perceived as deeply troubling by Rives, who ended his article with an active call for atheistic education of the vast children's group who were currently in a middle position in their world view.

The studies on childhood religiosity summarized here illustrate the high variability in the *style* and *starting perspective* of different investigators of that subject matter, which was of very high relevance to social policy in the USSR at the time. Basov's detached research interest in finding out *how* children's views on religion are organized at different grade levels is in great contrast with Rives' starting position of highly militant atheism (see also Rives, 1930). However, these vastly different studies of the very non-neutral subject matter of childhood religiosity seem to converge in one—the demonstration of the substantial (although minority) religiosity of Soviet children in the year 1929. In later years, the issue of religiosity in children's world view became a topic unavailable for any serious study, at the times when the *practical* efforts to eradicate the phenomenon from people's minds were at their maximum.

Understanding of social institutions and development of political ideologies

Children's understanding of social institutions can be expected to vary, depending upon their relations with these institutions. The context of the USSR in the 1920s provided a heterogeneous picture of classes of children whose relationship to a particular social institution were very different. The best example of how the child's perspective on institutions, set by the child's everyday activities, guides the child's understanding of them is the case of homeless children. Krasuskii and Makarovskii (1929) conducted a massive study with homeless children in Odessa in 1926 (N = 500, age range from under 8 years to over 18; most—92.4%—from age range 10–17 years). These children's relationship with social institutions like courts, militia (i.e., police), and prisons were obviously very different from 'ordinary' (i.e., home-living, school-going, and law-abiding) children. The homeless children, by their necessity to live, were in frequent conflictual contact with the institutions of law and order. Their answer to questions like 'who is a militiaman?', 'what is a prison?' and 'what is court?' revealed a clear reflection of their general life conditions. It was particularly dramatic in the case of answers to the questions about prisons:

Characteristically, only for 10.2% among the homeless and under-age lawbreakers did the understanding dawn that *our* [i.e., Soviet, as opposed to czarist] places of limitation of freedom are *correctional-work institutions*. Somewhat more frequently [14.8%] the responses characterize prison as the place for outliving the punishment. (Krasuskii & Makarovskii, 1929, p. 619, emphasis added)

The majority of homeless delinquents (59.8%) understood prison as the place for limitation of freedom. Given the nature of the sample, it is not surprising that the perspective from which the Soviet law-and-order officials would have liked children to view prison (as a correctional work institution) was highly discordant with the children's understanding of that part of society's organizational form. Likewise, only a minority of the children viewed courts in terms that fitted the self-reflection of Soviet state (7.4%—courts keep up public order; 4.6%—courts defend working people; 3.6%—courts solve disputes). The majority viewed the functions of courts as they appeared from their standpoint (30% 'for those who steal or kill'; 26.6%—court interrogates and judges; 13%—punishes).

The reflection of everyday life on children's understanding of the world is perhaps extreme in cases of extreme (in comparison with others') activities. Other studies of children's understanding of the world by Soviet psychologists in the 1920s revealed less extreme, but equally interesting effects of social environment. For example, Lozinskii's (1929) work on children's (9 17 years of age) understanding of poverty and affluence, performed in direct comparison with a similar study in France, revealed traces of ideas widely propagated in the Soviet society then (and until today). In dramatic contrast with French children, Soviet (Ukrainian) children mention *social* reasons as answers to the question 'why is it bad to be rich?' (57.6% of children in the Ukraine, 0% for French children), while *emotional* reasons were less prevalent (21% in the Ukraine, 65% in France). In the actual themes of responses, the Ukrainian children expressed a number of symptomatic ideas (which had no counterpart in the French data): it is sad to be rich, one can't work to earn one's living, lack of goals in life, a rich person is not the owner of the state, the rich have no influence, while rich there is no need to fight—but there is happiness in fighting, impossibility to work collectively, lack of working skills, to be rich is unhappy—better be middle-class, in the USSR there is no place for the rich, it is bad to be rich—the rich exploit others and does not work himself, the rich is incapable of work and lazy, it is bad to have everything knowing that others do not have minimal necessities, it is bad to be rich because everybody should be equal, the rich have many enemies, etc. (Lozinskii, 1929, p. 574). In these answers, the negative stereotype of the rich that was part of Soviet propaganda (and active efforts to expropriate the wealth of the rich) after 1917 finds its reflection in the Ukrainian children's world views.

The political angle of the world views of Soviet citizens is the 'core' of their socialization, as viewed from the perspective of the Soviet political system (Mead & Calas, 1955; Valsiner, 1984c). Thus the development of children's understanding of politics was a theme that interested Soviet paedologists of the 1920s. Investigations of large samples of schoolchildren were conducted by the Scientific-Pedagogical Institute of the Methods of School Work. The work by Gel'mont (1929) on schoolchildren's understanding of Soviet foreign policy is an illustration of the kind of work on children's political understanding that went on in the 1920s. Children (N = c.8,000) were (orally, but in a group situation) given a series of questions:

Q1. What are the relations between the USSR and bourgeois countries?
Q2. What should the relations between the USSR and bourgeois countries be like?

The massive questioning by Gel'mont of children from different ages (9–16 years) and social class background was cast in a context of clear expectancy as to the 'ideal' ways of children's thinking of foreign policy issues. That ideal emphasized children's identification with the particular ('progressive') social class (proletariat) *across* boundaries of countries, while the relationship to 'exploiting classes' was expected to be militant (likewise across state frontiers). Gel'mont's study, however, revealed a picture that was rather different from the author's proclaimed ideal (see Table VII.1).

Table VII.1 reveals a large challenge to Gel'mont's ideals for children's view of politics ('real/dialectical' cols 5 and 6) from both the 'pacifist' (cols 1 and 2) and 'militant' (cols 3 and 4) dominating views. 4.4% of all respondents viewed the USSR and bourgeois countries as living peacefully together in a friendly way, and 50.5% expressed the idea that the relationships should become that way. Gel'mont (1929, p. 607) labelled this 'unprincipled pacifism' (*bezprintsipnyi patsifizm*), with clear negative connotation. The case with children expressing militant ideals (77.5% of children, not surprisingly, viewed the USSR's relations with other countries as those between enemies, and 38% of the children wanted it to be so) did not deserve a similar opposite label (e.g., 'unprincipled militancy') from Gel'mont. Instead, Gel'mont views the 38% of militant answers as a positive, although not yet ideal (i.e., dialectically militant) view on foreign policy.

The age-group differences in Gel'mont's data are particularly interesting from the viewpoint of political socialization of children. Compared to younger children, the older groups demonstrated a drop in Gel'mont's 'unprincipled pacifism' (from 62.8% to 32.4%—col. 2, Q.2), while the ideal for unconditional militancy was observed to become more frequently endorsed (from 20.5% to 54.7%—col. 4, Q.2) when 9–10 and 15–16 year olds are

Table VII.1: Soviet schoolchildren's reasoning about relationships between the USSR and other countries

| | General type of reasoning about political relations | | | | | |
Sample	'Pacifist'		'Militant'		'Real'/'Dialectical'	
	Q.1	Q.2	Q.1	Q.2	Q.1	Q.2
TOTAL:	4.4	50.5	77.5	38.0	9.1	4.6
By sex:						
Boys	4.8	51.6	75.2	36.4	10.8	5.2
Girls	3.9	49.3	80.3	39.8	6.9	3.8
By age:						
(1) 9–10 yr.	6.8	62.8	67.3	20.5	1.2	0.3
(2) 11–12 yr.	5.2	59.7	78.4	31.0	4.7	1.9
(3) 13–14 yr.	3.6	51.6	79.1	37.3	9.5	5.1
(4) 15–16 yr.	3.1	32.4	77.9	54.7	16.9	9.0
By membership:						
Young Pioneers	3.5	47.2	77.2	38.0	12.5	6.3
Non-pioneers	4.7	51.2	77.7	35.2	7.5	4.0

Note: All figures in Table VII.1 are percentages from the total number of answers to Questions 1 and 2 (calculated separately). The percentages within-row & question do not total 100% because of the omission of some other ('indeterminate') response categories from Gel'mont's published data.

Source: Gel'mont (1929), pp. 600 and 606.

compared. The 'dialectical' viewpoint on USSR–other countries' relations (col. 6) likewise shows some increase with age.

Gel'mont's own discussion of these findings is characteristically flavoured by the data revealing a large gap between reality and the author's ideal ('dialectical') picture. It is especially the 'pacifist' sentiment that Gel'mont considers to be the antidote of *partiinost'* in children's political thinking. However, a Soviet educational official of Gel'mont's time, looking at his data, might have been pleased. After all, the data reveal that in the group 15–16 years of age, about two thirds (63.7%) of the respondents demonstrated their animosity to the 'enemies' of the USSR, either directly or in 'dialectically' militant ways. It must be remembered that Gel'mont's data were collected at the time when children must have been observers of class-conflicts within the USSR, where a 'dialectical' view of the 'enemies' of the working class was not particularly widespread, nor promoted. The children's knowledge about foreign policy matters was wholly a result of their school education, and must have been built upon notions of relationships between social classes inside the USSR.

One could, of course, view Gel'mont's data from a different angle—in older age groups, more children become reconciled with the perceived animosity between the USSR and other countries (as reflected in the reduced difference between percentages for questions 1 and 2, columns 3 and 4). Whatever the angle on the data, one basic result is worth remembering—Soviet children in the 1920s were already subjected to active (and in the majority of cases successful) socialization for ingroup (USSR)-outgroup (other, capitalist countries) relations along the model of *conditional animosity*. That animosity was to be latent rather than explicit. It need not be evoked in every situation, but is nevertheless present and creates the basis for the person's 'independently dependent' actions (Valsiner, 1984c). On the side of those whose goal it is to activate an appropriate action from a person, s/he could be set into action by the established psychological trigger mechanisms, coded into the children's internalized world view under the traditional themes of 'patriotism', 'love for fatherland', and identification of the self with the Soviet state. Viewed from the perspective of better understanding of children's political socialization, Gel'mont's data from the 1920s are of wider usefulness than just as analysis of the local Soviet life of that decade.

Conclusions: socialization of children's world views

The social transformation of culture in the USSR in the 1920s constituted a fertile ground for psychologists' acquisition of knowledge about how children's understanding of the world develops under the speedy transformation of their cultural environments. Partly because of their axiomatic basis that emphasized the unity of social and cognitive aspects of child development, partly thanks to the empirical phenomenology available in interviews and questionnaires administered to children from different backgrounds, Soviet developmental psychologists could attempt to transcend the traditional dichotomy between 'social' and 'cognitive' sides of development. The major conclusion from the studies on children's world views was expressed in concentrated form by Wolf Merlin:

The development of world view is conditionally determined [Russian *obuslovlivaetsia*, more exact translation: 'caused by setting up conditions'] by the development of the child's social life. The world view always lags behind the social life. (Merlin, 1929, p. 556)

The conditional-genetic role of the child's environment is the aspect of developmental theory in which psychologists in the USSR enriched contemporary (and subsequent) developmental psychology in other countries around the world. Like Vygotsky (Chapter IV) and Basov (Chapter V) in their respective theoretical systems, the investigators of children's world views (including those not close to Basov) in the 1920s who were largely empirically oriented, went beyond their Western-European counterparts particularly in their emphasis on the social environment's role in children's world views. The developing child, as an active agent in his relationships with the surrounding culturally meaningful environment (Basov, 1931a), assimilates culturally coded value-information from the environment while accommodating his thinking to the structural conditions of that environment. Children's world view is a product of the internalization of social experience. In its internalized form, the world view becomes a cognitive mediator (in Vygotsky's sense: see Chapter IV) in further dealings with the environment.

The social-cognitive *process* by which children's assimilation and accommodation of their relationships with the environment takes place includes an intricate synthesis of the previous state of children's world view with incoming new information. Generalized concepts of an abstract (i.e., context-free) kind have a crucial role in this, as described by Beliaev:

We are surrounded by a complex network of social behaviour. Before we react to one or another of these behavioural acts, we, in many cases, must conduct 'selective generalization' [V. Bekhterev's term], i.e., to differentiate, select that particular act from among others and relate it to previously known acts of a similar kind. As a result of that process a certain 'verbal label' is superimposed on the given act (e.g., this is 'theft'; that—'personal insult', etc.). Only after such labelling (qualification) does the corresponding positive or negative type of reaction follow. (M. Beliaev, 1929, p. 564)

The development of children's world views is thus important not as an end in itself, but rather as a means to other ends. Viewed from this perspective, it begins to make sense why labels of 'social class', 'atheism', 'internationalism', 'party', etc., and their semantic backgrounds, have been of central relevance for children's world view as seen by Soviet psychologists and educationalists. By active and redundant immersion of these labels and their associated values in different loci of the environments of developing children, the socializers can be certain that the majority of developing children internalize them in the process of their activity. In this sense, formation of children's world views is no simple 'brainwashing' as is often assumed by some Western political analysts of the USSR, especially by those of journalistic inclination. Instead, the educator sets up conditions for child-environment relationships *in such ways that the child (together with his peers) develops the prescribed world view as a result of his active interaction with the organized environment*. Soviet research on the development of world views in the 1920s provides some empirical data on the intermediate outcomes of that process, and some glimpses into the process by which the world views develop. The latter information is particularly interesting for developmental psychology as a whole, since the psychological mechanisms involved in the socialization of children's world view may lead to the understanding of basic principles of social development.

Individuals in collectives: social groups, their environments, and social development of children

It is not surprising that a special interest in forms of social organization of psychological phenomena has a longstanding important role in Soviet developmental psychology. Theoretically it emerges at the intersection of Marxist philosophy on the one hand, and European psychological thought on the other. Among the latter, the French sociological and mass-psychological works, together with an emphasis on the holistic nature of phenomena (from German Gestalt psychology—see Scheerer, 1980), served as catalysts for speedy and extensive development of social psychology of groups of human beings in the 1920s. The developmental emphasis in Marxist philosophy, together with pedagogical interest in children's social groups at different ages, led to the integration of developmental and social-psychological perspectives in early Soviet psychology. That integration has remained in force ever since—at its basis, contemporary Soviet social psychology has a developmental emphasis, and developmental psychology in the USSR is explicitly social in its approach to almost all psychological issues of child development.

Soviet social psychology of the 1920s: origins of the dynamic approach

Research on collective psychological phenomena has had two fertile periods in the history of Soviet psychology: the 1920s and the period from 1970s to the present. It is noteworthy that contemporary Soviet social psychology develops under conditions of appreciation of the work of the 1920s (Kolominskii, 1976; Kazakov, 1983; Lomov, 1980; Petrovskii, 1984a, 1984b, 1985). The results of empirical research from these periods are quite different in nature, reflecting the state of affairs in the society of the time. The research in the 1920s, largely facilitated by the work of Bekhterev (1921, 1976), covered a wide range of problems. In 1925, Bekhterev set the programmatic goals for social psychology, phrased in his reflexological terminology (Bekhterev, 1976, p. 45):

1. In what way, if any, do the reflexes of a collective as a whole differ from the reflexes of an individual, under the same general experimental conditions?

2. How do the reflexes of a collective change as a function of the collective's composition?

3. How do the reflexes of a collective change as a function of its internal and external conditions?

4. How do the reflexes of the individual change, i.e., how are they stimulated or inhibited, as a result of the effect of the collective on the individual, compared with analogous reflexes of the same individual outside the collective?

5. How do the reflexes of an individual in a collective vary as a function of the nature and composition of the collective?

6. How do the reflexes of a collective change under the influence of a particular individual?

7. What influences exerted by an individual on the collective are most effective, and under what conditions?

8. In what way and by what means does the collective act upon the individual through suggestion, persuasion, or other types of influence?

9. What are the specific features of any particular collective as assessed from its outward manifestations in the form of collective reflexes?

10. What are the major manifestations of the stimuli acting on a collective?

It is easy to see how Bekhterev's suggested research topics form certain thematic clusters. First, the *difference* between individuals as individuals, and individuals as members of a social unit (topics 1, 4, 5, 8) constitutes a major research issue. The roots of that issue are embedded in the contrast between individualistic European psychology of mass phenomena on the one hand, and the Russian tradition (see Chapter II on Kropotkin) of seeing individual people as integrated and interdependent parts of social units. Secondly, Bekhterev put forward the issue of *how collectives exist* as complex, dynamic holistic systems, as a function of their members (topics 2, 3, 6, 7) and by their collective action as a whole (9). Finally, Bekhterev raised the issue of *environments' influence* on the functioning of the collective (10).

These three major research themes have remained the basis for Soviet social-psychological interest in the functioning of social groups, even though Bekhterev's own reflexological terminology became extinct as the 1920s passed into history. In addition, of course, Soviet social-psychological research has also been borrowing from the cultural-historical traditions of Vygotsky, especially in the form of Leontiev's activity theory, and Zaluzhnyi's theoretical and empirical work on children's social group organization (Petrovskii, 1984b).

Bekhterev's interest in the study of collective psychology was not primarily oriented by a developmental aspect, although the latter was embedded in his general theoretical (dynamic-energetic) framework. Empirically, some of the experiments under his guidance were conducted with children's groups (e.g., Bekhterev, 1976), but the study of children was of no particular importance to him. However, it did influence a number of psychologists in the 1920s, leading them to the study of children's groups and collectives.

Environmental influence on the functioning of social groups of children was a particularly popular research issue among psychologists in 1920s. This can be explained by a combination of a number of reasons. First, in Soviet society of the 1920s, a high variety of children's social groups existed. Many of those were 'freely formed', i.e., had become functional by children's own activities and had not been organized by adults. Others—like the Soviet Young Pioneer movement, modelled on scouting traditions—were explicitly formed and organized by adults, with particular social and psychological goals in mind. Many of the freely-formed children's groups (for example, those of homeless children, child criminals, etc.) constituted a social 'problem' for the Soviet authorities. Secondly, differences between children's life in urban and rural areas of the USSR were huge. This was further accentuated by the socially set goals of reorganizing agriculture along Soviet political lines, and socializing rural children accordingly. Hence the increased interest of Soviet psychologists of the time in the differences between urban and peasant children (e.g., Fortunatov, 1929; Gershenzon & Likhachova, 1928; Levina & Gershenzon, 1928; Luria, 1978a–1930; Mikhlina & Nikitenko, 1928; Pokrovskaia, 1928; Rybnikov, 1929; Shapiro, 1928; Ul'man, 1928; Zeiliger, 1928), and their social life (Krasuskii, 1929). Thirdly, the Marxist axiom that the conditions of human psychological functioning depend upon their relationships with means of industrial or agricultural production led Soviet child psychologists to be interested in the work of children, and the role that their integration in work activities plays in their social development.

Given the conditions of the 1920s, many empirical research projects of that time look relatively 'exotic' from the perspective of the 1980s. For example, the occupation of newspaperboys (Chernikhova, 1929) no longer exists in the USSR. Nevertheless, research on the life of young newspaper sellers has enriched psychology's knowledge base of work-related adaptation of young children. Neither is it possible these days to address the issues of 'freely formed collectives of village youth' (Krasuskii, 1929), 'social images of homeless children' (Krasuskii & Makarovskii, 1929), or children's understanding of politics (Gel'mont, 1929). Since then, some of these social-psychological and cognitive phenomena have disappeared from the Soviet society, others have changed their nature. Research on child psychology has been adapted to changes in psychological phenomena in society. Contemporary developmental psychology in the USSR includes research on *adult-organized* social groups and collectives, mostly those that are a part of school life (social groups in classroom context, leadership in Young Pioneer groups, etc.—cf. Kolominskii, 1976). Contemporary interest in interdependence of the individual and the collective (Kon, 1978; Petrovskii, 1981a, 1984b, 1985; Porshnev, 1970, 1979), however, carries on the legacy of investigators from the 1920s (Artemov, 1929, Basov, 1931a, Ch. 27; Bekhterev, 1921, 1976; Beliaev, 1929, 1930a, 1930b; Fortunatov, 1925, 1929; Zaluzhnyi, 1929, 1930). Out of the immense variety of empirical research endeavours in Soviet developmental social psychology, both of the 1920s and of more recent times, a number of specific areas of interest are worthy of overview in the present context.

Collectives, social groups, and individuals: the problem of definition

The task of defining what 'collective' means was not simple for Soviet psychologists in the 1920s, nor is that question easily answered at the present time. In the 1920s, the issue of how to define this complex term was guided by the Soviet version of Marxist philosophy (mostly Bukharin, Deborin, etc.).

Three features have been important in Soviet psychologists' definitions of social units (organized groups and collectives). First, there is the emphasis on the *systemic nature* of these units. Secondly, the *refusal to reduce* the society or collective to its elements for analytic purposes is a feature widespread not only in Marxist philosophy but also in Gestalt psychological traditions to which psychology in the USSR was very close at that time. Thirdly, the people in society (the collective) are viewed as *occupying variable positions* within it as the holistic system, and as being related to one another by the defining characteristics of these positions (Beliaev, 1930a, 1930b). In Marxist social philosophy, the latter issue was defined as people's relationships to the means of production. In Soviet social psychology, it was reflected in different authors' emphases on activity, goals, needs, and value orientations. Different efforts to define 'the collective' existed in the 1920s. In Bekhterev's early conceptualization (Bekhterev, 1921, p. 41), the criteria for a social unit to be a 'collective' included unity of interests (that presuppose unity of goals) of the members, together with unity of the task which the collective is trying to accomplish, aside from mutual interactive influences. Zaluzhnyi defined the collective as an interacting group of persons that has revealed its capability for joint reaction to complexes of stimuli (Zaluzhnyi, 1928). That joint reaction is of an organized nature, and involves the understanding of collective goals, at least minimal planning of work and its distribution among members, and synthesis of the final collective reaction

(Zaluzhnyi, 1929). Another author from the same period, Artemov (1929, p. 470), considers three major points as defining a 'collective': (1) it emerges on the basis of children's play or work activity and constitutes a system, and not a sum, of its members; (2) its real functioning is expressed in interaction between children; (3) the individuals who make up a collective as a whole, acquire new characteristics as parts of the whole as they are its subordinates. Artemov's view on children's collectives is explicitly cast in terms of influences from Gestalt psychology. Finally, Basov arrives at the following general definition of the collective:

The collective is a social whole, that emerges on the basis of relationships of cooperation among people in the course of activity, directed towards a shared goal. (Basov, 1931a, p. 701)

These defining efforts of Soviet psychologists of the 1920s are in good agreement with views of contemporary authors. A. Petrovskii describes his differentiation of 'collective' from a 'diffuse social group' in similar terms:

In the collective, the defining characteristics are the interaction and mutual relationships between people that are mediated by goals, tasks, and values of their joint activity, i.e., its real content. From that perspective, a collective is a group in which interpersonal relationships are mediated by socially valued and personally meaningful content of joint activity. (Petrovskii, 1984b, p. 160)

Petrovskii's definition illustrates how the behaviour-oriented traditions of the 1920s of defining the collective as a *systematically organized* social group have been 'enculturated': the emphasis on cultural meanings and the personal sense of Vygotsky's tradition shows clearly through A. N. Leontiev's primary emphasis on *joint activity*. Whatever the differences between particular definitions of the term between different authors in Soviet psychology, a basic unifying ethos of these definitions remains: all of them emphasize the *systemic organization* of groups of people, as those *are active in a goal-directed manner* in particular environments.

Children's group organization and its devlopment

A number of Soviet psychologists of the 1920s were active in studying the group processes of children (A. Zaluzhnyi, S. Molozhavyi, P. Volobuev, B. Beliaev, V. Artemov, and others).

Among those, the Ukrainian investigator A.S. Zaluzhnyi may have provided the most extensive approach to children's collectives.

According to the most thorough researcher on children's social group organization in contemporary Soviet psychology, Iakov Kolominskii (1976, pp. 61–2), Zaluzhnyi's contribution in the 1920s to the empirical study of how children's collectives function has remained unsurpassed to the present time (as well as largely overlooked or forgotten: Zaluzhnyi, 1928, 1929, 1930, 1931a). Again, part of the slowness in contemporary Soviet psychologists' reference to Zaluznyi's work can be traced to the active criticism of his approach that was part of the wave of criticism in the early 1930s (see Chapter III). Zaluzhnyi, under such criticism, did not immediately succumb to the excessive self-criticism that some of his peers expected, but defended his position (see Zaluzhnyi, 1931b). However, as was the case with many serious believers in the Soviet system in the 1930s, he ended up as an active and aggressive critic of other paedologists a couple of years later (Zaluzhnyi, 1937). Nevertheless, relatively little detailed knowledge is available at the present time about his substantial empirical contribution to the study of the organization of social groups—long before social psychologists in other countries became actively interested in such topics.

The importance of Zaluzhnyi's work to understanding contemporary Soviet research on children's social groups lies in its role as the forerunner. His research may have been an influence on Anton Makarenko in his practical work in organizing children's groups in his work as director of a boarding school for young delinquents (see Kolominskii, 1976, p. 66). Makarenko's educational views, once they had become widespread in the USSR, have served as one of the bases for much of contemporary Soviet research (Petrovskii, 1985). Zaluzhnyi's work also seems to be a basis of Petrovskii's research programme.

Zaluzhnyi's approach to the study of children's groups has from the start been explicitly developmental. It involves a wide age-range of children (from 12 months to adolescence) and all the educational institutional frameworks in which children in the Ukrainian SSR participated in the 1920s. In a study of pre-schoolers' social groups, covering children from 1 to 4 years of age, Zaluzhnyi (1928) distinguished four types of social behaviour (defensive-negativistic, aggressive, primary-social, and collectively social), viewing these as a developmental sequence in children's social behaviour.

Furthermore, Zaluzhnyi (1930) outlined five stages in children's development of social relationships. The *first stage* involves the infant's distinguishing of the mother's face, while the appearance of another child in the infant's visual field is responded to in ways similar to that used in the case of physical objects. The *second stage* begins at about 6–7 months of age, when social interest in other children emerges. The interaction with other children has the form of 'passive-negativistic' (infant to the older child) or 'aggressive-despotic' (the older child towards the younger) behaviour. However, actions interpretable as mutual help already occur at this stage, all of which emerge under the influence of adults' actions. Two pathways in the development of children's actions are specified for that stage. First, the child learns to adapt his actions to those of other people. Secondly, the child repeats the actions of the adult.

At the *third stage*, children's socially-oriented actions begin to dominate over aggressive ones. The role of speech as a regulator of social interaction becomes particularly important at this stage. Both mutual help and competition are present in parallel. At the *fourth stage*, the child starts to take upon him/herself the organizing role not only in his relationships with the world of objects, but also in respect to his social world. It is at this stage that 'embryonic collectives' emerge in children's social interaction. Finally, at the *fifth stage* children start forming collectives in the full (from Zaluzhnyi's point of view) sense; they act together, criticize one another and give instructions for the 'right' behaviour. These 'play collectives' of older pre-schoolers are the basis of further advancement of 'work collectives' at school age and beyond.

Zaluzhnyi's emphasis on *organization* as the major aspect of children's collectives constitutes the core of his empirical research on schoolchildren's groups (Zaluzhnyi, 1929, 1930). His method of *natural experimentation* with social groups of schoolchildren involved eight different *types of task* that are given to a group, with subsequent documentation of the *process* by which these tasks are accomplished. The following group tasks were used by Zaluzhnyi (1929, pp. 480–1):

1. The group is asked to elect a representative for the upcoming conference of schoolchildren of the region/town.
2. The group is asked to elect one of its members to oversee the cleaning of the schoolyard.
3. The group is instructed to take sheets of paper from a table in an organized way, and every member of the group must write his/her name on every sheet.
4. The children are asked to write five numbers on the same sheets of paper (used in No. 3), so that one group member writes numbers 1–5, another 6–10, a third 11–15, etc.—so that in the end all the sheets are set in an order by these numbers, from the smaller to the larger ones.
5. The group is instructed to divide into subgroups of 3 members for the purpose of the activity of tree-planting.
6. The group is asked to plan for a school festival and to elect some of its members for fulfilling particular functions in connection with that.
7. The group is asked to prepare for a trip to the museum of the Revolution, and to prepare for discussions on the theme 'the October Revolution'.
8. The group (every member separately and anonymously) is asked to indicate names of 5 'disorganizers' (children who should improve their present conduct, if the group were to participate in a competition for the name of the best-organized group) amongst the group.

It is obvious that Zaluzhnyi's rationale for subjecting the groups to experimental (but ecologically valid) tasks was to reveal the organization of the group under the conditions of a set of task demands. Tasks 1 and 2 reveal the group's capacity for performing elections in an organized way. Tasks 3 and 4 address the capability of organizing distribution and coordination of problem-solving in the group. Task 5 reveals group members' mutual sympathies, as well as giving an indication of the speed with which the group can divide into task-oriented sub-units. Tasks 6 and 7 are meant to reveal the process whereby the group makes plans for future events. Finally, Task 8 is of particular interest for understanding social group actions in the context of Soviet society. It involves the issue of *criticism* of other persons, in the form of *anonymous* written indication. The task is formulated as improvement of the standing of the whole group, if some identified members of the group change their behaviour. It involves the feature of *reporting on one's peers* in the group by setting group goals above those of the reporting individual (who, as is well known to the children, remains unidentified) and his/her relationship with the identified 'target'. It is in respect to this task that Zaluzhnyi commented:

It is interesting to note that some older groups refuse to perform that task, claiming that among them everybody behaves well. However, such groups are an exception, all the others give their testimonies, and it often happens that a 'disorganiser', towards whom all others point in their anonymous messages, also writes about himself as a disorganiser and announces that he needs the most to improve his behaviour. (Zaluzhnyi, 1929, p. 487)

The peculiarities of the wave of criticism—writing anonymous accusations against others—and responses to allegations by (sometimes preemptive and voluntary) self-criticism that became very widespread in the Soviet society of the 1930s are embedded in the social interaction of collectives of Russian/Soviet schoolchildren long before that. Zaluzhnyi, with his knowledge of the reality of social interaction, made masterful use of that aspect of interpersonal relationships in children's groups in his empirical measurement system of group organization.

A somewhat different approach to the study of schoolchildren's collective organization was put forward by another Ukrainian psychologist P. Volobuev (1929), whose interest lay in describing how children's collectives can be observed to perform in pedagogical environments. Observers of classroom activity noted the occasions (in 5-minute consecutive intervals) in which children were 'off-duty' during the ongoing (teacher-organized) classroom activity. As a result, Volobuev defined a number of *types of working capabilities of children's groups*. At the same time it is symptomatic that Volobuev's observations do not include teachers' behaviour in the empirical research. Many of the temporal 'on-off task' working patterns that he attributed to the children's group are most likely results of ongoing students–teacher interaction, rather than attributable solely to children's behaviour.

Continuing the research traditions of Zaluzhnyi and his contemporaries, but claiming most direct affinity with Anton Makarenko's practical pedagogical work on children's collectives in the 1920s–30s, is at present Artur V. Petrovskii (1981a, 1984a, 1984b, 1985). Petrovskii's main interest is in the study of collectives as highly organized social units that are mediated by their members' activities and meaning systems (see his definition of a 'collective', above). He distinguishes such collectives from other groups, assigning to them the status of the highest organized type, from which other types differ as 'lower' ones. Five levels of organization of social groups, from the 'diffuse group' at the lowest, to the collective at the highest level, are charted out in Petrovskii's conceptual system, called by him 'stratometric' conceptualization of intra-group activity' (Petrovskii, 1984b, p. 164).

The hierarchy of levels of social group organization in Petrovskii's system is based on two dimensions. First, he uses the extent to which a group is mediated by activities of its members. Here, groups vary from a diffuse (minimal mediated state) to high (collective) organization. The second dimension that Petrovskii introduces is interesting in its value orientation: according to him, social units vary from those oriented towards 'social progress' (he immediately emphasizes that in the USSR this means 'building of communism'—Petrovskii, 1984b, p. 164), to those that are not oriented towards 'social progress' (e.g., mafia groups, anti-social groups, etc. in Petrovskii's view). Five types of social groups are defined by Petrovskii on the basis of his two-dimensional account: (1) collective, oriented towards 'social progress'; (2) collective, oriented away from 'social progress'; (3) groups with high development of social values but little mediation (e.g., a newly-formed group where joint activity is not yet established); (4) groups with low mediation and 'anti-social' values; the members of such groups 'have united for their own personal gains alone' (Petrovskii, 1985, p. 81).

Finally, there is type 5—the 'diffuse group' in which:

both the social value of mediating factors and the degree to which they are manifested in the system of interpersonal relations remain at zero. An excellent example of this is the experimental group chosen at random and given socially insignificant tasks to perform. (Petrovskii, 1985, p. 81)

The latter type of social group is undoubtedly the one most frequently studied by Western social psychologists. Petrovskii spares no words in demonstrating how misplaced for an adequate understanding of the functioning of social groups research on type-5 groups is, and he certainly has a valid basis for his criticism of the majority of Western practices of experimental social psychology.

At the same time, Petrovskii introduces the perspective of his own social background into the conceptualization of the types of group—the dimension of 'social progress-regress'. The way this dimension is set up by him represents the Soviet perspective, based on a particular social-political world view. A leader of a well-organized, highly activity-mediated, and ideologically 'progress-oriented' (by his sincere belief) mafia group may consider his own secret collective the highest form of social group, using exactly the same arguments as Petrovskii. The assignment of the most positive value to the type of group that is cherished by the investigator's social environment makes his science explicitly based on the perspective of that background (in this case, the Soviet Marxist world view). What may thus easily become lost is understanding of the relativity of *any* such perspective. When that understanding disappears, the given theory can easily become part of the culture on the basis of which it emerged in the first place.

Contemporary empirical research on children's groups

Most of the contemporary research on children's social groups in the USSR is related to environmental settings in which children's group activities are organized and directed towards different goals by their socializers. Very little interest in children's freely-forming groups (in great contrast with the 1920s) is evident in contemporary Soviet developmental psychology (an exception is Polonskii, 1973).

The most widespread issues of empirical research are related to the sociometric investigation of children's relationships within classrooms (cf. a very comprehensive overview by Kolominskii, 1976). The method of sociometry, since the translation of Moreno's *Sociometry* into Russian (in 1958) has been a target of active criticism from philosophers, while on the other hand it has slowly become a widely used research tool in psychologists' repertoire. The systemic view of social relationships shared by the majority of Soviet social psychologists has also led them to the understanding of the need to study individuals' development according to their simultaneous inclusion in a variety of groups (Kolominskii, 1983). Issues of the formation of group leadership and of factors in its change have been of interest to Soviet developmental psychologists (Krichevskii, 1977; Mal'kovskaia, 1973; Petrovskii, 1980; Petrovskii & Umanskii, 1978). In the phenomenon of group leadership, psychologists in the USSR are interested not in its status quo, but in the dynamic change over time that is wrought by the roles different group members carry out in conjunction with the tasks that the group as a whole is facing (e.g., Krichevskii, 1980). The leading role in the organization of children's groups is allotted to the actions of the pedagogues who take the group membership of the students into account in their activities (Liimets, 1982), and make use of children's suggestibility (Antonova & Khrustaleva, 1982). On the other hand, the development of identification with peer-group in adolescence among Russian children in the USSR, and their distancing of themselves from adults' influences, has been experimentally demonstrated as part of the 'real world' of children's collective activity in schools (Lavrinenko, 1970). These empirical findings illustrate that the reality of children's social development is a multi-faceted systemic process in which goal-directed efforts of adults (parents, teachers, etc.) and children's peer relations (group formation, interpersonal like and dislike, emergence of group norms) are related as a part of a complex system.

It is evident that traditional methods of psychology have very little to offer for the empirical study of such complexity. The understanding of the limited nature of these methods has been present in the thinking of Soviet social psychologists, who have often criticised these traditional methods for their theoretical limitations. However, at the same time, neither Soviet nor Western psychologists have provided a more positive research programme that would allow the self-evident complexity of the development of children's social groups in their everyday real-life context to be captured. From that perspective of empirical research, some of the ideas that have emerged in Soviet psychology may prove fruitful if developed further, rather than followed in their present state.

Social class, child development, and its environment

The theoretical notion that a person's social class membership results in a definite method of organization of the person's psychological processes was a widespread core idea around which the development of Marxist Soviet psychology took place in the 1920s. That notion was rooted in the inter-group (social class) conflict of the 1917 revolution and the following civil war, and was further intensified in the course of the 1920s when the previously 'lower' class of workers was put into the leadership position in society (see Chapter III). Not surprisingly, the social class background of children studied by Soviet psychologists in the 1920s was an important characteristic used in research, resulting in numerous comparisons of children of different social class backgrounds (Arkhangel'skii, 1929; Aryamov, Odintsova & Nechaeva, 1926; Fortunatov, 1929; Gel'mont, 1929; Rybnikov, 1929), and in descriptions of the attitudes or life of particular groups (Chernikhova, 1929; Vilenkina, 1930). Aside from providing information about the given state of affairs in samples of children from (or in) different social class and environmental settings, these studies were also aimed at finding ways of altering the status quo in a direction given by the social policy of the state at the time.

Fortunatov's (1929) questionnaire study of freely-formed collectives of adolescents in rural environments serves as a good example of how the Soviet 'fight' for winning over to their side the young generation of peasants could build upon children's own pastimes. The reality of children's life in rural areas was found to be full of inter-group fighting and theft of others' property:

The meaning of groupings of children from the same locality is stressed in the majority of answers very dramatically. The peasant boy or adolescent cannot safely go out onto the street or go to school, not to speak of trips further away, unless he belongs to a particular defensive and offensive group. Unfamiliar boys are to be beaten up without any guilt on behalf of these groups, but if the boy belongs to another gang, it is not safe to beat him. Fights and 'wars' occupy a major place in the lives of peasant boys. The children fight not only strangers but also their own closest peers in the gang. Describing a fight [within the gang] about some stolen birds, one of the respondents said: 'The fight did not disturb the collective, it even united it more, since heroes and leaders, as we knew them, were established in it.' (Fortunatov, 1929, p. 532)

It is on the basis of such free-ranging, trouble-making, and conflictful freely-formed children's collectives that the Soviet power started to redirect children's and adolescents' activities—by guiding their socially-created group agressiveness against *some* adults (e.g., peasants in the richer, so-called *kulak*, stratum; teachers of the older generation, and any 'enemies' or potential opponents of the Soviet system). The introduction of the Komsomol movement in rural areas accomplished exactly that goal. Fortunatov commented:

The Revolution reflected on the life of boys' groups very clearly. One of the groups, that consisted of well-performing pupils, at first was under a special influence of the village priest .... After the revolution, to the horror of the parents, these boys were working out 'the declaration for abandonment of god's law', obstructing the meetings held by the former 'father' (now called *pop*) [with negative connotations in Russian], and, finally, walking around in the village with revolutionary flags and songs .... The transition from fighting under the leadership of a *vozhak* ... to organized work of a Komsomol group is a typical phenomenon. *Komsomol ends the war between opposite ends of the village and begins the 'fight with adults who are against the formation of the [Komsomol] group'.* (Fortunatov, 1929, p. 533, emphasis added)

This description of the changes in children's social lives in the rural areas illustrates the social policy relevance to the young Soviet state of the work with freely-forming children's collectives. The social group phenomena (aggressive encounters within, and between, groups) which emerged spontaneously could be organized so as to serve a purpose. The benefit from such guidance was perceived to be there for both the adolescents (joining Komsomol) and their organizers:

The collective, to an extreme extent, makes it easier to select necessary experiences from the surrounding environment and provide necessary reactions to these experiences. Since that selection, by an emotionally volatile adolescent, is difficult, the help in selecting experiences and reactions serves as a factor that brings his nervous processes into order and makes them more productive. (Zalkind, 1930a, p. 22)

By providing an organizational framework for adolescents' collectives it becomes possible for adults to direct children towards some, rather than other, activities. However, that direction does not mean strict determination. This becomes clear from the studies of working-class youth (Vilenkina, 1930) in which their social interests were revealed. The simple label of social-class membership of any kind was clearly no guarantee that the given adolescent is taking the position expected of him by the Party, in the conditions of the social turmoil of the 1920s.

Going beyond the mere labels of social-class membership in determination of children's development was a task that a number of psychologists of the 1920s took seriously. That aspect of research involved careful recording of particular characteristics of the children's involvement in different activities. Research was conducted on the amount and kind of work that children of different ages were involved in (e.g., Arkhangel'skii, 1929; Chernikhova, 1929; Rybnikov, 1929), as well as chronometry of 'time budgets' for different activities of children, adolescents and young adults (Bernshtein, 1927; Kolesnikova & Pervova, 1927; Novikov, 1927; Semenov, 1927).

In the context of research on child–environment relationships, the issue of developmental transition from play to work activities was of particular interest to psychologists of the time (Basov, 1931a; Molozhavyi, 1929; Rybnikov, 1929; Vygotsky, 1966). It is in this respect that major differences were revealed between rural and urban children—the necessities of agricultural work made it natural for peasant children to become integrated in their families' economic (work) activities. It is through the necessities of everyday life that the child's environment sets absolute limits on the child's development, forcing the child either earlier or later (or in some cases of affluence, never) to become integrated into the world of work:

The environment, if it puts the child's activities into a certain framework, one way or another always reaches its goals, because it has all the necessary means for that. If it were not for that reason, the period of play in human ontogeny would last significantly longer; in reality for the overwhelming majority of human children this transformation of the type of activity takes place at an early age, since the conditions of life demand from them not play, but work. (Basov, 1931a, p. 670)

Basov's remark is useful for understanding how the question of the environment's role in child development can be asked in two ways. First, in the *general*-psychological sense, a developing child is always fully dependent on his/her particular environmental structure, which can be changed only relative to its previous state. Here, environment is equal to the child's total environment, a system of conditions for development. In contrast, the same question can be asked in the inter-systemic framework—what are the predominant effects of different types of environment on child development? From that perspective, contrasts between rural and urban, or between different social class backgrounds, are useful for research. It was the latter perspective that dominated Soviet developmental psychology in the 1920s, whereas when contemporary Soviet psychologists treat the matter they are more likely to use the general-psychological perspective.

Conclusions: lessons from Soviet research on social development

The issues of children's social development, as viewed by different researchers in the USSR and reviewed in this chapter, point to a number of general characteristics shared by otherwise widely divergent research traditions. First, the *social nature* of children's development of psychological functions of *both* social and cognitive kinds constitutes the axiomatic basis of most of Soviet child psychology. That social nature is exemplified in different forms: the gradual guidance of infants' neurological functions by care-givers in the direction of forming complex associations (Bekhterev), the transformation of the 'need for interaction' in the process of adult-child transaction (Lisina), the socially determined content of children's developing world views in middle and later childhood (Basov), the social determination of children's small-group and collective formation and functioning (Petrovskii), and so on.

Secondly, it is the emphasis on *change* that characterizes Soviet research on social development. This emphasis illustrates the depth of penetration of developmental ideas into the core of Soviet empirical research and theorizing—the mechanisms of children's development are understood only if we find out under what conditions a certain psychological phenomenon, social or cognitive, comes into being. Thus, children's world view can be studied as it emerges as a new cognitive structure, reflecting in some ways the changing conditions of children's social life environments. Or, a group of children that are brought together for the first time at the beginning of their summer camp as a 'diffuse group' proceed to form a 'collective' over the time they stay in the camp.

Thirdly, the research overviewed in the present chapter shares the *systemic view* of the processes of social development. The developing infant or toddler is viewed as a part of an organized system of child-care-giver relationships; the psychological phenomena observed in freely-forming children's collectives in the 1920s are viewed in the context of their relationships with the organized socio-economic conditions in which these social units exist. Furthermore, the structure of collectives is understood (in Petrovskii's case) as a multi-level system involving both actional and value-orientation components, rather than a simple conglomerate of multi-dimensional (mutually 'independent') 'variables'. That systemic emphasis makes it only natural that children's cognitive development is viewed in its relationships with social development. The logic of strict separation of child-psychological phenomenology into the 'cognitive' and the 'social' brands is alien to the basic meta-theoretical thinking on which psychology in the USSR is based. Viewed from that perspective, the segregation of materials overviewed in this, and the preceding, chapter is merely a heuristic feature used in the compositional organization of this book, rather than inherent in developmental psychology in the USSR—in its past or present state.

VIII Cultural Contexts of Child Development and Psychological Research

To an outside observer, it may justifiably seem that the multi-ethnic nature of the USSR could provide psychologists with remarkable opportunities for studying how different cultural backgrounds organize child development. However, very little research of a comparative-cultural nature has been conducted. Social reasons for psychologists' lack of enthusiasm for this research topic are not hard to find, especially if we consider the conditions in the 1920s that gave rise to a heightened interest in the issues of child development among Soviet 'national minorities', ethnic groups with non-Slavic cultural histories. That interest was eradicated from the official Soviet retrospect on their psychology, beginning with the wave of social changes in early 1930s (see Chapter III). Culturally oriented research of paedologists disappeared from Soviet psychology together with the official elimination of paedology. This fate is all the more ironic since it was in the context of paedology that criticism of the uncritical use of testing methods emerged. Paedologists who conducted research on children of non-Russian backgrounds at that time were among the ones who fought against uncritical use of borrowed tests in school practice, and other 'paedological distortions', as later ridiculed and eliminated by the 1936 Decree on Paedology. Culturally oriented research interests of psychologists in the USSR emerged, developed, and perished in the context of Soviet ideology that underwent its own transformation.

This chapter deals with the question of how psychologists in the USSR became interested in the study of child development in non-Russian ethnic contexts, and how the changes in Soviet society influenced the course and fate of these research efforts.

It must be clarified that only part of Soviet culturally-oriented developmental research can be viewed as similar to Western 'cross-cultural psychology'. Only the efforts of paedologists of the second half of 1920s to study children of non-Russian cultures in the context of extension of educational services to non-Russian traditional cultures may fit under that label. Paedological studies emphasized contrasts between Russian and 'national minority' cultures, and addressed the importance of the differences between these cultures for the progress of education. Other lines of research—Luria's studies in Central Asia in the 1930s and similar efforts later (Tulviste, 1984a), and Kon's ethnographic research on childhood (Kon, 1981a)—go far beyond the simple goal of finding the cross-cultural differences and similarities that characterize 'cross-cultural psychology'. Rather, these efforts constitute an extension of developmental psychology to the culturally varied life conditions of developing children.

The *natsmen* problem and psychological research in the 1920s

The paedological research on non-Russian children and their development was directly linked to the efforts of the Soviet government to introduce radical changes into the lifestyles of non-Russian ethnic groups within the USSR. This took place in the context of building a 'new society' where all the previously exploited people would be equal and (eventually) prosperous, and from where the remnants of the exploiting classes are eliminated.

The non-Russian national 'minorities' (*natsional'nyie menshinstva*, abbreviated 'natsmen') were considered to be at a lower level (stage) of cultural development than the Russians. The blame for this state of affairs was attributed to the colonialist policies of pre-1917 czarist Russia. Thus in post-1917 Russia, various efforts were undertaken to bring the cultural life of national minorities closer to that of Russia. These efforts varied. Some were aimed at helping the national minorities to develop their *own* new culture. Of course, a break with the past 'backward' traditions, especially religious ones, was implied. The history of the introduction of new alphabets by Soviet government to national minorities in the 1920s is interesting in this respect. Many of the 'new literacies' in the Caucasus and Central Asia were first based on the Latin alphabet, rather than the Cyrillic one. What these new alphabets helped to create was new *massive* literacy of people the majority of whom had been illiterate before.

A minority of the people in these cultures had been literate before, and continued to be—using the Arabic alphabet that had been in use in Islamic ethnic groups of Northern Caucasus and Central Asia. The 'liquidation of illiteracy' in conjunction with the new alphabet set the stage for future efforts of the Soviet government to facilitate the acceptance of *their* cultural and ideological messages (which the newly literate people could assimilate) in opposition to the traditional (religion-bound) messages (which were communicated in their written form in Arabic script to the few who could read). By eradicating the social religious institutions that would communicate the traditional messages to the masses of illiterate people, the Soviet government effectively replaced the oral religious cultural input by written government-controlled information that the people could themselves *actively* assimilate through their newly acquired reading skills. Just as the Reformation in sixteenth-century Europe led to the proliferation of literacy and to internalization of the ˈmessages decoded by people via reading the Bible on their own, the Soviet provision of new literacy to cultures in Central Asia and the Caucasus was part of efforts to guide cultural change in the direction favoured by the Soviet system. It is somewhat surprising, then, that the alphabets given in the 1920s to non-Russian cultures in the Soviet Union were based on the Latin script. This, however, was changed in the 1930s, when the Latin alphabet basis was changed to Cyrillic. Soviet literacy policies for the *natsmen* underwent a transition in the 1920s–30s that paralleled the changes in Soviety society as a whole.

Other efforts to 'bring the *natsmen* into line' with the rest of the USSR involved the introduction of Western-type compulsory school education to all areas in the USSR. The introduction of schools as an institution was a new development for the majority of *natsmen*; the problems involved were similar to those faced by European missionaries in their efforts to introduce Western schooling in Africa or Asia. It was in the context of the introduction of schooling that Soviet paedologists began to take an interest in the psychology of *natsmen's* children. That interest involved both research on children of ethnic minority groups who lived in overwhelmingly Russian regions (e.g., studies of Tatar schoolchildren in Moscow—Lavrova-Bikchentai, 1930), and the organization of paedological expeditions to regions of the USSR where non-Russian ethnic 'minorities' were actually the majority populations.

Paedological expeditions of 1929

As one of the initiators of psychological research on child development of *natsmen* cultures, Lev Vygotsky expressed his hope that 'the organization of paedological expeditions should become constant and necessary means of scientific investigation, like the method of "field study" in ethnography and ethnology' (Vygotsky, 1929b, p. 373). Soviet developmental psychologists of the 1920s certainly tried to accomplish that, at the height of their youthful energy.

In 1929, two paedological expeditions were organized by the Institute of the Methods of School Work. One of these involved the region of Northern Baikal where children of the Tungus ethnic group were studied. The other went to the Altai mountain region to study Oirot children. At the same time, an expedition from the Institute of the Preservation of Children's and Adolescents' Health was sent to the Buriat-Mongol Autonomic Republic for mostly anthropometric data gathering. At the same time, paedologists working at different universities in the non-Russian areas of the USSR were actively involved in the study of *natsmen* children (Baranova, 1930; Luria, 1931a, 1934; Ostrovskii, 1929). Descriptions of those expeditions by their participants, and the results reported by them, provide us with an interesting overview of ethnic childhoods in the USSR that are very different from the Russian cultural case. In addition to the descriptions of the 1929 expeditions, results of another field-trip to the same areas in 1966 add the possibility of finding out how conditions of child development, and children's performances, have changed through the decades (see Gurova, 1977, in English translation).

Childhood of the Tungus in the 1920s
The Tungus expedition worked in the region of Nizhneangarsk (on the Northern tip of Lake Baikal) in June-August 1929. It consisted of three members, all of whom were third-year students of paedology at the Second Moscow State University (Shepovalova, 1930, p. 172). One of the participants had previously worked

as a schoolteacher in the region. The goal of the expedition was to collect data on Tungus children's socialization and cognitive development using multiple methods taken from psychology and ethnography.

The Tungus at the end of 1920s were divided into three subgroups: mountain, riverbank, and sedentary Tungus. The first group—'mountain Tungus'—was nomadic in lifestyle (with temporarily sedentary life for the winter months), inhabiting inland and mountainous habitats. The subsistence of this group involved hunting, selling precious furs, and deer-herding. The 'riverbank Tungus' were settled on the banks of rivers around Lake Baikal and had made fishing their secondary subsistence activity (besides hunting). They also supplemented hunting and fishing with small-scale vegetable gardening.

The transition from 'mountain' to 'riverbank' group among the Tungus was reported to depend upon economic factors—in the case of insufficient income from hunting (selling furs), an impoverished Tungus could settle in a 'riverbank' Tungus settlement and try to make a living by fishing. The 'riverbank Tungus' had permanent winter huts, but preferred to live in yurts (Central Asian transportable round tents) in the summer, when the men went out on nomadic hunting trips while women and children stayed in the settlement. Finally, the 'sedentary Tungus' constituted a group with a completely sedentary lifestyle, where fishing cooperatives were organized by the Soviet system in conjunction with their socio-political goals and economic realities.

The traditional Tungus lifestyle had clear-cut demands for child socialization—the promotion of hunting-related skills in boys, and cattle/deer care and clothes-making knowledge in girls was an important goal for parents. The wealth of a Tungus family was determined by the number of hunters (father and hunting-age children) on the one hand, and the number of deer on the other. Literacy among Tungus adults was reported to be present in 9% of the adult population at the time (Usova, 1930).

The 'mountain' Tungus children at the time of the expedition were born without much help to the mother from other female relatives. The baby, starting from birth, was kept in a semi-sitting position in a special wooden box hung up in the yurt (so that it could be soothed by swinging), and which was set on back of a deer when the family was moving. Moss was used to furnish the interior of the cradle-box, and changed regularly to keep the infant clean. Infants were breast-fed until about two years of age, or more. The practices of the sedentary Tungus in that respect included other females' presence at childbirth, and regular washing of the infant (Shepovalova, 1930, p. 178). Smoking by young children was observed to be encouraged by many parents among the 'mountain Tungus', but largely discouraged by women among the 'riverbank' ones. Alcohol use was unknown to the Tungus at the time of the expedition.

The nomadic lifestyle of traditional Tungus put clear constraints on children's developmental environments. For travel, children under the age of six or seven were set to ride on the deer, but after that age mostly moved on foot. The lifestyle prepared them physically for long (5–6 hour) hikes, during which they could ride the deer only occasionally. Little planning of trips by adult Tungus was reported by the members of the expedition. Their impression was that a family could instantly decide to move on, dismantle the yurt immediately, expecting children to help in preparations for the journey. Children were observed to learn essential life skills of the Tungus—boys got their own rifles around the age of ten, while by the age of twelve to fourteen, girls could make clothes, milk deer, and perform other tasks at the level of adults. Religious socialization of Tungus children was observed to be of little intensity, constituting a mixture of indigenous beliefs with Russian Orthodox Christianity that had been introduced before 1917.

The social ecology and traditional lifestyle of the Tungus provided serious obstacles on the path of the Soviet government's efforts to introduce new school education for children and to teach literacy to adults. A school in the region, built and kept up by the Tungus tribal council, had been in operation since the end of the nineteenth century. In 1926 it became a boarding school, and from 1928 onwards it was united as a four-year institution with the Russian school of the region. Although Tungus children were taken into government schools, practically no Tungus child in 1928–29 was reported to finish the school (i.e., to reach 4th grade). The expedition documented a mismatch between Tungus children's home environment and the environment they encountered at school (Usova, 1930). In the latter, children were instructed under conditions of discipline-induced conformity to a classroom behaviour that was foreign and exhausting to them.

Escape from the boarding school by Tungus children was frequent, especially towards the end of the school year in the spring.

The expedition paid much attention to the study of Tungus children's general knowledge. Not surprisingly, they were generally knowledgeable about activities and objects that played important roles in the everyday lives of their families, whereas their knowledge about the world beyond their environment was scanty, and *depended upon their experience with some objects, persons, or activities that had become part of their immediate environments, often through symbolic and suggestive means.* Thus, the contrast between children's lack of knowledge of what 'USSR' means (20% of 61 children were familiar with the label, and 5%, all of whom had been to school or courses of literacy, knew the meaning of the abbreviation) and their knowledge of the portrait of Lenin (89% of children recognized it) is noteworthy (Bulanov, 1930, p. 199). The portraits of Lenin (and other Soviet leaders of the time, e.g., Rykov) were introduced to Tungus households by the state cooperatives that sold products to Tungus who had received their money for bringing in furs. These portraits were observed to occupy their symbolic places in Tungus yurts and huts—together with Russian Orthodox icons preserved from the pre-1917 times (Shepovalova, 1930). In contrast, the label 'USSR' was not introduced to the Tungus households through cooperative-introduced objects related to Tungus main economic activities, and was unfamiliar to those children who had not been exposed to it at a schooling institution. Likewise, children's knowledge of other ethnic groups included only those with whom they had some contact (Russians, Buriats) or about whom they had heard from other Tungus (25% had heard of the Chinese, 2–3% about Koreans, Chukchi, Samojeds, Yakuts, Germans, Jews, Englishmen, Japanese). The overwhelming majority of children (94.6%) could not name any foreign country (Bulanov, 1930, p. 198). The reliance on their immediate knowledge, based on their Tungus life environment and activities, was also demonstrated in the case of other topics that were studied (attitudes towards Russians, preferences for sex-role models, descriptions of action with money, etc.). The Tungus expedition collected a wide variety of data on the link between Tungus children's knowledge and behaviour, and their socio-cultural background. It brought the specificity and content of the thinking processes of traditional cultures to the attention of psychologists. The roots of later Soviet action-theoretical perspectives on human development can be found in the experiences of the investigators during the expedition. Indeed, the practical activities of the people, and children's actions with objects provided by the culture, constitute the factors responsible for children's knowledge (or lack of it) in different domains.

Childhood of Altais and Telengits in the Oirot region in the 1920s
The Oirot paedological expedition took place in parallel with the Tungus expedition. Its target—the Oirot region in the Altai mountains of Southern Siberia—was inhabited by a number of different ethnic groups at the time (48% of the population was made up of Telengits, Teleuts, Altais, Tatars; 50% were Russians, with 2% of other ethnic backgrounds). All the different indigenous ethnic groups are of Turkic origin, with languages sharing commonalities with Turkish. Before 1917, Russian colonial politics evicted the local population from their traditional habitats into higher mountain regions, which produced a long history of hostility against Russians. The indigenous population of the region is involved in cattle-breeding, hunting, and farming.

The three-member expedition to the Oirot region had to cope with language problems, as well as with the active uninterest of the local children in being tested by the researchers. The final results of the expedition included data from 86 children of two ethnic groups—Telengits (N=44) and Altais (N=42). These two groups of indigenous inhabitants of the Oirot region were described by the investigators as quite different from each other. The Telengits lived in the most remote areas of the region, yet despite their location, their culture had been exposed to considerable influence from Russian Orthodox missionaries. They were described by one member of the expedition as being 'by their traditions largely similar to Russians, although their lives are full of superstitions ...' (Golubeva, 1930, p. 209).

In contrast, the Altais were described as highly religious (shamanist) and highly restrictive of women's behaviour. The Altais were perceived by the Russian investigators as having less hygienic home environments than those of the Telengits. Literacy was more frequent among the Telengits as a result of the missions of the Orthodox Church, than among the Altais.

The adaptation of Oirot children to school conditions was found to encounter difficulties similar to those of the Tungus:

> They get exhausted quickly, they are bored by the school routines and the need for using effort. Oirots are children of nature and any kind of suppression of their personalities insults them and leads to escapes from school, all the more because parents do not protest against their escape and do not force the child to study. The Oirot child has great difficulty in adapting to the school and boarding-house regime: sit a few hours in the same place, get up, wash himself, change clothes. The child does not understand why he should lie down on the bed and not on the floor, and why he can't lie down in any bed he wants to and be there in coat and dirty boots. Unintelligible demands irritate children and lower their interest in school. (Golubeva, 1930, p. 219)

The home environment of children was also observed to set limits on the children's school attendance. In the autumn children were expected to herd the cattle, and return to that economic activity early in the spring. On the other hand, it was reported that some children (unfortunately unclear whether Altai or Telengit) ran away from home in order to attend school.

The investigators studied child socialization in families in the Oirot region by participant observations. Young children were seen to be integrated in the family's life activities, helped parents, and showed no capricious behaviour. The investigators were surprised by the quietness of Oirot children (Golubeva, 1930, pp. 212–13). Children were brought up with minimal pressure for differential sex-role development, and the social rule of sharing one's resources with other people was detected by the investigators. When tested for memory functions related to particular complex environments, Oirot children performed in superior ways that led the investigator (Zaporozhets, 1930) to hypothesize the presence of eidetic memory in those children.

Psychological testing versus research on psychological processes
Perhaps the most important empirical result that emerged as a result of the paedological studies of *natsmen* children was the understanding that Western intelligence tests, even after their adaptation to the local linguistic conditions, are useless as research tools and detrimental to practical work in schools. The children in the Oirot region were found to have IQ = 66.9 (standard deviation = 8.5) when the Russian-adapted Binet-Simon test was used, in

translation into the local languages (Zaporozhets, 1930, p. 233). Zaporozhets' vivid description of the process of testing Oirot children on Binet-Simon is worth closer attention:

Out of all methods that we used, the investigation with the Binet was especially difficult and exhausting for the Oirot child, and consequently also for the experimenters. It is enough to note that the duration of the investigation varied between 1.5 and 4 hours. Constant refusals, that sometimes were effective in nature (tears, attempt to hide in the mountains or *taiga*), to fulfill tasks; shyness of the child; unfavourable conditions for investigation (it took place in the yurts while the whole family of the child was present)—all these factors made the test-taking time very long. The verbally alien nature of questions led the child into an impasse. The goal of these questions provoked bewilderment in him. Why should a stranger know what he would do before making an important decision? ... The least difficulties were created by problems that required practical manipulation ... The test 'as many words as possible in 3 minutes' does not result in the minimum response given by Binet (60 words) in the majority of cases. Usually the child produces 30–40 words in 3 minutes. The words uttered by the child are either a list of objects in his immediate visual field during the experiment, or are taken by him from his experience, mainly from cattle-breeding, hunting, etc., that characterizes his interests. In this test, the Oirot child stops all the time and is in need of multiple repetitions of the instruction (6, 7, or more times) .... A special difficulty exists with tests that require the use of different logical operations. In defining objects, the Oirot child of any age group reveals a strong tendency to provide action-related definitions. Objects are defined by what they are used for. A child, in answer to the question—what is knife, chair, horse?—gives laconic answers: to cut, to sit, to ride. While answering abstract questions the child usually tries to bring them to the level of concreteness. The experimenter asks: 'what should be done if you break a thing that belongs to somebody else?' The child in his turn asks: 'Whose thing? What thing?' Evidently, depending on particular conditions, he is ready to act in one or another way. When asked: 'what do you do, before deciding upon an important task?' the child often asks 'which tasks?' If the experimenter is not careful enough and provides an example of a difficult task, then the child immediately solves the problem, but only in respect to that particular difficult task. (Zaporozhets, 1930, pp. 224–5)

In these difficulties in the administration of standardized psychological tests to *natsmen* children, the interference of the peculiarities of the thinking processes of children not exposed to formal Western-type education are evident. Zaporozhets' dissatisfaction with the use of tests is parallel to that of Piaget, who turned the difficulties which French schoolchildren had while answering standardized test questions into the object of investigation. It was clear to Zaporozhets and other participants in the paedological expeditions (Baranova, 1930; Bulanov, 1930; Schubert, 1930) that standardized tests are antithetical to the goal of understanding how the psychological *processes* of developing children are organized. Zaporozhets arrived at the conclusion that the use of intelligence tests to study the intellect of non-Western children is inappropriate because 'different psychological mechanisms underlie the solving of test items by European and Oirot children' (Zaporozhets, 1930, p. 232). The understanding that different cultural conditions of life are related to qualitatively (and not quantitatively) different mechanisms of thinking, which forms the backbone of the cultural-historical theory of psychology of Vygotsky and Luria (see Chapter IV), was illustrated by Zaporozhets' empirical research in Altai. It also makes the prevailing Soviet tendency towards exclusion of standardized tests from among acceptable methods of scientific psychology clearer and more meaningful. The 'de-standardization' and 'de-quantification' (see Brožek, 1972) of research methods in psychology in the USSR first emerged in the theoretical and empirical context of investigators' thinking about psychological phenomena, before it became the rule instituted by the 1936 Decree. The theoretical ideas that underlie Vygotsky's, Zaporozhets', Luria's, Piaget's, Köhler's and other European psychologists' deliberate decisions to avoid construction of quantitative data that obscure the psychological processes of the subjects are a serious, albeit forgotten, contribution to making psychology *more*, not less, scientific—in the sense that the data retain a clear connection with the reality. In this, Soviet developmental psychology shares with Jean Piaget the pioneering role of conducting careful qualitative observations and experiments on children's cognitive development.

'Cultural-historical' expeditions to Central Asia

For the cultural-historical school of thought in psychology (Chapter 4), the multi-cultural composition of Soviet society created a natural laboratory in which a number of propositions stemming from Vygotsky's theory could be studied in practice. The introduction of new cultural institutions by Soviet government in the non-Russian regions of the USSR created a number of 'teaching experiments' (in Vygotsky's sense). Efforts to 'teach' the 'more modern' ways of living (i.e., those of the Russian culture-in-transition) to traditional cultures that inhabited the geographical periphery of the Soviet Union were introduced as the basic social policy for the *natsmen*. In this context, psychologists' interest in the psychological changes that were wrought by new social policies was quite predictable. Thus, Soviet developmental psychology of the 1920s became interested in comparative-cultural research issues.

Strictly speaking, the research done by psychologists from the cultural-historical school in Central Asia in the early 1930s was not 'cross-cultural' in the contemporary sense of the term. Rather, it can be labelled 'cultural-developmental', since it parallels other Vygotskian ontogenetic research in differing cultural environments (Vygotsky, 1929b; Vygotsky & Luria, 1930b).

Applied to the study of psychological processes in developing cultures, this dialectical perspective on integration of different lines of development reveals why the plans for the two Central Asian expeditions were made up in the ways that they were (see Luria, 1931a, 1934, 1974, 1976a). Aside from addressing the issues of new developmental cognitive phenomena emerging as a result of cultural change, the expeditions also addressed issues of *connection* between the old traditions of the culture and newly introduced features. Vygotsky (1929b) put a special emphasis on that angle of research. Unfortunately, the old-to-new connection (e.g., data on the connection between traditional-religious belief systems and personality development) has remained hidden in the unpublished results of the expeditions, due to historical forces that rendered all the data from the research efforts unavailable to a wider public for many decades.

After forty years, some of the empirical data from the two expeditions organized by Alexander Luria to Central Asia (in the summers of 1931 and 1932) have become available (Luria, 1974), and accessible in the English language (Luria, 1976a). The theoretical background of these expeditions and the full scope of research activities involved have largely been ignored, both in the USSR and in the West.

In the first international announcement of the research in Central Asia, Luria described the goals of the first expedition:

The aim of the expedition was to investigate the variations in thought and other psychological processes of people living in a very primitive economic and social environment, and to record those changes which develop as a result of the introduction of higher and more complex forms of economic life and the raising of the general cultural level. One special task of the expedition was to develop new methods for evaluating intellectual status of individuals in very backward communities, because the usual methods of determining intelligence are inapplicable in the very special cultural conditions influencing the intellectual processes of the members of these groups. Another task was the preparation of educational methods which could be applied to these communities, such as the teaching of counting, reading, etc. (Luria, 1931a, p. 383)

The emphasis on the *backward-but-improving* status attributed to the Central Asian cultures is evident from this quote. The comparison basis for establishing the 'backwardness' of these cultures was the investigators' own cultural background of a European kind. Luria and other cultural-historical psychologists of his time had no egalitarian view of the traditional cultures in which they conducted their study. Instead, the 'backward' state of the cultures was equated with a developmentally lower stage from which, under certain environmental conditons, progression to higher stages can take place (e.g., Vygotsky & Luria, 1930, p. 58). The aim of the two Central Asian expeditions organized by Luria was to study the *development* of children *within cultures* that were at the time undergoing rapid transformation. Child development is inevitably intertwined with the developing culture, so Luria's cultural-historical research constitutes empirical developmental research *par excellence*.

The first expedition worked in Uzbek and Kirghiz areas (in the *kishlaks* of Shahimardan and Jordan in the Altai mountain region, and in Ust-Kurgan on the Naryn river). The list of topics covered by the programme of the first expedition was impressive:

1. Perception of colour, form, and optical illusions at various stages of people's cultural devlopment.
2. The configuration of vision in the system of visual thinking.
3. Structure of elementary thought processes at various stages of historical-psychological development.
4. Verbal-logical configurations in the system of visual thinking.
5. Concept formation at different levels of cultural development.
6. The development of causal thinking.
7. Traditional religious thought in the development of personality.
8. Perception of printed material in a system of visual thinking.

9. Numerical operations in a system of visual thinking.
10. Self-analysis and evaluation of others at various stages of personality development. [Luria, 1931a]

The second expedition organized by Luria took place in the summer of 1932. Kurt Koffka was the foreign participant in that expedition, although he left before the end due to illness (see Harrower, 1983). The expedition worked in the areas used in the previous summer (Shahimardan and Yordan, as well as the Altai region), and added the region of Palman (where Soviet efforts to get the peasants to join collective farms had largely succeeded by that time).

Results of the two expeditions revealed that the introduction of formal schooling and literacy training to Uzbek and Kirghiz peasants coincided with qualitative changes in their processes of thinking, perceiving, problem-solving, and self-reflection (Luria, 1974, 1976a). The results from analyses of one's own and others' selves had a special place in Luria's thinking about personality. In his autobiographical retrospect, Luria emphasized the relevance of the latter, since these demonstrated the cultural-developmental nature of the self:

We called these observations [on self-reflection] 'anti-cartesian experiments', since we found that critical relationship to one's self is the final stage of socially determined psychological development, and does not constitute its starting point, as would follow from Descartes' ideas. (Luria, 1982, p. 69)

The label of 'anti-cartesian experiments' fits well with most of the psychological research conducted by Luria and his colleagues, not only that carried out in Central Asia. In all research projects of the kind, the emphasis on the *development* of qualitatively new cultural, cognitive and behavioural phenomena is crucial. It was the process of the cultural development of personalities that Luria could observe in a cross-section of Central-Asian peasants whom the investigators met during the expeditions. Their basic finding included a demonstration of how internally-oriented self-evaluation develops in conjunction with new economic activities and exposure to formal schooling. The vehicle for that demonstration was questioning subjects about their 'shortcomings'. The Russian term used by Luria—*nedostatok*—can be applied *both* to external lack of something in terms of material goods, and to deficiences of one's character or personality. Luria's interviews with his subjects of variable exposure to culture contact with others (i.e., Russians) and different educational background revealed that greater exposure to formal schooling coincides with an increased readiness to talk about one's *psychological*, rather than material, 'shortcomings'. In other words, the concept of self as an entity that is separate from the social network of the individual and his activity context is a product of cultural history, rather than its starting datum (see Luria, 1974, pp. 148–62; Luria, 1976a, Ch. 7).

Other results of the two Central Asian expeditions are 'anti-cartesian' in a similar way. Luria's demonstration of changes in syllogistic reasoning, wrought by the cultural history of the time (Luria, 1974, pp. 108–37; Luria, 1976a, Ch. 4), and the demonstration of the cultural-historical nature of the process of generalization and abstraction (Luria, 1976a, Ch. 3) all reveal the same picture. Rapid changes in the organization of a traditional culture, brought about by culture contact that leads to a modified set of activities and to experience of formal schooling, are paralleled by transformation of the higher psychological functions of the members of the culture.

Extinction of psychological research on *natsmen* child development

The Soviet interpretation of the *natsmen* 'problem' was socially redefined at the beginning of the 1930s. According to the redefined version of the issue, all cultures of the USSR were now becoming homogeneous as the 'Soviet people'. Therefore any empirical demonstration of 'backwardness' of an ethnic group belonging to the 'Soviet people' could be considered 'insulting' to 'the most progressive society'; that of the USSR.

In such a context of social meanings, paedological and psychological research on non-Russian cultures in the USSR became at best irrelevant, and at worst contrary to the Soviet social-political goals of the 1930s. Thus, comparative-cultural research issues vanished from Soviet psychology for about forty years. Paedological 'abuses' in Samarkand were criticized by Leventeuv, himself an active member of Luria's expeditions to Central Asia. Leventuev (1931, p. 66) called for more direct control over paedology from 'proletarian revolutionaries' to avoid research that undermines the social-political goals of the Soviet system. In their turn, Luria's expeditions were criticized, since his results could be interpreted as revealing the *inherent* 'backwardness' of the peoples of Central Asia. That could be 'insulting' to these peoples, who were now (in the 1930s) building the 'new society' in full equality with Russians as belonging to the 'Soviet people' (Razmyslov, 1934). The developmental emphasis on differences *within* the ingroup of cultures inhabiting the USSR had vanished, and been replaced by the assertion that the 'Soviet people' is a unified homogenous population. This axiomatic idea rendered any demonstration of psychological differences between cultures in the USSR as undermining its own validity. To defend that axiom, comparative-cultural thinking and empirical research in the USSR became a forgotten and alien domain for psychologists' endeavours.

Re-emergence of comparative-cultural research in the 1970s

The results of the two Central Asian expeditions were published by Luria only in 1974, and became internationally available two years later (Luria, 1974, 1976a). An Estonian psychologist who received his higher education with Luria—Peeter Tulviste—became interested in replication and extension of Luria's cultural-historical work of the 1930s. At the same time, two other cross-culturally oriented empirical lines of research on child development emerged in the 1970s. First, the ethno-sociological perspective of Igor Kon has revived psychological interest in child development in different cultures, both inside the USSR and in other countries (Kon, 1983a, 1983b). This perspective is primarily connected with the work of ethnography, extending the Soviet ethnographic traditions towards the study of children's and parents' cognition and actions. Secondly, comparative-sociological research by the Estonian school of environmental psychology and urban sociology, led by Mati Heidmets, Jüri Kruusvall and Toomas Niit, emerged in the course of the 1970s (Heidmets, 1983a, 1983b, 1985; Kruusvall, 1983; Kruusvall & Heidmets, 1979; Niit & Lehtsaar, 1983; Niit,

Heidmets & Kruusvall, 1987). The main object of study of this
social-psychological school has been the organization and change
of families in different man-made environmental settings in urban
areas. The inclusion of urban areas from different regions of the
USSR in the empirical research projects has produced interesting
cross-cultural findings on child socialization.

Contemporary cultural-historical research on child development
The renewed interest in Luria's cultural-historical research in the
1970s led to the organization of a number of expeditions by
psychologists at Tartu University in Estonia to different cultural
areas in the USSR. All of these were undertaken at the intiative of
Peeter Tulviste. The first—in the summer of 1977—worked in the
Naryn area of Northern Kirghizia (Kazarman and Diurbel'dzin
regions). The second expedition visited Hant-speaking people on
the Ob River (Berezovo region) in Siberia. In addition, Tulviste
had previously done fieldwork on the Taimyr peninsula with
Nganassans.

The psychological problems addressed in the course of these
field trips largely replicated Luria's historical-cognitive research on
his two Central-Asian expeditions in the early 1930s. Both adults
(of different educational backgrounds) and children were studied as
to their ways of solving syllogistic reasoning tasks, and their self-
concepts were scrutinized in the context of an interview along lines
similar to those of Luria. A Piagetian task on the conservation of
the amount of liquid was also administered in field conditions. As a
special additional topic, children were studied with the help of an
animism questionnaire—a modified version of Wayne Dennis's
animistic reasoning inventory.

The major new issue, resulting from Tulviste's research, is
psychologists' understanding of the development of *relationships*
between deductive and inductive sides of thinking in connection
with subjects' cultural backgrounds and everyday activities.
Tulviste, like Luria about four decades before him, administered to
the subjects simple syllogistic reasoning tasks containing two types
of knowledge—the 'school' and 'everyday' types. In the study
conducted by Tulviste (1978) with Nganassan schoolchildren (age
range 8–15 years) in Taimyr, these two types of knowledge
inserted in the first figure of syllogism (Major premise: All X are
Y; minor premise: A is X; Question: is A—Y, or not?) were used

in 10 syllogistic items, 5 involving 'school' and 5 'everyday' knowledge. The difference between the two kinds of syllogism is exemplified in the contrast between the following two:

'EVERYDAY' CONTENT:
MAJOR PREMISE: 'Saiba and Nakupte [Ngnassan first names] always drink tea together'
MINOR PREMISE: 'Saiba drinks tea at 3 p.m.'
QUESTION: 'Does Nakupte drink tea at 3 p.m. or not?' 'Why do you think so?'

'SCHOOL' CONTENT:
MAJOR PREMISE: 'All precious metals are rustfree'
MINOR PREMISE: 'Molybdenum is a precious metal'
QUESTION: 'Does molybdenum rust or not?' 'Why do you think so?'

The rationale for using two different kinds of content in the same logical form of syllogism was to observe discrepancies in children's thinking between tasks they could learn only through school education (e.g., the molybdenum, and concepts of 'precious metal' did not occur in Nganassan's children's lives outside school), and tasks in which everyday knowledge was used. Two ways of constructing answers to the syllogisms could be used. The syllogisms could be answered on the basis of 'empirical' knowledge (through inductive reasoning mechanisms that generalize from empirical data collected by the subject in everyday life). Or, alternatively, they could be answered in terms of 'theoretical' knowledge (through deductive reasoning, following the logic of connecting the major and minor premises, never questioning the truthfulness of the major one).

Tulviste indeed found a discrepancy in how the majority of the children he studied operated with these two knowledge domains. These children (22 out of 35) were considered 'transitional' in the sense that they were assumed to be in the process of developing the use of deductive reasoning across many domains of thinking. Out of the 22 subjects who demonstrated different ways of thinking for the two knowledge domains, 17 children gave more 'theoretical' explanations for syllogisms with 'school' content. Three demonstrated equal use of 'theoretical' and 'empirical' response styles, and 2 used 'theoretical' ways of answering 'everyday'-content syllogisms more than the 'school'-content ones.

Tulviste's general interpretation of the syllogistic reasoning data extends the largely linear view of cognitive development, held by Luria and Vygotsky in the 1930s, to a multi-linear one:

there is no 'natural' human thinking and no one direction, in which it should inevitably develop in the course of its ontogenesis and cultural historical development. Rather, different kinds of theoretical activity produce different modes of verbal thinking that are necessary in creating (or generating), acquiring and using the respective modes of culture texts. (Tulviste, 1978, p. 16)

This general perspective was further extended in research done in Central Asia, where a study of similar syllogistic reasoning in elderly people who had received schooling in their youth but had subsequently returned to agricultural activities demonstrated that deductive reasoning was of little importance (Tamm & Tulviste, 1980). It was revealed that in many of these Kirghiz agriculturalists, the solution of syllogistic problems was consistently attempted using 'empirical' rather than 'theoretical' response strategies.

In different knowledge domains, the fate of 'theoretical' and 'empirical' ways of syllogistic reasoning varies. According to Tulviste, the exposure to formal schooling first promotes the use of the 'theoretical' (deductive) reasoning in respect to school-related knowledge, from which that new reasoning form is extended to different everyday-kinds of knowledge if schooling has a profound effect. If the schooled subject returns to activities that do not require the use of deductive reasoning, or where such reasoning is counterproductive (e.g., in everyday practical life tasks), the previous effects of schooling may be extinguished in the cognitive sphere. On the other hand, many people who have never been to school and who use 'empirical' (inductive) reasoning in all of their life situations, can advance their cognitive processes to a level where they depict reality with high accuracy, even if the subject steadfastly refuses to make a simple inference from a major premise of a syllogism in an experiment.

Tulviste's advancement of the Luria-Vygotsky line of research involves the recognition that the major set of activities in which a person is involved in everyday life is the final determiner of the ways deductive and inductive reasoning strategies are applied to a particular task. Formal schooling can play an important role in this, *if* the person has to use the reasoning strategies acquired at school in his life activities. For many people in industrialized cultures, a certain continuity exists between the demands on thinking promoted by school, and those required after formal education ends. For some, that continuity is absent, and the ways of thinking that rely on deduction from (un-questioned) major premises of figure-1 syllogisms vanish as they give way to dominance of inductive ways of thinking. Although the effects of formal schooling on cognitive development have been demonstrated beyond doubt (Cole *et al.*, 1971; Luria, 1974, 1976a; Ellis & Rogoff, 1986), the functioning of these effects in the context of people's everyday life remains largely unstudied (with rare exceptions—cf. Scribner & Cole, 1981). What Tulviste has demonstrated in cross-cultural studies, and what he has considered theoretically, is the *adaptational* nature of thinking in the context of activities. Different kinds of activity call for qualitatively different modes of thinking. The 'higher' or 'lower' status of these modes always remains relative to the given activity and cannot be determined in an absolute sense. This perspective is a decisive advancement in cognitive psychology of the cultural-historical line, in which Vygotsky's and Luria's emphasis on the development of higher psychological processes prevailed.

The research on animistic thinking in Kirghiz children (which is still unpublished) grew out of earlier efforts to study Estonian children in respect to personification of unliving objects (Tulviste & Lapp, 1978). Of 75 Estonian children in the age range of 3–7 years, 65 demonstrated animistic reasoning in tasks used originally by Margaret Mead for similar purposes. A parallel study of 30 parents revealed that 28 of them admitted using animistic explanations in *their* interaction with children (e.g., 'don't hit the bicycle, it's painful for it—imagine if somebody hit *you* like that!'—Tulviste, 1984a, p. 109). The origin of children's animistic thought is found in the cultural texts that older siblings and adults construct and narrate (Tulviste, 1977), and which the child internalizes.

The ethnographic approach to child development
The research orientation led by Igor Kon in contemporary social and developmental psychology in the USSR is the most closely related to the cross-cultural psychological and cultural-anthropological research around the world. This orientation involves the study of the *ethnography* of child development within cultural contexts. It is institutionally based on the ethnography

establishment (especially on the Institute of Ethnography of the Soviet Academy of Science) of the USSR, and has only occasional contact with Soviet 'mainstream' psychological schools and their publications.

Kon's ethno-sociological approach to child development has features that make his approach more erudite than its Western counterparts. Namely, his theoretical analysis integrates historical; semiotic, ethnographic and social-psychological knowledge in treating research issues (e.g., see Kon, 1980, 1984a, available in English). Of particular interest is the integration of semiotics and psychology in Kon's analyses of childhoods, since these two disciplines are very rarely in contact in Western-European and North-American developmental psychology. Kon's long-term interest in the sociology and social psychology of personality (Kon, 1967, 1978, 1981d, 1984b) is the basis on which his ethnological emphasis seems to have emerged.

The internationally-oriented and highly philosophically erudite thinking that permeates Kon's writing resembles the Russian psychological traditions of Vagner, Vygotsky, Basov and Severtsov, and is very different to the style of thinking that dominated Soviet psychology between the 1930s and 1970s. Kon's ethnography of childhood is a research orientation built along the lines of a cosmopolitan and internationally oriented science, rather than on Slavophilic grounds.

Kon's organizational work in publishing volumes of ethnography of childhood (Kon, 1983a, 1983b) and his own analyses of child socialization (Kon, 1978, 1981a, 1981b, 1983c) are explicitly developmental and systematic in nature. Three reference frames for the study of socialization are advocated by Kon. First, an analysis of cultures' concepts of children in the context of symbolism related to different age levels is called for. Secondly, he advocates a sociological analysis of children's position in the system of age stratification, research on age-specific activities of children, and interaction involving different child-socializing institutions. Finally, Kon expects the psychological analysis of children's actual development to be integrated into the system of interdisciplinary study of child development (Kon, 1978, 1981b). Explicit recognition of cultural variability (both intra- and inter-cultural) emerges from Kon's theoretical treatment of issues of child socialization. First, in his criticism of Bronfenbrenner's comparative research on Soviet and American childhoods (Russian translation of *Two worlds of childhood* appeared in 1976), Kon warns against simple contrasts between 'Soviet' and 'American' modal child-socialization mechanisms. According to Kon, interpretation of the 'school'/'family' distinction as the difference between Soviet and American 'typical' child socialization vehicles overlooks the systemic nature of 'family' *and* 'school' interaction in *both* cultures. Furthermore, in respect to any particular 'style' of child-rearing documented in any culture, Kon proposes:

Not a single one of those styles or, more exactly, value orientations, dominates on its own, especially when we consider the practice of child-rearing. In every society and at each level of its development, there coexist different styles and methods of child-rearing in which different social class, kin, regional, family, and other variations are reflected. Even the emotional relationship of the parents to the child, including its psychological defence mechanism, cannot be considered in isolation from other aspects of history, in particular—in isolation from the general style of interaction and interpersonal relations, values ascribed to individuality, etc. (Kon, 1981a, p. 5)

Kon is also one of the few social scientists in contemporary USSR who has repeatedly stressed that consideration of cultural differences between different regions of the USSR should be taken into account in social and family policy making (Kon, 1938c). It may be added that coming from an ethnographic institutional framework, that suggestion is well in line with ethnography's interest in cultures. Kon's extension of traditional ethnography to the psychosocial issues of personality development is a theoretical trend in contemporary social science in the USSR that deserves more interest than it has currently received from the international scientific community.

A number of ethnographical empirical projects have been conducted in the USSR, involving different ethnic areas. These studies have been devoted mostly to two topics—ethnopedagogics (cultures' child-rearing beliefs and practices) and children's folklore. The ethnopedagogical research in the USSR has resulted in the analyses of child-rearing among the Chuvash (Volkov, 1966), Azerbaidjanis (Gashimov, 1970), Ukrainians (Siavavko, 1974) and cultures of Siberia (Popov, 1984; Strakach, 1956). In research on children's folklore, mostly Russian children's oral creativity has been analyzed (Grechina & Osorina, 1981; Mamontova, 1981; Mel'nikov,

1970; Osorina, 1983). Contemporary interest in children's folklore has its historical roots in similar ethnographic research of the 1920s (Kapitsa, 1928; Vinogradov, 1925, 1930).

Soviet ethnography of recent decades also includes research on child-related cultural practices of Slavic and non-Slavic groups (e.g., child borrowing and adoption among the Yakuts—Evseeva, 1980; cultural organization of childbirth and children's health maintenance in Mordovia—Fedianovich, 1979). The problems of interethnic relations, similar to those whose study led to the disappearance of cross-cultural approaches in Soviet *psychology* in the 1930s, have been subjected to empirical investigation without much ado in ethnography. For instance, Sneshkova's (1982) thorough study of ethnic self-consciousness of children in the Ukraine (in Kiev and Karpathian mountain areas) takes Piaget's stage account of children's cognitive development as the basis from which to investigate the understanding by different-aged children of their own cultural backgrounds, as well as that of their neighbours.

The emergence in the recent decade of interests in the ethnography of child development in the USSR is not limited to cultures inhabiting the USSR. Efforts have been made to systematize and analyze child socialization in other areas of the world, most notably in the Middle East (Kon, 1983b) and East- and South-East Asia (Kon, 1983a). Some of this ethnography involves results of the authors' own fieldwork (with Afghans—Rahimov, 1983; Khmers—Kosikov, 1983).

The ethnographic approach to child socialization that is advancing in the framework of contemporary ethnography in the USSR is a small, but extremely interesting trend in cross-cultural psychology in the USSR. Serious integration of that trend with different tendencies in the frameworks of 'mainstream' psychological thinking in the USSR is unlikely to emerge. To that end, the Soviet psychological establishment at any time in history is as defensive of its discipline boundaries as its Western counterparts are of theirs.

Environmental psychology, urban sociology and child development

Data on child development in different cultural areas of the USSR emerge as a spin-off from the research programme of the Estonian environmental psychology and urban sociology group (Heidmets,

1983a, 1983b, 1985; Kruusvall, 1983, 1986; Kruusvall & Heidmets, 1979; Liik & Niit, 1986; Niit & Lehtsaar, 1983; Raudsepp, 1986). The Estonian group of environmental psychologists has been also instrumental in organizing the activities of environmental psychologists in the rest of the Soviet Union (see Niit, Heidmets, & Kruusvall, 1987).

The main object of empirical research by that group of younger-generation researchers is the actions people use to organize their life environments, at home, at work and in public places. Their research on families' organization of the space in their home territories (standard-size apartments) in a number of cities in the USSR has produced valuable data about the availability of home space for children in families of different cultural backgrounds. The areas involved in these studies in the years 1974–77 included two towns in the Russian Federation (Moscow, Pskov), and two in Estonia (Tallinn, Tartu). In 1978–81, a number of other cities (Liepaja, Ivano-Frankovsk, Kiev, Togliatti, Simferopol', Novosibirsk, Lvov, Tashkent and Leningrad) were added to the study (for results, see Heidmets, 1983b).

The theoretical basis for interpretation of the cross-cultural data on the development of children's need for space is Mati Heidmets' general theory of man–environment relationships (see Heidmets, 1983a, 1985). This theory integrates the interest in environment of contemporary environmental psychology in Europe and North America, with Soviet systemic and dialectical thinking about man–environment relations. Among the latter, Heidmets' theoretical system borrows from Igor Kon (see above), and Boris Porshnev (1974). Among internationally known environmental psychologists, Heidmets integrates ideas of Irwin Altman and Urie Bronfenbrenner into his theoretical system. However, Heidmets' theoretical system goes beyond all of his predecessors in its theoretical-empirical integrity (for a review in English see Heidmets, 1985). This is well reflected in his systemic description of the development of individual-enviroments relations:

The development of man-environment relations (in phylogenesis as well as in ontogenesis) is ... first and foremost man's differentiation of the world, i.e., in the process of development environment *differentiates* into internally and externally controlled, open and closed, 'own' and 'alien' environments. In those processes the dialectical character of development becomes evident, evolution does not proceed in one direction only but it is, as a rule, a balanced process. The increase of internal control in a certain sphere of environment brings about its decrease in other spheres, openness in one sphere brings about greater closedness in another .... (Heidmets, 1983a, p. 65, emphasis in original)

Heidmets' philosophical foundations go back to Herbert Spencer's emphasis on equilibration in nature and society. The Estonian school of environmental psychology approaches issues of children's development by studying the structural reorganization of children's micro-environments in the contexts of the family. The actual cultural structure of these families, as in the case of the cultural-historical school, remains beyond the scope of study in this sociological perspective.

Conclusions

The Soviet Union is a multi-cultural country where it is possible in principle to observe a great variety of culturally organized patterns of child development. However, the practical study of cross-cultural issues of child development has been rare. The emergence, disappearance, and re-emergence of comparative-cultural developmental research in the USSR has proceeded in close connection with the historical changes in the Soviet social system.

Despite the rarity of comparative-cultural developmental research in the USSR, some features of the existing (or formerly existing) research programmes are of theoretical relevance. First, the early paedological expeditions to non-Russian cultural regions demonstrated the inapplicability of standard tools of European-American psychological research methods across culture boundaries. Secondly, the *developmental* emphasis has been present in the majority of these research programme (Luria, Kon, Tulviste, Heidmets). That developmental emphasis is related to a systemic view on child development. In some cases (Kon's programme), that systemic view entails serious integration of knowledge about the cultural and historical development of the society with psychological knowledge about parental beliefs, thoughts and child-rearing actions. Comparative-cultural research on child development, even if rare, is conducted with an appreciation of the complexity caused by the integration of child development in a culture.

IX Cultural Heterogeneity of Developmental Psychology in the Soviet Union

In the process of its development mankind accumulated not only material but also spiritual values. The basis for the emergence of great human creations of the mind was, and forever remains, in the web of concrete cultures. As these creations crystallized within their cultures of origin, they become shared assets of the whole of mankind through the process of communication.

No single culture, however rich it may be, can encompass the whole variability present in the world, its 'immediate wholeness'. Every culture possesses a unique (and non-reconstructable by other cultures) view of the world.... Interaction of languages and cultures, their mutual enrichment, does not exclude the possibility of their partial integration and disappearance, as well as the emergence of new ones. In human society the complementarity of individualities, languages, and cultures has created preconditions for unlimited understanding and use of the world in all of its fullness and neverending richness. (Emil Shukurov, 1972, p. 39)

The Soviet Union is culturally heterogeneous, and so is psychology in the USSR. The cultural and geographical heterogeneity of Soviet psychology has usually been underestimated, both by Soviet description of its own psychology, and by international observers. In this chapter, after a brief analysis of the reasons that may underlie the lack of emphasis on heterogeneity in Soviet psychology as a whole, a brief overview of some selected traditions of developmental psychology in different cultural and geographic locations of the USSR is given.

Why is psychology in the USSR seen as homogeneous?

'Soviet psychology' is often presented to interested outsiders as a monolithic discipline, firmly grounded in the Marxist philosophical heritage and busily active in the service of 'Soviet society'. Understanding the geographical heterogeniety of psychology in the Soviet Union rarely proceeds beyond the recognition of different 'schools' of psychology in the 'major centres' (Moscow and Leningrad). Cultural heterogeneity of psychology in the USSR is usually considered sufficiently covered by mentioning the existence of the 'Georgian school' of psychology. In fact, the only clear (albeit not representative) recognition of cultural heterogeneity in Soviet psychology in published overviews in the West can be seen in the volume *Psychology around the world* (Sexton & Misiak, 1976), in which psychology in Armenia (Tutundjian, 1976) and 'Soviet Russia' (Brožek & Rahmani, 1976) are organized into separate chapters. Soviet reviews of their own psychology (e.g., Smirnov, 1975) refrain from treating the *cultural* heterogeneity of Soviet psychology, and present reviews of the *geographic-administrative* distribution of psychological research in different republics of the USSR. This displacement of emphasis follows directly from the socio-political axiom that different cultures in the USSR have by the present time become integrated into one 'Soviet culture' in which regional cultural differences have become homogenized—along the lines of Russian cultural models, of course—because the key policy-makers in the USSR are of Russian origin. Certainly that convenient 'blind spot' in Soviet perception of cultural heterogeneity in their psychological research helps to present 'Soviet psychology' as a monolithic discipline—all the more since references to it by Soviet authors contrast it with 'Western psychology', usually in a competitive (ingroup versus outgroup) kind of counterpoint. When such opposition between psychologies is set up, *both* the 'Soviet' and 'Western' psychologies come out far more homogeneous under their respective labels than is the case in reality.

Psychology of Western psychology's view of 'Soviet psychology'
Soviet self-perception of psychology in the USSR is thus very clear. It is equally interesting to try to understand the reasons behind international observers' similar views of 'Soviet psychology' as a geo-culturally homogeneous discipline. As curious as it may seem, the ingroup/outgroup separation of 'Western' and 'Soviet' psychology may be seen as one of its roots. But while the 'Soviet perspective' on the comparison of their psychology with that of Western countries starts from a critical stance, Western efforts to understand 'Soviet psychology' may be oriented more towards finding out information that is not easily accessible. This difficulty of access, paired with the presupposition that the political power of

the USSR in the world must somehow be matched with its inventive power in psychology, creates a situation similar to the 'Sputnik effect' of the late 1950s—when the Soviet launch of the first satellite ahead of the United States led to major efforts in American engineering education and technological progress.

As can be seen from previous chapters of this book, the unique status allotted in many Western views to 'Soviet psychology' as something different to its Western counterparts, is largely an illusion. That illusion is generated (and re-generated, over and over again!) by the *unhistoric* stance of Western interest in Soviet psychology. When compared directly, the status quo of 'Western' and 'Soviet' psychology in the 1980s, or 1970s, and of course even more so in the 1940s–1950s, seem vastly different. 'Soviet psychology' can be seen to differ from 'Western psychology' in almost every aspect of research: in the questions asked, the kinds of methods used, and in how inference is made from the data to general principles.

Nevertheless, when viewed from an historical standpoint, Soviet psychology of the present day is a result of the development of internationally widespread philosophical and psychological ideas of the past in directions canalized by the social history of the USSR. Many specific ideas of contemporary psychologists in the Soviet Union originate in the psychological traditions of the past, and are a further advancement of these 'old' ideas in ways divergent from the directions that psychological research (which may have originated in the same ideas) has taken in Western Europe and North America. In this historical sense, Soviet psychology is a 'distant relative' of Western psychology. The relatedness of these psychologies can be traced only through an historical analysis of both—and which is relatively rare both in the USSR and in present-day Western psychology. In the USSR, many of the original connections of 'Soviet' psychological ideas with their international roots have been purposefully played down over the past five decades, due to the social-political situation in society as a whole. In the West, psychology has been subject to the 'market economy' of fashions for different research topics, all studied by empirical research strategies that overlook the need for careful theoretical and historical analyses of the ideas that underlie these fashionable topics. As a result, both Soviet and Western views on psychological research have become historically myopic—

excluding history from actual research, and delegating it to the separate domain of the 'history of psychology'. The latter sub-discipline mostly deals with historical information as if it has little to offer to the advancement of psychological research. History, from this perspective, deals with things and ideas of the past, and has little relevance to the present, less so to the future.

It is ironic that it is exactly the *rejection* of this view of history's irrelevant role in psychology which could be crucial in learning from the work and life of psychologists in the Soviet Union. The canon of historicism is widely proclaimed in Soviet psychology, mostly in a declarative fashion mimicking the ideas of historical materialism, but sometimes also in conjunction with concrete psychological research. Developmental emphasis in psychology is thus perhaps one of the major theoretical tenets that Western psychology can learn from different theoretical systems present in Soviet psychology. While learning from the 'Soviets', however, it need not be forgotten that probably the learner is learning something from his own historical past. For example, a contemporary American psychologist who tries to use *Vygotsky's* thinking about internalization of interactive experience in his/her research, may not realize that by taking over some ideas of that 'Russian genius', it is actually the intellectual tradition of the Americans James Mark Baldwin and Josiah Royce within which his research is embedded. If a French psychologist attempted a similar endeavour, then it is the spirit of Pierre Janet that he resurrects. Or, if a German psychologist plans on using the 'Vygotsky-Sakharov classification method', or its American modification (Hanfmann-Kasanin test), then it is the methodological line of thinking of Narziss Ach that is being returned to its native land.

Likewise, the intellectual interdependence of psychological viewpoints within the heterogeneous 'Soviet psychology' has its own particular historical curiosities. Given the topic of this book, it is the developmental side of psychology that will be reviewed in the rest of this chapter. There are two (mutually interdependent) facets of the heterogeneity of developmental psychology in the USSR. First, the geographical distribution of developmental research is rather vast. Secondly, on many occasions the geographical diversity of developmental research intersects with the cultural and historical peculiarities of the geographical regions involved.

Geographical heterogeneity of developmental psychology in the USSR

As stated above, it would be a gross simplification to use the label 'Soviet psychology' when referring to different research orientations that have grown up in different parts of the Soviet Union. The difference in approach between some of such 'schools' of psychology may be very large, and they may be very different from what is usually accepted as 'Soviet psychology' in Europe and North America. The latter establishment of 'the typical' (or 'mainstream') Soviet psychology is usually biased by (a) limited access for foreigners to other than a few geographical locations in the USSR where psychology has developed; (b) the projection of the idea that the so-called 'prestigious' psychological centres represent the best of the state of the art, into Soviet conditions; and (c) Soviet psychologists' own presentation of their 'school' as the best in Soviet psychology. Thus, an international visitor who interacts with psychologists in Moscow may easily reach an understanding that Leontiev's activity theory is by far 'the' most respected theoretical system in Soviet psychology. Another visitor, who by some coincidence ends up visiting the Psychology Faculty of Leningrad University, may end up with a similar impression about Ananiev's systemic approach to the holistic study of the human being.

This problem of generalization about what is 'the' most important aspect of Soviet psychology is in essence one shared by anthropological investigators of other cultures who happen to visit different villages in the habitat of the given culture, and to talk to different informants in those villages. No solution to this problem other than abandonment of the problem itself—that is, of efforts to find 'the most typical' or 'widely shared' self-perception of the aboriginal population (or of Soviet psychologists)—can be envisaged. Instead, heterogeneity within a culture, or within a scientific community, is the name of the game, and an appropriate way to understand it is to know it.

Three 'schools' of contemporary Soviet psychology are relatively well known internationally: those of Leningrad, Moscow (Leontiev's 'school' as contrasted to that of Rubinshtein), and of Georgia (Uznadze's 'set-theoretic' school). Little known, but equally important are research paradigms of psychology currently developed in Estonia (Tartu and Tallinn), Kirghizia (Frunze), the Ukraine (Kiev), Lithuania (Vilnius and Kaunas) and Bielorussia (Minsk). The culturally heterogeneous nature of these schools is their important characteristic—the research approaches and traditions of psychologists in Estonia and Lithuania, for example, have more in common with European and North-American than with Soviet psychology.

The 'traditional' diversity of 'schools': Leningrad versus Moscow

The difference between Moscow and Leningrad 'schools' of psychology has its historical roots in the beginning of this century (cf. Chapter 3). The Moscow tradition emerged in the context of the Chelpanov-Kornilov-Vygotsky, Rubinshtein, Luria, Leontiev line of thinking, in conjunction with the Institute of Psychology at Moscow University (later connected with the Academy of Pedagogical Sciences). The Leningrad tradition has its roots in Bekhterev's theoretical and organizational influence in the first decades of this century. That influence has been most notable in the theoretical and empirical work led by Boris G. Ananiev (1907-1972) who was the Dean of Leningrad University Psychology Faculty in the 1960s and up to his death. Ananiev's work in psychology started from his association with Bekhterev's reflexological 'school' in the 1920s. Although he subsequently declared reflexology to be inappropriate for a 'Marxist psychology' (e.g., Ananiev, 1931), many of the ideas around which he built his theoretical system have a connection with the reflexological traditions (Ananiev, 1930a, 1930b). The most interesting indicator of this connection is Ananiev's emphasis on the study of correlational relationships (reminiscent of Bekhterevian associative relationships) within the structure of the human personality, and between the person and his environment. The emphasis on the study of correlational structures in Ananiev's thinking was also influenced by a Soviet biologist Schmal'gauzen (1938) who advanced a systemic theory of reorganization of holistic organisms in the course of evolution. Ananiev's general theory of 'human studies' is of wide interdisciplinary nature, integrating biological, anthropological, social and psychological approaches, with the goal of understanding human life and development. In that wide emphasis, Ananiev's theory and empirical work resembles the paedological traditions of the pre-1936 era to a great extent. The study of development, or 'ontopsychology', is one of the bases of Ananiev's 'human science'. Ananiev emphasized the role of guidance of the developing personality by his social others, claiming to follow one of the best-known Russian educationalists of the nineteenth century, K. Ushinsky (Ananiev, 1965, 1980). The issue of systemic interaction of the developing child and his/her purposefully organized social environment (that of educational settings) was of major interest to Ananiev all through his life (Ananiev, 1930b, 1935, 1957, 1966a, 1966b, 1968, 1980). Among these publications, the study of the psychology of evaluation of pupils in school contexts (Ananiev, 1935) is his major empirically oriented work in this research domain.

Ananiev's theoretical view on development was based on the themes of differentiation, the active role of the developing child in the environment, and heterochrony in the relationships of biological and social aspects of development. He consistently emphasized the structural, holistic nature of the developing organism and its environment (Ananiev, 1968)—a theme resembling the theoretical world view of Basov (see Chapter V). In the empirical domain, Ananiev's use of correlational statistical techniques to study the structural relationships in internal and external relations of the developing personality made it possible for statistical methodology to be accepted at Leningrad University in the post-1936 period, in great contrast with the anti-statistical ethos of the 'school' in Moscow. Ananiev's theoretical perspective made him (and the majority of psychologists of his 'school') interested not in the strength (or statistical significance) of individual correlation coefficients between variables, but in the *structure* of the multi-dimensional correlation patterns as a whole. The developmental emphasis found empirical expression in the interest of 'Ananievites' in the *change* in empirically established correlation structures over the subjects' age and transition through different social settings. Ananiev's relational view on organism–environment relationships was in some sense a parallel to Egon Brunswick's approach (see Hammond, 1966). However, the goal-directed nature of the environmental organization of the developing child makes Ananiev's approach kin to those of Vygotsky and Basov (see Ananiev, 1930a). In the tradition of Ushinskii, Ananiev viewed the developing human being as the object of education and child-rearing (*vospitanie*).

Aside from Ananiev, a number of other developmentally oriented psychologists have been connected with the 'Leningrad school' of Soviet psychology. First of all, there is the comparative and ontogenetic research of N. Tihh (1966, 1970) that follows the traditions of Vladimir Vagner and relies on the empirical observations of the 1920s (of Shchelovanov, Figurin, and Denisova). Other areas that border on developmental research in the 'Leningrad school' include social perception (Bodalev, 1982), perception and memory (Ananiev & Rybalko, 1964; Dvoriashina, 1966; Gizatullina, 1974; Troshikhina, 1973; Troshikhina & Gizatullina, 1979), self-evaluation (Kunitsyna, 1970), and speech (Akinshchkova, 1966).

In the 1980s the distinction between the Leningrad and Moscow 'schools' of psychology is becoming less evident. A number of Soviet psychologists from the Leningrad tradition have established themselves in key administrative positions in psychology institutions located in Moscow (e.g., Boris Lomov is Director of the Institute of Psychology of the USSR Academy of Sciences; Alexei Bodalev, the Dean of the Psychology Faculty at Moscow University). This fusion of the different Russian 'schools' seems to have reduced the traditional infighting of psychologists in the USSR. Perhaps more empirical research on child development will emerge as a result in the future. Thus far, the integration of the Leningrad and Moscow 'schools' in the Institute directed by Lomov has resulted in innovative work mostly on early ontogeny of perception (see Chapter 6).

The 'Georgian school' of psychology: *Einstellung* and *gantshoba*

While both Leningrad and Moscow traditions of Soviet psychology have been embedded in the Russian cultural environment, the third best-known 'school' of Soviet psychology differs in cultural background. The 'Uznadze school' of Georgian psychology has been described in a number of English-language publications in the last decades (see a special issue of *Soviet psychology*, 1968–69, 7, No. 2; also: Natadze, 1961, 1969), and the major work of its undoubted leader Dmitri Uznadze (sometimes transliterated as Usnadze) is available in English (Uznadze, 1966a).

The Georgian psychological tradition is another example of the international nature of a psychological paradigm that is subsumed under the label 'Soviet psychology' more or less due to the historical coincidence that Georgia in the trans-Caucasus geographical region became a part of the Soviet Union after the 1917 October revolution. Historically, the conceptual system of the 'Georgian school' originated in the German psychology of the beginning of this century. That history can be easily traced through the biography of the originator and passionately guarded *guru* of Georgian psychology—Uznadze himself. Uznadze was born in 1886 in Georgia (near Kutaisi), and went to Germany for his higher education. He studied at the universities of Leipzig and Halle, receiving his doctoral degree in philosophy from the latter in 1909 (on the study of the world view of Russian philosopher V. Soloviev). After returning to Georgia in 1910, he became one of the founders of Georgian university in Tbilisi (Tiflis), and later (in 1941) of the Institute of Psychology at the Georgian Academy of Sciences, which he led until his death in 1950.

Uznadze's theoretical views and experimental research are not products of any 'special' Georgian cultural conditions, but instead have their direct roots in Uznadze's education in Germany. The concept of 'set' (Georgian: *gantshoba*, Russian: *ustanovka*) was imported into Georgian psychology from Germany by Uznadze. It originated from Oswald Külpe's theoretical system, and more particularly from the concept of *Einstellung* (see Wellek, 1973). Uznadze's *gantshoba* is thus rooted in the same theoretical background as the Western concept of 'set' (Hritzuk, Unruh, & Hertzog, 1969; Hritzuk & Janzen, 1973).

Furthermore, Uznadze's work has been largely unavailable to other 'schools' in Soviet psychology, whereas it has been widely available internationally, at least among German-speaking psychologists. Its publication history illustrates this—all his major psychological writings became available earlier in German than in Russian. For example, his work on understanding of relationships in animals (Usnadze, 1927a), humans' understanding of meaning (Usnadze, 1927b) and naming (Usnadze, 1924), as well as his experiments with children (Usnadze, 1929a, 1929b) were all published in German psychological journals, prior to the appearance of the *first* publication of his work in Russian (Uznadze, 1930). A similar pattern of Uznadze's publications continued after 1930—he published first in Georgian and/or German (e.g., Usnadze, 1931, 1939), and his work was translated into Russian only after considerable delays (for example, his *Experimental foundations of the psychology of set* first appeared in Georgian in 1949, came out in Russian translation twelve years later and subsequently in English—Uznadze, 1966a). Uznadze's research on children appeared in Russian translation even later (Uznadze, 1966b, 1980).

The limited availability of Uznadze's writing in Russian (and in English) has provided a largely limited picture of his work in the area of child psychology. Uznadze wrote about issues of child psychology in conjunction with issues of pedagogical psychology all through his career— from 1912 to his death—in Georgian. However, his main available book includes only a two-page description of set formation in children of different ages (Uznadze, 1966a, pp. 76–8). Uznadze's earlier work was often carried out on children as subjects, although it would be impossible to consider him as basically a developmental psychologist. His research was nevertheless closely connected with the ideas of German developmetally oriented psychologists—Heinz Werner and William Stern at first, and also Edouard Claparède (Usnadze, 1924, 1929a, 1929b).

Uznadze's major excursion into the area of the study of issues relating to child development is represented mostly in his work on classification strategies of 3–8 year old children (Usnadze, 1929a, Uznadze, 1980). He demonstrated the difference between older and younger children's classification strategies within that age range: whereas the younger children's classification efforts were influenced by previously existing action tendencies, the older children could become free of those tendencies by devising a general classification principle to guide their actions.

Uznadze's basic idea of *gantshoba* has been developed in different directions by his numerous followers (Natadze, 1972; Prangishvili, 1967, 1973, 1975). The divergent nature of the 'Georgian school' of psychology from the rest of 'Soviet psychology' has performed a facilitating role in the re-emergence of interest in the question of unconscious psychological phenomena in recent years (Bassin, Prangishvili & Sherozia, 1978a, 1978b; Sherozia, 1979; Prangishvili, Sherozia, & Bassin, 1985). Thus 'Georgian psychology' has been quite internationally-minded, in both directions—towards both Western psychology and 'Soviet psychology' in the rest of the Soviet Union.

Despite Uznadze's original experimentation with children in the 1920s, only a few Georgian psychologists after him have been interested in issues of child development (e.g., Nioradze, 1974; Zarandia, 1971). First of all, existing contemporary research efforts on children have elaborated on Uznadze's classic study with pre-schoolers (Usnadze, 1929a, 1929b), demonstrating the gradual 'freeing' of the child's actions from the control of previously established action tendencies, as the child develops (Kezheradze, 1973). Not surprisingly (given the 'German connection' of Uznadze's theory), Georgian psychologists have done work on the development of volition and needs (Chkartishvili, 1963, 1974; Gobechia, 1981), and on development of children's interests (Sirbiladze, 1981). It is also interesting to point to some efforts by psychologists in Moscow who have tried to integrate Leontiev's activity theory with Uznadze's set-theoretic ideas (Asmolov, 1979). The historically divergent lines of development in psychology seem to be reintegrated in these efforts, since Leontiev's activity theory is grounded in the history of continental-European thought as thoroughly as Uznadze's *gantshoba* carries the heritage of *Einstellung* with it.

Psychology of interaction and philosophical semantics in Central Asia
One of the most interesting enclaves in the contemporary psychological scene of the Soviet Union is a group of highly erudite and constructive thinkers in Frunze (the capital of Kirghizian SSR) in the late 1960s. The basic theme on which the work of these thinkers has concentrated from that time until the present is social interaction, its development and functions, and its relations with human cognitive functioning. It is due to the activities of the researchers working in Kirghizia that the general topic of social cuteraction ('*obshchenie*') has become discussed and disputed in contemporary Soviet psychology (e.g., Sokovnin, 1968a, 1968b, 1974). Likewise, the research group in Frunze has made significant contributions to the studies of psychological semantics (Brudnyi, 1972) and phylogenetic developmental psychology (Shukurov, 1972).

Strictly speaking, the group of investigators working in Frunze contains three institutionally separate groups who share similar research interests but whose empirical research endeavours have been in slightly different directions. First, the Laboratory of the Problems of Pedagogics of Social Transaction at the Kirghizian Women's Pedagogic Institute, established by Vladimir Sokovnin in 1973, has emphasized the study of social transaction in conjunction with issues of pre-school (Ivanova, 1975; Dzhumalieva, 1983) and school-age education (Aksenenko & Sokovnin, 1975). The second group of investigators, led by Aaron Brudnyi and Emil' Shukurov, is attached to the Institute of Philosophy and Law of the Kirghizian Academy of Sciences, and has worked mainly on issues of psychological semantics, cognitive psychology, and theoretical issues of biological evolution (Brudnyi, 1972, 1975, 1983; Man'ko, 1976; Shukurov, 1972, 1976; Shukurov & Karakeyev, 1976; Sydygbekova, 1983). Since the beginning of the 1980s these two groups of investigators have become more closely integrated, as Aaron Brudnyi has assumed the role of the head of the Laboratory at the Pedagogic Institute (currently called 'The Laboratory of Problems of Intellect').

The third group of psychologists working in Frunze is attached to the Kirghizian Medical Institute and works on different problems of clinical psychology. This group is led by Valeri Solozhenkin and has concentrated on studying different aspects of social transaction in environmental contexts of clinical institutions (e.g., adolescents' regulation of personal space—Solozhenkin, Shilin, Sirota & Ivanenko, 1981).

The 'Estonian school' of psychology
In contrast with the group of psychologists in Kirghizia most of whom are non-natives in the region, the development of psychology in the Baltic state of Estonia is exclusively based on Estonian cultural and intellectual history. The latter has very little in common with the rest of the Soviet Union, and is highly international in nature. Culturally, Estonia shares a common history with Germany and with the Scandinavian countries. Politically, Estonia (like Latvia and Lithuania) was an independent country between the two world wars of this century. Its politically independent status is at least *de jure* recognized internationally, despite its (re)annexation by the Soviet Union at the end of the Second World War. However, even as a part of the Soviet Union, Estonian cultural heritage has managed to exist relatively independently of Soviet ideology, which has had its effect on the

rebirth of active psychological research in Estonia. The activities of psychologists in Estonia that have become prominent in the last two decades have a highly international perspective and would hardly fit into the scheme of any brand of 'Soviet psychology'. Started at Tartu University at the beginning of the 1970s, the active group of young-generation Estonian psychologists has mostly been interested in non-developmental issues of adult perception, cognition, and social psychology. However, on numerous occasions those interests have also had developmentally relevant outcomes. In this context, the development of children's drawings (Allik & Laak, 1985), conducted by psychologists in Tartu should be mentioned. The most active contemporary cultural-historical research on human development in the USSR is conducted in Tartu by Peeter Tulviste. This includes both theoretical (Tulviste, 1977, 1981a, 1981b, 1984a) and empirical work on cognitive development (Tulviste & Tulviste, 1985). Tulviste has also been the pioneer of revitalizing cross-cultural developmental research in the USSR (see Chapter 8). Developmental focus is also present in the work of Estonian environmental psychologists currently located at Tallinn Pedagogic Institute (cf. Heidmets, 1983a, 1985; Kruusvall & Heidmets, 1979; Niit & Lehtsaar, 1983; Niit, Heidmets, & Kruusvall, 1987). All of this research is conducted within theoretical perspectives that integrate some aspects of Soviet psychology with internationally prominent ideas and empirical findings.

Developmental psychology in Lithuania

Similarly to Estonian psychologists, Lithuanian psychologists' work is distinguished by its international orientation and largely empirical nature. In the recent decades, Lithuanian psychologists have played the pioneer role in re-introducing standardized clinical-psychological methods into Soviet psychology and psychiatry. A number of internationally known clinical-psychological methods have been standardized for the Lithuanian population at the Kaunas Medical Institute under the leadership of Antanas Goštautas. Some of the research with these methods has been conducted on adolescents (Goštautas, Berneris, & Jureviciute, 1983). Aside from the clinical-psychological research orientation (e.g., also Čepas, 1984, Lygis, 1981), a number of Lithuanian psychologists have been active in the framework of more theoretically oriented traditions of Soviet psychology (Gučas, 1981). Mostly the research efforts take place at Vilnius University where students can specialize in psychology. Aside from the University, psychological research is also carried out at pedagogical institutes (teachers' colleges) in Kaunas and Siauliai.

A number of research topics are worth mentioning in our small overview of contemporary Lithuanian psychology. Children's cognitive development within the Vygotskian frame of thought has been of interest, especially in the aspect of children's transition from the signal-using to symbol-using stage (Garbaćiauskiene, 1980; Garbaćiauskiene & Grigaite, 1980). Other investigators have followed the traditions of the 'Leningrad school' of psychology in the study of children's social groups (Lape, Abariunaite, & Gutauskiene, 1983; Talacka, 1980). Furthermore, efforts to study children's interests and their interdependence with adults' pedagogical activities seems to be persistent in Lithuanian psychology. Dževečka (1981a, 1981b, 1984) has investigated interests and memory of children in secondary school. The development of professional interests has been the topic of the work of S. Kregžde (1981). The role of parental attitudes in children's development of empathy has likewise been studied (Chomentauskiene, 1982). The role of the social environment in development of personality over childhood years has been of interest to Lithuanian psychologists (Miksyte, 1981), and the development of the self in the social role contexts has been investigated (Jacikevičius, 1984).

To summarize, contemporary Lithuanian psychology is perhaps less 'visible' on the pages of Soviet 'central' publications (published in Moscow and Leningrad) than its Estonian counterpart. International publications by Lithuanians are likewise very rare. Nevertheless, psychologists in Lithuania have developed their own, highly erudite, research traditions that they carry out in accordance with the European standards of scholarship. A number of aspects of the work by Lithuanian psychologists touch upon issues of development, and their exposure to the international readership in greater depth than is possible here would be clearly beneficial.

Conclusion: developmental psychology in the USSR is geo-culturally heterogeneous

This chapter has aimed to provide the reader with a perspective on the variability of geographical and cultural contexts in which different research groups and psychological 'schools' of thought have developed and exist. Even within the Russian cultural area, there are different 'schools' of psychology that have often been in quite fierce competition with one another (for example, the perspectives developed along divergent lines in Moscow and Leningrad). Fortunately, information about these 'major schools' of Soviet psychology has become available to international readers. At the same time, some other research groups located in the 'geographical periphery'—like the group in Frunze—are internationally almost totally unknown. The thinking of psychologists from these little-known research centres in the Soviet Union is often at least as (if not more) interesting than the better-known research that is easy to trace through major publications of Soviet psychology (which are largely dominated by 'central' psychological institutions).

Furthermore, the multi-cultural nature of the Soviet Union is closely related to the heterogeneity of psychological thought in 'Soviet psychology'. In this sense, the geographical (and linguistic) isolation of Georgian psychology has made it possible for the 'school' of thought originated by Uznadze to develop steadily from the 1920s to the present time, without the social-political intervention that upset the development of psychology in Russian areas in the 1930s. The cultural history of the 'Estonian school' of psychology (in conjunction with the European-type higher education at Tartu University) has made it possible for innovative and internationally open-minded research traditions to emerge in the 1970s.

The overview presented in this chapter is certainly not comprehensive. There are, of course, a number of other research centres in the USSR, besides the ones described above (e.g., see Holowinsky, 1978), where psychological research is carried out. Unfortunately, it is not possible in the present context to overview the specifically developmental aspects of psychological work at present being carried out in Minsk, Kiev, Kharkov, Krasnodar,

Iaroslavl, etc. A good example is the careful, thorough, and innovative work on children's social group organization that is carried out in Minsk (in Bielorussia) by Kolominskii (1976). The uneven international representation of Soviet work from 'the periphery' of the USSR (i.e., other than Moscow or Leningrad) is largely a matter of publication opportunities and their uneven distribution between the 'centres' and 'periphery' of Soviet psychology.

X Conclusions: Development of Developmental Psychology in the USSR

There have been two goals in writing this book. First, to analyze the historical development of developmental psychology in Russia (later the Soviet Union). Second, to provide an overview of the contemporary work of developmental psychologists in the Soviet Union. It is the explicit belief (or 'bias') of this author that the latter goal cannot fruitfully be attained without the former, which has been the basis of the organization of the material in this book. It has been demonstrated that the contemporary state of affairs in Soviet psychology is a result of a complex historical process of science–society relationships. It can be argued that the picture would be similar in case of psychology (or other social sciences) in any other country. It is through an explicitly historical analysis that we can understand the *present* (and, perhaps, future) state of a social science in any particular society.

The modernizing function of historical analysis

The thesis that an historical analysis can help us to understand the present state of our target of investigation hardly needs further proof. Nevertheless, the way in which history of psychology has often been viewed within the rest of that discipline seems to indicate that psychologists' current empirical research is only rarely guided by in-depth knowledge about the particular research tradition in history. As a result, psychologists of the present day are likely to re-invent not only ideas that have been prominent in the past, but also repeat entries into the *impasses* that have in the past already rendered useless outcomes. To elect to remain uninformed by one's past in a scientific discipline may easily lead to diminished chances for future development.

History of psychology, however, can be written in different ways, not all of which are equally productive in enlightening

325

psychologists' restless empirical activities of the present day. Writing history necessarily takes place from a certain basic position, the perspective of the writer. For example, Soviet sources on the history of Soviet psychology (e.g., Iaroshevskii, 1966, 1985; Petrovskii, 1967; Smirnov, 1975) have viewed the past of the discipline from the perspective of *partiinost'*. As a result, Soviet sources present a picture that largely resembles Soviet views of their whole society—that of constant progress, albeit fraught with conflict with different opponents at different times (from which the 'progressive' parties always emerge as 'winners'). As was seen in previous chapters, Soviet views on their history have purposefully overlooked some important contributions (e.g., research on children's social world views in the late 1920s), and contributors (e.g., Basov's theoretical heritage), that would not fit into the picture based on the *partiinost'* as it is perceived at the given historical period. Soviet self-presentation of Soviet psychology is far from an impartial rendering of 'basic facts'—in fact, every 'historical fact' in that presentation is embedded in the context of socio-political meanings that have been part and parcel of the development of Soviet society. Many of those meanings (such as the negative connotation of different kinds of 'errors' attributable to fellow psychologists' work) may be impossible to understand without an analysis of the social conditions that gave rise to these meanings.

In contrast, Western accounts of the history of Soviet psychology have attempted to present a 'dispassionate' account of the events over the past six decades. However, even the most uninvolved account of the history of Soviet psychology is given from a particular perspective—usually the one that the given Western historian of psychology has about what is important (and unimportant) to emphasize. With rare exceptions (e.g., Kozulin, 1984; McLeish, 1975), accounts of the history of Soviet psychology have largely taken the Soviet historical accounts of the discipline, tried to free them from the effects of *partiinost'*, and present the results as the objective view (e.g., Brožek and Slobin, 1972; London 1949; Rahmani, 1973). Or, alternatively, there have been numerous overviews of different aspects of Soviet psychology based either on Western political science frameworks (Bauer, 1952) or on the grounds of the Western contemporary interest in the status quo of the given issue in Soviet psychology (Brožek,

1962, 1963, 1964, 1966, 1972; London, 1954; O'Connor, 1966; Rahmani, 1966; Razran, 1935, 1958, 1965; Slobin, 1966). These different overviews of events in Soviet psychology have kept the Western readership informed about the superficial activities of Soviet psychologists—their empirical research and theoretical ideas in one or another area. However, these accounts have usually not penetrated the functioning of the mechanisms—conditions in the given society, and social-psychological organization of the given discipline—behind the obvious results of the work of Soviet psychologists. In contrast, studies of Soviet society in Western political science have rarely taken an interest in the history of Soviet psychology (a few exceptions are Bauer, 1952; Miller, 1986). This is understandable, since for the major task of understanding how Soviet society functions, the example of psychology is far too narrow a sphere from which generalizations could be made about society as a whole. Conversely, international psychologists' accounts of Soviet psychology may be designed to avoid analyses of society—a task most psychologists consider too complicated.

Nevertheless, an analysis of the social context of Soviet psychology is inevitable, if we are interested in 'making sense' of any aspect of that discipline. In this book, an effort has been made to present the history of Soviet developmental psychology *within* the context of changes in Soviet society as a whole. Undoubtedly the coverage of the society had to be narrowed down to allow for coverage of psychology. Therefore, only those aspects of social change in Russian/Soviet society that were considered to have the closest connection with the advancement of developmental ideas have been represented in the book. A special emphasis has been given to the social-psychological mechanisms by which change in Soviet philosophy and psychology was instigated in the early 1930s. As was demonstrated, the dramatic reformulation of psychology's theoretical and applied stance was a result of actions *both* from 'below' (the psychologists or philosophers themselves) and from 'above' (the decision-makers in the upper part of the social-political hierarchy). In this respect, the present historical account of Soviet developmental psychology constitutes a view on Soviet developmental psychology from the interactionist perspective. From that perspective, Soviet developmental psychology is viewed as a by-product of a systemic relationship between psychology as a social institution on the one hand, and society at large on the other. By careful analysis of the conditions of that systemic mechanism that have given rise to different outcomes in the past (in terms of ideas in developmental psychology), better understanding of the present state of the discipline can be obtained. History, from this perspective, ceases to be a discipline dealing with the past as such, and begins to give meaning to our understanding of the present. It is the history of psychology that can modernize the present state of the discipline, by enlightening it for further advancement.

The developmental nature of Soviet psychology

Developmental ideas have fared well in Soviet psychology. The reasons for this are hidden not in the minds of different scientists and their persistence, but in the interdependence of psychology and its social context.

The historically-oriented analysis of psychology-society interdependence that was attempted in this book revealed a small set of conditions that have facilitated the maintenance and flourishing of developmental ideas in Soviet psychology.

First, the close connections between pre-1917 Russian natural science and philosophical thought and its European scientific and cultural heritage made it possible for developmental ideas to establish a basis in society. Russian evolutionary biology and psychology, represented by the work of Vagner and Severtsov, built up the historical connection between the developmental emphasis in nineteenth-century natural science, and the emergence of Soviet developmental psychology in the 1920s. Furthermore, the Russian physiological traditions of Sechenov, Bekhterev and Pavlov provided their basic intellectual input into the development of a psychology that, first and foremost, makes *change* and *development* the core of psychological research. On the other hand, Russian contributions to European natural science and philosophy include substantial theoretical emphases, for instance on the cooperative factors operating in evolution (Kropotkin), and on the systemic nature of development (Bogdanov). Russian natural-scientific thought was both dependent on its European roots, and innovative in ways that went beyond those roots.

Second, the Russian traditions of natural science have largely emerged in conjunction with the continental-European traditions of holistic thinking, in contrast to the Anglo-Saxon associationistic traditions. Gray has captured that specificity of Soviet psychology very nicely:

To sum up those features of Soviet psychology which distinguish it most from its Anglo-Saxon counterpart, the former emphasizes the *active* part played by the subject (and especially the conscious human subject) in *structuring* his own environment and his own experience, in contrast to the traditional (though perhaps weakening) Anglo-Saxon insistence on a *passive* organism, in which associations are formed by the interplay of processes (such as temporal contiguity, and the occurrence of rewards and punishments) assuring successful *adaptation to* the environment. The reader with an interest in philosophy may have noticed in this formulation a parallel to the classic philosophical controversies between the British empiricist school (e.g., Locke, Hume, J. S. Mill), for whom the mind was a *tabula rasa* awaiting the impressions of repeated experience, and those continental philosophers, such as Leibniz, Kant, and Schopenhauer, who believed that our experience is shaped in important ways by the structure and activities of the mind. This parallel is certainly not an accidental one—both Soviet philosophy and Soviet psychology have European roots rather than Anglo-Saxon ones; and it is, I believe, the persistence of long-standing philosophical differences on the two sides of the English Channel which, more than anything else, accounts for the difficulties which the English or American reader encounters when he reads Soviet psychology. (Gray, 1966, pp. 1–2)

Indeed, all major developmental thinkers of the past (and present) in Soviet developmental psychology have invariably taken a systemic view of the psychological phenomena they have studied. Even the most emphatically associationistic thought systems— Sechenov's and Pavlov's thinking in neurophysiology—have emphasized the systemic nature of the formed associations. Bekhterev's associationism was closely intertwined with the all-encompassing systemic 'energetism' of his explanation of phenomena. Severtsov and Vagner emphasized the organism-environment interdependence, in which the organism was seen as playing an active role. A similar systemic emphasis on individual environment relationships was at the heart of Vygotsky's and Basov's explicitly developmental theories in developmental psychology *per se*.

Third, psychology in Russia (later the Soviet Union) has been closely connected with Western European psychological traditions all through its history. The developmental perspective in Soviet psychology has benefitted from the traditions of German psychology (particularly from its Gestalt traditions, and the developmental thinking of H. Werner, K. and Ch. Bühler, and W. Stern) and from the French/Swiss psychology of P. Janet, A. Binet, H. Wallon, J. Piaget, and E. Claparède. It has also been constructively aware of the American traditions of W. James, J. M. Baldwin, J. B. Watson, E. L. Thorndike and J. Dewey. The tradition of close educational and intellectual ties with continental Europe that dominated the lives of educated Russians in the nineteenth century is the basis for psychological thought systems in the USSR. In that respect, Soviet reliance on Marxist philosophy is just a particular example of interdependence with European thought. After all, it is useful to bear in mind that the ideology of the Soviet Union is rooted in the philosophical thought and political struggles of Western Europe in the nineteenth century.

Fourth, social change in Russian society—due to the 1917 bolshevik revolution—provided further direction that led developmental ideas to become centrally important in Soviet psychology. From 1917 onwards, Soviet psychology developed under conditions where the dissemination of Marxist philosophy as the only acceptable ideology for a society was taking place. Soviet psychologists' thinking along developmental lines was guided and facilitated by that ideological atmosphere in society. It helped scientists in the USSR to arrive at *both* the most interesting theoretical approaches in developmental psychology (e.g., those of Basov, Vygotsky, or Rubinshtein), and the most infamous travesties of science (Lysenko's biology; enforced 'Pavlovization' of Soviet psychology in the 1950s).

Nevertheless, the international intellectual ties of Soviet psychologists are not easy to trace at times in their writings, which are often less than precise in the provision of references to others' work. Here, too, the context-dependence of psychology is involved, in a paradoxical way. As was pointed out in Chapter II, fluctuation between 'Westernizing' and 'Slavophile' traditions in Russian society makes it predictable that ideas imported from Europe during the dominance of the former should become examples of 'indigenously Russian' progressive thinking when the latter ethos gains the upper hand. An historically oriented analytic perspective is necessary in order to understand where certain 'Soviet' ideas in psychology originate and what course of development has led to their contemporary form.

Study of child development in Soviet psychology

Developmental ideas have flourished in Soviet psychology at two levels. First, it would be fair to state that most of psychology in the USSR is 'developmental' in its theoretical core, even if at this general level it has little to do with any particular issues of development in human (or animal) ontogeny. Thus, investigations of the microgenetic aspects of visual perception (Zinchenko & Vergiles, 1969) or of the process of thinking in adults (Brushlinskii, 1979, 1983, 1984) need not deal with development of the subjects who participate in the study, but of particular psychological phenomena (images, solutions to problems, etc.) that emerge in the subjects' active relationships with the world. Even on a wider scale, developmental ideas have flourished in the non-empirical sphere of Soviet psychology, largely in conjunction with reiteration of the basic principles of Marxist dialectics in psychologists' discourse.

Secondly, at the more specific level, developmental ideas have been prominent in Soviet child psychology ever since the 1920s. In the present book, two historical periods in which active empirical research has been carried out in Soviet developmental psychology have been singled out for in-depth analysis. The research findings on child development from the 1920s and early 1930s were analyzed in some detail. Likewise, contemporary (1970s–80s) activities of child psychologists in the USSR were overviewed. The present coverage bypassed the specific research by Soviet developmentalists in the period in between the two (1940s–60s) without greater analysis, or any attempt at an overview of the extent of research done in these decades. Two reasons for this can be mentioned. First, it is in the context of the social events of the 1920s and early 1930s that Soviet developmental research of today has its foundations. The decades 1940s–60s largely maintained those original foundations which were developed in directions quite closely guided by the social discourse of the time. (For example, the increasingly evident emphasis on 'practice' in psychological theorizing of the 'Kharkov school'—see Chapter VI —emerged at a time when the 'need for closer ties with the practice' of life was propagated in Soviet society—(see Chapter III). It was in the 1970s that Soviet research on child development again 'opened up' more to international connections. As was seen from our historical analysis, it is that internationalism of science that allows for new solutions to old problems to emerge.

Secondly, the period 1940s–60s in Soviet research on child development is quite widely overviewed in available reviews of specific issues in the discipline (see Brožek, 1966; Rahmani, 1966; Slobin, 1966). Likewise, extensive translations of original writings by Soviet child psychologists, covering that period, are available in English (Cole, 1977, 1978; Cole & Maltzman, 1969; Winn, 1961; Zaporozhets & El'konin, 1971). These sources, together with the translations in the journal *Soviet Psychology* provide a comprehensive overview of major development research done during those decades. It is the newest *and* the oldest (i.e., that from the 1920s) information about Soviet research on child development that has been of limited access to international readers who rely on materials available in English. Hopefully, this book has helped to fill in some gaps in our knowledge about these selected periods of Soviet developmental research.

Heterogeneity of paradigms, and its social regulation

Aside from the history of developmental ideas, the information presented in this book discusses the *internal heterogeneity* of what is subsumed under the label 'Soviet psychology'. It has often been the case that both Soviet psychologists themselves and their international counterparts are eager to present and perceive 'Soviet psychology' as if it were a monolithic system of ideas and research practices. In fact, at any time in the history of Soviet psychology, there have been active (sometimes aggressive) disputes between different viewpoints within the same general (since 1920s, Marxist) paradigm in psychology. Extra-scientific authority has regularly been used to settle these disputes in Soviet psychology, as was described in Chapter III. Kuhn's description of the ways in which scientists solve their disputes were found not to function in the history of Soviet psychology. Even in Western social sciences, it is doubtful that the directions in which these disciplines move is merely determined by the scientific community alone. The complicated process of allocation of research funds for research of some, rather than other, topics in the social sciences in any

Western country may demonstrate the interdependence of the science and its background society. Of course, these cases might never take the form of the excessive infighting of interested sides that have been so characteristic of Soviet philosophy and psychology (see Chapter III).

Geographical and cultural heterogeneity of developmental psychology in the Soviet Union

The heterogeneity of Soviet developmental psychology also has a geographical dimension that is related to the cultural heterogeneity of the USSR. Contrary to the claims made by the promoters of the official Soviet viewpoint, the Soviet Union is not inhabited by 'Soviet people' for whom national and cultural identity has ceased to be important. The 'New Soviet Man'—a dedicated 'soldier' for the 'cause of communism', and against his own cultural and family ties—has not emerged in the USSR. Instead, the scene of intellectual pursuits in the Soviet Union includes individuals of highly varied cultural backgrounds. The geographical distribution of research centres on psychology partly coincides with the cultural differences between researchers. The cultural background of the 'Georgian school' of psychology has kept that European tradition of psychological thought intact over decades, and immune to possible interventions on behalf of the psychological 'schools' dominating ethnically 'Russian' geographical areas. The special situation of Estonia has made it possible for psychologists there to develop their theoretical and empirical research in ways that innovatively integrate Western and Soviet psychological traditions. Developmental psychology in the Soviet Union is a heterogeneous discipline, distributed over the vast territory of the USSR, even if unevenly. To take any particular research tradition of Soviet psychology—for example, that emanating from Moscow or Leningrad—as 'the typical' 'Soviet developmental psychology' amounts to taking a part of a highly differentiated whole for the whole in full. It may indeed be difficult or confusing to chart out the whole picture, but avoidance of that difficulty may result in our own limited understanding of what is *really* happening in Soviet psychology.

General conclusions: society and the science of development

Science is inevitably intertwined with the cultural history within which it has developed. This is true, although not always directly observable, of natural sciences. In the social sciences, the connection between the science and society is particularly strong. The history of the society guides the development of the given branch of social science, and that science produces results which, in principle, fit the expectations of the society. Thomas Kuhn's view on scientific progress that concentrates on factors inherent to science therefore lacks a crucial aspect—an analysis of how the internal structure of 'scientific revolutions' is interdependent with its environment of social history.

The topic analyzed in this book—how developmental ideas and empirical research on child development have been advanced in Soviet psychology—is an interesting case history of a discipline that has been closely related to changes in society over decades. The *socio-political* idea that 'new psychology' *must be* built on the grounds of Marxist philosophy set many Soviet child psychologists working in a direction that made development the core of, rather than a peripheral addition to, ordinary 'child psychology'. As I tried to demonstrate, not one, but many different particular views of child development have emerged in the context of Marxism-based psychology in the USSR. The majority of these theoretical views have clear connections with international psychology, if not always of the given time then definitely with some historically 'older' perspectives. The 'old-fashioned' character of Soviet developmental psychology does not mean that it is 'lagging behind' its Western counterparts. In fact, from our contemporary view of psychological issues in the 1980s we are often ready to become fascinated with *some* ideas of earlier Soviet psychologists (Vygotsky is a perfect example here). While praising Vygotsky for 'being ahead of his time' we are likely to overlook the simple fact that he, in his turn, developed in the social and intellectual context of his time. Perhaps we would be better off praising (also) that intellectual context—of ideas that we might otherwise label 'outmoded' or 'old-fashioned'. A thinker is always embedded in his environment and develops in interaction with it—so overlooking that environment may lead us to attribute credit for the ideas to the individual, rather than to individual-environment relationships. That would amount to the application of the transactionist thinking (similar to the ideas of Vygotsky, or Basov) to the development of particular ideas in Soviet psychology.

Finally, there remains the difficulty of understanding the actual bases of developmental ideas in Soviet psychology. These ideas are historically related to their international counterparts. Due to social-political transformations in Soviet society, these international links have at times been carefully hidden from the view of others. The voluminous discourse of Soviet psychology has often been rather aggressive towards internationally originated or shared ideas. However, that 'Sovietophilic' facade need not stop interested readers from the tedious but rewarding effort of figuring out the actual international connections of ideas that are claimed to be 'Soviet' in origin. No simple solution exists to this problem. It is detective work of a sort—unlikely to become a major pastime for those psychologists who believe in movement of their discipline along a linearly progressive line, based on reaching greater knowledge through accumulation of empirical data over time. The history of Soviet developmental psychology (and of the society as a whole) may caution us about believing in the unlimited and guaranteed progress of our science. Instead, a careful look into the past history of our own, and Soviet, developmental psychologies might help us to move forward more cautiously, and in ways that take our own cultural histories into account.

Bibliography

Abel'skaia, R. & Neopikhonova, Ia.S. (1932). 'The problem of development in German psychology and its influence on Soviet paedology and psychology'. *Paedologia*, No. 4, 27–36.

Adams, M. (1980). 'Severtsov and Schmalhausen: Russian morphology and the evolutionary synthesis'. In E. Mayr & W.B. Provine (Eds), *The evolutionary synthesis: Perspectives on the unification of biology* (pp. 193–225). Cambridge, Ma.: Harvard University Press.

Agol, I. (1928). 'Neo-vitalism and Marxism'. *Pod znamenem Marksizma*, No. 3, 202–37.

Akinshchikova, G.I. (1966). 'The relation of motorics and speech in childhood'. In B.G. Ananiev & B.F. Lomov (Eds), *Problems of general, social, and engineering psychology* (Problemy obshchei, sotsial'noi, i inzenernoi psikhologii) (pp. 14–22). Leningrad: Izd. LGU.

Aksenenko, S.E. & Sokovnin, V.M. (1975). 'The problem situation of social transaction and the process of education'. In V.M. Sokovnin (Ed.), *Problems of pedagogics and psychology of social transaction* (Problemy pedagogiki i psikhologii obshchenia). Frunze: Mektep.

Allik, J. & Laak, T. (1985). 'The head is smaller than the body: but how does it join on?' In N.H. Freeman & M.V. Cox (Eds), *Visual order: The nature and development of pictorial representation* (pp. 266–86). Cambridge: Cambridge University Press.

Ananiev, B.G. (1930a). 'On the problem of the foundation of behaviour'. *Voprosy izuchenia i vospitania lichnosti*, 9, 1–2, 12–18.

Ananiev, B.G. (1930b). 'A sociogenetic theory of the development of human behaviour'. *Voprosy izuchenia i vospitania lichnosti*, 9, No.4., 27–43.

Ananiev, B.G. (1931). 'On some questions of Marxist-Leninist reconstruction of psychology'. *Psikhologia*, No. 3–4, 325–44.

Ananiev, B.G. (1935). *Psychology of pedagogical evaluation*. Leningrad: Institut Mozga (also available in: Ananiev, 1980, Vol. 2, pp. 128–272).

Ananiev, B.G. (1957). 'On the development of children in the process of instruction'. *Sovetskaia pedagogika*, 21, 7, 12–24.

Ananiev, B.G. (1965). 'Man as the object of education'. *Sovetskaia pedagogika*, 29, 1, 24–36.

Ananiev, B.G. (1966a). 'Problems of pedagogical anthropology'. *Sovetskaia pedagogika, 30,* 5, 27–37.
Ananiev, B.G. (1966b). 'An important problem of contemporary pedagogical anthropology'. *Sovetskaia pedagogika, 30,* 1, 33–53.
Ananiev, B.G. (1968). 'The structure of individual development as a problem of contemporary pedagogical anthropology'. *Sovetskaia pedagogika, 32,* 1, 21–31.
Ananiev, B.G. (1980). *Selected psychological works* (Izbrannyie psikhologicheskie trudy), Vols. 1–2. Moscow: Pedagogika.
Ananiev, B.G. & Rybalko, E.F. (1964). *Characteristics of children's perception of space* (Osobennosti vospriatia prostranstva u detei). Moscow: Prosveshchenie.
Antonova, G.P. & Khrustaleva, N.V. (1982). 'Characteristics of suggestibility among preschoolers and lower-grade schoolchildren'. *Voprosy psikhologii,* No. 3, 50–5.
Antsyferova, L.I. (1981). 'On the dynamic approach to the psychological study of personality'. *Psikhologicheskii zhurnal,* 2, 2, 8–18.
Arkhangel'skii, P.V. (1929). 'The urban child and work'. *Paedologia,* Nos. 1–2, 178–93.
Artemov, V.A. (1929). 'Social psychology and the study of children's collectives'. *Paedologia,* No. 4, 462–77.
Aryamov, I.A., Odintsova, L.I. & Nechaeva, E.I. (1926). *The child of the worker* (Ditia rabochego). Moscow: Gosizdat.
Asmolov, A.G. (1977). 'Activity and levels of set'. *Vestnik Moskovskogo Universiteta. ser. 14. psikhologia,* No. 1, 3–12.
Asmolov, A.G. (1979). *Activity and set* (Deitel'nost' i ustanovka). Moscow: Izdatel'stvo MGU.
Asmolov, A.G., Bratus', B.S., Zeigarnik, B.W., Petrovskii, V.A., Subbotskii, E.B., Kharash, A.U. & Tsvetkova, L.S. (1979). 'On some perspectives of the study of sense formations of personality'. *Voprosy psikhologii,* No. 4, 35–46.
Asmolov, A.G. & Petrovskii, V.A. (1978). 'On the dynamic approach to psychological analysis of activity'. *Voprosy psikhologii,* No. 1, 70–80.
Asnin, V.A. (1979–80). 'The development of visual-operational thinking in children'. *Soviet psychology,* 18, 223–36.
Asnin, V.A. (1980–81). 'The conditions for reliability of a psychological experiment'. *Soviet psychology,* 19, 2, 80–99.

Babich, N. (1984). 'The development of questions of preschoolers'. *Voprosy psikhologii,* No. 2, 67–74.
Babkin, B.P. (1949). *Pavlov: A biography.* Chicago: University of Chicago Press.
Bakanov, E.N. (1977). 'Stages in the development of volitional processes'.

Vestnik Moskovskogo Universiteta. ser. 14. psikhologia, No. 4, 12–22.
Baldwin, J. M. (1892). 'Suggestion in infancy'. *International Congress of Experimental Psychology,* second session (pp. 49–56). London: Williams & Norgate.
Baldwin, J. M. (1894). 'Personality-suggestion'. *Psychological review, 1,* 274–9.
Baldwin, J. M. (1895). 'The origin of a "thing" and its nature'. *Psychological review, 2,* 551–73.
Baldwin, J. M. (1906). *Thought and things.* Vol. 1: *Functional logic, or genetic theory of knowledge.* London: Swan Sonnenschein & Co.
Baldwin, J. M. (1915). *Genetic theory of reality.* New York: Putnam.
Baldwin, J. M. (1930). 'James Mark Baldwin'. In C. Murchison (Ed.), *A history of psychology in autobiography.* Vol. 1 (pp. 1–30). New York: Russett & Russell.
Baranova, T. (1930). 'Adaptation of a test method and measurement of intellectual development to the conditions of Central Asia'. *Paedologia,* No. 2, 255–62.
Bartlett, F. C. (1932). *Remembering.* Cambridge: Cambridge University Press.
Basov, M. Ia. (1920). 'The problems of functional psychology in the approach of A. F. Lazurskii'. *Voprosy izucheniia i vospitania lichnosti,* No. 2, 219–29.
Basov, M. Ia. (1922). *Will as the object of functional psychology* (Volya kak predmet funktsional' noi psikhologii). Petrograd: Nachatki znanii.
Basov, M. Ia. (1923). *The experience of the method of psychological observation and its application to preschool children.* Moscow-Leningrad: Gosudarstvennoe Izadatel'stvo.
Basov, M. Ia. (Ed.) (1924a). *The experience of objective study of childhood* (Opyt ob'ektivnogo izuchenia detstva). Leningrad: Gosizdat.
Basov, M. Ia. (1924b). 'The method of objective observation in child psychology and pedagogics'. In Basov (Ed.) (1924a) (pp. 5–20).
Basov, M. Ia. (Ed.) (1925a). *The pedagogue and research on children* (Pedagog i issledovatel'skaia rabota nad det'mi). Leningrad: Gosizdat.
Basov, M. Ia. (1925b). 'What does it mean to observe the behaviour of a children's collective?' In Basov (Ed.) (1925a) (pp. 114–44).
Basov, M. Ia. (1928a). *General foundations of paedology* (Obshchie osnovy pedologii), Moscow-Leningrad: Gosudarstvennoe izdatel'stvo.
Basov, M. Ia. (1928b). 'The structural analysis of behavioural processes as the major problem and tool of paedological psychology'. *Paedologia,* No. 1, 40–8.
Basov, M. Ia. (1929a). 'Structural analysis in psychology from the standpoint of behavior'. *Journal of genetic psychology, 36,* 267–90.
Basov, M. Ia. (1929b). 'New problems of psychology'. *Estestvoznanie i*

marksizm, No. 3, 54–82 (also in Basov, 1930).

Basov, M. Ia., Ed. (1930). *Current problems of paedology* (Ocherednyie problemy pedologii). Moscow: Gosizdat.

Basov, M. Ia. (1931a). *General foundations of paedology* (Obshchie osnovy pedologii). 2nd edn. Moscow-Leningrad: Gosizdat.

Basov, M. Ia. (1931b). 'On some tasks of the forthcoming reorganization of paedology'. *Paedologia*, No. 5–6, 3–28.

Basov, M. Ia. (1975). *Selected psychological writings* (Izbrannye psikhologicheskie issledovania). Moscow: Pedagogika.

Basov, M. Ia. & Gerke, E. (1924). 'On the question of individual specificities and culture of observers in objective psychological observations'. In Basov (Ed.) (1924a) (pp. 132–62).

Basov, M. Ia. & Nadol'skaya, M. (1913). 'Individual peculiarities of movement-volitional processes'. *Vestnik psikhologii*, No. 3.

Bassin, F. V., Prangishvili, A. S. & Sherozia, A. E. (Eds) (1978a). *The unconscious*. Vol. 1: *Development of the idea*. Tbilisi: Metsniereba.

Bassin, F. V., Prangishvili, A. S. & Sherozia, A. E. (Eds) (1978b). *The unconscious*. Vol. 2: *Sleep, clinic, creativity*. Tbilisi: Metsniereba.

Bateson, G. (1971). 'The message "this is play"'. In R. E. Herron & B. Sutton-Smith (Eds), *Child's play*. New York: Wiley.

Bauer, R. A. (1949). 'The genetics controversy and the psychological sciences in the USSR'. *American psychologist*, 4, 10, 418–21.

Bauer, R. A. (1952). *The new man in Soviet psychology*. Cambridge, Ma.: Harvard University Press.

Bechterev, V. M. (1932). *General principles of human reflexology*. New York: International Publishers (English trans. of *Obshchie osnovy refleksologii cheloveka*, 4th edn—see Bekhterev, 1928).

Bechterew, W. M. (1926). *Allgemeine Grundlagen den Reflexologie des Menschen*. Leipzig: Deuticke.

Behrens, P. J. (1985). 'The application of Pavlovian conditioning procedures in child and developmental psychology'. In G. Eckardt, W. Bringmann & L. Sprung (Eds), *Contributions to a history of developmental psychology* (pp. 329–40). Berlin: Mouton.

Bekhterev, V. M. (1896). *On the localization of the conscious activity in animals and humans* (O lokalizatsii soznatel'noi deiatel'nosti u zivotnykh i cheloveka). St Petersburg: K. Rikker.

Bekhterev, V. M. (1904). *The psyche and life* (Psikhika i zizn'). 2nd edn. St Petersburg: K. Rikker.

Bekhterev, V. M. (1907). *Objective psychology*. Vol. 1. St Petersburg: P. P. Soikin.

Bekhterev, V. M. (1909). 'The problems of child-rearing at the age of first childhood' (Voprosy vospitania v vozraste pervogo detstva). St Petersburg.

Bekhterev, V. M. (1910). *The original evolutions of children's drawing in the light of objective study* (Pervonachal'nyie evoliutsii detskogo risunka v ob'ektivnom izuchenii). St Petersburg: P. P. Soikin.

Bekhterev, V. M. (1912). 'On the development of neuro-psychic activity in the first half-year of a child's life'. *Vestnik pskiholgii, kriminal'noi antropologii, i gipnotizma*, 9, 2, 1–48.

Bekhterev, V. M. (1916). 'On the role of music in the aesthetic rearing of children, starting from their first days'. St Petersburg: P. P. Soikin.

Bekhterev, V. M. (1917). *General foundations of human reflexology* (Obshcie osnovy refleksologii cheloveka). 1st edn. Petrograd: Kolos.

Bekhterev, V. M. (1921). *Collective reflexology*. Petrograd: Kolos.

Bekhterev, V. M. (1925). *Psychology, reflexology, and Marxism*. Leningrad: Izadtel'stvo Gosudarstvennogo refleksologischeskogo Instituta.

Bekhterev, V. M. (1926). *General foundations of human reflexology*. 3rd edn. Leningrad: Gosizdat.

Bekhterev, V. M. (1928). *General foundations of human reflexology*. 4th edn. Moscow: Gosizdat.

Bekhterev, V. M. (1976). 'Some empirical data in the area of collective reflexology'. *Soviet psychology*, 14, 4, 3–41 (Russian original, 1925).

Bekhterev, V. M. & Dubrovskii, A. B. (1926). 'Dialectical materialism and reflexology'. *Pod znamenem Marksizma*, No. 7–8, 69–94.

Bekhterev, V. M. & Shchelovanov, N. M. (1969). 'Toward the establishment of a developmental reflexology'. *Soviet psychology*, 8, 1, 7–25 (Russian original 1925).

Beliaev, B. V. (1929). 'The problem of the collective and its experimental-psychological study'. *Psikhologia*, 2, 2, 179–214.

Beliaev, B. V. (1930a). 'The problem of collective and its experimental-psychological study (Overview of experimental studies)'. *Psikhologia*, 3, 3, 336–74.

Beliaev, B. V. (1930b). 'The problem of collective and its experimental study (The method and results of experimental investigation)'. *Psikhologia*, 3, 4, 488–549.

Beliaev, M. F. (1929). 'Types of social expressions in youth and adolescence'. *Paedologia*, No. 4, 558–69.

Beliaev, M. F. & Lukina, A. M. (1932). 'Sociotypes of the difficult-to-educate children (leaders, followers, loners, unstables) in the individual reflexological experiment'. *Voprosy izuchenia i vospitania lichnosti*, 10, 27–40.

Bel'tiukov, V. I. (1964). *On the acquisition of speech sounds by children* (Ob usvoenii det'mi zvukov rechi). Moscow: Prosveshchenie.

Bel'tiukov, V. I. (1977). *Interaction of analyzers in the process of perception and acquisition of speech* (Vzaimodeistvie analizatorov v protsesse vospriatia i usvoenia ustnoi rechi). Moscow: Pedagogika.

Bel'tiukov, V.I. & Salakhova, A.D. (1973). 'The babbling of the hearing child'. *Voprosy psikhologii*, No. 2, 105–16 (English trans. in Cole, 1977, pp. 587–605).

Bel'tiukov, V.I. & Salakhova, A.D. (1975). 'On the acquisition of the sound (phonemic) system of language by the child'. *Voprosy psikhologii*, No. 4, 71–80 (English trans. in *Soviet psychology*, 1976, *15*, 1, 59–73).

Benigni, L. & Valsiner, J. (1985). 'Developmental psychology without the study of processes of development?' *Newsletter of the International Society for the Study of Behavioural Development*, No. 1.

Bernshtein, M.S. (1927). 'About what do our figures speak?' In M.S. Bernshtein & N.A. Rybnikov (Eds), *The time budget of our youth* (Biudzet vremeni nashego moldniaka), pp. 111–36. Leningrad: Gosizdat.

Bernshtein, N.A. (1947). *On the construction of movements* (O postroenii dvizhenii). Moscow: Medgiz.

Bernshtein, N.A. (1966). *Etudes on the philosophy of movement and physiology of activity* (Ocherki po fiziologii dvizenii i fiziologii aktivnosti). Moscow: Meditsina.

Bertalanffy, L. von (1955). 'An essay on the relativity of categories'. *Philosophy of science*, *22*, 4, 243–63.

Bertalanffy, L. von (1981). *A systems view of man*. Boulder, Co.: Westview Press.

Beteleva, T.G., Dubrovinskaya, N.V. & Farber, D.A. (1977). *The sensory mechanisms of the developing brain*. (Sensornye mekhanizmi razvivaiushchegosya mozga). Moskva: Nauka.

Bibrikh, R.R. (1978). 'From the history of the problem of determinism in the psychology of motivation'. *Vestnik Moskovskogo Universiteta, seria. 14, psikhologia*, No. 2, 75–87.

Bil'chugov, S.Iu. (1978). 'On some characteristics of the experimental method of J. Piaget'. *Vestnik Moskovskogo Universiteta. Seria 14. Psikhologia*, No. 1, 18–25.

Black, J.L. (1979). *Citizens for the fatherland: education, educators, and pedagogical ideas in 18th-century Russia*. Boulder, Co.: East European Quarterly.

Blonski, P.P. (1920). *The reform of science* (Reforma nauki). Moscow: Izdatel'stvo Otdela narodnogo obrazovania Moskovskogo Soveta.

Blonski, P.P. (1921). *Essays on scientific psychology* (Ocherki nauchnoi psikhologii). Moscow: Gosizdat.

Blonski, P.P. (1927). *Psychological essays* (Psikhologicheskie ocherki). Moscow: Novaia Moskva.

Blonski, P.P. (1928). 'The subject of psychology and psychopathology from a genetic standpoint'. *Pedagogical seminary and journal of genetic psychology*, 35, 356–73.

Blonski, P.P. (1935). *Development of the schoolchild's thinking* (Razvitie myshlenia shkol'nika). Moscow: Uchpedigz.

Bloom, A. (1981). *The linguistic shaping of thought*. Hillsdale, NJ: Erlbaum.

Bodalev, A.A. (1967). 'The contribution of psychologists from the city of Lenin to the development of Soviet psychology'. *Voprosy psikhologii*, No. 5, 149–58.

Bodalev, A.A. (1982). *Perception and understanding of person by person* (Vospriatie i ponimanie cheloveka chelovekom). Moscow: Izdatel'-stvo MGU.

Bodalev, A.A. (1983). 'Educational psychology and moral education'. *Soviet psychology*, 22, 1, 13–19.

Bodalev, A.A., Lomov, B.F. & Matiushkin, A. (1984). 'Psychological sciences to school reform'. *Voprosy psikhologii*, No. 3, 12–24.

Bogdanov, A. (1899). *The main elements of the historical perspective on nature* (Osnovnyie elementy istoricheskogo vzgliada na prirodu). St Petersburg: Sankt-Peterburgskoe Aktsionernoe Obshchestvo pechatnykh del 'Izdatel''.

Bogdanov, A. (1922). *Tektology: the general organizational science* (Tektologia: vseobshchaia organizatsionnaia nauka). Peterburg-Moscow-Berlin: Izdatel'stvo Z.I. Grzebina.

Bohannan, L. (1976). 'Shakespeare in the bush'. In J. Friedl (Ed.), *Cultural anthropology*. New York: Harper & Row.

Boiko, E.I. (1952). 'Some questions about the rebuilding of psychology on the basis of I.P. Pavlov's teaching'. *Voprosy filosofii*, No. 1, 162–8.

Borovski, V.M. (1929). 'Psychology in the USSR'. *Journal of general psychology*, 2, 177–86.

Bozhovich, L.I. (1968). *Personality and its formation in childhood* (Lichnost' i ee formirovanie v detskom vozraste). Moscow: Prosvetchenie.

Bozhovich, L.I. (1969). 'The personality of schoolchildren and problems of education'. In M. Cole & I. Maltzman (1969) (pp. 209–48).

Bozhovich, L.I. (1978). 'Stages in the formation of personality in ontogeny'. *Voprosy psikhologii*, No. 4, 23–35. (English trans. *Soviet psychology*, 1979, 17, 3, 3–24).

Bozhovich, L.I. (1979a). 'Stages in the formation of personality in ontogeny'. *Voprosy psikhologii*, No. 2, 47–56. (English trans. *Soviet psychology*, 1980–81, 19, 2, 61–79).

Bozhovich, L.I. (1979b). 'Stages in the formation of personality in ontogeny'. *Voprosy psikhologii*, No. 4, 23–34.

Bozhovich, L.I. & Slavina, L.S. (1967). 'Fifty years of Soviet psychology of childrearing'. *Voprosy psikhologii*, No. 5, 51–70 (English trans. *Soviet psychology*, 1968, 7, 1, 3–22).

Bozhovich, L. I. & Zinchenko, P. I. (1979–80). 'The psychology of acquiring factual knowledge by schoolchildren'. *Soviet psychology, 18*, 2, 67–83.

Bratus', B. S. (1977a). 'On one mechanism of goal-formation'. *Voprosy psikhologii*, No. 2, 121–4.

Bratus', B. S. (1977b). *Psychological aspects of the moral development of personality* (Psikhologicheskie aspekty nravstvennogo razvitia lichnosti). Moscow: Izdatel'stvo MGU.

Brazelton, T. B., Koslowski, B. & Main, M. (1974). 'The origins of reciprocity'. In M. Lewis & L. Rosenbloom (Eds), *The effect of the infant on its caregiver*. New York: Wiley.

Bronfenbrenner, U. (1979). *The ecology of human development*. Cambridge, Ma.: Harvard University Press.

Brožek, J. (1962). 'Current status of psychology in the U.S.S.R.' *Annual review of psychology, 13*, 515–66.

Brožek, J. (1963). 'Soviet psychology'. In M. H. Marx & W. A. Hillis (Eds), *Systems and theories in psychology* (pp. 438–55). New York: McGraw-Hill.

Brožek, J. (1964). 'Recent developments in Soviet psychology'. *Annual review of psychology, 15*, 493–594.

Brožek, J. (1966). 'Contemporary Soviet psychology'. In N. O'Connor (Ed.), *Present-day Russian psychology* (pp. 178–98). Oxford: Pergamon Press.

Brožek, J. (1972). 'To test or not to test: trends in Soviet views'. *Journal of the History of the Behavioural Sciences, 8*, 243–8.

Brožek, J. & Slobin, D. (Eds) (1972). *Psychology in the USSR: An historical perspective*. White Plains, NY: International Arts & Sciences Press.

Brožek, J. & Rahmani, L. (1976). 'Soviet Russia'. In Sexton & Misiak (1976) (pp. 370–88).

Brudnyi, A. A. (1972). *The semantics of language and human psychology*. (Semantika iazyka i psikhologia cheloveka). Frunze: Ilim.

Brudnyi, A. A. (1975). 'Understanding as a philosophical-psychological problem'. *Voprosy filosofii*, No. 10, 109–17.

Brudnyi, A. A. (1983). 'On intellect and its functions'. In A. A. Brudnyi (Ed.), *Problems of the psychology of intellect* (Problemy psikhologii intellekta). Frunze: Kirghiszkii Gosudarstvennyi Universitet.

Bruner, J. (1983). *In search of mind*. New York: Harper & Row.

Bruner, J. (1984). 'Vygotsky: a historical and conceptual perspective'. In J. V. Wertsch (Ed.), *Culture, communication, and cognition: Vygotskian perspectives* (pp. 21–34). Cambridge: Cambridge University Press.

Brushlinskii, A. V. (1968). *The cultural-historical theory of thinking* (Kul'turno-istoricheskaia teoria myshlenia). Moscow: Vyshhaia shkola.
Brushlinskii, A. V. (1979). *Thinking and prediction* (Myshlenie i prognozirovanie). Moscow: Mysl'.
Brushlinskii, A. V. (1983). *Psychology of thinking and problem-based instruction* (Psikhologia myshlenia i problenoie obuchenie). Moscow: Pedagogika.
Brushlinskii, A. V. (1984). 'Activity, act, and the psychological as a process'. *Voprosy psikhologii*, No. 5, 17–29.
Budilova, E. A. (1972). *Philosophical problems in Soviet psychology* (Filosofskie problemy v sovetskoi psikhologii), Moscow: Nauka.
Bulanov, I. (1930). 'Results on the study of behaviour of the Tunguz child'. *Paedologia*, No. 2, 194–207.
Burmenskaia, G. V. (1978). 'The understanding of the invariance of the amount as an index of the mental development of the child'. *Voprosy psikhologii*, No. 6, 142–52.

Cairns, R. B. (1983). 'The emergence of developmental psychology'. In P. H. Mussen (Ed.) *Handbook of child psychology*. Vol. 1: *History, theory, and methods* (pp. 41–102). New York: Wiley.
Cairns, R. B. & Valsiner, J. (1982). 'The cultural context of developmental psychology'. Paper presented at the 90th Annual Convention of the American Psychological Association.
Čepas, V. (1984). 'Psychogenetic research of intelligence: methods, problems, and results'. *Lievtuvos TSR auykš'tuju mokyklu mokslo darbai. Psichologija*, 5, 73–88.
Chernakov, E. T. (1948). 'Against idealism and metaphysics in psychology'. *Voprosy filosofii*, No. 3, 301–15.
Chernikhova, L. B. (1929). 'Newspaper-children and their environment'. *Paedologia*, No. 1–2, 167–77.
Chkhartishvili, S. N. (1963). 'On the problem of the will of first-graders'. *Voprosy psikhologii*, No. 12, 109–16.
Chkhartishvili, S. N. (Ed.) (1974). *Some problems of psychology and pedagogics of sociogenic needs* (Nekotoryie voprosy psikhologii i pedagogiki sotsiogennykh potrebnostei). Tbilisi: Metsniereba.
Chomentauskiene, R. (1982). 'The influence of general attitude of parents towards child on the development of his empathy'. *Lietuvos TSR aukš'tuju mokyklu mokslo darbai. Psichologija*, 3, 117–30.
Cole, M. (Ed.) (1977). *Soviet developmental psychology: An anthology.* While Plains, NY: M. E. Sharpe.
Cole, M. (Ed.) (1978). *The selected writings of A. R. Luria.* White Plains, NY: M. E. Sharpe.

Cole, M. (1979-80). 'Introduction: The Kharkov school of developmental psychology'. *Soviet psychology*, 18, 2, 3-8.

Cole, M., Gay, J., Glick, J. & Sharp, D. (1971). *The cultural context of learning and thinking*. New York: Basic Books.

Cole, M. & Maltzman, I. (Eds) (1969). *A handbook of contemporary Soviet psychology*. New York: Basic Books.

Davydov, V. V. (1957). 'The formation of the basic concept of quantity in children'. *Voprosy psikhologii*, No. 2, 82-96.

Davydov, V. V. (1962). 'The analysis of the structure of counting as the precursor of a programme of arithmetics'. In D. B. El'konin & V. V. Davydov (Eds), *Problems of psychology of learning by younger schoolchildren* (Voprosy psikhologii uchebnoi deiatel'nosti mladshikh shkol'nikov) pp. 50-184. Moscow: Prosveshchenie.

Davydov, V. V. (Ed.) (1969). *Psychological possibilities of younger schoolchildren for the study of mathematics* (Psikhologicheskie vozmoznosti mladshikh shkol'nikov v usvoenii matematiki). Moscow: Prosveshchenie.

Davydov, V. V. (1972). *Kinds of generalization in instruction* (Vidy obobstchenia v obuchenii). Moscow: Pedagogika.

Davydov, V. V. (1983). 'Results and prospects of the scientific activity of the Institute of General and Pedagogical Psychology'. *Voprosy psikhologii*, No. 1, 5-22.

Davydov, V. V. & Andronov, V. P. (1979). 'Psychological conditions of the emergence of ideal actions'. *Voprosy psikhologii*, No. 5, 40-54.

Davydov, V. V. & Radzikhovskii, L. A. (1981). 'The theory of L.S. Vygotsky and the activity approach in psychology'. *Voprosy psikhologii*, No. 1, 67-80.

Davydov, V. V. & Zinchenko, V. P. (1980). 'The principle of development in psychology'. *Voprosy filosofii*, No. 12, 47-60.

Denisova, M. P. & Figurin, N. L. (1969). 'Experimental reflexological research on the newborn'. *Soviet psychology*, 8, 1, 50-62 (Russian original, 1924).

Dobzhansky, T. (1955). 'The crisis in Soviet biology'. In E. J. Simmons (Ed.), *Continuity and change in Russian and Soviet thought* (pp. 329-46). Cambridge, Ma.: Harvard University Press.

Draguns, J. G. (1984). 'Microgenesis by any other name ....' In W. D. Froehlich, G. Smith, J. Draguns & U. Hentschel (Eds), *Psychological processes in cognition and personality* (pp. 3-17). Washington, DC: Hemisphere Publishing Co.

Dvoriashina, M. D. (1966). 'On some individual characteristics of adolescents' perceptual constancy'. In B. G. Ananiev & B. F. Lomov (Eds), *Problems of general, social, and engineering psychology*

(Problemy obshchei, sotsial'noi i inzenernoi psikhologii) (pp. 23–31). Leningrad: Izdatel'stvo LGU.

Dževečka, A. (1981a). 'Correlation analysis of relations between the interests of senior pupils to teaching subjects and the peculiarities of memory and thinking'. *Lietuvos TSR aukštuju mokyklu mokslo darbai. Psichologija*, 2, 9–16.

Dževečka, A. (1981b). 'The investigation of senior form pupils' interests to teaching subjects'. *Lietuvos TSR aukštuju mokyklu mokslo darbai. Psichologija*, 2, 17–26.

Dževečka, A. (1984). 'The motives of learning activity and intellect of students'. *Lietuvos TSR aukštuju mokyklu mokslo darbai. Psichologija*, 5, 14–25.

Dzhumalieva, Zh.M. (1983). 'Experimental investigation of early forms and levels of critical thinking'. In A.A. Brudnyi (Ed.), *Problems of the psychology of intellect*. (Problemy psikhologii intellekta). Frunze: Kirghizskii Gosudarstvennyi Universitet.

Egorov, B.F. (1973). 'Slavophilia, westernizing, and culturology'. *Trudy po znakovym sistemam* (Tartu University). Vol. 6 (pp. 265–75). Tartu: Tartu University Press.

Elagina, M.G. (1974). 'The influence of the need for practical cooperation with adults on the development of active speech in young children'. In Lisina (1974b, pp. 114–27).

Elagina, M. (1975). 'Some characteristics of the interaction of young children with adults that facilitate the emergence of speech communication'. In V.N. Pushkin (Ed.), *Experimental investigations on problems of general and educational psychology* (Eksperimental'nye issledovania po problemam obshchei i pedagogicheskoi psikhologii) (pp. 38–47). Moscow: NII Obshchei Pedagogiki.

El'konin, D.B. (1960). *Child psychology* (Detskaia psikhologia). Moscow: Uchpedgiz.

El'konin, D.B. (1971). 'Development of speech'. In Zaporozhets & El'konin (1971) (pp. 111–85).

El'konin, D.B. (1974). *The psychology of instruction of the younger schoolchild* (Psikhologia obuchenia mladshego shkol'nika). Moscow: Znannie.

El'konin, D.B. (1978). *The psychology of play* (Psikhologia igry). Moscow: Pedagogika.

Ellis, S. & Rogoff, B. (1986). 'Problem solving in children's management of instruction'. In E. Mueller & C. Cooper (Eds), *Process and outcome in peer relations* (pp. 301–25). Orlando, Fl.: Academic Press.

Ermilov, V. (1906). *Betskoi and Novikov* (Betskoi i Novikov). Moscow: Sytin.

Ermolaev, H. (1963). 'Soviet literary theories 1917–1934'. *University of California Publications in Modern Philology.* Vol. 69. Berkeley-Los Angeles: University of California Press.

Evseeva, N.S. (1980). '*Atalychestvo* and adoption among Yakuts'. *Sovetskaia etnografia,* No. 1, 105–8.

Fabri, K.E. (1975). 'On the zoopsychological, ethological, and comparative-psychological approaches to the study of animal behaviour'. In K.E. Fabri (Ed.), *Problems of zoopsychology, ethology and comparative psychology* (Voprosy zoopsikhologii, etologii, i sravnitel'noi psikhologii) (pp. 3–8). Moscow: Izdatel'stvo MGU.

Fabri, K.E. (1978). 'On the lawfulness of psychological development in animal ontogeny. In L.I. Antsyferova (Ed.), *The principle of development in psychology* (Printsip razvitia v psikhologii—pp. 337–66). Moscow: Nauka.

Fabri, K.E. (1982). 'The play of animals and children'. *Voprosy psikhologii,* No. 3, 26–34.

Fam Min Hak & Radzikhovsky, L.A. (1977). 'Early papers by L.S. Vigotsky and the development of Soviet psychology'. *Vestnik MGU, seria 14, psihologia,* 3, 11–20.

Fedianovich, T.P. (1979). 'Mordova cultural rites, connected with the birth of a child'. *Sovetskaia etnografia,* No. 2, 79–89.

Fel'dshtein, D.I. (1980). 'Psychological problems of socially useful activity as a condition of the formation of an adolescent's personality' *Voprosy psikhologii,* No. 4, 69–78.

Fel'dshtein, D.I. (1982). *Psychological characteristics of socially useful activity of adolescents* (Psikhologicheskie osobennosti obshchestvenno poleznoi deiatel'nosti podrostkov). Moscow: Pedagogika.

Fel'dshtein, D.I. (1983). 'Psychological aspects of the study of the contemporary adolescent'. *Voprosy psikhologii,* No. 1, 33–42.

Feodorov, S.I. & Nikol'skii, V.N. (1930). 'The study of characteristics of work processes in difficult-to-raise adolescents'. *Voprosy izuchenia i vospitania lichnosti,* 9, 1–2, 80–5.

Feofanov, M.P. (1931). 'The methodological foundations of the School of Basov'. *Paedologia,* No. 3 (whole No. 18), 27–43.

Feofanov, M.P. (1932). 'The theory of cultural development in paedology as an eclectic concept that has mostly idealistic roots'. *Paedologia,* No. 1–2, 21–34.

Festinger, L., Riecken, H.W., & Schachter, S. (1956). *When prophecy fails.* Minneapolis, Mn.: University of Minnesota Press.

Feyerabend, P. (1975). *Against method.* London: NLB.

Feyerabend, P. (1976). 'On the critique of scientific reason'. In R.S. Cohen, P. Feyerabend & M. Wartofsky (Eds), *Essays in memory of*

Imre Lakatos (pp. 109–43). Dordrecht: Reidel.

Figurin, N.L. & Denisova, M.P. (1949). *Stages in the development of children's behaviour from birth to 1 year* (Etapy razvitia povedenia detei ot rozhdenia do l goda). Moscow: Medgiz.

Figurin, N.L. & Denisova, M.P. (1969). 'Experimental reflexological study of early discrimination of combinative reflexes in infancy'. *Soviet psychology*, 8 1, 63–78 (Russian original 1925).

Filosofova, L.I. (1924). 'Comparative-psychological observations on the problem of sensory culture of the Montessori system'. In Basov (1924a), (pp. 103–31).

Fitzpatrick, S. (1979). *Education and social mobility in the Soviet Union 1921-1934*. Cambridge: Cambridge University Press.

Flavell, J. (1967). *Genetic psychology of J. Piaget* (Geneticheskaia psikhologia Zana Piaze). Moscow: Prosveschchenie.

Fonarev, A.M. (1977). *The development of orienting reactions in children*. (Razvitie orientirovochnyh reaktsii v detei). Moscow: Pedagogika.

Fortunatov, G.A. (1925). 'The study of children's collectives'. *Vestnik prosveshchenia*, No. 4, 45–54.

Fortunatov, G.A. (1929). 'Freely emerging groups of adolescents'. *Paedologia*, No. 4., 525–39.

Foucault, M. (1983). *This is not a pipe*. Berkeley: University of California Press.

Fradkina, F.I. (1949). 'Stages in the development of play in early age'. In *Stages in the development of play and actions with objects in early childhood* (Etapy razvitia igry i deistvii s predmetami v rannem detstve) (pp. 41–73). Moscow: Izdatel'stvo APN RSFSR.

Frolov, Y.P. (1937). *Pavlov and his school*. Oxford, New York: Oxford University Press.

Gal'perin, P.Ia. (1959). 'Development of studies on the formation of mental operations'. In B.G. Ananiev (Ed.), *Psychological science in the USSR* (Psikhologicheskaia nauka v SSSR). Vol. 1 (pp. 441–69). Moscow: Izdatel'stvo APN RSFSR.

Gal'perin, P.Ia. (1966). 'On the idea of interiorization'. *Voprosy psikhologii*, No. 4, 128–35.

Gal'perin, P.Ia. (1968). 'Towards research of the intellectual development of the child'. *International journal of psychology*, 3, 257–71.

Gal'perin, P.Ia. (1969). 'Stages in the development of mental acts'. In M. Cole & I. Maltzman (1969), (pp. 249–73).

Gal'perin, P.Ia. (1979–80). 'The role of orientation in thought'. *Soviet psychology*, 18, 2, 84–99.

Gal'perin, P.Ia. (1980). 'The functional difference between tool and means'. In I.I. Il'iasov & V.Ia.Liaudis (Eds), *Khrestomatia po vozrastnoi i pedagogicheskoi psikhologii* (pp. 195–203). Moscow: Izdatel'stvo MGU.

Gal'perin, P.Ia. (1982). 'Intellectual capabilities among older preschool children: On the problem of training and mental development'. In W.W. Hartup (Ed.), *Review of child development research*. Vol. 6 (pp. 526–46). Chicago: University of Chicago Press.

Gal'perin, P.Ia & Danilova, V.L. (1980). 'Rearing of systematic thinking in the process of solution of little creative problems'. *Voprosy psikhologii*, No. 1, 31–8.

Gal'perin, P.Ia. & Georgiev, L.S. (1960a). 'Psychological analysis of contemporary methods for training concepts in arithmetics'. *Doklady APN RSFSR*, No. 1, 31–6.

Gal'perin, P.Ia. & Georgiev, L.S. (1960b). 'Basic sequence of actions resulting in the formation of elementary mathematical concepts'. *Doklady APN RSFSR*, No. 3, 37–42.

Gal'perin, P.Ia. & Georgiev, L.S. (1960c). 'The basic contents of a program of formation of elementary mathematical concepts using methods based on measures'. *Doklady APN RSFSR*, No. 4, 49–52.

Gal'perin, P.Ia. & Georgiev, L.S. (1960d). 'The results of formation of the elementary mathematical concepts using methods based on measures'. *Doklady APN RSFSR*, No. 5, 41–4.

Gal'perin, P.Ia. & Georgiev, L.S. (1961). 'Psychological aspects of formation of elementary concepts of mathematics in children'. *Doklady APN RSFSR*, No. 7, 63–6.

Gal'perin, P.Ia. & Kabyl'nitskaia, S.L. (1974). *Experimental formation of attention* (Eksperinental'noie formirovanie vnimania). Moscow: Izdatel'stvo MGU.

Gal'perin, P.Ia., & Talyzina, N.F. (1968). *The formation of knowledge and skills on the basis of stage-theory of formation of mental operations* (Formiriovanie znaii i umenii na osnove teorii poetapnogo usvoenia umstvennykh deistvii). Moscow: Izdatelistvo MGU.

Garbačiauskiene, M. (1980). 'Some theoretical questions of studying the development of conceptual thinking'. *Lietuvos TSR aukštuju mokyklu mokslo darbai. Psichologija*, 1, 3–22.

Garbačiauskiene, M. & Grigaite, B. (1980). 'Mastering of written language as one of the conditions of transition from pre-conceptual to conceptual thinking'. *Lietuvos TSR aukštuju mokyklu mokslo darbai. Psichologija*, 1, 24–36.

Gashimov, L.Sh. (1970). *Azerbaijdian ethnopedagogics* (Azerbaidzanskaia narodnaia pedagogika). Baku.

Gel'mont, A.M. (1929). 'Children and politics'. *Paedologia*, No. 4, 595–611.

Gel'mont A.M. (1931). 'For Marxist-Leninist paedology (about the errors of P.P. Blonski)'. *Paedologia*, No. 4, 37–51.

Gergen, M.M. & Gergen, K.J. (1984). 'The social construction of narrative accounts'. In K.J. Gergen & M.M. Gergen (Eds), *Historical social psychology* (pp. 173–89). Hillsdale, NJ: Erlbaum.

Gershenzon, E.A. & Likhachova, A.S. (1928). 'The speech of the peasant child'. In Zeiliger (1928) (pp. 83–103).

Ghiselin, M. (1976). 'The nomenclature of correspondence: a new look at "homology" and "analogy". In R.B. Masterton, W. Hodos & H. Jerison (Eds), *Evolution, brain, and behavior: persistent problems* (pp. 129–42). Hillsdale, NJ: Erlbaum.

Gippenreiter, Iu.B. (1983). 'The meaning of personality in the works of A.N. Leontiev and the problem of the study of character'. *Vestnik Moskovskogo Universiteta. ser.14. psikhologia*, No. 4, 7–22.

Gizatullina, D.H. (1974). 'On the dynamics of the development of short-term memory in children of early age'. In *Voprosy teoreticheskoi i prikladnoi psikhologii*. Leningrad: Izdatel'stvo LGU.

Glotova, G.A. & Salmina, N.G. (1983). 'of spontaneous comprehension of semiotic aspects of speech, play, and drawing by children'. *Vestnik Moskovskogo Universiteta. ser. 14. psikhologia*, No. 2, 47–57.

Gobechia, F.V. (1981). 'Deviant behaviour of the under-aged and some sociogenic needs'. In S.N. Chkhartishvili, V.L. Kakabadze & N.I. Sarjveladze (Eds), *The problems of formation of sociogenic needs* (Problemy formirovania sotsigennykh potrebnostei) (pp. 146–9). Tbilisi: Uznadze Institute of Psychology.

Godovikova, D. (1974). 'The coordination of children's activity in interaction with adults during exploration of novel objects'. In M.I. Lisina (Ed.), *Interaction and its influence on the psychological development of the preschooler* (pp. 162–80). Moscow: NII Obshchei Pedagogiki.

Goer, A.E. & Goer, G. (1927). 'The first period of language activity of the child'. In Rybnikov (1927).

Golubeva, A.P. (1930). 'A study of the Oirot child in Altai'. *Paedologia*, No. 2, 208–21.

Goštautas, A., Berneris, V. & Jureviciute, E. (1983). 'Standardization of questionnaire methods (MMPI and 16PF) for adolescent examination'. *Lietuvos TSR aukš'tuju mokyklu mokslo darbai. Psichologija*, 4, 41–6.

Graham, L.R. (1967). *The Soviet Academy of Sciences and the Communist Party, 1927–1932*. Princeton, NJ: Princeton University Press.

Granat, E.E. & Zagorzel'skaia, E.I. (1930). 'Medical-paedological expedition to Buriat-Mongolia'. *Paedologia*, No. 2, 235–54.

Gray, J.A. (1966). 'Attention, consciousness and voluntary control of behaviour in Soviet psychology: Philosophical roots and research branches'. In O'Connor (1966) (pp. 1–38).

Grechina, O.N. & Osorina, M.V. (1981). 'Contemporary folklore prose of children'. In *Russian folklore: folklore and historic reality* (Russkii fol'klor: Fol'klor i istoricheskaia real'lost'). Vol. 20. Leningrad: Nauka.

Gučas, A. (1981). *Child psychology* (Vaiko psichologija). Kaunas: Sviesa.

Gureeva, N.M. & Chebysheva, N.A. (1969). *An account of the life and activities of the academician I.P. Pavlov*. Vol. 1. Leningrad: Nauka.

Gurian, W. (1955). '*Partiinost*' and knowledge'. In E.J. Simmons (Ed.), *Continuity and change in Russian and Soviet thought* (pp. 298–306). Cambridge, Ma.: Harvard University Press.

Gurova, R.G. (1977). 'A study of the influence of sociohistorical conditions on child development' (comparative investigation, 1929 and 1966). In Cole (1977) (pp. 369–92).

Guthrie, E.R. (1930). 'Conditioning as a principle of learning'. *Psychological review, 37,* 412–28.

Gvozdev, A.N. (1927). 'The acquisition of mother tongue by child'. In Rybnikov (1927).

Gvozdev, A.N. (1948). *Acquisition of the acoustic side of Russian by the child* (Usvoenie rebenkom zvukovoi storony russkogo iazyka). Moscow: Izdatel'stvo Akademii Pedagogicheskikh Nauk RSFSR.

Hammond, K.R. (Ed.) (1966). *The psychology of Egon Brunswick.* New York: Holt, Rinehart & Winston.

Harrower, M. (1983). *Kurt Koffka: an unwitting self-portrait.* Gainesville, Fl: Univ. Presses of Florida.

Heidmets, M. (1983a). 'Subject and environment'. In H. Mikkin (Ed.), *Problems in practical psychology: studies in social psychology* (pp. 38–66). Tallinn: Tallinn Pedagogic Institute Press.

Heidmets, M. (1983b). 'The "subjectness" of family and its demands for lodgings'. In E.-M. Vernik (Ed.), *Psychological conditions for social interaction* (pp. 5–16). Tallinn: Tallinn Pedagogic Institute Press.

Heidmets, M. (1985). 'Environment as the mediator of human relationships: Historical and ontogenetic aspects'. In T. Gärling & J. Valsiner (Eds), *Children within environments: toward a psychology of accident prevention* (pp. 217–27). New York: Plenum.

Hertzog, R.L. & Unruh, W.R. (1973). 'Toward a unification of the Uznadze theory of set and Western theories of human functioning'. In A.S. Prangishvili (Ed.), *Psychological investigations* (pp. 132–9). Tbilisi: Metsniereba.

Holowinsky, I.Z. (1978). 'Contemporary psychology in the Ukrainian Soviet Socialist Republic'. *American Psychologist, 33,* 185–9.

Hritzuk, J. & Janzen, H. (1973). 'A comparison of *ustanovka* and

Einstellung: Uznadze and Luchins'. In Prangishvili (1973) (pp. 140–6).

Hritzuk, J., Unruh, W. & Hertzog, R. (1969). 'Some Soviet approaches to the study of personality'. *Canadian psychologist*, 10, 32–48.

Iagunkova, V.P. (1953). 'About the major principles of the reflex theory of academician I.P. Pavlov'. *Voprosy filosfii*, No. 3, 109–19.

Iakobson, S.G. (1979). 'Analysis of psychological mechanisms of the ethical regulation of behavior in children'. *Voprosy psikhologii*, No. 1, 38–48.

Iakobson, S.G. & Pocherevina, L.P. (1982). 'The role of subjective attitude toward ethical models in the regulation of preschoolers' moral conduct'. *Voprosy psikhologii*, No. 1, 40–9 (English trans. *Soviet psychology*, 22, 1, 20–37.)

Iakobson, S.G. & Shchur, V.G. (1977). 'Psychological mechanisms of children's acquisition of ethical norms'. In *Psychological problems of ethical rearing of children* (Psikhologicheskie problemy nravstvennogo vospitania detei). Moscow: IOPP.

Iarmolenko, A.V. (1930). 'The motorics of preschool age'. *Paedologia*, 4, 463–7.

Iarmolenko, A.V. & Belikova, M.M. (1930). 'The study of the motor sphere of blind children'. *Voprosy izuchenia i vospitania lichnosti*, 9, 1–2, 90–8.

Iaroshevskii, M.G. (1947). 'The bourgeois psychologists of the USA in the fight for elimination of consciousness'. *Voprosy filosofii*, No. 3, 280–93.

Iaroshevskii, M.G. (1966). *History of psychology* (Istoria psikhologii). Moscow: Mysl'.

Iaroshevskii, M.G. (1968). *Ivan Mikhailovich Sechenov*. Leningrad: Nauka.

Iaroshevskii, M.G. (1971). *Psychology in the 20th century* (Psikhologia v XX stoletii). Moscow: Politizdat.

Iaroshevskii, M.G. (1985). *History of psychology* (Istoria psikhologii). 2nd edn Moscow: Mysl'.

Iaroshevskii, M.G. & Gurgenidze, G.S. (1981). 'L.S. Vygotsky on the nature of the psyche'. *Voprsoi filosofii*, No. 1, 142–54.

Ignjatović-Savić, N., Kovač-Cerovic, T., Plut, D. & Pesikan, A. (1985). 'Patterns of mother-infant interaction'. Paper presented at the 8th biennial meeting of the International Society for the Study of Behavioural Development, Tours, France.

Istomina, Z.M. (1948). 'The development of voluntary memory in preschool age'. In *Problems of psychology of preschool-age children* (Voprosy psikhologii rebenka doshkol'nogo vozrasta). Moscow: APN

RSFSR (English trans., *Soviet psychology, 13*, 4, 5–64).

Ivanov-Smolenskii, A.G. (1933). *The method of the study of the conditional reflexes in man* (Metodika issledovania uslovnykh refleksov u cheloveka). Moscow: Medgiz.

Ivanov-Smolenskii, A.G. (1934). *On the road to the study of highest forms of neurodynamics in man* (Na puti k izucheniu vysshikh form neirodinamiki cheloveka). Moscow: Gosmedizdat.

Ivanov-Smolenskii, A.G. (1935). 'Experimental study of the higher nervous activity of the child'. *Fiziologicheskii zhurnal*, No. 1.

Ivanov-Smolenskii, A.G. (1954). *Essays on the patho-physiology of the higher nervous activity*. Moscow: Foreign Language Publishing House (in English).

Ivanova, V.P. (1975). 'On some difficulties of transaction among preschool children'. In V.M. Sokovnin (Ed.), *Problems of pedagogics and psychology of social transaction* (Problemy pedagogiki i psihologii obshchenia). Frunze: Mektep.

Jacikevičius, A. (1984). 'Some peculiarities of self-appraisal of personality by future teachers'. *Lietuvos TSR aukštuju mokyklu mokslo darbai. Psichologija 5*, 3–13.

Janet, P. (1921). 'The fear of action'. *Journal of abnormal psychology and social psychology, 16*, 2–3, 150–60.

Jevons, W.S. (1958). *The principles of science*. New York: Dover (original in 1873).

John-Steiner, V., Cole, M., Souberman, E. & Scribner, S. (1978). 'Editors' preface'. In L.S. Vygotsky, *Mind in society* (pp. ix–xi). Cambridge, Ma.: Harvard University Press.

Joravsky, D. (1961). *Soviet Marxism and natural science 1917–1932*. New York: Columbia University Press.

Joravsky, D. (1978). 'The construction of the Stalinist psyche. In S. Fitzpatrick (Ed.), *Cultural revolution in Russia, 1928–1931* (pp. 105–28). Bloomington: Indiana University Press.

Joravsky, D. (1985). 'Cultural revolution and the fortress mentality'. In A. Gleason, P. Kenez and R. Stites (Eds), *Bolshevik culture* (pp. 93–113). Bloomington: Indiana University Press.

Juviler, P.H. (1985). 'Contradictions of revolution: juvenile crime and rehabilitation'. In A. Gleason, P. Kenez & R. Stites (Eds.), *Bolshevik culture* (pp. 261–78). Bloomington: Indiana University Press.

Kaidanovskaia, I.A. (1984). 'Experimental-genetic analysis of cognition in the works of J. Piaget'. *Vestnik Moskovskogo Universiteta. seria 14. psikhologia*. No. 3, 36–40.

Kairov, I.A. & Bogdanova, O.C. (Eds) (1979). *Moral development of younger schoolchildren in the process of education* (Nravstvennoie razvitie mladshikh shkol'nikov v protsesse vospitania). Moscow: Pedagogika.

Kaloshina, I.P. & Kharicheva, G.I. (1975). 'On the development of means of logic in thinking'. *Sovetskaia pedagogika*, No. 4, 97–104.

Kanicheva, R.A. (1930). 'On the influence of the central nervous system on the vegetative nervous system of psychoneurotic children'. *Voprosy izuchenia i vospitania lichnosti*, 9, 1–2, 56–61.

Kapitsa, O.I. (1928). *Children's folklore* (Detskii fol'klor). Leningrad.

Karpova, S.N. & Petrushina, L.G. (1981). 'Significance of games involving a plot and role-playing for the development of moral behaviour'. *Vestnik Moskovskogo Universiteta. ser.14. psikhologia*, No. 3, 22–30 (English trans., *Soviet psychology*, 1982, 21, 1, 18–31).

Kasatkin, N.I. (1935). 'Development of acoustic and visual conditional reflexes and their differentiation in infants'. *Sovetskaia paediatria*, No. 8.

Kasatkin, N.I. (1948). *Early conditional reflexes in the human ontogeny* (Rannyie uslovnyie refleksy v ontogeneze cheloveka). Moscow: Medgiz.

Kasatkin, N.I. (1951). *Treatise on the development of higher nervous activity in the child at early age* (Ocherk razvitia v.n.d. u rebenka rannego vozrasta). Moscow: Medgiz.

Kazakov, V.G. (1983). 'The development of applied problems of social psychology in Soviet science'. In E.V. Shorokhova & V.P. Levkovich (Eds), *Applied problems of social psychology* (Prikladnyie problemy sotsial'noi psikhologii) (pp. 5–23). Moscow: Nauka.

Kezheradze, E.D. (1973). 'The cognitive operation of generalization and rigidity in the preschool age'. In Prangishvili (1973) (pp. 159–65).

Khomenko, K.E. (1979–80). 'The emergence of visual-imagic thought in the child'. *Soviet psychology*, 18, 2, 37–46.

Khomenko, K.E. (1980). 'The understanding of literary images of early-age children'. In I.I.Il'iasov & V.Ia. Liaudis (Eds), *Khrestomatia po vozrasstnoi i pedagogicheskoi psikhologii* (p. 276). Moscow: Izdatel'stvo MGU.

Kline, G.L. (1955). 'Darwinism and the Russian Orthodox Church'. In E.J. Simmons (Ed.), *Continuity and change in Russian and Soviet thought* (pp. 306–28). Cambridge, Ma.: Harvard University Press.

Kniaz'kov, S.A. & Serbov, N.I. (1910). *Ocherk istorii narodnago obrazovaniia v Rossii do epokhi reform Aleksandra II.* Moscow: V. Antin' & Co.

Köhler, W. (1927/1973). *The mentality of apes.* New York: Liveright.

Köhler, W. (1928). 'Intelligence in apes'. In C. Murchison (Ed.),

Psychologies of 1925. (pp. 145–61). Worcester, Ma.: Clark University Press.

Köhler, W. (1971). *The selected papers of Wolfgang Köhler*. New York: Liveright.

Kolbanovskii, V. (1939). 'The matter and consciousness'. *Pod znamenem Marksizma*, No. 8, 39–61.

Kolesnikova, A. & Pervova, T. (1927). 'The time budget of students of the Profintern pedagogical school'. In M.S. Bernshtein & N.A. Rybnikov (Eds), *The time budget of our youth* (Biudzet vremeni nashego molodniaka) (pp. 86–102). Leningrad: Gosizdat.

Kolominskii, Ia I. (1976). *Psychology of interrelationships in small groups* (Psikhologia vzaimootnoshenii v malykh gruppakh). Minsk: Izd. Belorusskogo Gosudarstvennogo Universiteta.

Kolominskii, Ia.L. (1983). 'Developmental and pedagogical social psychology in the light of problems of child-rearing'. In E.V. Shorokhova & V.P. Levkovich (Eds), *Applied problems of social psychology* (Prikladnyie problemy sotsial'noi psikhologii) (pp. 255–70). Moscow: Nauka.

Kol'tsova, M.M. (1958). *On the formation of higher nervous activity of the child* (O formirovanii vyshhei nervnoi deiatel'nosti rebenka). Leningrad: Medgiz.

Kon, I.S. (1967). *Sociology of personality* (Sotsiologia lichnosti). Moscow: Politizdat.

Kon, I.S. (1978). 'Age categories in sciences studying man and society'. *Sociological investigations*, No. 3, 76–86.

Kon, I.S. (1979). *Psychology of youth* (Psikhologia iunosheskogo vozrasta). Moscow: Politizdat.

Kon, I.S. (1980). 'Ethnography and psychology'. In E. Gellner (Ed.), *Soviet and Western anthropology* (pp. 217–30). London: Duckworth.

Kon, IS. (1981a). 'Ethnography of childhood'. *Sovetskaia etnografia*, No. 5, 3–13.

Kon, I.S. (1981b). 'On the problem of age symbolism'. *Sovetskaia etnografia* No. 6, 98–106.

Kon, I.S. (1981c). 'The category of self in psychology'. *Psikhologicheskii zhurnal*, No. 3, 25–38.

Kon, I.S. (1981d). 'Psychology of sex differences'. *Voprosy psikhologii*, No. 2, 47–57.

Kon, I.S. (Ed.) (1983a). *Ethnography of childhood: traditional forms of rearing children and adolescents among peoples of East and South-East Asia*. Moscow: Nauka (in Russian).

Kon, I.S. (Ed.) (1983b). *Ethnography of childhood: traditional forms of rearing children and adolescents among peoples of Middle East and South Asia*. Moscow: Nauka (in Russian).

Kon, I.S. (1983c). 'Ethnography and the problems of sex'. *Sovetskaia etnografia*, No. 3, 25–34.

Kon, I.S. (1984a). 'The self as a historical-cultural and ethnopsychological phenomenon'. In L. Strickland (Ed.), *Directions in Soviet social psychology* (pp. 29–46). New York: Springer.

Kon, I.S.(1984b). *In the search of Self* (V poiskakh sebia). Moscow: Politizdat.

Korneeva, G.A. (1978). 'The role of actions-with-objects in the formation of number concept in preschoolers'. *Voprosy psikhologii*, No. 2, 91–101.

Korner, A.F. (1979). 'Maternal rhythms and waterbeds'. In E.B. Thoman (Ed.), *Origins of infant's social responsiveness*. Hillsdale, N.J.: Erlbaum.

Kornilov, K.N. (1921) *Theory of human reactions* (Uchenie o reaktsiakh cheloveka). Moscow-Leningrad: Gosudarstvennoie Izdatel'stvo.

Kornilov, K.N. (1923a). 'Contemporary psychology and Marxism, I.' *Pod znamenem Marksizma*, No. 1, 41–50.

Kornilov, K.N. (1923b). 'Contemporary psychology and Marxism, II.' *Pod znamenem Marksizma*, No. 4–5, 86–114.

Kornilov, K.N. (1924). 'The dialectical method in psychology'. *Pod znamenem Marksizma*, No. 1, 107–13.

Kornilov, K.N. (Ed.) (1925). *Psychology and Marxism* (Psikhologia i marksizm). Leningrad: Gosizdat.

Kornilov, K.N. (1927). 'The contemporary state of psychology in the USSR'. *Pod znamenem Marksizma*, No. 10–11, 195–217.

Kornilov, K.N. (1930). 'Psychology in the light of dialectic materialism'. In C. Murchison (Ed.), *Psychologies of 1930* (pp. 243–78). Worcester, Ma.: Clark University Press.

Kosikov, I.G. (1983). 'Traditional institutions of child-rearing in Khmer society'. In I. Kon (Ed.), (1983a) (pp. 128–171).

Kovalev, V.I. (1981). 'On the problem of motives.' *Psikhologicheskii zhurnal*, 2, 1, 29–44.

Kozlova, Y.V. (1978). 'Early ontogeny of the binocular vision in humans'. Unpublished dissertation of the Candidate of Sciences degree, Moscow: Institute of Psychology of the Academy of Sciences. (cf. published results in Kozlova & Mit'kin, 1977).

Kozlova, Y.V. & Mit'kin, A.A. (1977). 'Development of oculomotor activity in the early ontogeny of bipolar vision'. *Studies psychologica*, 19, 4, 301–3.

Kozulin, A. (1984). *Psychology in utopia*. Cambridge, Ma.: MIT Press.

Kozulin, A. (1986). 'The concept of activity in Soviet psychology'. *American psychologist*, 41, 3, 264–74.

Krasnobaev, I.M. (1960). *Formation of moral beliefs in upper-level schoolchildren* (Formirovanie nravstvennykh ubezdenii u starsheklassnikov). Moscow: Pedagogika.

Krasnogorskii, N.I. (1907). 'Experiment on the formation of artificial conditional reflexes in children of early age'. *Russkii vrach*, No. 35, 1245.

Krasnogorskii, N.I. (1908). 'On conditional reflexes in children'. *Russkii vrach*, No. 28, pp. 930–932; and No. 29, pp. 969–977.

Krasnogorskii, N.I. (1935). *Development of the teaching of the physiological activity of children's brains* (Razvitie uchenia o fiziologicheskoi deiatelnosti mozga u detei). Leningrad: Biomedgiz.

Krasuskii, V.S. (1929). 'Free collectives of peasant children'. *Paedologia*, No. 4, 508–24.

Krasuskii, V.S. & Makarovskii, D.B. (1929). 'Social knowledge of homeless children'. *Paedologia*, No. 4, 612–21.

Kregžde, S. (1981). *Psychology of the formation of professional interests* (Psikhologia formirovania professional'nykh interesov). Vilnius.

Kreps, E.M. (Ed.) (1975). *Unpublished and little-known materials of I.P. Pavlov* (Neopublikovannyie i maloizvestnye materialy I.P. Pavlova). Leningrad: Nauka.

Krichevskii, R.L. (1977). 'On some mechanisms of leadership in collectives of higher-grade children'. *Novyie issledovania v psikhologii*, No. 1, 57–61.

Krichevskii, R.L. (1980). 'The dynamics of group leadership'. *Voprosy psikhologii*, No. 2, 42–52.

Kropotkin, P.A. (1908). *Mutual aid: a factor of evolution.* London: Heinemann.

Kropotkin, P.A. (1920). *Contemporary science and anarchy.* (Sovremennaia nauka i anarkhia). St Petersburg & Moscow: "Golos Truda".

Kruusvall, J. (1983). 'A comparative analysis of room use in city apartments'. In H. Mikkin (Ed.), *Problems in practical psychology: studies in social psychology* (pp. 79–105). Tallinn: Tallinn Pedagogic Institute Press.

Kruusvall, J. (1986). 'The informational function of social communication'. In J. Orn & T. Niit (Eds), *People, social interaction and the living environment* (pp. 85–102). Tallinn: Tallinn Pedagogic Institute Press.

Kruusvall, J. & Heidmets, M. (1979). 'Family life in multi-storied apartment houses'. In M. Heidmets, R. Kilgas, J. Kruusvall & J. Valsiner, *Man, environment, space* (pp. 43–81). Tartu: Tartu University Press.

Kruusvall, J., Niit, T. & Heidmets, M. (1984). 'Mass housing and psychological research'. A keynote address at the meeting of the International Association for the Study of People and their Physical

Surroundings, West Berlin, July.

Kuhn, T.S. (1962). *The structure of scientific revolutions*, Chicago: University of Chicago Press.

Kuhn, T.S. (1970). *The structure of scientific revolutions*, 2nd edn. Chicago: University of Chicago Press.

Kumarin, V. (Ed.). (1976). *Anton Makarenko. His life and his work in education*. Moscow: Progress.

Kunitsyna, V.N. (1966). 'On the problem of estimation of another person's age by adolescents'. In B.G. Ananiev & B.F. Lomov (Eds), *Problems of general, social, and engineering psychology* (Problemy obshchei, sotsial'noi, i inzenernoi psikhologii) (pp. 43–51). Leningrad: Izdatel'stvo LGU.

Kunitsyna, V.N. (1970). 'On the question of self-evaluation of the adolescent'. *Uchenyie Zapiski LGU. seria psikhologii*, No. 2 (Whole No. 352), 62–69.

Kurazov, I.F. (1930). 'Methodological conclusions of the Behaviorist congress'. *Voprosy izuchenia i vospitania lichnosti*, 9, 1–2, 1–8.

Kussmann, T. (1974). *Sowjetische Psychologie: Auf der Suche nach der Methode*. Bern: H.Huber.

Kvasova, D.G. & Fedorova-Grot, A.K. (1967). *The physiological school of I.P. Pavlov* (Fiziologicheskaia shkola I.P. Pavlova). Leningrad: Nauka.

Ladygina-Kots, N.N. (1935). *The child of the chimpanzee and the human child in their instincts, emotions, games, habits, and emotional movements*. (Ditia shimpanze i ditia cheloveka v ih instinktah, emotsiyah, igrah, privytskah i vyrazitel'nih dvizeniyah). Moscow: Trudy Darvinskogo Muzeia.

Lakatos, I. & Musgrave, A. (Eds) (1970). *Criticism and the growth of knowledge*. Cambridge: Cambridge University Press.

Lape, J., Abariunaite, A., & Gutauskiene, L. (1983). 'Investigation of group interests structure'. *Lietuvos TSR aukštuju mokyklu mokslo darbai. Psichologija, 4*, 47–58.

Lashley, K.S. (1930). 'Basic neural mechanisms in behavior'. *Psychological review, 37*, 1, 1–24.

Lavrinenko, A.I. (1970). 'On the problem of stability of schoolchildren's moral reasoning'. *Voprosy psikhologii*, No. 3, 94–104.

Lavrova-Bikchentai, Z.G. (1930). 'Physical development of Tatar schoolchildren in Moscow'. *Paedologia*, No. 2, 263–71.

Lazurskii, A. (1906). *Treatise on the science of characters* (Ocherk nauki o kharakterakh). St Petersburg: I.N. Skorokhodov.

Lefebvre, V.A. (1980). 'An algebraic model of ethical cognition'. *Journal of Mathematical Psychology, 22*, 83–120.

Lehtman, Ia. B. (1953). 'For rebuilding psychology on the basis of I. P. Pavlov's teaching'. *Voprosy filosofii*, No. 2, 219–24.

Lenin, V. I. (1970). 'On the meaning of militant materialism'. In V. I. Lenin, *Sobranie sochinenii, 45* (5th edn), 23–33, Moscow (original: March 1922 in *Pod znamenem Marksizma*).

Leontiev, A. A. (1974). *Psychology of interaction* (Psikhologia obshchenia). Tartu: Tartu University Press.

Leontiev, A. A. (1983). 'The creative path of Aleksei Nikolaevich Leontiev'. In A. Zaporozhets, V. P. Zinchenko, O. Ovchinnikova & O. Tikhomirov (Eds), *A. N. Leontiev and contemporary psychology* (A. N. Leontiev i sovremennaia psikhologia) (pp. 6–39). Moscow: Moscow University Press.

Leontiev, A. N. (1931). *Development of memory* (Razvitie pamiati). Moscow: Gosizdat.

Leontiev, A. N. (1932). 'The development of voluntary attention in the child'. *Journal of genetic psychology, 40,* 52–83.

Leontiev, A. N. (1944). 'Psychological foundations of preschoolers' play'. *Sovetskaia pedagogika*, No. 8–9, 37–47.

Leontiev, A. N. (1946). 'On some psychological questions of the conscious nature of learning'. *Sovetskaia pedagogika*, No. 1–2.

Leontiev, A. N. (1947). 'Problems of child and pedagogical psychology'. *Sovetskaia pedagogika, 11,* 6, 103–10.

Leontiev, A. N. (1950). *Mental development of the child* (Umstvennoie razvitie rebenka). Moscow (stenographed lecture—in English see Winn (1961)).

Leontiev, A. N. (1972a). 'The problem of activity in psychology'. *Voprosy filosofii*, No. 9, 95–108 (English trans. in J. Wertsch (Ed.), *The concept of activity in Soviet psychology* (pp. 37–71). Armonk, NY: M. E. Sharpe.)

Leontiev, A. N. (1972b). 'Activity and consciousness'. *Voprosy filosofii*, No. 12, 129–40.

Leontiev, A. N. (1974a). 'General notion of activity'. In A. A. Leontiev (Ed.), *Foundations of the theory of speech activity* (Osnovy teorii rechevoi deiatel'nosti) (pp. 5–20). Moscow: Nauka.

Leontiev, A. N. (1974b). 'Activity and personality'. *Voprosy filosofii*, I: No. 4, 87–97; II: No. 5, 65–78.

Leontiev, A. N. (1975). *Activity, consciousness, personality* (Deiatel'nost', soznanie, lichnost'). Moscow: Izdatel'stvo Politicheskoi Literatury.

Leontiev, A. N. (1978). *Activity, consciousness, and personality.* Englewood Cliffs, NJ: Prentice-Hall (English trans. of Leontiev, 1975).

Leontiev, A. N. (1980). 'The mastery of scientific concepts by pupils as a problem of pedagogical psychology'. In I. I. Il'iasov & V. Ia. Liaudis (Eds), *Reader on developmental and pedagogical psychology*

(Khrestomatia po vozrastnoi i pedagogicheskoi psikhologii) (pp. 161–94). Moscow: Moscow University Press. (presented at a conference in 1935).

Leontiev, A.N. (1981). *Problems of the development of the mind.* Moscow: Progress (in English trans. of *Problemy razvitia psikhiki*).

Leontiev, A.N. & Gal'perin, P.Ia. (1964). 'The theory of mastery of knowledge and programmed learning'. *Sovetskaia pedagogika*, No. 10, 56–65.

Leontiev, A.N. & Rozanova, T.V. (1951). 'The dependence of association formation on the content of activity'. *Sovetskaia pedagogika*, No. 10, 60–78.

Leventuev, P. (1931). 'Political falsification in paedology'. *Paedologia*, No. 3 (Whole No. 15), 63–6.

Levina, M.A. (1925). 'On the question of the meaning of the method of psychological observations on children in the system of pedagogical education.' In Basov (1925a), (pp. 92–113).

Levina, M.A. & El'konin, D.B. (1931). 'For struggle for Marxist-Leninist paedology'. *Paedologia*, No. 5–6, 29–40.

Levina, M.A. & Gershenzon, E.A. (1928). 'Social expressions of the peasant child'. In Zeiliger (1928), (pp. 102–18).

Levina, R.E. (1968). 'Ideas of L.S. Vygotsky about the planning speech of the child'. *Voprosy psikhologii, 14*, No. 4, 105–15.

Levina, R.E. (1979). 'L.S. Vygotsky's ideas about the planning function of speech in children'. In J. Wertsch (Ed.), *The concept of activity in Soviety psychology* (pp. 279–99). Armonk, NY: M.E. Sharpe.

Levitin, K. (1982). *One is not born a personality.* Moscow: Progress.

Lewin, K., Lippitt, R. & White, R.K. (1939). 'Patterns of aggressive behaviour in experimentally created "social climates"'. *Journal of social psychology, 10*, 271–99.

Liders, A.G. (1978a). 'Development of a generalized method of comparison of sets in preschool children'. *Vestnik Moskovskogo Universiteta. ser. 14. psikhologia*, No. 3, 26–37.

Liders, A.G. (1978b). 'On the analysis of the use of logical models in Piaget's study of intellect'. In *Psychology of cognitive activity (Psikhologia poznavatel'noi deiatel'nosti) (pp. 11–18).* Moscow: Izdatel'stvo MGU.

Liders, A.G. (1980a). 'Piaget's phenomena and their real origins'. *Vestnik Moskovskogo Universiteta. seria 14. psikhologia*, No. 3, 18–31.

Liders, A.G. (1980b). 'Perception and phenomena of nonconservation'. *Voprosy psikhologii*, No. 4, 129–32.

Lygis, D. (1981). 'The investigation of attention properties in normal and abnormal children'. *Lietuvos TSR aukš̆tuju mokyklu mokslo darbai. Psichologija, 2*, 41–51.

Liik, K. & Niit, T. (1986). 'Intimacy and family relationships'. In J. Orn and T. Niit (Eds.), *People, social interaction and the living environment* (pp. 154–77). Tallinn: Tallinn Pedagogic Institute (in Russian).

Liimets, H. (1982). *How does the process of instruction rear children?* (Kak vospityvaet protsess obuchenia). Moscow: Znanie.

Lipkina, A.I. (1980). 'Child psychology and the formation of moral components of the child's world view'. *Voprosy psikhologii*, No. 1, 11–21.

Lisina, M.I. (1961). 'Influence of the interaction with close people on early child development'. *Voprosi psikhologii*, No. 3, 117–125.

Lisina, M.I. (1974a). *Development of interaction in preschoolers* (Razvitie obshchenia u doshkol'nikov). Moscow: Pedagogika.

Lisina, M.I. (1974b). 'The child's interaction with adults as activity'. In M.I. Lisina (Ed.), *Interaction and its effect on the psychological development of the preschooler* (Obshchenie i ego vliyanie na razvitie psikhiki doshkol'nika). Moscow: NII Obshchei Pedagogiki APN SSSR.

Lisina, M.I. (1976). 'On the mechanism of change in children's leading activity in the first seven years of life'. In *Problems of periodization of ontogenetic psychological development*. Moscow: IOPP.

Lisina, M.I. (1978a). 'On the mechanisms of change in children's leading activity in the first seven years'. *Voprosi psikhologii*, No. 5.

Lisina, M.I. (1978b). 'Interaction between adults and children in their first seven years'. In V. Davydov (Ed), *Problems of general, developmental, and pedagogical psychology*. (Problemy obshchei vozrastnoi, i pedagogicheskoi psikhologii (pp. 237–52). Moscow: Pedagogika.

Lisina, M.I. (1980). 'The study of interaction with surrounding people among children of early and preschool age'. *Sovetskaia pedagogika*, No. 1 63–70.

Lisina, M.I. (1982a). 'The development of interaction in the first seven years of life'. In W.W. Hartup (Ed.), *Review of child development research*. Vol. 6 (pp. 133–74). Chicago: University of Chicago Press.

Lisina, M.I. (1982b). 'The development of cognitive activity of children in the process of interaction with adults and peers'. *Voprosy psikhologii*, No. 4, 18–35.

Lisina, M.I. (Ed.). (1985). *Interaction and speech: children's speech development in interaction with adults* (Obshchenie i rech: razvitie rechi u detei v obshchenii so vzroslymi). Moscow: Pedagogika.

Lisina, M. & Bedel'baeva, H.T. (1974). 'Characteristics of preschoolers' behaviour during perception of persons or objects'. In Lisina, 1974b (pp. 147–161).

Lisina, M.I., Vetrova, V.V. & Smirnova, Y.O. (1974). 'On the influence of need in interaction with adults on the child's relationship with adults'

speech directed towards them'. In Lisina (Ed.), 1974b (pp. 128–48).
Lomov, B.F. (1975). 'Interaction as a problem of general psychology'. In
    E.V. Shorokhova (Ed.), *Methodological problems of social psychology*
    (Metodologicheskie problemy sotsial'noi psikhologii) (pp. 124–35).
    Moscow: Nauka.
Lomov, B.F. (1976). 'Interaction and social regulation of individual's
    behaviour'. In B.F. Lomov (Ed.), *Psychological problems of social
    regulation of behaviour* (Psikhologicheskie problemy sotsial'noi
    reguliatsii povedenia) (pp. 64–93). Moscow: Nauka.
Lomov, B.F. (1980). 'Characteristics of cognitive processes in conditions
    of interaction'. *Psikhologicheskii zhurnal, 1*, 5, 26–42.
Lomov, B.F. (1981). 'Personality in the system of social relations'.
    Psikhologicheskii zhurnal, 2, 1, 3–17.
London, I.D. (1949). 'A historical survey of psychology in the Soviet
    Union'. *Psychological bulletin, 46*, 241–77.
London, I.D. (1954). 'Researches on sensory interaction in the Soviet
    Union'. *Psychological bulletin, 51*, 531–68.
Lozinskii, S.O. (1929). 'Reasoning of children about poverty and
    affluence'. *Paedologia*, No. 4, 571–6.
Luria, A.R. (1925). 'Psychoanalysis as a system of monistic psychology'. In
    K. Kornilov (Ed.), *Psychology and marxism* (Psikhologia i marksizm)
    (pp. 47–80). Leningrad: Gosudarstvennoe Izdatel'stvo.
Luria, A.R. (1928a). 'Psychology in Russia'. *Pedagogical seminary and
    journal of genetic psychology, 35*, 3, 347–55.
Luria, A.R. (1928b). 'The problem of the cultural behaviour of the child'.
    Pedagogical seminary and journal of genetic psychology, 35, 493–506.
Luria, A.R. (1928c). 'On the system of psychology of behaviour'.
    Psikhologia, 1, 1, 53–65.
Luria, A.R. (1928d). *Speech and intellect in child development* (Rech i
    intellekt v razvitii rebenka). Moscow: Gosizdat.
Luria, A.R. (1930a). 'On the structure of reactive processes'. *Psikhologia,
    3*, 2, 241–8.
Luria, A.R. (1930b). Book review: M. Basov, *General Principles of
    Paedology*, Moscow-Leningrad, 1928. *Journal of genetic psychology
    37*, 176–8.
Luria, A.R. (1931a). 'Psychological expedition to Central Asia'. *Science,
    74*, No. 1920, 383–4.
Luria, A.R. (1931b). 'On the problem of neurodynamic development of
    the child'. *Paedologia*, No. 2 (Whole No. 14), 18–29.
Luria, A.R. (1932). *The nature of human conflicts*. New York: Liveright.
Luria, A.R. (1934). 'The second psychological expedition to Central Asia'.
    Journal of genetic psychology, 44, 255–9.
Luria, A.R. (1936). 'The development of mental functions in twins'.

Character and personality, 5, 35–47.

Luria, A. R. (1947). Traumatic aphasia (Travmaticheskaia afazia). Moscow: Izdatel'stvo Akademii Meditsinskikh Nauk.

Luria, A. R. (Ed.) (1956). Problems of higher nervous activity of normal and abnormal child (Problemy vyshhei nervnoi deiatel'nosti normal'nogo i anormal'nogo rebenka). Vol. 1. Moscow: Izdatel'stvo APN RSFSR.

Luria, A. R. (Ed.) (1958). Problems of higher nervous activity of normal and abnormal child. Vol. 2. Moscow: Izdatel'stvo APN RSFSR.

Luria, A. R. (1960). The role of speech in the regulation of normal and abnormal behaviour. Oxford: Pergamon Press.

Luria, A. R. (1961). 'An objective approach to the study of the abnormal child'. American Journal of Orthopsychiatry, 31, 1, 1–16.

Luria, A. R. (Ed.) (1963). The mentally retarded child. New York: Macmillan.

Luria, A. R. (1966). Human brain and psychological processes. New York: Harper & Row.

Luria, A. R. (1974). On the historical development of cognitive processes (Ob istoricheskom razvitii poznavatel'nykh protsessov). Moscow: Nauka.

Luria, A. R. (1976a). Cognitive development: its cultural and social foundations. Cambridge, Ma.: Harvard University Press.

Luria, A. R. (1976b). Basic problems of neurolinguistics. The Hague: Mouton.

Luria, A. R. (1978a). 'A child's speech responses and the social environment'. In Cole (1978) (pp. 45–77). (Russian original published in USSR in 1930).

Luria, A. R. (1978b). 'The development of writing in the child'. In Cole (1978) (pp. 145–94). (Russian original, 1928).

Luria, A. R. (1979). Language and consciousness (Iazyk i soznanie). Moscow: Izdatel'stvo MGU. (English trans.: Language and cognition, New York: Wiley, 1982).

Luria, A. R. (1982). Stages of the past journey (Etapy proidennogo put'i). Moscow: Izdatel'stvo MGU.

Luria, A. R. & Iudovich, F. Ia. (1956). Speech and the development of psychological processes in children (Rech i razvitie psikhicheskikh protesessov u detei). Moscow: Izdatel'stvo APN RSFSR. (English trans.: Speech and the development of mental processes in the child, London: Staples Press, 1959).

Luria, A. R. & Tsvetkova, L. S. (1966). Neuropsychological analysis of problem solving (Neiropsikhologicheskii analiz reshenia zadach). Moscow: Prosveshchenie.

Luria, A. R. & Vinogradova, O. S. (1959). 'An objective investigation of the dynamics of semantic systems'. *British Journal of Psychology*, 50, 2, 89–105.

Maksimov, L.K. (1979). 'The dependence of development of schoolchildren's mathematical thinking on the nature of instruction'. *Voprosy psikhologii*, No. 2, 57–65.

Malakhovskaia, D.B. (1975). 'On the history of the study of bird behaviour'. In K.E. Fabri (Ed.), *Problems of zoopsychology, ethology, and comparative psychology* (pp. 79–80). Moscow: Izdatel'stvo MGU.

Mal'kovskaia, T.N. (1973). 'The development of leaders among older schoolchildren'. In B.D. Parygin (Ed.), *Administration and leadership* (Rukovodstvo i liderstvo) (pp. 94–119). Leningrad: LGPI.

Mamontova, G.I. (1981). 'Cultural-historical and psychological bases of children's horror stories'. In *Siberian folklore* (Sibirskii fol'klor) (pp. 55–62). Novosibirsk: Novosibirsk Pedagogic Institute.

Man'ko, Yu. V. (1976). 'Semantic analysis of the concept "deiatel'nost"'. In A.A. Brudnyi & E. Shukhurov (Eds), *Semantics and social psychology* (Semantika i sotsial'naya psikhologia). Frunze: Ilim.

Mansurov, N.S. (1952). 'For the use and development of the teaching of I.P. Pavlov in psychology'. *Voprosy filosofii*, No. 1, 153–61.

Markova, A.K. (1979). 'The problem of the development of the motivation of the learning activity'. *Sovetskaia Pedagogika*, No. 11, 63–71.

Markova, A.K. (1980). 'Paths for the study of schoolchildren's motivation for learning activity'. *Voprosy psikhologii*, No. 6, 25–34.

Markova, A.K. (Ed.). (1986). *The formation of study interests in schoolchildren* (Formirovanie interesa k ucheniu u shkol'nikov). Moscow: Pedagogika.

Markova, I. (1982). *Paradigms, thought, and language*. Chichester: Wiley.

Maslina, M.N. (1947). 'For bolshevik *partiinost*' in questions of psychology'. *Voprosy filosofii*, No. 2, 334–7.

Matiushkin, A.M. (1983). 'The psychological structure, dynamics, and development of cognitive activity'. *Soviet psychology*, 21, 4, 91–115.

McLeish, J. (1975). *Soviet psychology: history, theory, content*. London: Methuen.

Mead, M. & Calas, E. (1955). 'Child-rearing in postrevolutionary Russia'. In M.Mead & M. Wolfenstein (Eds), *Childhood in contemporary cultures*. Chicago: University of Chicago Press.

Medevedev, Z.A. (1969). *The rise and fall of T.D. Lysenko*. New York: Columbia University Press.

Medvedev, Z.A. (1979). *Soviet science*. Oxford: Oxford University Press.

Mel'nikov, M.N. (1970). *Russian child folklore of Siberia* (Russkii detskii fol'klor Sibiri). Novosibirsk: Nauka.

Menchinskaia, N.A. (1975). 'The ways of realization in psychology of the principle of unity of childrearing and instruction'. *Sovetskaia pedagogika*, No. 9, 8–17.

Menchinskaia, N.A. (1978). 'Psychological regularities in the formation of the communist world view in schoolchildren'. In *The formation of the communist world view of schoolchildren* (Formirovanie kommunisticheskogo mirovozrenia u shkol'nikov) (pp. 60–6). Moscow: Pedagogika.

Merlin, V. (1929). 'On the evolution of the social world view in children'. *Paedologia*, No. 4, 541–57.

Merlin, V. (1965). 'From the history of Soviet psychological thought (On the question of psychological heritage of Professor M.Ia. Basov)'. *Voprosy psikhologii*, No. 5, 28–35.

Merlin, V. & Khriakova, M. (1930). *Problems of the development of children's social world view* (Voprosy razvitia sotsial'nogo mirovozrenia u detei). Moscow-Leningrad: Gosizdat.

Meshcheryakova, S.Y. (1974). 'Behaviour of the child in an unfamiliar setting in the presence of a known adult'. In Lisina (1974b) (pp. 24–40).

Meshcheryakova, S.Y. (1975a). 'Characteristics of the animation complex in infants stimulated by objects and interaction with adults'. *Voprosy psikhologii*, No. 5, 82–88.

Meshcheryakova, S.Y. (1975b). 'On the problem of the nature of the animation complex'. In V.N. Pushkin (Ed.), *Experimental investigations on the problems of general and pedagogical psychology* (Eksperimental'nyie issledovania po problemam obshchei i pedagogicheskoi psikhologii) (pp. 57–66). Moscow: NII Obshchei pedagogiki APN SSSR.

Miasishchev, V.N. (1925). 'On the relationship of the external and internal reactions'. *Novoe v refleksologii*, No. 1.

Miasishchev, V.N. (1930). 'On the relationship of vegetative and animalic reactions'. *Voprosy izuchenia i vospitania lichnosti*, 9, 1–2, 24–32.

Miasishchev, V.N. (1932). 'On the types of behaviour and the types of the nervous system'. *Voprosy izuchenia i vospitania lichnosti*, 10, 5–12.

Mikhlina, E.S. & Nikitenko, N.I. (1928). 'Play activity of the peasant child'. In Zeiliger (1928) (pp. 43–68).

Miksyte, G. (1981). 'Training of a creative personality and the problem of intellectual activity of pupils'. *Lietuvos TSR aukštuju mokyklu mokslo darbai. Psichologija*, 2, 3–8.

Miliavskaia, V.O. (1932). 'Experimental data on the issue of working ability in connection with the typical characteristics of behaviour'. *Voprosy izuchenia i vospitania lichnosti*, 10, 13–27.

Miller, M.A. (1986). 'The origins and development of Russian psychoanalysis'. *Journal of the American Academy of Psychoanalysis*,

14, 1, 125–35.

Mitin, M. (1931). 'New tasks of the work on the philosophical front, in connection with the results of the discussion'. *Pod znamenem Marksizma*, No. 3, 12–35.

Mitin, M., Ral'tsevich, V. & Iudin, P. (1930). 'About new tasks of Marxist-Leninist philosophy'. *Pravda*, 7 June, pp. 3–4.

Mit'kin, A.A. (1981). 'Visual-vestibular interaction in infancy'. *Psikhologiceskii zhurnal*, *2*, 4, 68–79.

Mit'kin, A.A., Kozlova, Y.V., Sergienko, Y.A. & Yamshchikov, A.N. (1978). 'On some questions of the early ontogenesis of sensorimotor functions'. In *Eye movements and visual perception* (Dvizenie glaz i zritel'noye vospriatie) (pp. 9–70). Moscow: Nauka.

Mit'kin, A.A., Sergienko, Y.A. & Yamshchikov, A.N. (1978). 'The dynamics of the development of oculomotor activity in infants'. In B. Lomov & I. Ravisscth-Stscherbo (Eds), *Problems of genetic psychophysiology of the man* (Problemy geneticheskoi psikhofiziologii cheloveka) (pp. 170–81). Moscow: Nauka.

Mit'kin, A.A., Sergienko, Y.A. & Yamshchikov, A.N. (1979). 'Some forms of oculomotor behaviour in early human ontogeny'. In K.K. Sudakov, V.B. Zvyrkov & D.G. Shevchenko (Eds), *Systems analysis of mechanism of behaviour* (Sistemnyi analiz mehanizmov povedenia) (pp. 143–53). Moscow: Nauka.

Mit'kin, A.A. & Yamshchikov, A.N. (1978). 'On the problem of the mechanisms of eye movements'. *Fiziologia cheloveka*, *4*, 6, 963–70.

Molozhavyi, S.S. (Ed.). (1929). *Play and work in preschool age* (Igra i trud v doshkol'nom vozraste). Moscow-Leningrad: Gosudarstvennoe Isdatel'stvo.

Morgun, V.F. (1976). 'Psychological problems of study motivation'. *Voprosy psikhologii*, No. 6, 54–63.

Natadze, R.G. (1961). 'Studies on thought and speech problems by psychologists of the Georgian SSR'. In N. O'Connor (Ed.), *Recent Soviet psychology* (pp. 304–26). New York: Liveright.

Natadze, R.G. (1969). 'Experimental foundations of Uznadze's theory'. In Cole & Maltzmann (1969) (pp. 603–24).

Natadze, R.G. (1972). *Imagination as a factor of behaviour* (Voobrazhenie kak faktor povedenia). Tbilisi: Metsniereba (in Russian).

Nekliudova, A.I. (1924). 'On the problem of the development of perception among preschoolers'. In Basov (1924a) (pp. 54–102).

Nekliudova, A.I. & Vol'berg, V.Ia. (1930). 'Forms of social relationships of preschool children and their development'. In Basov (1930), pp. 112–52.

Nepomniastschaia, V.I., Kanevskaia, M.E., Pakhomova, O.N., Barchalkina, V.V., Rubtsova, S.N. & Muze, E.N. (1980). 'Valuation as the central component of the psychological structure of personality'. *Voprosy psikhologii*, No. 1, 22–30.

Niit, T., Heidmets, M. & Kruusvall, J. (1987). 'Environmental psychology in the Soviet Union'. In D. Stokols (Ed.), *Handbook of environmental psychology*. New York: Wiley.

Niit, T. & Lehtsaar, T. (1983). 'Privacy preferences of family members'. In H. Mikkin (Ed.), *Problems in practical psychology: studies in social psychology* (pp. 124–32). Tallinn: Tallinn Pedagogic Institute Press.

Nikolaeva, E.F. (1979). 'On the role of actions-with-objects of the child in the synthesis of his logical operations'. *Voprosy psikhologii*, No. 5, 113–16.

Nikol'skaia, A.A. (1975). 'General review of translated literature on child and pedagogical psychology in pre-revolutionary Russia'. *Voprosy psikhologii*, No. 1, 151–62.

Nioradze, V.G. (1974). 'The structure of the cursive of handwriting as the foundation for formation of graphic habits of schoolchildren'. *Voprosy psikhologii*, 4, 59–70.

Nisbett, R.E., Krantz, D.H., Jepson, C. & Kunda, Z. (1983). 'The use of statistical heuristics in everyday inductive reasoning'. *Psychological review*, 90, 4, 339–63.

Nosulenko, V.N. (1979). 'Characteristics of reception and processing of acoustic information under conditions of interaction between operators'. In *Problems of engineering psychology*. Moscow: Nauka.

Novikov, V.M. (1927). 'The time budget of the students of Trotsky Pedagogical School in Moscow'. In M.S. Bernshtein & N.A. Rybnikov (Eds), *The time budget of our youth* (Biudzet vremeni nashego molodniaka) (pp. 73–85). Leningrad: Gosizdat.

Novoselova, S.L. (1978). *Development of thinking in early age* (Razvitie myshlenia v rannem vozraste). Moscow: Pedagogika.

Obukhova, L.F. (1972). *Stages in the development of children's thinking* (Etapy razvitia detskogo myshlenia). Moscow: Izdatel'stvo MGU.

O'Connor, N. (Ed.) (1966). *Present-day Russian psychology*. Oxford: Pergamon Press.

Osipova, V.N. (1926). 'The speed of formation of associative reflex at school age'. *Nervnoi sistemy. Novoie v refleksologii fiziologii*, No. 2.

Osipova, V.N. (1927). 'About the lack of extinguishability of associative reflexes in children'. *Voprosy izuchenia i vospitania lichnosti*, No. 1–2.

Osipova, V.N. (1928). 'The School of V.M. Bekhterev and paedology'. *Paedologia*, 1, 10–26.

Osipova, V.N. (1929). 'On the problem of speech command and

integrative versions of the work of central nervous system of children, based on the speech commands'. *Novoe v refleksologii i fiziologii nervnoi sistemy*, 3, 274–84.

Osorina, M.V. (1983). 'Contemporary children's folklore as an object of interdisciplinary research (on the ethnography of childhood)'. *Sovetskaia etnografia*, No. 3, 34–45.

Ostrovskii, A.D. (1929). 'The study of environment and everyday life in national minority regions of Northern Caucasus'. *Paedologia*, No. 1–2, 214–20.

Patiaeva, E.Iu. (1983). 'Situational development and motivation levels'. *Vestnik Moskovskogo Universiteta. ser. 14. psikhologia*, No. 4, 23–32.

Paulhan F. (1928). 'Qu'est-ce que le sens des mots?' *Journal de psychologie*, 25, 289–329.

Pavlov, I.P. (1906). 'Scientific study of so-called psychical processes of higher animals'. *Science*, 24, 613–19.

Pavlov, I.P. (1927), *Conditioned reflexes: an investigation of the physiological activity of the cerebral cortex*. Oxford: Oxford University Press.

Pavlov, I.P. (1928). *Lectures on conditioned reflexes*. Vol. 1: *Twenty-five years of objective study of the higher nervous activity (behaviour) of animals*. New York: International Publishers.

Pavlov, I.P. (1930). 'A brief outline of the higher nervous activity'. In C. Murchison (Ed.), *Psychologies of 1930* (pp. 207–20). Worcester, Ma.: Clark University Press.

Pavlov, I.P. (1932). 'The reply of a physiologist to psychologists'. *Psychological review*, 39, 2, 91–127.

Pavlov, I.P. (1941). *Lectures on conditioned reflexes*. Vol. 2: *Conditioned reflexes and psychiatry*. New York: International Publishers.

Payne, T.R. (1968). *S.L. Rubinshtein and the philosophical foundations of Soviet psychology*. Dordrecht: D. Reidel.

Petrovskii, A.V. (1953a). 'On the results of the session on psychology'. *Voprosy filosofii*, No. 5, 261–4.

Petrovskii, A.V. (1953b). 'About the objective nature of psychological laws'. *Voprosy filosofii*, No. 3, 173–7.

Petrovskii, A.V. (1964). 'The psychological views of P.P. Blonski'. *Sovetskaia pedagogika*, 28, 5, 113–21.

Petrovskii, A.V. (1967). *History of Soviet psychology* (Istoria sovetskoi psikhologii). Moscow: Prosveshchenie.

Petrovskii, A.V. (1980). 'Theory of activity-based mediation and the problem of leadership'. *Voprosy psikhologii*, No. 2, 29–41.

Petrovskii, A.V. (1981a). 'The collective, interaction, and personality development'. In I.I. Il'iasov & V.Ia. Liaudis (Eds), *Khrestomatia po vozrastnoi i pedagogicheskoi psikhologii* (pp. 138–42). Moscow: Izd. MGU.

Petrovskii, A. V. (1981b). 'Personality in psychology from the position of a systems approach'. *Voprosy psikhologii*, No. 1, 57–66.

Petrovskii, A. V. (1984a). 'The theory of activity mediation in interpersonal relations'. In L. H. Strickland (Ed.), *Directions in Soviet social psychology* (pp. 99–112). New York: Springer.

Petrovskii, A. V. (1984b). *Questions of the history and theory of psychology* (Voprosy istorii i teorii psikhologii). Moscow: Pedagogika.

Petrovskii, A. V. (1985). *Studies in psychology: the collective and the individual.* Moscow: Progress (in English).

Petrovskii, A. V. & Petrovskii, V. A. (1982). 'The individual and his need to be a personality'. *Voprosy filosofii*, No. 3, 44–53.

Petrovskii, A. V. & Umanskii, L. I. (Eds) (1978). *Psychology of age collectives* (Psikhologia vozrastnykh kollektivov). Moscow: Pedagogika.

Petrovskii, V. A. (1975). 'On the psychology of activeness of personality'. *Voprosy psikhologii*, No. 3, 26–38.

Piaget, J. (1926). *The language and thought of the child.* London: Routledge & Kegan Paul.

Piager, J. (1932). *Rech i myshlenie rebenka* (Russian edn of Piaget, 1926). Leningrad: Gosizdat.

Piaget, J. (1956). 'Some impression of a visit to Soviet psychologists'. *American Psychologist, 11,* 343–5.

Piaget, J. (1959). *The language and thought of the child.* London: Routledge & Kegan Paul.

Piaget, J. (1969). *Selected psychological works* (Izbrannyie psikhologicheskie trudy). Moscow: Prosveshchenie.

Piaget, J. (1970). 'Piaget's theory'. In P. H. Mussen (Ed.), *Carmichael's manual of child psychology.* 3rd edn, Vol. 1 (pp. 703–22). New York: Wilcy.

Piaget, J. (1977). *The development of thought.* New York: Viking.

Piaget, J. & Inhelder, B. (1963). *The genesis of elementary logical structures* (Genezis elementarnykh logicheskikh struktur). Moscow: Inostrannaia Literatura.

Piskun, V. M. & Tkachenko, A. N. (1981). 'L. S. Vygotsky and A. A. Potebnya'. In V. V. Davydov (Ed.), *The Scientific heritage of L.S. Vygotsky and contemporary psychology* (Nauchnoie tvorchestvo L. S. Vygotskogo i sovremennaia psikhologia) (pp. 125–8). Moscow: IOPP.

Poddiakov, N. N. (1977). *The thinking of the preschooler* (Myshlenie doshkol'nika). Moscow: Pedagogika.

Poddiakov, N. N. (1981). 'On the problem of the intellectual development of the child'. In V. V. Davydov (Ed.), *The scientific heritage of L. S.*

Vygotsky and contemporary psychology (Nauchnoie tvorchestvo L.S. Vygotskogo i sovremennaia psikhologia, pp. 128–30). Moscow: I.O.P.P.

Podgoretskaia, N.A. (1974). 'The study of logical thinking of adults'. *Sovetskaia pedagogika, 37*, 3, 31–40.

Podgoretskaia, N.A. (1977). 'Study of spontaenously formed logical thinking'. *Vestnik Moskovskogo Universiteta, seria psikhologia*, No. 2, 44–52.

Pokrovskaia, E.I. (1928). 'The environment of the peasant child'. In Zeiliger (1928) (pp. 12–25). Moscow-Leningrad: Gosizdat.

Polikanina, R.I. (1966). *The development of higher nervous activity in premature infants in early life* (Razvitie vyshhei nervnoi deyatel'nosti u nedonoshennyh detei v rannem vozraste). Leningrad: Meditsina.

Polonskii, I.S. (1973). 'Methods of the study of spontaneous-group interaction of adolescents and youth'. In: *Measurements in the studies of educational problems* (Izmerenia v issledovanii problem vospitania). Tartu: Tartu University Press.

Popov, A.A. (1984). *The Nganassans: social organizations and beliefs* (Nganassany: sotsial'noe ustroistvo i verovania). Leningrad: Nauka.

Porshnev, B.F. (1970). *Social psychology and history.* Moscow: Progress (in English)

Porshnev, B.F. (1974). *On the beginning of human history (problems of paleopsychology)* (O nachale chelovecheskoi istorii (problemy paleopsikhologii). Moscow: Mysl'.

Porshnev, B.F. (1979). *Social psychology and history* (Sotsial'naia psikhologia i istoria). 2nd edn. Moscow: Nauka.

Potebnya, A.A. (1926). *Thought and language* (Mysl' i iazyk). 5th edn. Kharkov: Gosudarstvennoe Izdatel'stvo Ukrainy.

Prangishvili, A.S. (1967). *Studies in the psychology of set* (Issledovania po psikhologii ustanovki). Tbilisi: Metsniereba (in Russian).

Prangishvili, A.S. (Ed.) (1973). *Psychological investigations: a commemorative volume dedicated to the 85th anniversary of the birth of D. Uznadze.* Tbilisi: Metsniereba.

Prangishvili, A.S. (1975). *Psychological etudes* (Psikhologicheskie ocherki). Tbilisi: Metsniereba.

Prangishvili, A.S., Sherozia, A.E. & Bassin, F.V. (Eds) (1978). *The unconscious.* Vol. 3: *Cognition, communication, personality.* Tbilisi: Metsniereba.

Prangishvili, A.S., Sherozia, A.E. & Bassin, F.V. (Eds) (1985). *The unconscious.* Vol. 4: *Results of the discussion.* Tbilisi: Metsniereba.

Protopopov, V.P. (1909). *On the associative motor reaction to acoustic stimulus.* (O sochetatel'noi dvigatel'noi reaktsii na zvukovyie razdrazhenia). St Petersburg: Tovarishchestvo Khudozestvennoi Pechati.

Protopopov, V.P. (1928). *V.M. Bekhterev as a reflexologist* (V.M. Bekhterev kak refleksolog). Harkov.

Protopopov, V.P. (1946). *Patophysiological foundations of rational therapy of schizophrenia* (Patofiziologicheskie osnovy ratsional'noi terapii shizofrenii). Kiev: Gosmedizdat.

Protopopov, V.P. (1948). *Ivan Petrovich Pavlov: his teaching about higher nervous activity.* (Ivan Petrovich Pavlov: ego uchenie o vyshei nervnoi deiatel'nosti). Kiev: Gosmedizdat.

Protopopov, V.P. (1950). *The study of higher nervous activity in the natural experiment* (Issledovanie vyshei nervnoi deiatel'nosti v estestvennom eksperimente). Kiev: Gosmedizdat.

Radzikhovsky, L.A. (1979). 'Analysis of L.S. Vygotsky's works in Soviet psychology'. *Voprosi psikhologii, 6,* 58–67.

Radzikhovsky, L.A. (1982). 'Commentaries to L. Vygotsky's *Myshlenie i rech*'. In L.S. Vygotsky, *Sobranie sochinenii.* Vol. 2: *Problemy obshchei psikhologii.* Moscow: Pedagogika.

Radzikhovsky, L.A. & Homskaya, E.D. (1981). 'A.R. Luria and L.S. Vygotsky (early years of collaboration)'. *Vestnik Moskovskogo Universiteta. Seria 14. Psikhologia 2,* 66–76.

Rahimov, R.R. (1983). 'Children and adolescents in Afgan society'. In Kon (1983a) (pp. 89–117).

Rahmani, L. (1966). 'Studies on the mental development of the child'. In O'Connor (1966) (pp. 152–77).

Rahmani, L. (1973). *Soviet psychology: philosophical, theoretical, and experimental issues.* New York: International Universities Press.

Raikov, B.E. (1961). *Karl Baer: his life and works* (Karl Ber: ego zizn' i trudy). Moscow-Leningrad: Izdatel'stvo Akademii Nauk.

Raudsepp, M. (1986). 'Social-psychological effectiveness of living space'. In J. Orn & T. Niit (Eds), *People, social interaction and the living environment* (pp. 115–53). Tallinn: Tallinn Pedagogic Institute (in Russian).

Razmyslov, P.I. (1934). 'On the "cultural-historical theory of psychology" of Vygotsky and Luria'. *Kniga i proletar'skaia revolutsia,* No. 4, 78–86.

Razran, G. (1935). 'Psychology in the USSR'. *Journal of philosophy, 32,* 19–24.

Razran, G. (1942). 'Current psychological theory in the USSR'. *Psychological bulletin, 39,* 445–6.

Razran, G. (1957). 'Soviet psychology since 1950'. *Science, 126,* 1100–7.

Razran, G. (1958). 'Soviet psychology and physiology'. *Science, 128,* 1187–94.

Razran, G. (1965). 'Russian physiologists' psychology and American experimental psychology'. *Psychological bulletin, 63,* 42–64.

Rives, S. M. (1929). 'Children and religion'. *Paedologia,* No. 4, 577–93.

Rives, S. M. (1930). *Religiosity and antireligiosity in children's environment* (Religioznost' i antireligioznost' v detskoi srede). Moscow: Rabotnik Prosveshchenia.

Rogoff, B. & Wertsch, J. (Eds.) (1984). 'Children's learning in the "Zone of Proximal Development"'. *New Directions for Child Development,* No. 23.

Roll-Hansen, N. (1985). 'A new perspective on Lysenko?', *Annals of science, 42,* 261–78.

Rosch, E. (1978). 'Principles of categorization'. In E. Rosch & B. Lloyd (Eds), *Cognition and categorization* (pp. 27–48). Hillsdale, NJ: Erlbaum.

Rozengart-Pupko, G. L. (1948). *The formation of speech in early age children* (Formirovanie rechi u detei rannego vozrasta). Moscow: Izdatel'stvo APN RSFSR.

Rozov, A. I. (1953). 'Reflections by an ordinary psychologist'. *Voprosy filosofii,* No. 3, 177–79.

Rubinshtein, S. L. (1934). 'Problems of psychology in the works of K. Marx'. *Sovetskaia psikhotekhnika, 7,* 3–20.

Rubinshtein, S. L. (1935). *Foundations of psychology* (Osnovy psikhologii). Moscow: Uchpedgiz.

Rubinshtein, S. L. (1940). *Foundations of general psychology* (Osnovy obschei psikhologii). Moscow: Academy of Sciences Publishing House.

Rubinshtein, S. L. (1943). 'Soviet psychology in the conditions of the Great Patriotic War'. *Pod znamenem Marksizma,* No. 9/10, 45–61.

Rubinshtein, S. L. (1946). *Foundations of general psychology.* 2nd edn. Moscow: Uchpedgiz.

Rubinshtein, S. L. (1957). *Being and consciousness* (Bytie i soznanie). Moscow: Izdatel'stvo Akademii Nauk.

Rubinštejn, S. L. (1987). 'Problems of psychology in the works of Karl Marx'. *Studies in Soviet Thought, 33,* 111–30.

Rubtsov, V. V. (1980). 'The role of cooperation in the development of children's intellect'. *Voprosy psikhologii,* No. 4, 79–89.

Ruzskaya, A. G. (1974). 'The influence of the emotional contact with the adult on the emergence of first words among children at the end of the first and the beginning of the second year of life'. In M. I. Lisina (Ed.), *Interaction and its influence on the psychological development of the preschooler* (Obshchenie i ego vliyanie na razvitie psihiki doshkol'nika) (pp. 95–113). Moscow: NII obshchei pedagogiki APN SSSR.

Rybnikov, N. A. (1926). *Child's language* (Iazyk rebenka). Moscow-

Leningrad: Gosizdat.

Rybnikov, N.A. (Ed.) (1927). *Child's speech* (Detskaia rech). Moscow: Institute of Experimental Psychology.

Rybnikov, N. (Ed.) (1928). *The fairy tale and the child* (Skazka i rebenok: pedologicheskii sbornik). Moscow-Leningrad: Gosizdat.

Rybnikov, N.A. (1929). 'The urban and rural child: the peasant child'. *Paedologia,* No. 1–2, 117–32.

Ryle, G. (1949). *The concept of mind.* London: Hutchinson.

Safin, V.F. (1982). 'The dynamics of evaluation models in the adolescents and youth'. *Voprosy psikhologii,* No. 1, 69–75.

Sakharov, I..S. (1930). 'On the methods of the study of concepts'. *Psikhologia, 3,* 1, 3–33.

Salmina, N.G. & Kolmogorova, L.S. (1980). 'The mastery of elementary mathematical concepts in different conditions of materialized objects and action tools'. *Voprosy psikhologii,* No. 1, 47–56.

Sapir, I.D. (1926). 'Freudianism and Marxism'. *Pod znamenem Marksizma,* No. 11, 59–87.

Scheerer, E. (1980). 'Gestalt psychology in the Soviet Union'. *Psychological research, 41,* 113–32.

Schiff, Z.I. (1935). *Development of scientific concepts in schoolchild* (Razvitie nauchnykh poniatii u shkol'nika). Moscow-Leningrad: Gosudarstvennoe Uchebno-Pedagogicheskoe Izdatel'stvo.

Schmal'gauzen, I.I. (1938). *The organism as a whole in individual and historical development* (Organizm kak tseloe v individual'nom i istoricheskom razvitii). Moscow-Leningrad: Izdatel'stvo Nauk SSSR.

Schniermann, A.L. (1928). 'Present-day tendencies in Russian psychology'. *Journal of general psychology, 1,* 397–404.

Schniermann, A.L. (1930a). 'Bekhterev's reflexological school'. In C. Murchison (Ed.), *Psychologies of 1930* (pp. 221–42). Worcester, Ma.: Clark University Press.

Schniermann, A.L. (1930b). 'On the object and method of reflexology as a science of coordinative activity'. *Voprosy izuchenia i vospitania lichnosti, 9,* 1–2, 8–11.

Schubert, A.M. (1930). 'Experience of the paedological-pedagogical expeditions on the study of peoples of far-off border regions'. *Paedologia,* No. 2, 167–71.

Scribner, S. & Cole, M. (1981). *The psychology of literacy.* Cambridge, Ma.: Harvard University Press.

Sechenov, I.M. (1866). *Refleksy golovnago mozga.* St Petersburg: Tipografia A. Golovachova.

Sechenov, I.M. (1907). *Autobiograficheskia zapiski Ivana Mikhailovicha Sechenova.* Moscow: Izdanie 'Nauchnago slova'.

Semenov, M. (1927). 'The time budget of the Moscow rabfak student'. In M.S. Bernshtein & N.A. Rybnikov (Eds), *The time budget of our youth* (Biudzet vremeni nashego molodniaka) (pp. 57–72). Leningrad: Gosizdat.

Sergienko, Y.A. (1981). 'Infant oculomotor activity under complex movement stimulation'. *Psikhologicheskii zhurnal*, 2, 6, 57–64.

Severtsov, A.N. (1921). *Etiudy po teorii evoliutsii: individual'noie razvitie i evoliutsia*. 2nd edn. Berlin: Gosudarstvennoie Izdatel'stvo RSFSR.

Severtsov, A.N. (1922). *Evoliutsia i psikhika*. Moscow: Izdatel'stvo Sabashnikovykh.

Severtsov, A.N. (1934). *Glavnye napravleniia evoliutsionnogo protsessa: morfobiologicheskaia teoria evolitsii*. Moscow-Leningrad: Gosudarstvennoie Izdatel'stvo.

Sewertzoff, A.N. (1929). 'Direction of evolution'. *Acta zoologica*, 10, 59–141.

Sexton, V.S. & Misiak, H. (Eds) (1976). *Psychology around the world.* Monterey, Ca.: Brooks/Cole.

Shakirova, G.M. (1981). 'On the goal-directed formation of moral beliefs in schoolchildren'. *Voprosy psikhologii*, No. 6, 47–58.

Shapiro, S.A. (1928). 'Some characteristics of the work activity of the peasant child'. In Zeiliger (1928) (pp. 25–43).

Shapiro, S.A. & Gerke, E.D. (1930). 'The process of adaptation to the environmental conditions in the behaviour of the child'. In Basov (1930) pp. 73–112.

Shchelovanov, N.M. (1938). 'On the rearing in infant homes'. *Voprosy materinstva i mladenchestva*, No. 13.

Shchelovanov, N.M. (1948). *Development and education of children of early age in children's institutions* (Razvitie i vospitanie detei rannego vozrasta v detskih utchrezdeniyah). Moscow: Izd. APN RSFSR.

Shchelovanov, N.M. (1969). 'Methods in developmental reflexology'. *Soviet psychology*, 8, 1, 26–49. (Russian, original 1925).

Shchelovanov, N.M. & Aksarina, N.M. (Eds) (1939). *Child-rearing in nurseries* (Vospitanie detei v yasl'yah). Moscow: Medgiz.

Shepovalova, A. (1930). 'The social everyday environment of Tunguz children in Northern Baikal'. *Paedologia*, No. 2, 172–186.

Sherozia, A.E. (1979). *The psyche, consciousness, unconscious.* Tbilisi: Metsniereba.

Shukurov, E. (1972). 'The concept of complementarity and the problem of the genesis of social transaction'. *Voprosy filosofii*, No. 4, 35–9.

Shukurov, E. (1976). 'Social transaction and concept'. (Obshchenie i ponyatie). In A.A. Brudnyi & E. Shukurov (Eds), *Semantics and social psychology* (Semantika i sotsial'naya psikhologia). Frunze: Ilim.

Shukurov, E. & Karakeyev, T.D. (1976). 'Systems analysis in the study of semantic elements of civiliations'. In A.A. Brudnyi & E. Shukurov (Eds), *Semantics and social psychology* (Semantika i sotsial'naya psikhologia). Frunze: Ilim.

Siavavko, E.G. (1974). *Ukrainian ethnopedagogics in its historical development*. Kiev: Naukova Dumka (in Ukrainian).

Simonov, P.V. (1953). 'On the term "higher nervous activity of the man"'. *Voprosy filosofii*, No. 4, 213–15.

Sirbiladze, P.G. (1981). 'On the study of cognitive interests of schoolchildren'. In S.N. Chkhartishvili, V.L. Kakabadze & N. Sarjveladze (Eds), *The problems of formation of sociogenic needs* (Problemy formirovania sotsiogennykh potrebnostei) (pp. 206–9). Tbilisi: Uznadze Institute of Psychology.

Slobin, D.I. (1966). 'Soviet psycholinguistics'. In O'Connor (1966) (pp. 109–51).

Slobodchikov, V.I. (1982). 'Problems of theory and diagnostics of psychological development'. *Voprosy psikhologii*, No. 1, 19–28.

Smirnov, A.A. (Ed). (1967). *Age and individual differences in memory* (Vozrastnye i individuaal'nye razlichia v pamiati). Moscow: Prosveshchenie.

Smirnov, A.A. (1975). *Development and the contemporary state of psychological sciences in the USSR* (Razvitie i sovremennoe sostoianie psikhologicheskoi nauki v SSSR). Moscow: Pedagogika.

Smirnov, A.A. (1978). 'The general theory of psychological activity and N.A. Bernstein's conception'. *Vestnik Moskovskogo Universiteta. ser. 14. psikhologia*, No. 2, 14–25.

Smirnova, Y.O. (1974). 'The relationship of child to adult and its influence on memory encoding'. In M.I. Lisina (Ed.), *Interaction and its influence on the psychological development of the preschooler* (Obshchenie i ego vliyanie na razvitie psikhiki doshkol'nika) (pp. 181–98). Moscow: NII obshchei pedagogiki APN SSSR.

Smokler, H. (1983). 'Institutional rationality: the complex norms of science'. *Synthese*, 57, 129–38.

Snezhkova, I.A. (1982). 'On the problem of the study of ethnic self-consciousness among children and adolescents'. *Sovetskaia etnografia*, No. 1, 80–8.

Sokhina, V.P. (1968). 'Psychological foundations of the formation of primary mathematical concepts'. In Gal'perin & Talyzina (1968) (pp. 117–34).

Sokovnin, V.M. (1968a). '"Obshchenie" and its means'. In: *Consciousness and transaction* (Soznanie i obshchenie). Frunze: Ilim.

Sokovnin, V.M. (1968b). 'Human transaction and ideology'. *Ideology and social psychology* (Ideologia i obshchestvennaia psikhologia). Frunze: Ilim.

Sokovnin, V. M. (1973). *On the nature of human interaction* (O prirode chelovecheskovo obshchenia). Frunze: Mektep.
Sokovnin, V.M. (1974). *On the nature of human interaction.* (O prirode chelovecheskovo obshchenia). 2nd edn. Frunze: Mektep.
Sokovnin, V.M. (1975). 'Socialization, social transaction, pedagogics'. In V. M. Sokovnin (Ed.) *Problems of pedagogics and psychology of social transaction* (Voprosy pedagogiki i psikhologii obshchenia). Frunze: Mektep.
Solozhenkin, V. V., Shilin, V. A., Sirota, N. A. and Ivanenko, V. V. (1981). 'Factors of the social regulation of behaviour and parameters of environment mediated by territorial behaviour of adolescents'. In T. Niit, M. Heidmets & J. Kruusvall (Eds), *Man and environment: psychological aspects.* Tallinn: Estonian Branch of the Soviet Psychological Association.
Strakach, Iu. B. (1956). *Popular traditions and the preparation of industrial-agricultural cadres* (Narodnyie traditsii i podgotovka promyshlenno-sel skohoziaistvennykh kadrov). Novosibirski: Nauca.
Subbotskii, E. V. (1976). *Psychology of partnership relations in preschoolers* (Psikhologia otnoshenii partnerstva u doshkol'nikov). Moscow: Izd. MGU.
Subbotskii, E. V. (1977). 'The study of sense formations in children'. *Vestnik Moskovskogo Universiteta. ser. 14. psikhologia,* No. 1, 62–72.
Subbotskii, E. V. (1978a). 'On the subjectivity of "childish" reasoning'. *Voprosy psikhologii,* No. 2, 81–90.
Subbotskii, E. V. (1978b). 'The development of moral behaviour in preschoolers'. *Vestnik Moskovskogo Universiteta. ser. 14. psikhologia,* No. 3, 13–25.
Subbotskii, E. V. (1979). 'The formation of moral action in the child'. *Voprosy psikhologii,* No. 3, 47–55.
Subbotskii, E. V. (1981a). 'The development of personality-type behaviour of preschoolers and their interaction style'. *Voprosy psikhologii,* No. 2, 68–78.
Subbotskii, E. V. (1981b). 'Development of moral behaviour in preschoolers in a psychological-pedagogical experiment'. *Vestnik Moskovskogo Universiteta. ser. 14. psikhologia,* No. 2, 56–65. (English trans.: *Soviet psychology,* 1981, *20,* 1, 62–80).
Subbotskii, E. V. (1983). 'The moral development of the preschool child'. *Voprosy psikhologii,* No. 4, 29–38. (English trans.: *Soviet psychology,* 1984, *22,* 3, 3–19).
Subbotskii, E. V. (1984). 'Perception by pre-school children of unusual phenomena'. *Vestnik MGU. seria 14. psikhologia,* No. 1, 17–29.
Sydygbekova, D. T. (1983). 'Understanding of text as intellectual operation'. In A. A. Brudnyi (Ed.), *Problems of the psychology of*

intellect. Frunze: Kirghizskii gosudarstvennyi universitet.

Talacka, V. (1980). 'Influence of group size on the degree of individual learning'. *Lietuvos TSR aukštuju mokyklu mokslo darbai. Psichologija, 1*, 37–42.

Talyzina, N.F. (1969). *Theoretic problems of programmed instruction* (Teoreticheskie problemy programmirovannogo obuchenia). Moscow: Izd. MGU.

Tamm, T. & Tulviste, P. (1980). 'Theoretic syllogistic reasoning—regressing when not used?' *Acta et commentationes universitatis Tartuensis*, 522 (pp. 50–9). Tartu: Tartu University Press.

Tihh, N.A. (1966). *Early ontogenesis of primate behaviour* (Rannii ontogenez povediniya primatov). Leningrad: Izdatel'stvo LGU.

Tihh, N.A. (1970). *Prehistory of society* (Predistoria obshchestva). Leningrad: Izdatel'stvo LGU.

Toulmin, S. (1978). 'Mozart in psychology'. *New York Review of Books, 25*, 14, 51–7.

Troshikhina, J.G. (1973). *The evolution of the memory functions* (Evoliutsia mnemicheskoi funktsii). Leningrad: Nauka.

Troshikhina, J.G. & Gizatullina, D.H. (1979). 'Development of short-term memory of children at early age'. *Voprosi psikhologii*, No. 4, 127–30.

Tudge, J. (1983). 'Moral development in the Soviet Union: a conceptual framework'. *Soviet psychology, 22*, 1, 3–12.

Tulviste, P. (1977). 'The type of text and the type of thinking'. *Acta et commentationes universitatis Tartuensis*, 411 (pp. 90–102). Tartu: Tartu University Press.

Tulviste, P. (1978). 'On the origins of theoretic syllogistic reasoning in culture and in the child'. *Acta et commentationes universitatis Tartuensis*, 474 (pp. 3–22). Tartu: Tartu University Press.

Tulviste, P. (1981a). 'Is there a form of verbal thought specific to childhood?' *Voprosy psikhologii*, No. 5, 34–42. (English trans.: *Soviet psychology*, 1982, *21*, 1, 3–17).

Tulviste, P. (1981b). 'On the problem of typology of verbal thinking'. In V.V. Davydov (Ed.), *The scientific heritage of L.S. Vygotsky and contemporary psychology* (Nauchnoie tvorchestvo L.S. Vygotskogo i sovremennaia psikhologia) (pp. 154–7). Moscow: Institute of Psychology of APN.

Tulviste, P. (1981c). 'On the historical-psychological approach to human needs'. In Sh. N. Chkhartishvili, V.L. Kakabadze & N.I. Sardjveladze (Eds), *Problems of formation of sociogenic needs* (pp. 82–6). Tbilisi: Uznadze Institute of Psychology.

Tulviste, P. (1984a). *The change of thinking in history* (Mõtlemise muutumisest ajaloos). Tallinn: Valgus (in Estonian).

Tulviste, P. (1984b). 'Short essay on the history of Estonian psychology'. *Acta et commentationes universitatis Tartuensis*, 691 (pp. 3–16). Tartu: Tartu University Press.

Tulviste, P. & Lapp, A. (1978). 'Could Margaret Mead's methods reveal animism in Manus children? A partial replication study in a European culture'. *Acta et commentationes universitatis Tartuensis*, 474 (pp. 23–30). Tartu: Tartu University Press.

Tulviste, T. & Tulviste, P. (1985). 'On the relationship between the character of units and operations in verbal thinking: experimental proof of Vygotsky's hypothesis'. In R. M. Frumkina (Ed.), *Linguistic and psycholinguistic structures of speech* (Lingvisticheskie i psikholingvisticheskie struktury rechi) (pp. 109–15). Moscow: Institut Iazykoznania AN SSSR.

Tutundjian, H. (1976). 'Armenia'. In Sexton & Misiak (1976) (pp. 29–33).

Ul'man, E. E. (1928). 'The constructive activity of the peasant child'. In Zeiliger (1928) (pp. 68–82). Moscow-Leningrad: Gosizdat.

Umanskii, L. I. (Ed.) (1975). *Social-psychological aspects of the social activity of personality and collectives of schoolchildren and students* (Sotsial'no-psikhologicheskie aspekty obshchestvennoi aktivnosti lichnosti i kollektiva shkol'nikov i studentov). Iaroslavl: Izdatel'stvo Iaroslavlskogo GU.

Usnadze, D. (1924). 'Ein experimenteller Beitrag zum Problem der psychologischen Grundlagen der Namengebung'. *Psychologische Forschung, 5*, 24–43.

Usnadze, D. (1927a). 'Zum Problem der Relationserfassung beim Tier'. *Archiv für die Gesamte Psychologie, 60*, 361–90.

Usnadze, D. (1927b). 'Zum Problem der Bedeutungserfassung'. *Archiv für die Gesamte Psychologie, 58*, 163–86.

Usnadze, D. (1929a). 'Gruppenbildungsversuche bei vorschulpflichtigen Kindern'. *Archiv für die Gesamte Psychologie, 73*, 217–48.

Usnadze, D. (1929b). 'Die Begriffsbildung im vorschulpflichtigen Alter'. *Zeitschrift für angewandte Psychologie.*

Usnadze, D. (1931). 'Über die Gewichtstauschung und ihre Analoga'. *Psychologie Forschung, 14*, 366–79.

Usnadze, D. (1939). 'Unterschungen zur Psychologie der Einstellung'. *Acta psychologica, 4.*

Usova, K. I. (1930). 'The Tunguz child at school'. *Paedologia*, No. 2, 187–92.

Uznadze, D. N. (1930). 'On the questions of the principal law of set change'. *Psikhologia, 3*, 3, 316–335 (in Russian).

Uznadze, D. N. (1966a). *The psychology of set*. New York: Consultants Bureau. (Russian trans. 1961; Georgian original, 1949).

Uznadze, D. N. (1966b). *Psychological investigations* (Psikhologicheskie issledovania). Moscow: Nauka.

Uznadze, D. N. (1980). 'The formation of concepts in preschool age'. In I. I. Il'iasov & V. Ia. Liaudis (Eds), *Reader on developmental and pedagogical psychology* (Khrestomatia po vozrastnoi i pedagogicheskoi psikhologii). Vol. 1. (pp. 121–30). Moscow: Izdatel'stovo MGU.

Vagner, V. A. (1890). 'Observations on *Araneina*'. *Trudy imperatorskogo Sankt-Peterburgskogo Obshchestva Estestvoispytatelei*, 21.

Vagner, V. A. (1896). *Problems of zoopsychology* (Voprosy zoopsikhologii). St Petersburg: Izdatel'stvo Panteleeva.

Vagner, V. A. (1901). 'The biological method in zoopsychology' (Biologicheskii metod v zoopsikhologii). *Trudy imperatoskogo Sankt-Peterburgskogo Obshchestva Estestvoispytatelei*, 33, 2, 1–96.

Vagner, V. A. (1907). 'Psycho-biologische Unterschungen an Hummeln mit Bezugnahme auf die Frage der Geselligkeit im Tierreiche'. *Zoologica: Originale-Abhandlungen aus dem Gesammtgebiete der Zoologie*, 46.

Vagner, V. A. (1910). *The biological foundations of comparative psychology* (Biologicheskie osnovania sravnitel'noi psikhologii). Vol. 1. Moscow: M. O. Wolf.

Vagner, V. A. (1913). *The biological foundations of comparative psychology* (Biologicheskie osnovania sravnitel'noi psikhologii). Vol. 2 Moscow: M. O. Wolf.

Vagner, V. A. (1924–29). *Etudes in comparative psychology* (Etiudy po sravnitel'noi psikhologii). Leningrad: Nachatki Znanii.

Vagner, V. A. (1925). *From reflexes to instincts* (Ot refleksov—do instinktov). *Etiudy po sravnitel'noi psikhologii*. Vol. 3. Leningrad: Nachatki Znanii.

Vagner, V. A. (1929). *Psychological types and collective psychology* (Psikhologicheskie tipy i kollektivnaia psikhologia). Leningrad: Nachatki Znanii.

Valsiner, J. (1981). 'The father's role in the social network of a Soviet child'. In M. Lamb (Ed.), *The role of the father in child development* (pp. 187–201). New York: Wiley.

Valsiner, J. (1984a). 'Conceptualizing intelligence: from an internal static attribution to the study of process structure of organism-environment relationships'. *International journal of psychology*, 19, 363–89.

Valsiner, J. (1984b). 'Two alternative epistemological frameworks in psychology: the typological and variational modes of thinking'. *Journal of mind and behavior*, 5, 4, 449–70.

Valsiner, J. (1984c). 'The childhood of the Soviet citizen: socialization for loyalty'. Ottawa: Carlton University Press.

Valsiner, J. & Van der Veer, R. (1987 in press). 'A history of the sociogenetic perspective: common roots of Lev Vygotsky and George Herbert Mead'. *Journal for the Theory of Social Behaviour.*

Van IJzendoorn, M. H. & van der Veer, R. (1984). *Main currents of critical psychology*. New York: Irvington.

Van der Veer, R. (1983). 'Early periods in the work of L. S. Vygotsky: The influence of Spinoza'. Paper presented at the conference 'Teaching on a scientific basis', Aarhus, Denmark, January.

Van der Veer, R. (1984). *Cultuur en cognitie*. Groningen: Wolters-Noordhoff. (in Dutch).

Van der Veer, R. (1986). 'Vygotsky's developmental psychology'. *Psychological reports*, 59. 527–36.

Van der Veer, R. & Valsiner, J. (1987 in press). 'Connections between Lev Vygotsky and Pierre Janet'. *Developmental Review.*

van Rappard, J. F. H. & van der Sijde, P. C. (1982). 'Aktiviteit en mensbeeld'. *Gedrag – Tijdschrift voor psychologie*, 10, 5, 337–53 (in Dutch).

Varjun, J. (1981). 'On some methodological problems of the study of individual differences in cognitive needs of infants'. In Sh. N. Chkhartishvili, W. L. Kakabadze & N. I. Sarjveladze (Eds), *The problems of formation of sociogenic needs* (Problemy formirovania sochiogennyh potrebnostei) (pp. 236–41). Tbilisi: Usnadze Institute of Psychology.

Venger, L. A. (1969). *Perception and instruction* (Vospriatie i obuchenie). Moscow: Prosveshchenie. (partial English trans.: *Soviet psychology*, 1971, 10, 5–108).

Venger, L. A. (1974). 'On the qualitative approach to the diagnostics of mental development'. *Voprosy psikhologii*, No. 1, 116–22.

Venger, L. A. (1982). 'Studies on the development of abilities in children'. In W. W. Hartup (Ed.), *Review of child development research*. Vol. 6 (pp. 501–25). Chicago: University of Chicago Press.

Venger, L. A. (1983). 'The mastery of mediated solution of cognitive problems and the development of cognitive abilities of the child'. *Voprosy psikhologii*, No. 2, 43–50.

Venger, L. A. & Kholmovskaia, V. V. (Eds.) (1978). *Diagnostics of mental development in preschool children* (Diagnostika umstvennogo razvitia doshkol'nikov). Moscow: Pedagogika.

Vilenkina, R. G. (1930). 'On the characteristics of feelings of working-class adolescents'. *Paedologia*, No. 1, 81–97.

Viljunas, V. K. (1976). *Psychology of emotional phenomena* (Psikhologia

emotsional'nykh iavlenii). Moscow: Izdatel'stvo MGU.
Vinogradov, G.S. (1925). *Children's satiric lyrics* (Detskaia satiricheskaia lirika). Irkutsk: Izdanie Vostochno-Sibirskogo otdela Russkogo Geograficheskogo Obstcestva.
Vinogradov, G.S. (1930). *Russian children's folklore* (Russkii detskii fol'klor). Irkutsk: Izdanie Irkutskoi sektsii nauchnykh rabotnikov.
Volkov, N.G. (1966). *Ethnopedagogics of the Chuvash* (Etnopedagogika Chuvasskogo naroda). Cheboksary: Chuvashknigoizdat.
Volobuev, P. (1929). 'Working capability of children's collectives at preschool age'. *Paedologia*, No. 4, 490–501.
Vol'tsis, K.Ia. (1974). 'Characteristics of goal-setting in play among 4-year-olds'. *Novyie issledovania v psikhologii*, No. 1 (Whole No.9), 27–8.
Vygotsky, L.S. (1925). 'The principles of social education of deaf and dumb children in Russia'. *Proceedings of the International Conference on the Education of the Deaf* (pp. 227–37). London.
Vygotski, L.S. (1929a). 'The problem of the cultural development of the child'. *Journal of genetic psychology, 36*, 415–34.
Vygotsky, L.S. (1929b). 'On the problem of the plan of scientific-investigative work on paedology of national minorities'. *Paedologia*, No. 3, 367–77.
Vygotsky, L.S. (1934). 'Thought in schizophrenia'. *Archives of neurology and psychiatry, 31*, 1063–77.
Vygotsky, L.S. (1939). 'Thought and speech'. *Psychiatry, 2*, 29–54.
Vygotsky, L.S. (1956). *Thinking and speech. Selected psychological studies* (Myshlenie i rech. Izbrannie psihologicheskie issledovania). Moscow: Izdatel'stvo APN RSFSR.
Vygotsky, L.S. (1960). *Development of higher psychical functions* (Razvitie vyshhikh psikhicheskih funktsii). Moscow: APN.
Vygotsky, L.S. (1961). 'Thought and speech'. In S. Saporta (Ed.), *Psycholinguistics* (pp. 509–37). New York: Holt, Rinehart & Winston.
Vygotsky, L.S. (1962). *Thought and language.* Cambridge, Ma.: MIT Press.
Vygotsky, L.S. (1963). 'The problem of learning and mental development at school age'. In B. & J. Simon (Eds), *Educational psychology in the USSR* (pp. 21–34). London: Routledge & Kegan Paul.
Vygotsky, L.S. (1965). 'Psychology and localization of functions'. *Neuropsychologia, 3*, 381–6.
Vygotsky, L.S. (1966). 'Play and its role in the psychological development of the child'. *Voprosy psikhologii, 12*, 6, 62–76.
Vygotsky, L.S. (1967). 'Play and its role in the mental development of the child'. *Soviet psychology and psychiatry, 5*, 3, 6–18.
Vygotsky, L.S. (1970). 'Spinoza and his teaching of emotions in the light of contemporary psychoneurology'. *Voprosy filosfii*, No. 6, 119–30.

Vygotsky, L.S. (1971). *The psychology of art*. Cambridge, Ma.: MIT Press.
Vygotsky, L.S. (1977). 'Development of higher psychological functions'. *Soviet psychology,* 15, 3, 60–73.
Vygotsky, L.S. (1978). *Mind in society*. Cambridge, Ma.: Harvard University Press.
Vygotsky, L.S. (1979a). 'Consciousness as a problem in the psychology of behaviour'. *Soviet psychology, 17*, 4, 3–35.
Vygotsky, L.S. (1979b). 'On the development of higher forms of attention in childhood'. *Soviet psychology, 18*, 1, 67–115.
Vygotsky, L.S. (1981a). 'The genesis of higher mental functions'. In J. Wertsch (Ed.), *The concept of activity in Soviet psychology* (pp. 144–88). Armonk, NY: M.E. Sharpe.
Vygotsky, L.S. (1981b). 'The development of higher forms of attention in childhood'. In J. Wertsch (Ed.), *The concept of activity in Soviet psychology* (pp. 189–240). Armonk, NY: M.E. Sharpe.
Vygotsky, L.S. (1981c). 'The instrumental method in psychology'. In J. Wertsch (Ed.), *The concept of activity in Soviet psychology* (pp. 134–43). Armonk, NY: M.E. Sharpe.
Vygotsky, L.S. (1982a). *Historical sense of the psychological crisis* (Istoricheskii smysl psikhologiceskogo krizisa). In L.S. Vygotsky, *Collected works* (Sobranie sochinenii). Vol. 1 (pp. 291–436). Moscow: Pedagogika.
Vygotsky, L.S. (1982b). *Thinking and speech* (Myshlenie i rech). In L.S. Vygotsky, *Collected works* (Sobranie sochinenii). Vol. 2 (pp. 5–361). Moscow: Pedagogika.
Vygotsky, L.S. (1986a). *Thought and language*. 2nd revised edn. Cambridge, Ma.: MIT Press.
Vygotsky, L.S. ['The concrete psychology of man'] (unpublished manuscript). *Vestnik Moskovskogo Universiteta. seria 14. Psikhologia,* No. 1, 52–65.
Vygotsky, L.S. & Luria, A.R. (1930a). 'The function and fate of egocentric speech'. *Proceedings and papers of the 9th International Congress of Psychology* (pp. 464–5). Princeton: The Psychological Review.
Vygotsky, L.S. & Luria, A.R. (1930b). *Etudes on the history of behaviour* (Etiudy po istorii povedenia). Moscow-Leningrad: Gosizdat.

Watson, J.B. (1916). 'The place of the conditioned-reflex in psychology'. *Psychological review, 23*, 2, 89–116.
Watson, J.B. (1919). *Psychology from the standpoint of a behaviorist.* Philadelphia: J.B. Lippincott.
Wellek, A. (1973). 'The theories of ustanovka (*Einstellung*) and structure'. In Prangishvili (1973) (pp. 105–7).
Werner, H. (1937). 'Process and achievement: a basic problem of

education and developmental psychology'. *Harvard educational review*, 7, 353-68.

Werner, H. (1957). 'The concept of development from a comparative and organismic point of view'. In D.B. Harris (Ed.), *The concept of development* (pp. 125-48). Minneapolis: University of Minnesota Press.

Werner, H. & Kaplan, B. (1963). *Symbol formation*. New York: Wiley.

Wertsch, J. (1981). 'The concept of activity in Soviet psychology'. In J. Wertsch (Ed.), *The concept of activity in Soviet psychology* (pp. 3-36). Armonk, NY: M.E. Sharpe.

Wertsch, J. (1985). *Vygotsky and the social formation of the mind*. Cambridge, Ma.: Harvard University Press.

Wertsch, J. & Rogoff, B. (1984). 'Editors' notes'. *New directions for child development*, No. 23, 1-5.

Wertsch, J. & Stone, C.A. (1985). 'The concept of internalization in Vygotsky's account of the genesis of higher mental functions'. In J. Wertsch (Ed.), *Culture, communication, and cognition: Vygotskian perspectives* (pp. 162-97). Cambridge: Cambridge University Press.

Wilder, L. (1975-76). 'The verbal control of behaviour'. *Soviet psychology*, 14, 1-2, 3-12.

Williams, L.P. (1973). 'Kant, Naturphilosophie, and scientific method'. In R.N. Giere & R.S. Westfall (Eds), *Foundation of scientific method* (pp. 3-22). Bloomington: Indiania University Press.

Windholz, G. (1983) 'Pavlov's position towards American behaviourism'. *Journal of the history of the behavioural science*, 19, 394-407.

Windholz, G. (1984a). 'Pavlov and the demise of the influence of Gestalt psychology in the Soviet Union'. *Psychological research*, 46, 187-206.

Windholz, G. (1984b). 'Pavlov's little-known primate research'. *Pavlovian journal of biological science*, 19, 1, 23-31.

Windholz, G. & Lamal, P.A. (1986). 'Pavlov and the concept of association'. *Pavlovian journal of biological science*, 21, 1, 12-15.

Winn, R.B. (Ed.) (1961). *Soviet psychology*. New York: Philosophical Library.

Wortis, J. (1950). *Soviet psychiatry*. Baltimore: Williams & Wilkins.

Wozniak, R.H. (1972). 'Verbal regulation of motor behaviour: Soviet research and non-Soviet replications'. *Human development*, 15, 13-57.

Wozniak, R.H. (1975). 'A dialectical paradigm for psychological research: Implications drawn from the history of psychology in the Soviet Union'. *Human development*, 18, 18-34.

Wozniak, R.H. (1983). 'Lev Semenovich Vygotsky (1896-1934)'. *APA division 26 Newsletter*, May.

Zabrodin, Iu.M. & Nosulenko, V.N. (1979). 'Characteristics of the estimation of loudness of tone signals in interaction conditions'. *Voprosy psikhologii*, No. 4, 118–21.

Zak, A.Z. (1978). 'Experimental study of reflection in young schoolchildren'. *Voprosy psikhologii*, No. 2, 102–10.

Zakharov, A.I. (1982). 'Psychological characteristics of children's viewing of the role of parents'. *Voprosy psikhologii*, No. 1, 59–68.

Zalkind, A.B. (1924). 'Psychoneurology and revolution'. *Pravda*, No. 8 (24 January), p. 1.

Zalkind, A.B. (1930a). 'Main features of the transitional age'. *Paedologia*, No. 1, 3–25.

Zalkind, A.B. (1930b). 'On the psychoneurological study of national minorities'. *Paedologia*, No. 2, 165–6.

Zalkind, A.B. (1931a). 'The psychoneurological front and psychological discussion'. *Paedologia*, No. 3 (Whole No. 15), 1–6.

Zalkind, A.B. (1931b). 'Differentiation on the paedological front'. *Paedologia*, No. 3 (Whole No. 15), 7–14.

Zalkind, A.B. (1932). 'For Marxist-Leninist methodology in paedology: about "Sex education"'. *Paedologia*, No. 1–2, 11–20.

Zaluzhnyi, A.S. (1928). 'The nature of social relationships in pre-kindergarten children'. In *Major problems of paedology in the USSR* (Osnovnyie problemy pedologii v SSSR). Moscow: Gosizdat.

Zaluzhnyi, A.S. (1929). 'Organization of school groups'. *Paedologia*, No. 4, 478–89.

Zaluzhnyi, A.S. (1930). *Treatise about the collective, methodology, children's collective* (Uchenie o kollektive. Metodologia. Detskii kollektiv). Moscow-Leningrad: Rabotnik Prosveshchenia.

Zaluzhnyi, A.S. (1931a). *Children's collective and ways of its study* (Detskii kollektiv i metody ego izuchenia). Moscow-Leningrad.

Zaluzhnyi, A.S. (1931b). 'For the Marxist-Leninist approach to the problem of children's collectives'. *Paedologia*, No. 3, 44–57.

Zaluzhnyi, A.S. (1937). *The pseudo-science paedology in the 'works' of Zalkind* (Lzenauka pedologia v 'trudakh' Zalkinda). Moscow: Gos. uch-ped izdatel'stvo.

Zaporozhets, A.V. (1930). 'Intellectual development and psychological characteristics of Oirot children'. *Paedologia*, No. 2, 222–34.

Zaporozhets, A.V. (1948). 'The change in the motorics of the preschool child in connection with the motives of his activity'. *Izvestia APN RSFSR*, *14*, 125–66.

Zaporozhets, A.V. (1960). *Development of voluntary movements* (Razvitie proizvol'nykh dvizhenii). Moscow: Izdatel'stvo APN RSRSR.

Zaporozhets, A.V. (1967). 'Development of perception and activity'. *Voprosy psikhologii*, No. 1, 11–16.

Zaporozhets, A.V. (1969). 'Some of the psychological problems of sensory training in early childhood and the preschool period'. In Cole & Maltzman (1969) (Eds) (pp. 86–120).

Zaporozhets, A.V. (1977a). 'The development of logical thinking in the preschool-age child'. *Soviet psychology, 15*, 4, 45–59. (Russian original 1948).

Zaporozhets, A.V. (1977b). 'A psychological study of the development of motor activity in the preschool-age child'. *Soviet psychology, 15*, 4, 60–72. (Russian original, 1948).

Zaporozhets, A.V. (1978). 'The meaning of earlier periods of childhood for the formation of personality'. In L. Antsyferova (Ed.), *The principle of development in psychology* (Printsip razvitia v psikhologii) (pp. 243–65). Moscow: Nauka.

Zaporozhets, A.V. (1979–80). 'Thought and activity in children'. *Soviet psychology, 18*, 2, 9–22. (Ukrainian original, 1941).

Zaporozhets, A.V. (1980). 'The role of elements of practice and speech in the development of thinking in children'. In I.I. Il'iasov & V.Ia. Liaudis (Eds), *Reader in developmental and pedagogical psychology* (Khrestomatia po vozrastnoi i pedagogicheskoi psikhologii) (pp. 228–44). Moscow: Izdatel'stvo MGU.

Zaporozhets, A.V. & El'konin, D.B. (Eds.) (1971). *The psychology of preschool children.* Cambridge, Ma.: MIT Press.

Zaporozhets, A.V. & Lukov, U.D. (1979–80). 'The development of reasoning in young children'. *Soviet psychology, 18*, 2, 47–66.

Zaporozhets, A.V., Venger, L.A., Zinchenko, V.P. & Ruzskaia, A.G. (1967). *Perception and action* (Vospriatie i deistvie). Moscow: Prosveshchenie.

Zarandia, M.I. (1971). 'On the development of mental operations in children of preschool age'. *Voprosy psikhologii*, No. 5, 100–9.

Zeiliger, E.O. (1925). 'Psychological investigation of the child in the process of preschool pedagogical work'. In Basov (1925a) (pp. 38–91).

Zeiliger, E.O. (Ed.) (1928). *The peasant child* (Krestianskii rebenok: materialy k ego izuchenia). Moscow-Leningrad: Gosizdat.

Zeiliger, E.O. & Levina, M.A. (1924). 'The experience of the study of preschoolers' free play with objective observational methods'. In M.Ia. Basov (Ed.), *Experience of the objective study of the child* (pp. 21–53). Leningrad: Gosizdat.

Zeiliger, E.O. & Levina, M.A. (1930). 'Structural analysis and internal mechanisms of preschoolers' play'. In Basov (1930), (pp. 38–72).

Zender, M.A. & Zender, B.F. (1974). 'Vygotsky's view about age periodization of child development'. *Human development, 17*, 24–40. [pp. 27–40 trans. of: Vygotsky, L.S., 'The problem of age periodization of child development', from *Voprosy psikhologii*, 1972).

Zhukovskaia, Z. M. (1930). 'The study of active haptic manipulation by blind children'. *Voprosy izuchenia i vospitania lichnosti*, 9, 1–2, 86–90.

Zimmerman, C. C. (1968). *Sorokin, the world's greatest sociologist*. Saskatoon: University of Saskatchewan Press.

Zinchenko, P. I. (1961). *Involuntary remembering* (Neproizvol'noe zapominanie). Moscow: Izd. ANP RSFSR.

Zinchenko, P. I. (1983–84). 'The problem of involuntary memory'. *Soviet psychology*, 22, 2, 55–111 (Russian original, 1939).

Zinchenko, V. P., Van-Tzi Tsin, & Tararkanov, V. V. (1962). 'The formation and development of perceptual actions'. *Voprosi psihologii*, No. 3.

Zinchenko, V. P. & Vergiles, N. Yu. (1969). *The formation of the visual image*. (Formirovanie zritel'nogo obraza). Moskva: Izdatel'stvo MGU.

APPENDIX A: A Programme for an Interview with Children for the Study of their Social Knowledge*

The first part

I. Physical causality
1. (a) Where does wind come from? (b) Why does it blow?
2. You have seen clouds moving in the sky. Why do they move? How does it happen?
3. (a) Does the Sun move or not? Why does it move? How does it happen? (b) Does the moon move or not? Why does it move? What makes it move? (c) Do the stars move or not? Do the clouds move or not?
4. (about shadow): (a) Do you know what this is? (b) Why did the shadow appear? (c) Can you make a shadow with a book? How should one do it? Where will the shadow from the book fall? Why?
5. (a) Why does this thing fall? What makes it fall? (b) Why don't colourful air ballons that are sold in the street fall? What holds them up in the air? (c) Is an aeroplane heavy or light? (d) Why does it not fall? (e) Why do the sun, the moon and the stars not fall on to Earth? What holds them up?

II. Boundaries and features of life and being alive
(What is considered alive and not alive. What objects have consciousness and capability of feeling pain).
1. Which objects are called 'living' and which 'not-living'?
2. Are the following living or not living: a stone, a stick, a tree, a flower, a worm, a fly, water, clouds, the Moon, an aeroplane? Why?
3. Can the following objects think: (same list as above)? Why?
4. Will the following objects feel pain, if one hits them: (same list as above)? Why?

*Source: Basov (1931a), pp. 747–50.

5. What do you want: to live or to die? Why? For what purpose do you want to live?
6. Do other people want to live or not? Why do you think so? For what purpose do they want to live?
7. Do animals want to live or not? Why do you think so? (If answer is that they do): For what purpose do they want to live? Do they know, for what purpose they live? Why do you think so?
8. Do plants live or not? Why do you think so? (If yes): Do they want to live? For what purpose? Do they know for what purpose they live? Why do you think so?

III.   The origins of things existing
1. Where do people originate (come from)? Where did you come from? Where did your father come from? Where did other people come from?
2. Where did horses, birds, fish, flies ... come from?
3. Where did grass, trees come from?
4. Where do earth, stones come from? Where do iron and glass come from?
5. Where do clouds originate? How did they appear in the sky? Where is the sky from? Where is the snow, rain from?
6. Where do rivers originate? Where did water come from? Where did seas come from?
7. Where did the Sun originate? How did it appear in the sky? Where did the Moon originate? Where did the stars originate? Have they always been the way they are today? Have the following always been like today: people, animals, plants, the Sun, the Moon, stars, or Earth? Was there a time when there was nothing? (If yes): What was then?

IV.   The psychological and the physical
1. Can you think?
2. Think now about something.
3. What did you think about?
4. How do you think?
5. With the help of what do you think?
6. Can one think with closed mouth, ears, eyes?
7. Can you see your thoughts? Can you touch them with your hands? Why can you not do it?
8. Can I see your thoughts?
9. How do you know what you are thinking about?

10. Have you dreamed in your sleep? How did you see it—as you can see now, or in a different way?
11. Can one see with closed eyes, while not sleeping? Why?
12. What you dream about—can you touch it with your hands? Why?
13. What is it that you dream about in your sleep?
14. Have you heard about the soul? Do you have a soul? What is it like? Where is it?
15. Do the plants have souls? Where are they located?
16. And other objects?
17. (If the soul is said to exist): Does it die together with the person (animal), or plant?
18. (If not), what happens to it after death? How does it survive after death?

V. Religion
1. What is the sky? Has it always existed? How did it emerge?
2. Does God exist? Why do you think so? (If yes: What is he like? Where is he? What does he do? Does he work?.) Is there anything that is created by God? What exactly?
3. Should one pray to God? Why? Can God punish people? For what? How?
4. Do all people believe that God exists and pray to him? (If no: Which people do you like better? Why?).
5. Does the devil exist? Why do you think so? If 'yes': What is he like? Where is he? What does he do? Does he work? Is there anything that is created by the devil? What exactly? Can the devil punish people? How? For what? What should one do to avoid punishment?

The second part

I. Work
1. Does your father (mother) work? Do you work? How?
2. What does it mean 'to work'? Does the teacher work? Why do you think so? Does an engineer work? An artist? A militiaman (while on duty)? Why do you think so? Do children work? When do they work and when do they not work? Do they work when they are playing ball or checkers, or something else? Why do you think so?

3. Why do people work? If all people had as much money as they want, could they live without working? Why do you think so?
4. Do all people work? Who does not work? Why is it that some work and others don't? (If the first question is answered 'all'): Has it always been in our country that everybody works? When was it different? Who did not work then? Why?
5. Do all people abroad (in other countries) work? Who does not work? Why?
6. Can everybody do the work they want to? Why do you think so? Can anybody be taught to do any work? Why do you think so?
7. When you grow up—how would you like to live: with work (working) or without work, doing nothing? If you had enough money to last for your whole life, would you want to work? Why? What would you do then?

II. Class society
1. Who are called 'bourgeoisie', 'worker', 'peasant'? What do they do?
2. Who are you: bourgeoisie, worker, or peasant? And your father? Your mother? Why do you think so?
3. Which of the groups (bourgeoisie, workers, peasants) do the teachers belong to? Artists? Militiamen? Red Army soldiers? Why do you think so (in every case)?
4. Who is called rich, poor?
5. Why are some people rich and others poor? Are there rich and poor in every country all the time? Why do you think so? Can all people be equally rich? (If 'no': Why do you think so?; if 'yes': When does that happen? What must be done to achieve that?).
6. Is the bourgeoisie the same as the rich, or not? Bourgeoisie, workers, peasants—which of these are richer, who poorer? Can a bourgeois be poor? Why? Can workers be rich? In what way? Can peasants be rich? Why can they be so? Is a rich worker a bourgeois, or not? Or a rich peasant? Why do you think so?
7. Can it be that there are no bourgeoisie, workers, and peasants, and all people will be alike? (If 'not': Why do you think so?; if 'yes': When will that happen? What must be done to achieve that?).

8. Whom would you like to be most—rich or poor? Why? Bourgeois, worker, or peasant? Why?

III. Class struggle

1. Do the workers and bourgeoisie live in harmony? Why? How do workers and peasants get along with each other—are they in harmony or not? Why? How do peasants and the bourgeoisie live—in harmony or not? Why?
2. Do you know what a revolution is? What happens during a revolution? What revolutions do you know? What happened in our country during the February Revolution? What happened during the October Revolution? Why did the February Revolution happen? Who made it? Why did the October Revolution take place? Who made it? Who won in that revolution? Why did they win?
3. In other countries, abroad—are people happy or not that the October Revolution occurred in our country? Is everybody glad (or not) equally about it? Who is glad? Who is not glad? Why? Can a similar revolution take place there, like the one we had? Why do you think so? If that happens—will people in our USSR be happy or not? Why?
4. Are you glad that the October Revolution took place in our country? Why? When do you think it is better—now, or before the Revolution? Why? Would you like a new revolution to take place? Why?
5. What do you think: are revolution and war the same thing or not? What is the difference? Did our country have a war long ago? With whom did we fight? Who won? Who was defeated? What did the winners and losers gain? Why do wars occur? Can we have another war? Why? With whom will we then fight? Do the workers of other countries want to fight with us? Why? And the bourgeoisie? Why? And peasants? Why? Can it be, that people will never have wars with one another? (If 'not': Why do you think so?; if 'yes': When will that happen? What must be done to achieve that?).

IV. Political parties

1. Do you know what a party is? Which parties do you know? How do parties emerge? For what are they formed?
2. Which parties do you know in the USSR? Who is called a

communist? For what purpose did the communists organize their party? Can everybody be a communist? Who benefits from communists—the bourgeoisie, workers, or peasants? Whom do they harm? Are all workers communists? Why? And peasants? Why? And bourgeoisie? Why? Do the communists accept any kind of a person into their party? (If 'no': Who are not accepted? Why?).

3. Are there communist parties abroad? What do foreign communists want? Are there other parties too? What do they want? Do the communists live in harmony with other parties? Why? And our communists with foreign ones—are they in harmony or not? Why? Do our communists meet foreign ones? Why do they meet? What is Komintern?

4. Can a communist in all cases act as he wishes? But if the party orders him to act in the opposite way, what should he do? Why? If a communist acts as he wishes and not according to the wish of the party, what should happen? Why?

5. What is the leader of the party called? Why do parties have leaders? Which leaders of communist parties do you know? Why did they become leaders? Who was the first and the highest leader of the communist party during the Revolution? Who is now? If the communists had no Lenin, could the Revolution have taken place?

6. Do you want to be a communist? Why? And a Komsomol? A Pioneer? Why? (If already a member: Are you satisfied with being a member of the organization? What are you satisfied with, and with what are you dissatisfied?).

V.   The nationality question

1. What nationalities do you know?

2. Which nationality you consider the best? Why do you think so? And which nationality is the next best? Why? And the next? And which nationality is the least good? Why do you think so? What other nationality is not good? Why?

3. Are all nationalities in the USSR equal, or are some against others? (If unequal: Which nationality is pushing others aside? Why? Who are being pushed aside? Why do you think so?). Was it the same before the Revolution as it is now? How was it then? Why?

4. Do all nationalities have their bourgeoisie, workers, and

peasants? The Russians have their workers and bourgeoisie, the French and the Germans have them too—so tell us whom do Russian workers like more: Russian bourgeoisie or German or French workers? Why do you think so? Whom do German or French workers like best—their own bourgeoisie or Russian workers? Why?

5. To which nationality do you belong? To which would you like to belong? Why?

VI. The state

1. Why do militiamen stand in the streets? Who set them out there? If somebody rides in a streetcar and jumps off when it is moving, a militiaman charges him 1 rouble—why does he do that? Who permitted him to take money from people? Can one not listen to him and not give him money? What will he do then? Why? Will he be right, or not? Why?

2. What do the Red Army soldiers do? How did they become soldiers? For what purpose does the Red Army exist? Who organized it? Who gives money for it? Do all people become soldiers? If one does not want to be a soldier, can he not go to serve in the Red Army, or not? Why? Could the Army not exist? Why (If 'yes' then: When will that happen? What must be done for that?).

3. Do you know what the court is? What is done in court? For what reasons are people tried? Who made up courts? Why? Is it possible to live without courts? What is a prison? Who, and for what, is sent to prison?

4. Do you know what laws are? Who makes laws? For what? Do all people have to follow laws? Can one not follow them? Why?

5. What are the Soviets? What is done in the Soviets? How are Soviets made up? Who works in the Soviets? Have the Soviets always existed? If 'no' then: When were they not present and why? Are there Soviets like ours in other countries? If 'no': Why not? Will there be some time? When?

6. What is the name of our country? Who directs our country? Whom do you know in our government? Why do they direct everything, and others follow them? Can one not follow an order from the government? Why?

7. Who has more power in our government: the bourgeoisie, the

workers, or peasants? Why do you think so? In other countries, abroad, is it the same as in ours or different? Why?

VII.   Morality and law

1. Have you ever been punished? Who did it? For what? How? Were they right to punish you? Why? Do other children get punished? Who do? For what? How? Is it right that they get punished? Why? Are adults punished? Who are? For what? Is that right? Why?
2. May one lie? Why do you think so? Should one always tell the truth? If your comrade in class did something wrong (e.g., spoiled a thing), would you tell your teacher about it? Why? (If 'no' then: But what if the teacher asks you who did it—what will you say then? Why?)
3. May one take another's things without permission (steal)? May one take communal (public) property without permission? Why? But if another person has many of such things and he has no need for those, may one take (steal) them without permission? Why? If one person has much bread and the other none at all and is starving—may he steal bread from the first? Is it good to do so or not? Why? During the revolution the workers took factories from the bourgeoisie— did they act properly doing so? Why?
4. May one kill people? Why? Is it prohibited to kill any people? (If not all: Who can be killed? Who may kill them?). May you kill a person? (If 'no': But if you were a soldier in war, could you kill or not? Would you act properly if you killed a person during war? Why?). Can the court order the killing of a person? (If 'no': Why?; if 'yes': When can it do so? Is that good, or not? Why?)
5. Are people always put to prison for bad deeds? Can one be sent to prison for a good deed? (If 'yes': Who can? For what good deed?). Are communists these days sent to prison or not? Why? Is it well done that they are not imprisoned? But before the Revolution, under the czar, were they sent to prison or not? Why? Was it well done that they were imprisoned? (If 'not well done' then: Who did it then in such a bad way? Why were they not sent to prison?). In our country, communists are not now imprisoned, but how is it in other countries? Why? Do they act in a good way abroad? Why do you think so?

Index

activity 53
  theory of (Leontiev) 216–22
attention
  involuntary, 150
  voluntary, 150
analysis
  conditional-genetic 130
  into elements
    'differential' 174–6
    'real' 174–6
  and synthesis 178
  into units (minimal gestalts)
    130, 173–9
aromorphosis 47

behaviourism 85–6
  integration with cognitive/-
    affective study, 169, 179,
    186–8
  overcoming of 88–9
Bekhterev's 'principles'
  of continuous change 57–8
  differentiation 59
  of evolution 58–9
  of historical sequence 59
'biogenetic law', the (Haeckel)
  44

children
  drawings 53, 197, 321
  in early Soviet Union 68–71
  homeless 69–70, 260–1
  play 148–9, 169, 180, 199,
    201–2
  religiosity 256–9

understanding of social
  phenomena, 254, 260–4,
  387–94
cognition 207–8
  'actional' (Basov) 172
  and action 146–7, 208–12,
    216–22
  cultural dependence of 293, 298,
    300–3
  formation of 212–16
    world views 253–4, 264–6
  and interaction 248–51
  moral 223–6
  Piagetian studies 222–3
collectives
  definition 270–1
  organization of 275–7
  reflexological approaches to,
    267–8
complexity 130, 182–3
consciousness 106–7, 109–10,
  186–8

degeneration 47
development
  active construction of 132, 137,
    139, 254–5
  concept of 14, 115–16
  conditional nature of 132
  constraints in understanding of
    logical 13–15
    entification 15–16
    homogenization 16–17
  dialectical thinking about 17–18,
    48